ENGINEERED IN JAPAN

ENGINEERED IN JAPAN

Japanese Technology-Management Practices

Editors
Jeffrey K. Liker,
John E. Ettlie,
and John C. Campbell

New York   Oxford
OXFORD UNIVERSITY PRESS
1995

Oxford University Press

Oxford   New York
Athens   Auckland   Bangkok   Bombay
Calcutta   Cape Town   Dar es Salaam   Delhi
Florence   Hong Kong   Instanbul   Karachi
Kuala Lumpur   Madras   Madrid   Melbourne
Mexico City   Nairobi   Paris   Singapore
Taipei   Tokyo   Toronto

and associated companies in
Berlin   Ibadan

Published in 1995 by Oxford University Press, Inc.
198 Madison Avenue, New York, New York 10016

Oxford is a registered trademark of Oxford University Press

Library of Congress Cataloging-in-Publication Data
Engineered in Japan : Japanese technology-management practices /
Jeffrey K. Liker, John E. Ettlie, and John C. Campbell, editors.
p. cm.   Includes bibliographical references and index.
ISBN 0-19-509555-3
1. Research, Industrial—Japan—Management.
2. Research, Industrial—United States—Management.
3. Technology—Japan—Management.   4. Technology—United States—Management.
I. Liker, Jeffrey K.   II. Ettlie, John E.   III. Campbell, John Creighton.
T177.J3E64   1995
607'.273—dc20   94-39020

9 8 7 6 5 4 3 2 1

Printed in the United States of America
on acid-free paper

Preface

In 1991, at the instigation of Senator Jeff Bingeman of New Mexico, the U.S. Congress provided $10 million to the secretary of defense to establish a program for U.S.–Japan industry and technology management training. Its goal was to improve U.S. industrial competitiveness by learning from Japan the best practices in manufacturing and the management of technology. The Air Force Office of Scientific Research (AFOSR) agreed to administer the new program. Twenty-five universities competed to create programs to research, educate, and train in the area of Japanese technology management. Four universities were awarded two-year grants: the Massachusetts Institute of Technology, Vanderbilt University, the University of Michigan, and the University of Wisconsin on behalf of a consortium including the National Technological University and the Engineering Alliance for Engineering Education (EAGLE). Since that time, an additional $10 million in funding was allocated to the program each year from 1992 to 1994; three of the four original grantees were renewed for two more years, another 10 universities were granted awards (several of these were consortia); and another $5 million funding is pending at the time of this writing.

The three objectives of the program are to increase understanding of Japanese industry and technology-management methods; provide U.S. citizens and permanent resident scientists, engineers, managers, and students of industry and technology management training in the Japanese language, business practices, and culture; and give program participants opportunities to be directly involved in Japanese scientific research, engineering development, and management activities. All these activities were aimed at increasing the flow of technical and management knowledge from Japan to the United States. Although there has been much emphasis in the media on one-sided flows of goods, services, and dollars, there has been less emphasis on the intellectual imbalance that the United States has created through lack of interest in investment in human resources with the capacity to deal effectively with the Japanese, particularly technical personnel. The programs have evolved in different ways at each university, but overall, they are vigorous, with many students involved, continuing education courses developed, students and professional internships in Japan created, and research conducted.*

This book evolved from the research activities of the University of Michigan's Japan Technology Management Program from 1991 to 1993. Scholars were brought together from engineering, business, and liberal arts to investigate Japanese technology management from different vantage points. Some researchers had devoted their careers to studying Japanese technology management and related issues. Other researchers specialized in technology management and examined Japanese approaches within their areas of expertise. To fill in gaps in the research coverage of our faculty, we also drew on researchers outside the University of Michigan who were already doing important research on some aspect of Japanese technology management.

After the research was conducted and the draft chapters written, all the authors of this book met for an intensive two-day conference in Ann Arbor in the summer of 1993. Each chapter was assigned at least two peer reviewers from the group to critique the chapter and suggest improvements. The peer reviews and ensuing discussions at the conference in every case led to significant improvements in the chapters and also provided opportunities for the writers of the pieces to see the whole. In this way, the fragmented pieces became one volume.

Many books have been written about Japanese design practices and manufacturing methods. Why is another book needed? Most writings have focused on shop-floor practices; a few have emphasized Japanese basic research and product-development methods, concentrating on the rapid time to market of Japanese companies. But until now, not a single, comprehensive book has covered the entire technology life cycle. Moreover, many books on Japanese methods are how-to books; focusing on a specific technique or method and describing it in normative terms: "Follow this eight-step process that excellent Japanese companies use and you too can be competitive." Such books can be useful, but they are not based on research and often give misleading impressions about how Japanese companies, even the best ones, really work. *Engineered in Japan* is different:

1. It covers the entire life cycle from basic R&D, to development engineering, to manufacturing processes, and to learning from the Japanese.
2. It is based on recent, original research by scholars, all writing about the subfields they know best.
3. The chapters go beyond superficial descriptions of stylized practices to look in depth at particular issues, often contradicting or qualifying the conventional wisdom. For example, Chapter 10 by Hammett, Hancock, and Baron gives an illustration of where Japanese companies intentionally do not use much statisti-

---

* For further information on the AFOSR program, see *Learning from Japan: Improving knowledge of Japanese technology management practices*, Committee to assess U.S.–Japan Industry and Technology Management Training Programs, Manufacturing Studies Board, National Research Council, Washington, DC, 1994.

cal process control (SPC), a technique that has become almost synonomous with Japanese quality methods.

This book was written for scholars interested in Japanese business, engineering, and management and for practicing engineers and technology managers. It includes statistical studies, conceptual arguments, and in-depth case studies. We avoided methodological jargon and specialized technical discussions, though we assume some familiarity with basic concepts of Japanese manufacturing methods (e.g., SPC and JIT) and general management practices (e.g., lifetime employment, slow promotion, small-group activities) because so much has been written about these topics. When we do mention such basic concepts as SPC, JIT, lifetime employment, and small-group responsibility, it is to further elaborate, clarify, or refute myths that have little basis in reality. Each chapter of the book is a stand-alone article that can be read on its own, but as a whole the book covers the technology-development life cycle and is suitable for a graduate-level course. Each grouping of chapters could be used as a module in the course.

Many people and organizations made this book possible. We thank the Air Force Office of Scientific Research for its financial support and, in particular, Lieutenant Colonel Claude Cavender for his thoughtful guidance. We deeply appreciate the hard work and persistent dedication of Heidi Tietjen, associate director of the Japan Technology Management Program, who has held the organization together and kept us all honest. The book is quite readable thanks to the high-quality editing by Lee Meiser and Lynnette Porter. Finally, we thank our many colleagues at the University of Michigan in engineering, business, and the Center for Japanese Studies, who collectively create an intellectual environment that fosters excellent research.

Ann Arbor
October 1994

J. K. L.
J. E. E.
J. C. C.

Contents

Contributors

Howard E. Aldrich, Professor of Sociology, University of North Carolina at Chapel Hill

Jay S. Baron, Manager of Manufacturing Systems Research, Office for the Study of Automotive Transportation, University of Michigan

C. Christopher Baughn, Visiting Assistant Professor of Management and Organization Sciences, Wayne State University

Mary Yoko Brannen, Assistant Professor of International Business, Organizational Behavior and Human Resource Management, University of Michigan

John Creighton Campbell, Professor of Political Science and co-Director of Japan Technology Management Program, University of Michigan

Thomas Y. Choi, Assistant Professor of Management, Bowling Green State University

Robert E. Cole, Professor of Sociology and Business Administration, University of California at Berkeley

John J. Cristiano, Graduate Research Assistant, Industrial and Operations Engineering, University of Michigan

Izak Duenyas, Assistant Professor of Industrial and Operations Engineering, University of Michigan

John E. Ettlie, Associate Professor of Operations Management and Director, Manufacturing Management Research, University of Michigan

John W. Fowler, Operations Modeling Department, SEMATECH

W. Mark Fruin, Hong Kong Bank of Canada Professor and Director, Institute of Asian Research, University of British Columbia

Patrick C. Hammett, Graduate Research Assistant, Industrial and Operations Engineering, University of Michigan

Walton M. Hancock, William Clay Ford Professor of Product Manufacturing and Professor of Industrial and Operations Engineering, University of Michigan

Rajan R. Kamath, Assistant Professor of Corporate Strategy, University of Cincinnati

Jeffrey K. Liker, Associate Professor of Industrial and Operations Engineering and Director of Japan Technology Management Program, University of Michigan

David T. Methé, Assistant Professor of Corporate Strategy, University of Michigan

Will Mitchell, Assistant Professor of Corporate Strategy, University of Michigan

Mitsuo Nagamachi, Professor of Industrial and Systems Engineering, Hiroshima University

Richard N. Osborn, Professor of Management and Organization Sciences, Wayne State University

Thomas Roehl, Assistant Professor of International Business, University of Illinois

Toshihiro Sasaki, Professor of Management, Kyoto Sangyo University

Lee Schruben, Professor of Operations Research and Industrial Engineering, Cornell University

Ronald J. Slattery, Graduate Research Assistant, Business Administration, University of Michigan

Durward K. Sobek II, Graduate Research Assistant, Industrial and Operations Engineering, University of Michigan

Peter Swan, Graduate Research Assistant, Operations Management, University of Michigan

Allen C. Ward, Assistant Professor of Mechanical Engineering and Applied Mechanics, University of Michigan

S. Nazli Wasti, Graduate Research Assistant, Industrial and Operations Engineering, University of Michigan

Daniel E. Whitney, Principal Research Associate, Center for Technology, Policy, and Industrial Development, Massachusetts Institute of Technology

ENGINEERED IN JAPAN

1

Engineered in Japan:
Introduction and Overview

JEFFREY K. LIKER,
JOHN E. ETTLIE,
AND JOHN CREIGHTON CAMPBELL

One might ask why yet another book on Japanese management would appear on the shelves at this late date. After all, haven't U.S. managers learned all they need to know about Japanese approaches, from the voluminous literature appearing in the 1980s? We learned all about JIT, TQM, TPM, SPC, QFD, and the product-development *shusa*. We know about lean manufacturing, and we have been busily adopting what we can of Japan's quality methods. Our plants have become leaner and more productive, and in many cases, the quality of our products approaches Japanese quality. We have been reducing product-development time through a variety of organizational and technical concurrent engineering approaches. We have been gaining market share, and at the time of this writing, our economy seems to be strengthening as the Japanese economy is still struggling to emerge from recession.

Despite these signs of growing strength in the U.S. economy and the apparent stalling of the Japanese system, we believe it is just a matter of time before the Japanese economy gets back on its feet and Japanese firms emerge with new methods, approaches, and competitive strategies. Part of this new order will undoubtedly involve new and renewed technology strategies.

As one of the three most economically competitive nations in the world today, Japan will continue to play a central role as a competitor, as a market for our products, as a business partner, and as a source of ideas for innovative practices. The fact that the manufacturing world has been taking Japan seriously for about the last decade is a beginning, not an end. It is true that some of the aura of Japanese quality has been demystified as we have found that, yes, many ideas originated in some form in the United

States, and yes, when we put our mind to it, we can make those sensible ideas work here. But it is also true that many U.S. companies are still struggling to implement basic methods like control charts and JIT and that the success of Japanese companies goes beyond the plethora of alphabet soup techniques that are applied on the shop floor. Noteworthy Japanese approaches also go beyond human resource–management methods, like the use of cross-functional teams, lifetime employment, and intensive training.

We believe that the fundamental strength of Japan's best companies will not be depleted by the current recession. At least for large Japanese companies, this strength is in the form of technological infrastructure, business and engineering expertise, and organizational routines that are deeply embedded in relatively stable enterprises. Equity sharing and the capital-formation capacity of the *keiretsu* system in Japan protects large Japanese companies from failure (Dore, 1986; Miyashita & Russell, 1994). Although we are seeing large companies downsize, close plants, and cut back on basic research, we are not seeing them shut their doors. Nor are we seeing the level of instability—for example, through mergers and acquisitions—characteristic of U.S. companies in economic downturns. The relative stability of Japanese companies and of the employees of those companies means that established routines and infrastructure can weather the storm of rocky economic times. If anything, hard times create further external pressure to reduce costs and become more competitive, encouraging the type of organizational learning that Cole (Chapter 16) argues characterizes Japanese companies.

This book is about how Japanese companies manage critical aspects of the technology-management process. We have selected issues over the total life cycle, from basic research to product conception to product development to shop-floor methods. We also devote some attention to discussing what U.S. companies can learn from Japanese methods and how culture affects the ability of U.S. companies to learn.

The title of this book, *Engineered in Japan,* appropriately credits the Japanese with creating innovative management approaches, tools and techniques, and technologies. Engineering is the design and implementation of solutions to solve problems. Good engineers take basic scientific principles and ideas from wherever they can get them. They are less interested in creating a new basic technology or theory for its own sake and more interested in creatively applying science and technology. We have found many excellent engineers in Japan—not just those with engineering degrees—but individual persons and collections of persons who have worked long and hard to develop and implement innovations and improve on those innovations. We can perhaps learn more from the process of creation in Japan and the organizational structures that support innovation than from the particular approaches, tools, and technologies created.

The book is an edited collection. The individual chapters together cover the various stages of the R&D and product life cycle. In all cases, the chapters go beyond past observations about this technique or that process.

Each author in some way digs below the surface of Japanese management approaches, by looking more closely than has been done before at how a particular method is applied, identifying some new practices that have not heretofore been highlighted in books on Japanese methods, presenting more recent data that contradict some conventional thinking about U.S.–Japanese differences, or looking at an old technique from a new perspective.

This book is organized into four parts, roughly following the technology life cycle: applied R&D, product–process development, manufacturing methods and management, and technology deployment and organizational learning. We will briefly summarize each chapter.

APPLIED R&D

It is well known that compared with the United States, a larger portion of Japanese research and development emanates from industry, as opposed to universities and government labs. The university infrastructure for research lags far behind that of U.S. research universities. In private Japanese companies through the 1980s, there was an increased emphasis on expenditures for more fundamental research. Methé, in Chapter 2, describes fundamental research as being somewhere between basic research and engineering development; it is the platform from which many specific products can be developed. There is some evidence of a backlash in the recession of the 1990s, with less emphasis on increasing basic research and more emphasis in Japanese industries on developing specific products. But at the same time there is a continuing struggle to find a balance between fundamental research and product development. The authors of the first two chapters in Part I delve into this issue in some depth, looking at R&D management in electronics and pharmaceuticals. The second two chapters describe interorganizational consortia and alliances as they influence the development and flow of technology.

In "Basic Research in Japanese Electronics Companies" (Chapter 2), Methé builds on his 1991 book on Japan's semiconductor industry, entitled *Technological Competition in Global Industries,* with new research evidence. In the past, we Americans viewed the Japanese as adopters and modifiers of existing technology who depended on the United States for basic research. But Methé focuses on the efforts of Japanese semiconductor manufacturers to develop an internal capability for fundamental research and to incorporate their discoveries into commercial products. "Fundamental" research, as he defines it, is not basic or applied research but generic research on particular problems that can become the launching point for a variety of new products. The challenge is to develop new "routines" that make innovation an established process that can be continually improved in the way that shop-floor learning has been successfully institutionalized. Methé explores the management approaches that are allowing

Japan to progress rapidly in basic technological innovation as well as the barriers they are facing. He also examines the dynamic tension between developing internal capabilities to create innovative new products and then pushing them into new, marketable products *(pushing on a string)*, and deploying able research scientists and engineers into the more routine development of specific products with short time horizons *(pulling on a string)*.

In "R&D Investment Growth and Organizational Changes by Japanese Pharmaceutical Firms, 1975–1993" (Chapter 3), Roehl, Mitchell, and Slattery make observations strikingly similar to Methé's but, in this case, in the Japanese pharmaceutical industry. While many authors in this book emphasize U.S.–Japanese differences, this chapter points out differences in the R&D intensity and focus among pharmaceutical firms within Japan. The study is based on archival sources of Japanese innovation over the last 15 years and interviews with 15 Japanese pharmaceutical companies and several industry analysts in Japan in August 1992. The authors note that Japanese pharmaceutical companies are finding innovative ways to develop a better basic research capability, as they can no longer profitably copy from the West—the basic research in this field is progressing too fast for successful companies to remain followers. And there are greater barriers to borrowing technology from other companies.

In "Governance Structure and Technology Transfer Management in R&D Consortia in the United States and Japan" (Chapter 4), Aldrich and Sasaki look at the governance structure of R&D consortia. This chapter is based on a comparative survey of 39 U.S. and 54 Japanese R&D consortia registered through 1990 in the United States and 1991 in Japan. U.S. companies typically create consortia as separate organizations with a general charter in their own offices; they attempt to tie together companies, the government, and universities. Japanese consortia are more company centered: They typically do not have separate offices but reside in member companies and concentrate on specific technological issues rather than a general charter. The authors compare practices for membership management, conflict management, and technology transfer. Although there are no performance data, and thus no prescriptive statements made about the superiority of one organizational form over another, the rapid recent growth of consortia foundings in the United States suggests that there is an opportunity for research on consortia to help shape the new emerging population.

In "Governing United States–Japan High-Technology Alliances" (Chapter 5), Osborn and Baughn summarize the results of their five-year research program on this topic. They find three major governance forms for alliances—dominance, turbulence, and international hybridization—which have different implications for the management of the alliances. From data on 725 alliances from 1984 to 1989, they identify the main characteristics of these three types. Only international hybridization leads to balanced patterns of trade flows, which is the pattern, the authors argue, that has the greatest potential in technical areas in which each actor brings to the table a distinctive and complementary competency needed to serve global markets.

PRODUCT–PROCESS DEVELOPMENT PRACTICES

Product development is a critical lever for industrial competitiveness, and many companies in the United States and Japan have discovered that high-speed and quality product-development practices depend on the concurrent engineering of products and processes, and thus product development and manufacturing are intimately connected. There is an explosion of new practices in the United States to implement concurrent engineering, many of them based on vague conceptions of Japan's best practices. The key issue is integration. How can we integrate the development of a product with the development of a manufacturing system to optimize the overall system design? How can we integrate the development of components of the overall product so that they fit together, even though they have been developed by different engineering groups, perhaps even by engineers from different parts suppliers? How can we make integration a strategic advantage? All four chapters in this part focus on different aspects of integrating the development process.

In "Nippondenso Co. Ltd." (Chapter 6), Whitney synthesizes what he learned from seven visits over a 17–year period to Nippondenso (ND), a first-tier supplier of electromechanical components to Toyota and other auto companies and arguably Japan's foremost automotive parts manufacturer. He describes how ND learned to use design to achieve the strategic goal of meeting the demands of Toyota, its dominant customer. These included demands for rapid new product introductions, an extreme level of product diversity, and orders with very short lead times. Whitney provides a comprehensive analysis of many facets of ND's approach, including how it categorizes problems of assembly automation into distinct classes and develops solutions to problems within each class, uses robots as a strategic resource, and manages concurrent engineering to achieve breakthrough product development on prescheduled time lines.

In "Integrating Suppliers into Fast-Cycle Product Development" (Chapter 7), Liker, Kamath, Wasti, and Nagamachi look at the well-known Japanese practice of involving parts suppliers in the early stages of product development. The authors report results from one of the largest studies ever undertaken of U.S.–Japanese differences in involving suppliers in design. The study combines in-depth interviews at three auto companies and seven suppliers and a survey of about 150 Japanese suppliers and 200 U.S. suppliers. They describe how the Japanese "design-in" system enables auto companies to manage the information complexity and risk associated with involving a large number of outside suppliers in product development. They found that U.S. auto companies have, in fact, adopted many features of Japanese supplier management, though there still are some critical differences. They observe that black-box sourcing is more than a matter of sourcing early and giving suppliers design responsibility. The ability to use black-box sourcing effectively depends on excellence in systems engineering; it is not a replacement for this skill. Although U.S. companies are rapidly adopting many structural features of the Japanese black-box sourcing system, it is less clear whether they are also developing the underlying competencies and institutional arrangements that make black box-sourcing work.

In "Toyota, Concurrent Engineering, and Set-Based Design" (Chapter 8), Ward, Sobek, Cristiano, and Liker analyze a new paradigm of design they call *set-based design.* In the conventional point-based approach, designers quickly develop a particular design solution—a point in the design space—and then iterate from that starting point until they achieve a satisfactory solution. The authors argue that effective, truly concurrent design requires shifting to a set-based paradigm in which the design team defines and communicates about sets of designs—regions in the design space. The authors conducted interviews with U.S. and Japanese automakers and parts suppliers to test the hypothesis that the Japanese are more set based than U.S. designers are. Instead, however, they found the set-based approach characterizes only Toyota, the most successful Japanese automaker. The set-based approach is indeed a fundamentally new paradigm for design and has potentially revolutionary implications for how concurrent engineering is practiced.

In "Competing in the Old-Fashioned Way" (Chapter 9), Fruin examines the product–process development approach of Toshiba, a leading Japanese manufacturer of a diverse range of products (e.g., home appliances, consumer electronics, computers, photocopiers, and automatic mail-sorting equipment). He analyzes Toshiba's use of development factories—knowledge works—to bring together all resources in one place to rapidly develop and manufacture new products. Fruin argues that successful time-based competition depends on localizing and integrating knowledge resources around a single dominant product or, at best, a few related product lines (i.e., competing in the old-fashioned way). In this regard, the M-form (i.e., multidivisional) organization characteristic of large U.S. corporations has a disadvantage over the more traditional U-form, or unitary, firms organized around a single dominant product or a few related product lines. Toshiba has managed to retain the product organization in its knowledge works despite becoming a large multinational player.

MANUFACTURING METHODS AND MANAGEMENT

Japanese factories remain the world benchmark for quality and productivity, though there has been major progress in the United States, based in large part on competition and lessons learned from Japan. Because much has been written about the generic manufacturing practices that are typical of the best Japanese factories (e.g., in-process quality checks, *kaizen,* pull systems), we focus here on practices that either elaborate on the Japanese manufacturing approach or contradict common views of best practice.

In "Producing a World-Class Automotive Body" (Chapter 10), Hammett, Hancock, and Baron focus on one manufacturing process and, in so doing, provide a level of depth often missing from discussions of Japanese manufacturing practices. The world leaders in auto-body development have managed to understand the sources of variation in the body and to reduce variation through careful design and extreme standardization of the production process. Interestingly, in this context, classic statistical process control methods do not work well. If the process gets out of control, there are no simple adjustments that can be made to the dies and presses to bring the process back into control. Therefore, the dies and equipment must be so well designed and maintained that they will not go out of control. The standardization of processes, die and press maintenance, setup, and die design can actually eliminate the need for statistical process control during production.

Hammett and his colleagues also identify an innovative approach used by leading Japanese companies for product–process development, known as *functional build*. Traditional developers start with a blueprint, or database, of the body and then, in die tryout, spend a great deal of time grinding the dies until they stamp out parts that precisely meet the nominal dimensions of the body designers. By contrast, functional build treats the original body design as a general target. The dies are made as closely as possible to the original body dimensions, but then in die tryout, a body is assembled, tested, and approved as long as it meets the design intent, even if it does not precisely match the original nominal dimensions. This approach provides flexibility to deviate from the blueprint and, through trial and error, to arrive at the final die and body design simultaneously. This method explicitly recognizes that the whole is more than the sum of the parts.

In "Japanese Development of Scheduling Methods for Semiconductor Manufacturing" (Chapter 11), Duenyas, Fowler, and Schruben discuss an interesting instance of a manufacturing system too complex for *kanban* systems to work effectively. They find that leading Japanese wafer manufacturers use scheduling software developed in house. They also identify several common characteristics of the scheduling methods in all the Japanese companies they visited: Technical projects are viewed as part of long-term continuous improvement, not one-shot efforts; there is an emphasis on developing their own software using relatively simple simulation procedures; and there is a strong emphasis on involving plant managers and operators early in the development of the scheduling tools.

In "U.S.–Japanese Manufacturing Joint Ventures and Equity Relationships" (Chapter 12), Ettlie and Swan analyze more than 300 cases of direct investment by Japanese firms in the United States and extend their findings with a close-up look at four cases of U.S.–Japanese manufacturing joint ventures. They find that the stereotype of the Japanese manufacturing partner bringing production know-how and the U.S. partner bringing product and marketing presence to a joint venture is generally true of these cases. They also find that Japan's high standards of manufacturing quality are usually maintained and extended by the joint ventures. The cases provide a rich picture of the complexities and conflicts in managing joint ventures, particularly when equity is equally shared and neither partner dominates the relationship. The joint venture rarely delivers on the original goals, but often as it evolves, new, equally important objectives are emphasized. An issue for both parties is how to learn from the joint venture and to bring those lessons back to the parent organizations. A new management form that leverages U.S. and Japanese technology that typically surpasses the parent organizations is emerging in these alliances. A number of these joint ventures (e.g., NUMMI) are the leaders in their industry.

TECHNOLOGY DEPLOYMENT AND
ORGANIZATIONAL LEARNING

Ultimately, to be useful, technology must be deployed, and the organization should continuously improve the technology and learn from its experiences. Part IV focuses on the ability of U.S. firms to learn from the successful practices observed in Japan. All five authors take the position that much can be learned from Japanese practices and that the potential for improvements in productivity and quality are enormous. There do not seem to be any inherent cultural barriers that make impossible the transfer of practices from Japan to the United States. On the other hand, learning from Japan, and organizational learning in general, is difficult, particularly given the many barriers to learning in U.S. manufacturing firms.

In "Culture, Innovative Borrowing, and Technology Management" (Chapter 13), Campbell argues that culture need not be an obstacle to adopting Japanese practices, that in fact, many characteristics of Japanese company culture that Americans assume are the key to the success of the Japanese manufacturing system are simply not true. Using survey data, he shows that compared with the United States, Japanese employees may be less committed to their organizations, less satisfied with their jobs, less willing to sacrifice personal goals for the sake of the organization, and more distrustful of the motives of others. On the other hand, much of the Japanese success in management can be attributed to their strong belief that relationships matter. Indeed this belief is so strong that Japanese go to great lengths to manage relationships, including finding structural means to force the right people to work together (but only when needed) and to reduce the likelihood of unproductive conflict. Campbell likens the Japanese use of institutional structures to foster harmonious relationships to that of the U.S. Marines using methods like selection screening, intense socialization, disciplined procedures, an emphasis on the work group as the social unit, and strong group leaders. He contends that we should and can learn the importance of relationships and how to structure our organizations to utilize the power of relationships in organizations.

In "Does Culture Matter?" (Chapter 14), Brannen looks at an increasingly common and important worldwide phenomenon—bicultural organizations. Through an intensive case study of an American paper plant that was bought out and managed by the Japanese, she traces the complex dynamics as each side learns to adjust and create a new "culture of work." Ultimately, the new Japanese managers were successful in improving the productivity and quality of the plant, using many core features of their Japanese production system. But this was only after considerable conflict, adjustment of expectations, and learning to live and work together by both sides. Brannen argues that to be effective, one group cannot try to impose its culture on the joint organization. In fact, whether or not the leaders like it, a new hybrid culture will be negotiated and evolve over time. Leaders who are sensitive to cultural issues can help guide the evolution in a way that plays on the strengths of each culture.

In "Institutional Pressures and Organizational Learning" (Chapter 15), Choi and Wasti paint a somewhat less optimistic picture when they examine the success of purely U.S. companies in learning Japanese manufacturing methods. The authors report in-depth case studies of six U.S. automotive-parts suppliers who have tried to adopt Japanese production methods. They conducted interviews with managers and shop-floor employees and discovered that only one of the six companies had effectively implemented the Japanese production methods. Most companies were driven to adopt these approaches by institutional pressures, primarily from their major automotive customers. Choi and Wasti observe three levels of learning—no learning, single-loop (mechanistic) learning, and double-loop (systems) learning. In single-loop learning, companies simply focus on one production method at a time and mechanistically get the employees to use the method. In these cases, the method generally has little impact, and the employees do not understand how the method fits into a broader system of production. In double-loop learning, the employees see a new system of management and understand how individual technologies fit into this system. Only one company qualified as a double-loop learner, and this company made far greater improvements than the other companies did. U.S. companies have the opportunity to learn from the Japanese, but if adoption is driven only by external pressures to conform, such learning is likely to be limited to superficial adoption. To be effective, learning must be double-loop learning with an understanding of the underlying systemic relationships among the parts. This systemic understanding must be pushed all the way down to first-line managers and workers on the shop floor.

In "Reflections on Organizational Learning in U.S. and Japanese Industry" (Chapter 16), Cole offers a candid analysis of the failure of U.S. companies to learn new practices at an organizational level. He distinguishes between individual learning and organizational learning, which often do not go hand in hand. In the modal U.S. firm, the systems and culture support learning by individual persons, but this learning tends not to be shared and is not applied to ongoing organizational routines. Thus although the individual person may benefit and be very good at doing a task, this learning does not spill over to other individual's work and will disappear when that person leaves the department or company. By contrast, the modal Japanese firm is able to combine both individual and organizational learning, though often individual learning and creativity are either sacrificed or channeled solely toward corporate ends. A key to organizational adaptation and even innovation in the Japanese firm is standardization, something that Americans seem to resist and assume is antithetical to learning and innovation. Cole argues that in the more turbulent environments of the future, corporate success will increasingly go to firms that develop their potential to maximize both individual and organizational learning. Japanese firms face the challenge of tapping individual creativity and have much to learn from the United States in this regard. The challenge for the U.S. firm is focusing on a higher conversion rate from individual to organizational learning, and Japan has much to offer on how this can be accomplished.

COMMON THEMES

When we, the editors, looked over the chapters, one overarching theme stood out: Japanese managers tend to think in terms of *systems*. That is, whereas U.S. managers concentrate on individual skills, techniques, departments, and components, Japanese managers focus on the connections among them. In the final chapter of the book, "Managing Technology Systemically," we explore the major subthemes that are part of the systems approach that we observed in Japan.

The chapters in this book illustrate different aspects of this systems emphasis, partly depending on the disciplinary background of their authors. For example, the social scientists emphasized the importance that Japanese managers place on social relationships and interorganizational linkages, and the engineers on our team were struck by their skill in systems design. Five interrelated themes, however, cut across the individual chapters.

Developing Broad Internal Competencies

Japanese business organizations seem to focus on developing core internal strategic capabilities as a means of integrating the parts of their companies. Technical skill becomes a central organizing agent rather than a specialist commodity. Thus breadth is encouraged in addition to depth.

Being Flexible Within Clear Boundaries

Japanese companies combine organizational innovation and creativity with highly disciplined processes. The relatively organic, integrated systems observed in Japan are certainly not free-for-alls; instead, there are clear boundaries and often very strict conformance to those boundaries. This is true for many kinds of boundaries—target specifications for products, boundaries between levels of the hierarchy, boundaries between departments or sections, standardized ways to perform jobs, target goals and dates for R&D projects, and boundaries on appropriate social behavior.

Carefully Constructing Social Boundaries

Successful Japanese companies have developed the capability to effectively manage part–whole relationships. Even when the division of labor among engineers is extensive, they are able to develop products that function well as a whole. The U.S. interpretation of this situation is often that Japanese are more "teamy" and naturally cooperate toward a common goal, even with "partners" in other firms, government, and education. But Campbell (Chapter 13) argues that this is far from the truth. If anything, cooperation across boundaries happens more "naturally" in the United States. Because the Japanese believe that people and organizations are naturally self-serving, they pay much attention to carefully constructing boundaries and working to create strong relationships across boundaries, but only when these are strategically important.

Regarding "Japanese Methods" as Consequences of Attention to Designing Systems for Local Conditions, Not as Stand-Alone Tools

"Japanese techniques" are not universally practiced in Japan, nor are they essential in and of themselves. In fact, Japanese managers and engineers are often surprised to find that the world is so interested in "Japanese" methods. Japanese managers typically view their culture and internal organizations as unique and work at developing a strong internal culture and adapting tools and methods to local circumstances (Campbell, 1988). U.S. managers, however, often borrow the techniques and miss the structural and cultural conditions that make the techniques effective.

Increasing Global Connectivity

Japan has historically been a very insulated, homogeneous society; clearly that was the case, by design, before the Meiji era (1868–1911). Yet there is evidence in many chapters of this book that Japanese companies are becoming increasingly connected globally and have become formidable global competitors.

This book should not be viewed as a description of typical Japanese practices of typical Japanese companies. We fully intended to search for best practices and document them. Companies like Toyota, Nippondenso, Hitachi, and Toshiba all are top corporate players in the world, including

Japan. This book provides a close look at many technology-management practices that have contributed to the remarkable gains in Japan's competitiveness over the last several decades. The descriptions of practices are intended to stimulate thinking and suggest ideas, not to be copied. We also saw evidence that Japanese companies are far from invincible: They are run by fallible, self-interested managers, as are companies throughout the world. But they contain many gems of innovative practice that we can learn.

REFERENCES

Campbell, J. C. (1988). *Politics and culture in Japan.* Ann Arbor: Center for Political Studies, Institute for Social Research, University of Michigan.

Dore, R. (1986). *Flexible rigidities: Industrial policy and structural adjustment in the Japanese economy, 1970–80.* Stanford, CA: Standford University Press.

Methé, D. T. (1991). *Technological competition in global industries: Marketing and planning strategies for American industry.* Westport, CT: Quorum Books.

Miyashita, K., & Russell, D. (1994). *Keiretsu: Inside the hidden Japanese conglomerates.* New York: McGraw-Hill.

I

APPLIED R&D

2

Basic Research in Japanese Electronic Companies: An Attempt at Establishing New Organizational Routines

DAVID T. METHÉ

Knowledge, along with the traditional resources of land, labor, and capital, has always been important to determining a firm's competitive success. A fundamental shift is occurring in the composition of these elements, however. From the beginning of this century, knowledge began to play a more dominant role in a firm's success in industrial competition (Betz, 1987). With the pace of that domination accelerating as this century draws to a close, scholars and practitioners alike are recognizing the important role that knowledge plays in competitive success. The resulting strategic attention has generated a plethora of management concepts ranging from first-mover advantage and transaction costs to core competency and organizational learning, among many others. Much of this strategic attention has centered on the question of how to apply resources to generate, organize, and utilize technical knowledge so it will result in an innovation, that is, a new product or process or an improvement of an existing product or process that better meets market needs. The management of this process is called *technology management* or the *management of innovation*.

The question of how Japanese companies manage technology or the innovation process is central to this chapter, for two reasons. First, most of the competitive challenge confronting U.S. electronics companies has come and will continue to come from their Japanese counterparts (Methé, 1992). Second, in spite of the many efforts of scholars and practitioners to study the management of innovation, our knowledge is still elemental. An examination of approaches taken by Japanese companies toward the management of technology and innovation represents a unique opportunity to study models of innovation that have developed differently from those generally studied by U.S. management scholars. By exploring the approaches taken by Japanese firms toward innovation, we can gain not only important insights into how Japanese companies innovate but also insights into technology management issues in general.

CHOICE OF THE ELECTRONICS INDUSTRY

I chose the electronics industry for my examination for a number of reasons. The growing strength of Japanese technological capabilities is widely acknowledged (Arrison, Bergson, Graham, & Harris, 1992). Although Japanese companies are equally strong in the automobile industry and are growing in strength in industries such as pharmaceuticals, the first and most crucial test of Japanese innovative capabilities will come in the electronics industry. The reason is that the pace of technological change in the electronics industry, as exhibited by the revolution in numbers and variety of products, has pushed the electronics industry further and faster than other industries. This pace of change continues today and will continue unabated well into the next century. Consequently, companies in the electronics industry, whether Japanese or American, are being confronted with the obsolescence of technological knowledge bases at a pace unheard of in other industries. Witness the current upheaval in the computer industry because of the movement from mainframes to networked personal computers and the rapid change in microprocessor and operating systems technology.

In addition, many industries that are or are becoming global, such as the automobile and pharmaceutical industries, are becoming more dependent on technological change in the electronics industry as a driver of technological innovation in their own industry (Methé, 1992). Although these industries will maintain a core set of technologies that will remain independent of electronics-based technologies, companies' abilities to initiate and leverage innovations in those core technological areas will increasingly depend on attendant electronic technologies in design and manufacturing equipment. As a result, one study in Japan of the influence of electronics on 84 industries for 1975, 1980, and 1985 showed the increasing importance of direct electronics input during each year for all industries (Management and Coordination Agency, 1975, 1980, 1985).

TECHNOLOGICAL CHALLENGES
IN THE ELECTRONICS INDUSTRY

As noted earlier, the pace of technological change is presenting a tremendous challenge to firms in the electronics industry. This technological challenge is occurring on two fronts, the increasing miniaturization of components and the greater systematization of products. At the component level, the impact of increasing miniaturization is especially evident in the development of integrated circuits. The progression of technological innovation into the 256M DRAM and beyond is pushing the technology horizon for the design and fabrication of integrated circuits past the solid-state physics knowledge base that has supported all previous integrated circuit innovation and into quantum physics. The uncertainty of when, and possibly if, the shift from solid-state physics to quantum physics will occur has generated a sense of urgency among integrated circuit manufacturers and the upstream firms that supply them in planning for new chip development.

This sense of urgency is further heightened by the trend toward greater systematization. The boundaries between a component and a system are blurring at an accelerating pace. This process began with the first microprocessor and is hitting its stride with the emergence of the new 64–bit microprocessors. The impact of this process is being felt most strongly in the downstream industries that use these microprocessors. The emergence of the multimedia field is a result of these innovations.

Multimedia are indicative of both the promises and problems confronting companies that wish to compete in the electronics industry. The blurring of component and system occurring in the technology is mirrored in the blurring boundaries between what were once considered separate industries. Not only are the functions of computers and communication beginning to merge in the nascent form of multimedia, but so too are the industrial and consumer applications of electronics. Add a little from the entertainment industry, by way of programs, and a close approximation of what multimedia may become is apparent.

Even if multimedia did not exist on the horizon, the higher degree of systematization would be fed from another source: the increasing interdependence of innovation in the hardware and software areas of electronics. The ability to sell electronic products to an increasingly sophisticated and satiated consumer depends more on the product's ease of use, not only as a stand-alone but also as part of a broader network of products in which it can interact. To provide such capabilities, more powerful systems software and object technology (object-oriented operating systems) need to be developed (Boyd, 1993). To make them work, these new software innovations will require even greater sophistication in both memory and microprocessor technologies. Consequently, the need to produce even more systemic products will further push components into miniaturization.

JAPAN'S RESPONSE TO TECHNOLOGY CHALLENGES

This positive feedback cycle between systemization and miniaturization is beginning to lead electronic companies into uncharted technological waters. Not only is the underlying knowledge base for integrated-circuit production shifting, but also the skills needed to design and produce the networked, user-friendly multimedia products of the future have pushed electronics companies into deeper explorations of such fundamental areas of science as the nature of intelligence, language, and learning. These technological waters are uncharted in the United States as well as Japan. Couple these facts with the speed of technological catch-up by Japanese companies, which has already occurred, and the result is that many Japanese companies no longer are confronted with the comfortable choice of "making or buying" the technology. The knowledge on which twenty-first-century electronics products will be based is now being developed, and Japanese companies are aware that they must be a part of the process that "makes" or generates this knowledge or they will be left behind in the competition for emerging markets. The rise in the number of "basic research" institutes in Japan, as seen in Table 2.1, is indicative of Japanese companies' strategic understanding of the situation.

In the remainder of this chapter, I examine issues surrounding the emergence of basic research in Japan. To understand the process by which basic research has emerged in Japan and how it is being integrated into already existing research and development systems, a general understanding of the status of science and technology in Japan is necessary. Following this, I offer a definition of basic research as it applies to industrial company settings in general and Japanese company settings in particular. The main discussion of basic research in Japanese companies focuses first on the strategic motivations behind setting up these institutes and then on the institutional arrangements of the institutes themselves. Following that, I discuss the themes and organizational routines for doing basic research. Finally, I present some general conclusions.

The discussion on basic research and science in Japan is not intended to put forth any value judgments as to the proper way to carry out scientific or basic research. I did not try to determine whether the Japanese way of conducting research is correct, incorrect, or even "better" than the way research is conducted in the United States, however that is defined. It is important that the institutional setting in which research is conducted and some of the forces that act on this research be explained. Through an

Table 2.1. Number of Basic Research Institutes Established in Japan

Year	Number	Year	Number
1976	2	1983	6
1977	1	1984	7
1978	1	1985	6
1979	1	1986	5
1980	1	1987	6
1981	4	1988	13
1982	1	1989	11

Source: Chogin, 1991, p. 10.

understanding of the institutional forces affecting research in the Japanese context, the conclusions drawn can highlight areas of potential problems to be avoided as well as learning, for both the United States and Japan.

DEFINITIONS OF BASIC RESEARCH

Discussions of basic research in Japan usually include the copious use of quotation marks. This is a consequence of both the historic conditions of Japanese science and technology and the pragmatic and problem-driven approach taken by business people in general and Japanese business people in particular toward research and development issues. It is beyond the scope of this chapter to discuss the history of science and technology in Japan (see Odagiri & Goto, 1993). However, several salient points need to be highlighted.

SOME HISTORICAL CONSIDERATIONS

First, like many other concepts, science as it is practiced in the West, using theory-based hypotheses evaluated by empirical data testing, was imported into Japan. The growth of a strong independent tradition of scientific inquiry was truncated by the rise of militarism and the advent of the World War II. After the war, Japan began again the process of importing knowledge. This importation process had two implications for the subsequent development of technology in Japan.

First, from both a policy and an institutional resources point of view, it was more efficient to acquire, modify, and use knowledge generated elsewhere than to attempt to generate it internally. Second, both scientific and technological knowledge were being imported at the same time. As a result, what in the West would be distinguished as scientific knowledge, as opposed to technological knowledge, was to the Japanese simply that knowledge needed to solve problems. The clear distinction between science and technology thus became blurred. As a result, the Japanese term *kagakugijutsu* appears as often as do *kagaku* and *gijutsu* in discussions of science and technology. *Kagakujiutsu* often is translated into English as "science and technology," with the "and" made explicit in English but absent in Japanese.

This lack of distinction between what would be considered the appropriate domain of science in the West, that is, "knowledge for knowledge's sake," and the appropriate domain for technology, that is, "knowledge to solve a problem," may account as much for the confusion over what is considered basic research in Japan as the fact that Japanese technology has just recently approached the frontiers of scientific knowledge. But another factor, which goes beyond the historical setting of Japan and relates to the historical development of science and technology itself, is also at work.

The distinction between science and technology is blurring because of a process begun in the early part of the twentieth century. With the founding of the first company-supported research institutes in the United States and Europe, scientific knowledge and methods were first applied to industrial problems (Betz, 1987). This process has culminated in the late twentieth century in the electronics and biotechnology industries, among others, in which technology drives science as much as science drives technology. In an interesting twist of history, the perspective offered in the term *kagakug-ijutsu* may more accurately match the "scientific technology" on which modern industrial products and competition are based.

It is not surprising that the Japanese researchers from business laboratories that I interviewed for this study responded to questions about definitions of basic research with pragmatic and problem/solution–oriented answers. Distinctions among "basic," "applied," and "developmental" research were made less on purpose and more on process. These process distinctions were directed more to the time horizon of the research yielding a commercial product, the level of uncertainty or risk in developing a product, and the extent to which the research used information at the frontier of knowledge or required the generation of new knowledge to create a product in the future. Although this mind-set considers method more than motive, most of the Japanese interviewees commented that some of their research, especially what they termed *long-range basic research*, could be supported if it could solve problems that would benefit humankind, if not the company directly. They further noted, however, that the nature of business being what it is, the majority of projects would have to more than recoup the effort in resources expended; that is, they would have to make a profit.

These findings are in line with what other researchers have found when examining the nature of basic research in Japanese companies (Hicks & Hirooka, 1991). In discussions with U.S. researchers working for U.S. companies, similar sentiments emerged. Although I make no attempt to present these findings as the result of rigorous investigation, they do point to a preliminary conclusion that current definitions used by the National Science Foundation (NSF) or the Organization for Economic Cooperation and Development (OECD), when applied to business-sponsored research, are inadequate at best and misleading at worst. The source of misdirection is that the NSF's and OECD's definitions for basic research spring from the assumption that the researchers are motivated by "knowledge for knowledge's sake" and imply a strong and clear separation between science and technology. When discussing basic research, business people neither assume this motivation nor recognize such a clear separation between science and technology. For purposes of this study, then, the definition of basic research follows from the empirical data gathered through interviews rather than the definition used by the OECD or NSF. Basic research is any research that requires a long time frame in which to conduct it and requires the creation of new knowledge to solve problems. These problems may be practical, such as the creation of a product, or conceptual, such as the creation of a theory. This type of research is also characterized by a high degree of uncertainty in reaching conclusions, whether practical or conceptual.

THE INSTITUTIONAL SETTING FOR BASIC RESEARCH IN JAPAN

Three major Japanese institutions can conduct basic research in any modern capitalist setting: business, universities, and research institutes, whether government or private. Although most figures that measure the level of effort expended by these three institutions in Japan appear to indicate that the lion's share of basic research is carried out by universities and research institutes, as would be expected, in the case of Japan this may be somewhat misleading.

It has become somewhat fashionable to point to the failings in research of Japanese academic institutions and universities. Many Japanese are quick to point out the inadequate facilities (Ishii, 1993; Oka, 1993), and many privately admit to the problems with the *kozasei* system. Many Japanese academics and business people interviewed for this study noted that as a force for driving science in Japanese society, universities are the weak siblings of the three institutions. Although there are talented and creative researchers in Japanese universities, they are not in an institutional position to take a leadership role in guiding the development of science and basic research in Japan. In part, the interviewees pointed out that universities were established as knowledge disseminators, not knowledge generators, and in this capacity along with the primary and secondary education institutions, they have provided a steady stream of educated and disciplined workers. As such, Japanese universities are valued by Japanese companies more for their graduates than for their research.

Research institutes, especially government-supported research institutes, could fill the void left by universities, but here also, these institutions must contend with their history. In many cases these institutes were established inside a functioning ministry, such as the Ministry of International Trade and Industry (MITI), to help in the import and assimilation of foreign technology. These institutes have been described as constrained by the yearly budget system and bogged down in bureaucratic red tape (Muto & Hirano, 1991). Consequently, in their present form, these institutes are not likely to play a key role in establishing science in Japan.

This leaves, by default, business as the only institution with the resources and motivation to carry out scientific endeavors. However, the primary motivation of business is to make a profit from its efforts. This is a far cry from the "knowledge for knowledge's sake" motivation that science in the West is typically thought of as having as its raison d' être. In terms of papers published, Japanese researchers in business laboratories are conducting research that is considered of high scientific quality by scientists around the world (Hicks & Hirooka, 1991). It is also indicated in this and other reports that scientific research is often jointly conducted by business, university, and government research institutes (Hicks & Hirooka, 1991; JICST, 1992). This first leads us to four caveats that need to be understood before we examine the research and development system of Japanese businesses.

SOME IMPORTANT CAVEATS

Although the business sector is taking and will continue to take the leading role in defining science and basic research in Japan, business will not do it alone. The measure of technological and scientific infrastructure in an economic system cannot be determined solely by the number of business laboratories. This leads us to our first caveat, changes in the university–business relationship in science and technology.

Creative talent does exist in Japanese universities, and programs are being put in place for that talent to be channeled into doing research. These programs range from informal contact between university researchers and business laboratories to more formal institutional arrangements such as the Research Center for Advanced Science and Technology (RCAST) at the University of Tokyo. Formally inaugurated in 1987 with funding from the Ministry of Education and also from the business community, this institute was established to stimulate research into a broad range of topics, from developing new photonic materials to studying of the role of ethics in science and technology. What is important to the development of this institution is the presence of business in establishing the organization. Also, a business presence is maintained through contract research. The RCAST program was established as a way to provide greater flexibility in establishing and maintaining over the long term the university–business relationships necessary to carry out high-risk projects. The extent to which that relationship is weighted more toward business interests has yet to be determined. Other, similar programs have been established by the Ministry of Education in about 28 universities, and with these the number of joint projects stood at 1,139 in 1991 (Weber, 1993).

A parallel situation exists concerning the current government laboratories and research institutes and leads us to our second caveat. Similar flexibility and long-term perspectives are the hallmark of programs being established directly by government agencies such as the Agency of Industrial Science and Technology (AIST), currently connected with MITI, and the Research Development Corporation of Japan (JRDC), as part of the Science and Technology Agency (STA). The number and variety of programs that have been established through these and other ministries are too large and complicated to chronicle in this chapter. However, we should pay some attention to two projects as illustrative of the type of projects under way: one related to AIST and the other to STA.

In 1986 much interest was generated in the area of high-temperature superconductivity, by a discovery made by two researchers in IBM's Zurich laboratory. The International Superconductivity Technology Center (ISTEC) was established in 1988 through AIST's guidance as part of the Research and Development Project on Basic Technologies for Future Industries and administered by the New Energy and Industrial Technology Development Organization (NEDO). ISTEC is a nonprofit foundation that receives funding from NEDO and, currently, 112 private companies. The companies are large and small, industrial and non-industrial, and include non-Japanese companies. There are two types of members, general members who pay a yearly fee to join and receive periodic updates on ISTEC findings and special supporting members who pay a higher yearly fee but can send researchers from their companies to one of ISTEC's laboratories. Researchers from these special member organizations usually stay at IS-TEC's Superconductive Research Laboratory (SRL) from one to three years. Foreign researchers also participate in some projects.

Again, as in the case of the universities, business is part of in this basic-research endeavor. Because of the very nature of the problems related to high-temperature superconductivity, much of the early research conducted at SRL was exploratory and aimed at creating new knowledge. However, in recent interviews with the heads of SRC, they pointed out a shift in the research focus. That is, the goal of much of the research now is to develop a product or process that will be useful to business. The research conducted at this center, as with the cooperative university programs, can and will have scientific import and is appearing in academic journals, but the directed nature of the research also is important to note. The research will directly contribute to some company's "bottom line." Again, we should repeat that no value judgment is being presented. What is important is the institutional setting and the effect this has on the type and outcome of the research. That effect will most likely be to drive the work done at SRL further from the conceptual, knowledge-based work of science and more toward the solution of practical, product-based problems.

Another and slightly different type of project is the Exploratory Research for Advanced Technology (ERATO) projects that are administered by JRDC as part of STA. Like the ISTEC organization for superconductivity, the JRDC can fund ERATO projects for five years and, as a result, is able to get around the year-to-year budget constraints at those laboratories connected directly to the ministries. JRDC, like NEDO, is a statutory corporation of the Japanese government and, as such, can plan and fund projects over a longer time frame than simply year to year.

The ERATO program began in 1981 and is continuing. The program is made up of a number of projects that run for five years. In total, as of July 1992, about 638 researchers from 180 different organizations had participated in an ERATO project, including some 283 research personnel from 137 companies. Unlike ISTEC, the JRDC-run ERATO projects have no permanent laboratory and thus depend on the laboratory facilities of the participating organizations. The projects usually have a project leader, who may be from a university, government research institute, or private company. This leader picks a team of researchers who then carry out the research in their own or shared laboratory. JRDC provides the funding, and the participating organizations provide the laboratories and personnel. Again, flexibility is built into the system in terms of budgetary and organizational arrangements. Although the research team leaders are invited, usually because of their reputation and accomplishments in their respective fields, they have wide latitude in choosing members of the research team, which may include researchers from foreign companies.

Another program set up by the JRDC to encourage basic research is the Precursory Research for Embryonic Science and Technology (PRESTO) program. This program was established in 1991 and has accepted 72 researchers into three field areas. Unlike ERATO, these researchers work individually on projects for three-year periods as employees of JRDC at laboratories provided by JRDC. What is different about PRESTO is that it is centered on individual researchers, rather than teams of researchers, and allows these individuals to follow their own research agenda.

Some member organizations of these various quasi-governmental bodies are at least medium-size firms. This brings us to our third caveat, the role of supplier firms, usually small and medium-size firms, which cannot afford large research laboratories. The strength of the large Japanese firms that so often compete with U.S. companies depends directly on the health of their small supplier firms. That health is in turn becoming more dependent on these small and medium-size firms keeping up with technological change (Methé, 1985, 1991). Many medium-size supplier firms, such as Nikon and JEOL, are able to gain insights into future technologies through programs such ERATO and ISTEC. In this way, even these companies can keep up with the basic-research activities of their larger brethren. Likewise, small companies can take advantage of prefectural and local government support and a network of some 170 public centers established to support technological improvement in small companies (Shapira, 1992). These *kosetsushi* act very much like the agricultural extension system in the United States, but the crucial difference is the generation and dissemination of new technology to small manufacturing firms (Shapira, 1992). As a result of these programs, small and medium-size firms are able to keep up with and, in the case of some medium-size firms, create next-generation technology.

The final caveat is the increasingly apparent fact that research and development activities are taking place in a global environment (Gibbs, 1994). Many Japanese companies have established research and development facilities overseas, and many more are planning to do so (Methé, 1991). The activities of these facilities range from the basic-research activities of NEC's Princeton Laboratory and Hitachi's Cambridge Center to the advanced technology work of Sony's Advanced Video Technology Center or Toshiba's Advanced Television Technology Center, both in the United States, to numerous design centers for customizing products to fit the local market. This internationalization of research facilities, especially at the high end of the research spectrum, is another and crucial way in which Japanese companies can develop basic-research capabilities. By tapping into the talent available, the different approaches to research routines represented by different countries, and the network of available contacts, Japanese companies can gain immediate access to basic-research capabilities. In this respect, the "make or buy" decision reemerges, but in a drastically different form. It is no longer make or buy the technological information, but make or buy the research talent and attendant research routines.

MOTIVATIONS FOR BASIC RESEARCH IN JAPAN

Having discussed definitional issues and the overall complexity of the technological infrastructure related to research and development activities in Japan, I now turn to the organizational routines of research and development in several large Japanese electronics companies and the emerging role of basic research in those companies. In this study, an organizational routine means the way in which a task is conducted by the members of an organization. Routines represent the summation over time of individual actions as they work in conjunction with other individual actions in the organization to solve problems. These actions are retained by the organization and can be taught to other members. The routines need not be codified and can be taught experientially. A routine exists independently of any individual person or group that is carrying it out but is subject to interpretation. Through this interpretation, organizational routines can be changed. The value of this change and its retention and diffusion throughout the organization, however, are often beyond the control of the person or group that originated the change. One organizational routine, the "make or buy" decision, has been a reinterpreted by Japanese companies. In the fast-paced competition in the electronics industry, waiting to "buy" new technological information is simply untenable. A gain of three to six months on a competitor can often spell the difference between a profit and merely breaking even, with larger time gains translating into larger profits.

Concern was raised publicly in Japan beginning in the mid-1980s that Japanese companies needed to concentrate more on generating new technological knowledge (Methé, 1991). This discussion was motivated primarily by the "make or buy" situation. Part of the motivation for the discussion, however, arose from the recognition that for all the technological prowess available in Japan, Japanese companies were seen as imitators and free riders on the scientific efforts of U.S. and European companies. The often-voiced laments by the Japanese about a "Nobel Prize gap" was one manifestation of this awareness. Several Japanese writers and researchers also noted the need for greater "creativity" on the part of Japanese companies if they were going to be able to contribute to the future of humankind, let alone survive in the competition of the future (Murakami & Nishiwaki, 1991). Even in the interviews I conducted for this report over the past two years, Japanese researchers raised the issues of whether they were creative or even capable of creativity in the sense of a truly groundbreaking invention or discovery. Although it is beyond the scope of this research to be able to answer that question definitively, I will offer a comment.

Part of the reason for this perception lies in Japan's latecomer status. What is innovative to the latecomer can be perceived as mere imitation to the already established player. Often what is lost in this observation is the creative way in which the product may have been copied. A lot of ingenuity can go into new ways to manufacture an old product, as one example. This confusion over the content and process aspects of technological change contributed to U.S. companies' misinterpretation of the competitive capabilities of Japanese companies.

Furthermore, creativity can manifest itself in a variety of ways. Terms such as *radical, major,* or *incremental innovation* (Methé, 1985) and *frame-breaking* or *frame-bending change* (Tushman, Newman, & Romanelli, 1986) are examples of the deeper understanding of the innovation process as it relates to the strategic management of business. Sony was very creative in developing and marketing the Walkman. Sharp was equally so in its efforts to use LCDs in its products. Nintendo perhaps takes the prize for being able to creatively rearrange existing technologies and gain a dominant position in a market. In each case, creativity was exhibited along the different dimensions of competition, which are, in turn, technological, product, and market. Japanese companies have creatively been able to use existing technologies in products and sell them to markets that U.S. companies had either overlooked or felt were not large enough to enter. Japanese companies are currently confronting the necessity of developing new technologies that can be used in products to sell to markets. This is most evident in the case of multimedia, an industry concept in search of a product to define it.

RESEARCH AND DEVELOPMENT ROUTINES IN JAPAN

The institutional arrangements for basic-research facilities in Japanese companies can be seen as an outgrowth of the overall approach to research and development that already exists in these companies. The linear approach most often discussed in the United States, of basic research's providing the fundamental knowledge that applied research then turns into a prototype that can be further refined into a successful product through developmental research, is turned on its head in Japanese companies. Rather than "push on a string," the Japanese "pull on it." The approach is problem driven, in which a particular market need must be met by a product that is often a combination of technologies. These two approaches are presented in Figure 2.1.

This approach of "pulling on the string" was well suited to the market share–driven strategy of Japanese companies, because it allowed a large variety of products to be developed efficiently from a well-mapped body of technical knowledge. This approach has also been observed in the introduction of both software and hardware products in the computer industry (Choy, 1994). This research and development system places a larger emphasis on development and a smaller emphasis on research, because the knowledge needed was almost always available or could be acquired. The ability of Japanese companies to turn out large varieties of products is seen in Table 2.2.

Table 2.2 shows the number of new product introductions each year for a selected group of consumer electronic and durable white goods. The timing of the product introductions coincided with the semiannual payment of bonuses. Organizationally, this "innovation treadmill" required a close connection between those actually making the product and those designing and developing it. Often laboratories were located on the same grounds as factories, which facilitated their sharing of technical information. This practice has led some observers to comment that Japanese factories, or *works,* as they are called, are intelligent (Fruin, 1992). Perhaps the most noted is the Toshiba works at Ome, which was responsible for developing that company's laptop computer.

What is considered research and development in Japanese companies often differs from that of their U.S. counterparts. For instance, one company in 1992 considered activities on photolithographic steppers for the 64M DRAM and 256M DRAM "design" work and not true research. True research was being carried out on photolithographic equipment for 1G DRAM and greater. This means that the level of work being done in

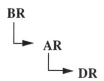 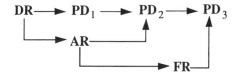

U.S. APPROACH:

JAPANESE APPROACH:

BR: Basic Research **FR:** Fundamental Research
AR: Applied Research **PD$_i$:** Product Developed at i
DR: Developmental Research

Figure 2.1. Comparison of U.S. and Japanese approaches to research and development in companies.

Table 2.2.   Number of New Product Introductions,
Selected Products over Several Years

	1987	1988	1989
Color TVs	277	286	296
VTRs	154	202	184
Personal computers	135	214	166
Air conditioners	337	452	536
Refrigerators	189	235	228
Washing machines	115	145	145

Source: Adapted from Nikkei Electronics, 1992, p. 122.

the research laboratories of this company may be equivalent to that done
in the engineering departments of U.S. universities, an observation that has
been made in other companies (Hicks & Hirooka, 1991).

Not only is the physical location of the research facility a factor, but the
system for allocating resources internally must also be structured to help
keep this system going. Although the standard research and development
routines of Japanese companies vary from company to company, these
practices emphasize efficiency. Generally, the approach taken by Japanese
companies in the past 40 years has been predicated on the assumption that
they were dealing with a known technology trajectory, whether it was basic oxygen furnaces (BOF) in steel processing or metal oxide semiconductors (MOS) in integrated-circuit processing. Efficiency in moving along
each trajectory is key in the research process. This explains why one of the
first steps a Japanese researcher takes when handed an assignment is to
study the relevant patent database to determine whether a useful answer
already exists. This also helps explain why many research laboratories in
Japan have their own patent library on site, even with space at a premium.
These research and development routines can suffer from an extreme form
of Greshem's law. The drive for efficiency, especially in the use of time for
speeding a product to market, tends to focus researchers' attention on
finding an answer rather than allowing them the luxury of pursuing interesting questions. These interesting questions may open up new avenues of
research, which in turn raise even more questions. Consequently, "question raising," or exploratory research, is crowded out by "question-
answering research." Japanese companies have been aware of this problem
for some time and have attempted to put in place different routines for
conducting special or advanced research.

ATTEMPTS TO DEVELOP NEW RESEARCH ROUTINES

Perhaps one of the best examples of how a new research and development
routine was put in place to supplement the activities of the structured research and development process is provided by one large integrated electronics manufacturer. An intricate system of *tokubetsu kenkyu* (*tokken*),

or special research projects, was established. These projects were carried out in addition to regular research activities and received special attention by top management, in that *tokken* project managers reported directly to top management. *Tokken* projects were usually corporate-level, large-scale projects related to urgent research and development matters. Resources were flexibly assigned and may have come from a wide variety of sources within the company. Two types of *tokken* categories were established. The first, *tokken A*, usually had a shorter time frame and were related more to immediate business unit needs. The second, *tokken B*, were longer-range research projects that tapped into future technologies. A typical *tokken A* project might be carried out by a works, a divisional laboratory, and a corporate laboratory, whereas the *tokken B* would usually be done at one or more corporate laboratories. There were about 40 *tokken* projects running at the time of this interview in 1992. Although they increased the flexibility of the research routines, these *tokken* projects were still driven by the efficiency ethos of the overall research organization. Exploratory or question-raising research was still being crowded out.

To put into some perspective the strategic change effort undertaken by these projects, there are nine corporate laboratories and 26 divisional laboratories in this large integrated electronics manufacturer, with 4,300 people doing research at the corporate laboratories and 8,600 people at the divisional and works laboratories. This attempt to break up some of the established research routines by the use of *tokken* projects is spread across the entire company. However, of the nine corporate laboratories, eight are closely tied into the divisions' day-to-day activities. About 70 percent of their research budget is from contract research from the divisions and works. The other 30 percent comes from corporate coffers. The Central Research Laboratory, which in many ways acts as a hub for the other corporate laboratories, receives about 50 percent of its research funds from the corporation and the remaining 50 percent from the divisions and works. All these can be called on to participate in *tokken* projects.

BASIC RESEARCH AT ONE JAPANESE COMPANY

The *tokken* system did increase the company's flexibility and responsiveness, but it was felt that many technological areas that would become important sources of products were being overlooked. The company needed to establish a new set of organizational routines for conducting exploratory research. As a result, it decided to establish a new laboratory, the Advanced Research Laboratory (ARL). In doing so, the company decided that 100 percent of the ARL's funding would come from corporate headquarters. Consequently, it is the only laboratory in this large integrated electronics manufacturer's research system that is structured to be totally independent from the day-to-day activities of the operating units. It is also physically quite far from the rest of the company's laboratories and factories. The ARL is dedicated to the long-range, high-risk, new techno-logical knowledge–generating projects that make up basic research in Japan.

In discussing why the ARL was established, several important factors were mentioned. The ARL was established in 1985. Before that time, the company recognized that it needed to begin developing its own technologi-cal area, much as ATST had done when it developed the transistor in 1948. Only in this way, it was felt, could the company survive in future competitive contests. It was being squeezed by companies from the devel-oping nations of South Korea and Taiwan on one end and was tied to waiting for new technology from the United States and Europe. This situa-tion would lead to strategic decline, it was felt. Consequently, a new ap-proach using different research routines had to be started.

The ARL was originally placed in this company's research campus, which houses the Central Research Laboratory (CRL) and other related facilities. This was initially done more because of space considerations and the fact that the new laboratory's building and equipment had not yet been completed. Part of the reason for establishing the ARL was because of the overwhelming attractive pull exerted on the researchers by the daily research challenges of the operating units. Even the CRL, which at one time was responsible for conducting the company's long-range research, was seen as being too enmeshed in the "day-to-day" research routines, of "pulling on the string."

Moreover, although the *tokken* projects did add flexibility to the stan-dard research and development system, they lacked a degree of continuity and were not an appropriate vehicle to provide strategic direction to this company's research efforts. Consequently, it was felt that by setting up a laboratory that was organizationally separate from the rest of the research system, this laboratory's researchers would be less likely to be "captured" by the lure of "pulling on the string." The ARL was moved from the original site at the company's research campus to a physical location away from the rest of the company's activities. Considerations such as space and the cost of land were important. However, the sense that by placing the ARL away from other research laboratories, researchers could truly focus on their question-raising research and not be caught by sociometric forces drawing them into question-answering research was given weight by the decision makers.

In the efforts to insulate the ARL, however, concern was expressed that it not become isolated from the rest of the organization. Unlike planets in a solar system, researchers often do benefit when they stray from their usual "orbits" and "collide" with one another. The trick with the ARL was to control the number of collisions. A delicate balancing act must be performed, it was stated, to allow the researchers to concentrate on their work and also be open to outside influence. This feat must be accom-plished not only between the ARL and the rest of the company's research and operating units but also between the ARL and the rest of the world.

Part of the balancing act can be accomplished by conducting conferences and seminars for both the company's researchers and those from outside the company. In addition, guest researchers can be brought in for lectures and seminars, and some foreign researchers are participating in research at the ARL. There are currently about 100 researchers at the ARL, of whom about four are not Japanese. In time the number of researchers should expand to 200. There also are hopes of internationalizing the research agenda and increasing the number of non-Japanese researchers to about 10. In addition to conferences, contact with the outside is through publishing papers and joint research. For example, one of the ARL senior researchers is currently participating in an ERATO project. In addition, some ARL researchers may leave for other laboratories in the company or may leave the company completely. Some have gone into academic institutions, but none has entered another company. Finally, the choice of projects plays a role in controlling the degree of connection to the rest of the company.

It was stated that the ARL belongs to the company and is not a university laboratory. As such, the type of projects suggested and selected should have some kind of product or process application to the company. What distinguishes the ARL from other laboratories, and even from the *tokken* system, is the time frame and degree, in terms of both the difficulty and the number of knowledge-generating activities involved. All projects may have a 10- to 20-year or longer time frame before the knowledge generated is expected to be converted into products. Also, each project is concerned with advancing knowledge in one of four main areas: electron/radiation beam physics, software science, biotech, and materials science. Currently, 16 projects are spread across these areas and include electron holography, synchrotron radiation, natural-language understanding, automatic program production, protein engineering, measurement and analysis of biological materials, conducting polymers and atomic structure calculation of semiconductors, and high-temperature superconductors. These projects are expected to result in papers and patents, in that order. Products were not expected to be a direct result of research, although other laboratories were expected to use the knowledge gained to develop products. In conducting some research in electron physics, it was necessary to develop new tools, one of which, a holography electron microscope, could result in a marketable product, it was thought.

Each project team is led by a senior researcher. In addition to conducting research, the senior researcher offers guidance to the other team members in pursuing individual research. Because the ARL was part of a business, it could not afford to let its researchers run off in every possible direction and thus become too dispersed. This was seen as wasting resources. But it was recognized that in basic research, individual creativity is crucial to success. Again, the company is attempting to strike a balance between individual work and team work in developing a new research routine. In the other laboratories in this company, most research is carried out by a team, and the team's result is evaluated. Each researcher in ARL is evaluated formally once a year, but real results, in terms of papers, are not expected for three to five years. Part of this formal evaluation is an assessment from the team leader. In addition, an informal review of each researcher is conducted once a year by the director of the ARL. But even if a researcher totally fails in the ARL, he or she is not fired but is simply moved to another laboratory in the company's system, on the assumption that even though he or she cannot do basic research, he or she will be able to do more applied research.

To enhance further the freedom to pursue individual research efforts in the ARL, attempts are made to keep the laboratory organization as flat and small as possible. This is a way to avoid the *kozasei,* which exists in universities and is seen as stifling to research creativity. In other laboratories in this company, a kind of *kozasei* does exist, as senior researchers assume a greater role in actually running the laboratories. However, in the ARL the senior researchers are there to guide and coordinate the research activities of younger researchers. Furthermore, there are no technicians, lab assistants, or secretarial staff for the researchers. In theory, each researcher must act as his or her own technician or lab assistant. In practice, however, some hierarchy has crept in, in that freshman researchers act as lab assistants to senior researchers. This occurs more often in the "hard" science areas such as electron/radiation beam physics and not at all in the software science area.

At first glance it may appear as somewhat wasteful to have younger researchers running lab tests and calibrating equipment, but this often can lead to improvements in how the tests are done. Younger researchers want to develop more efficient and effective ways to run the tests so that they can get on with their own research. Also, new insights can be gained by having well-trained researchers running the tests. They may spot interesting phenomena that a technician concerned merely with accurately running the test might miss.

From a budgetary point of view, most of what researchers need can be acquired without onerous administrative red tape. For the most part, the researchers can assume that they will be funded at the level needed to complete their research, over the necessary time frame. This is especially true in the software sciences, for which very expensive equipment, such as computers, is already in place. Occasionally, in the hard sciences, new and expensive equipment must be acquired. In that case, the decision can be made by the director of the ARL. Only rarely does it need to go higher in the organization. Budgetary constraints for projects usually do not kick in until the $1 million to $2 million level on a yearly basis.

Although the ARL has been in existence since 1985, it has been in its new facilities for only the past few years. It is too soon to tell if any research projects will meet the expectations of the researchers or the company, although every attempt is being made to maintain the new research routines that have been established at the ARL. This is true in spite of the recession currently plaguing the Japanese economy and electronics producers in particular.

A LOOK AT OTHER JAPANESE COMPANIES' EXPERIENCES

Other Japanese companies in the same industry are also attempting to develop new organizational routines for research and development. I found in the research for this chapter that each company has taken a different approach to this endeavor. Space does not permit as detailed a report for each company as the one given previously (Methé, 1994), but I shall present some general observations.

The structure of the basic-research laboratory varies from company to company. In one company it appears to have evolved in the central research laboratory as more and more corporate laboratories dedicated to specific technology areas are established. These dedicated technology laboratories appear to take on more of the longer-term product-development activities that were once done by the central research laboratory. As a result, the central research laboratory has more freedom to pursue even broader-ranging and longer-term technology projects.

Another company has established a basic-research facility as a brand new laboratory away from other laboratories, but it has included several applied-research labs inside the new basic-research laboratory. In this case, the new basic-research laboratory is separate, both physically and in terms of funding, but it is not totally dedicated to basic research, in that some facilities and researchers have as their explicit charge the development of products or work on processes.

In yet a third case, no physical basic-research laboratory was established at all, or at least none was called by that name. In its place a number of systems allowing researchers to receive resources to follow difficult and challenging research projects that might result in products or processes for the company were put in place. This process was true at least for the hardware end of this computer and electronics manufacturer. For the software end, a new laboratory was established to examine such questions as Where and how will the information society progress? What kind of "tools" will people use in the twenty-first century? How do Japanese people recognize *kanji* (Japanese characters or syllables), and how is the pattern physiologically processed and stored? In addition, some hard science is being done in this laboratory in fields such as biosensors.

In still another company, part of its central research laboratory was set aside for basic research. In this case, the company admitted that the kind of basic research being conducted in the first company described in this chapter was unlikely to be done in this setting, but it hoped that this approach would allow the companies' several laboratories to coordinate to do advanced technological research and to assimilate results from various scientific fields.

CONCLUSIONS

Several general factors come into play in the cases of these companies as they attempt to develop new organizational research routines. The first is an awareness that there is a dynamic tension that must be balanced between generating knowledge and allowing researchers to follow their research agenda and generating a product or process useful to the company that requires exploiting knowledge and follows from the company's research agenda. The second is balancing the dynamic tension between connecting the basic-research group to the organization and insulating researchers from the pressures that such connections will bring. The third is balancing the dynamic tension between producing something useful in the near term that has a relatively small risk and waiting for something even more useful in the far term that has a relatively great risk.

The challenge confronting Japanese management is one common to any organization that must replace tried and successful routines with ones that are untried and speculative in their outcomes. This challenge is made even more complicated because not only the research routines are untried and speculative but also the nature of the research being conducted is more open ended and uncertain. Confronted with the unknowns of these new routines as well as the unknowns inherent in any kind of exploratory research, mistakes and even failures are inevitable. How these situations are handled will determine which way the balance will trip along the three dimensions discussed earlier.

Another factor common to all the companies that further complicates the balancing act between "old" and "new" routines is that none of the companies I surveyed had had experience doing this kind of research. In each company I examined, individual researchers and research managers had had experience working in such research institutes as Bell Laboratories in the United States, but on a companywide basis, this was a small percentage. As a result, the cumulative experience inside these companies is quite small, and although the need for this kind of research is recognized, there is still a very small constituency supporting it. The test comes with the failures that are inevitable in this type of research. Pressures to justify this type of research already are mounting because of the current recession. Justification can be given now for continued support, because the programs are still young and results are not yet forthcoming, but such explanations have a very short half-life, if U.S. and European business experience is any guide.

It is likely, however, that enough Japanese companies will be successful in establishing these new routines because of the environment in which Japanese companies currently find themselves. As noted earlier in this chapter, they must develop knowledge-generating capabilities. And these companies are not working alone on building these capabilities. In some cases the university, governmental, and international aspects of Japan's growing technological infrastructure can compensate for or enhance the activities of individual companies. This can occur in two ways. The first is with the knowledge that is created by these programs. The second relates more to the process of doing exploratory research.

In an examination first of the process issue, an important contribution that the various government–industry programs such as ISTEC and ERATO are making is training a generation of researchers experienced in the difficulties of conducting basic or question-raising research. Although the number of researchers going through these programs is not large relative to the total number of researchers in Japanese organizations, their training and experience are an added source of learning that can be used to alter the organizational routines currently used by Japanese companies. Given the relatively small size of the basic, exploratory research being conducted in companies, the effect of these researchers may be disproportionately larger than their numbers would indicate. Similar effects could be derived from the university–business connections. The international research activities are also a way to expose researchers to new ways of conducting exploratory research. These various ways of conducting basic research raise other issues in and of themselves, however, because their influence can run both ways. Because university laboratories and government research institutes have been tied to business from the start, a tradition of research independent of business influence is weak. Consequently, the very success of establishing these new routines in a context dominated by a business ethos could lead to more vexing problems. Perhaps the most salient issue is that of questions over the ownership of intellectual property rights. This is important not only to the cooperative research carried out among industry, government, and universities but especially because of the globalization of research activities. This is where the very business-oriented approach taken by Japan toward basic research could have its most troubling effect.

Ideally, scientific knowledge is seen by scientists as the fruit of basic research and also as a public good. But businesses, whether Japanese or non-Japanese, think first of ownership. In the United States and Europe, other institutions can act somewhat to counter this tendency of businesses to restrict on the flow of knowledge. Even in these economies, the powerful allure of profit for individual researchers and the call for increasing competitiveness by focusing university and government institutes' research on more near-term results useful to business have been difficult to resist. In Japan, these other institutions are weaker. Consequently, a new form of "trade dispute" could arise in the future, as Japan's more business-oriented basic research efforts begin, as they most certainly will, to bear fruit.

This issue over the free flow of scientific and technological information is not just a matter for government trade negotiators or business managers. Rather, it is a matter that can affect all scientific research and the progress of humankind itself. Both scientific and technological knowledge are closer to living, breathing organisms than they are to mechanical entities. This type of knowledge must be continually refreshed, challenged, and updated, or it will die; that is, it will lose its value-generating capacity. It would be ironic if one of the consequences, albeit unintended, of the recent strategic attention on the importance of knowledge in creating products with greater value were to miss this organic view of knowledge and lead to restrictions that constrained the growth of knowledge. As managers of companies, whether Japanese or non-Japanese, become more involved in technological research, they must keep in mind that successful innovation is built on the efforts of many who often belong to different and independent organizations. If many companies close themselves off, then the great endeavor that is science could slow and perhaps cease.

It is difficult to assess the outcome of such a situation, but an image from antiquity may be useful for these modern times and issues. It is one image of hell in Buddhist cosmology, in which a great banquet is displayed on a table. Around the table sitting opposite each other are a number of people. Each person has a pair of chopsticks, which, however, are too long, to pick up any food and place it into the person's mouth. The chopsticks are, however, long enough to feed the person across the table. What makes this an image of hell is that no one will feed the person opposite him or her, and so all are slowly starving.

As long as Japan, and also South Korea, Taiwan, Malaysia, Thailand, and other countries, develop the capabilities to pursue advanced scientific endeavors in this capitalist system, the image of this Buddhist hell will probably be kept from becoming a reality. The free flow of information required for continued progress in science and technology must be balanced with the need for proprietary information to be protected as more companies begin to engage in knowledge-generating activities. This will be a difficult balancing act, but one that must be achieved if we are to solve the increasingly global challenges of environment, health, and economic development.

REFERENCES

Arrison, T. S., Bergsten, C. F., Graham, E. M., & Harris, M. C. (Eds.). (1992). *Japan's growing technological capability: Implications for the U.S. economy.* Washington, DC: National Academy Press.

Betz, F. (1987). *Managing technology: Competing through new ventures, innovation and corporate research.* Englewood Cliffs, NJ: Prentice-Hall.

Boyd, J. (1993, July 19). The computer world according to sun. *Japan Times,* p. 9.

Chogin, S. K. (1991). *R&D globalization activities: The path from a country-based industry to a world-based industry,* (in Japanese). Tokyo: Nihon choki shinyo ginko.

Choy, J. (1994, April 1). *Japan's computer software market: Where are the Japanese?* JEI Report No. 13A. Tokyo: Japan Economic Institute.

Fruin, M. (1992, November 13). *Organizational architecture and innovation: Knowledge works at Toshiba.* Unpublished paper, University of Michigan.

Gibbs, W. W. (1994, April). Basic strategies: Japanese companies cultivate research labs sown in the U.S. *Scientific American*, pp. 114–15.

Hicks, D., & Hirooka, M. (1991, September). *Defining basic research in Japanese companies and science in Japanese companies: A preliminary analysis.* Tokyo: National Institute of Science and Technology Policy.

Hirano, Y., & Nishigata, C. (1990, January). *Basic research in major companies of Japan.* Tokyo: National Institute of Science and Technology Policy.

Ishii, Y. (1993, Spring). A neglect of research may doom Japan's future. *Economic Eye, 14,* 9–11.

JICST (1992). *Company research and development information map* (in Japanese). Tokyo: Nihon kagaku gijutsu joho center.

Management and Coordination Agency (1975). *Linked input–output tables.* Tokyo: Management Coordination Agency.

Management and Coordination Agency (1980). *Linked input–output tables.* Tokyo: Management Coordination Agency.

Management and Coordination Agency (1985). *Linked input–output tables.* Tokyo: Management Coordination Agency.

Methé, D. T. (1985). *Technology, transaction costs, and the diffusion of innovation: The evolution of the United States and Japanese DRAM integrated circuit industries.* Unpublished doctoral dissertation, University of California at Irvine.

Methé, D. T. (1991). *Technological competition in global industries: Marketing and planning strategies for American industry.* Westport, CT: Quorum Books.

Methé, D. T. (1992). Techno-global competition in the integrated circuit industry. *Advances in applied business strategy* (Vol. 3). Greenwich, CT: JAI Press.

Methé, D. T. (1994). *Differences in approach taken by Japanese companies in the establishment of new organizational routines for basic research and enhancing creativity.* Unpublished working paper, University of Michigan.

Murakami, T., & Nishiwaki, T. (1991). *Strategy for creation.* Cambridge: Woodhead Publishing.

Muto, E., & Hirano, Y. (1991, September). *Government laboratories and basic research: Towards the promotion of basic research in government laboratories.* Tokyo: National Institute of Science and Technology Policy.

Nikkei Electronics. (1992, July 6). *Home appliance makers' movements focus on consumers and retail stores* (in Japanese). Report No. 558. Tokyo: Nikkei Electronics.

Odagiri, H., & Goto, A. (1993). The Japanese system of innovation: Past, present and future. In R. R. Nelson (Ed.), *National innovation systems: A corporative analysis* (pp. 76–114). New York: Oxford University Press.

Oka, H. (1993, Spring). The industrial's sector's expectations of engineering education. *Economic Eye, 14,* 12–15.

Shapira, P. (1992, Spring). Lessons from Japan: Helping small manufacturers. *Issues in Science and Technology, 8,* 66–72.

Tushman, M. L., Newman, W. H., & Romanelli, E. (1986, Fall). Convergence and upheaval: Managing the unsteady pace of organizational evolution. *California Management Review, 29,* 29–44.

Weber, H. (1993). *University–industry cooperative research centers in national universities in Japan.* Report Memorandum No. 93–7. Tokyo: Tokyo Office of U.S. National Science Foundation.

3

The Growth of R&D Investment and Organizational Changes by Japanese Pharmaceutical Firms, 1975–1993

THOMAS ROEHL,
WILL MITCHELL,
AND RONALD J. SLATTERY

In this chapter we examine the growth of R&D investment and organizational changes undertaken by Japanese pharmaceutical manufacturers during the past two decades. Many firms in the Japanese pharmaceutical industry have taken great strides toward world levels of R&D intensity and product output, but contrary to many other industries discussed elsewhere in this volume, the industry leaders remain below the sales volume of leading global players in the industry. In 1990, for example, the largest Japanese firm spent about $350 million (9% of sales) on R&D, whereas Bristol-Myers Squibb spent $854 million (9% of sales) and Merck spent $881 million (11% of sales). Given their smaller revenue base, the Japanese firms cannot match the current level of R&D expenditure of the leading European and American rivals. Thus, rather than starting from a position of international strength, the firms in this industry must find a way to improve their current, relatively weak international competitive position while at the same time responding to environmental stimuli that are forcing change on the worldwide pharmaceutical industry. Not being dominant global firms, these companies might have much to say to American firms that also are struggling to assume strong positions in their industries.

In 1990, Japanese pharmaceutical production totaled about ¥5,600 billion, exports reached ¥36 billion, and imports amounted to ¥469 billion (Japan Economic Institute, 1992; Table 3.1). Japanese-owned companies distributed about 90 percent of pharmaceutical sales in Japan; about 10 percent of sales in Japan were accounted for by foreign-owned distribution subsidiaries (Nakagawa, 1992). Drugs distributed by Japanese-owned companies included drugs developed and produced in Japan, drugs produced in Japan under license from non-Japanese companies, and imported pharmaceuticals. Drugs made in Japan from primarily imported bulk ingredients amounted to about 25 percent of production in 1990 (Japan Economic Institute, 1992). Foreign-owned firms accounted for almost 25 percent of sales in 1990, but more than half of this was distributed by an independent Japanese firm or with a Japanese joint-venture partner (Nakagawa, 1992).

Recently, several researchers identified major changes that are taking place in the Japanese pharmaceutical industry. Several analysts found that R&D expenditures, the output of new chemical entities (NCEs), and the emphasis on basic science all are increasing in the Japanese pharmaceutical industry (e.g., Campbell, Mitchell, & Roehl, 1995; *Economist,* 1987; Grabowski, 1990; Hawkins & Reich, 1992; Ikegami, Mitchell, & Penner-Hahn, 1994; Industrial Bank of Japan, 1992; James, 1990; Mitchell, Roehl, & Slattery, in press; Nakamura, 1991; Nikko Research Center, 1991; Reich, 1990; Salomon Brothers Asia Limited, 1992; Suguro, 1990; Yoshikawa, 1989). Indeed, more new NCEs originated in Japan than in any other country between 1981 and 1989. An unpublished study by the consulting group of Japan Pharma shows that of the 443 NCEs introduced between 1981 and 1989, 117 originated in Japan, 107 in the United States, and 36 in Germany. Some analysts argue that products developed in Japan have been more likely to advance existing technology incrementally than to push biomedical science onto new frontiers, but commentators have noted an increase in the number of corporate research units that emphasize open-ended basic biomedical research rather than targeted product development. These trends point to the potential for some Japanese pharmaceutical companies to emerge as major global players in the next decade.

This chapter is based on information gathered from public sources and interviews conducted in Japan with 15 pharmaceutical companies and several industry analysts during July and August 1992 and follow-up interviews with firms in the summer of 1993. We report an industrywide trend of increasing investment in R&D, greater numbers of researchers, and the creation of new organizational units specifically devoted to research and development. At the same time, we report substantial firm-based differences in R&D investment growth, research focus, and research organization. The chapter will help broaden the understanding of the role that might be played by different Japanese companies in the global pharmaceutical industry during the next decade. More generally, we address the importance of examining firm-specific differences that have major implications for competition within an industry and show the limitations of the all too common "Japanese industry" approach to studying technology management in Japan.

R&D TRENDS IN THE JAPANESE
PHARMACEUTICAL INDUSTRY

The pharmaceutical R&D process can be categorized in terms of basic biomedical research, drug discovery, and preclinical product development. Basic research identifies opportunities for pharmaceutical therapy. Drug discovery refers to finding and testing development candidates from existing and newly synthesized chemical entities. Preclinical development describes a particular drug and carries out toxicology studies. After preclinical trials, drugs undergo several rounds of clinical testing on human subjects before they are introduced commercially. The earliest parts of the sequence are closest to basic science, and the latest parts are closest to applied product development, with early-stage drug discovery lying at the basic-research end of the continuum and later-stage discovery being part of product development.

Historically, the Japanese pharmaceutical industry has been characterized as being less research intensive than are the pharmaceutical industries in the United States and western Europe. Instead, they are perceived as being much more focused on the discovery of incrementally improved drugs and their preclinical development than on basic biomedical research and early-stage drug discovery. Traditionally, most companies emphasized identifying and testing development candidates from existing and newly synthesized chemical entities rather than finding new opportunities for pharmaceutical therapy. For instance, Halliday, Walker, and Lumley (1992) reported that the 11 leading Japanese pharmaceutical firms they surveyed undertook fewer high-risk projects than did the leading American and European pharmaceutical companies, and they were slightly more likely to concentrate on modifying products than on carrying out more basic research and development. During the past two decades, however, environmental influences on the R&D practices of Japanese pharmaceutical manufacturers have changed drastically, and as a result, the intensity and focus of R&D activity also have changed and are continuing to change.

Three Key Environmental Changes

Three environmental influences that have caused R&D practices to change stand out: (1) changes in the domestic regulatory and health cost payment environment, (2) changes in the competitive environment, and (3) increases in the cost of R&D after the 1960s. The changes on the demand side of the market, in the competitive environment, and on the supply side of the industry provided the stimulus for changes by the firms and formed the basis for understanding the industrywide and company-specific responses that are the theme of this chapter. In particular, the changes dramatically increased the incentives for Japanese pharmaceutical companies to carry out more basic research and early-stage drug discovery to compete effectively in Japan and throughout the world.

Changes in Domestic Regulatory Conditions

Two major regulatory changes affected R&D incentives in the pharmaceutical industry during the past two decades. First, until 1976, Japanese patent law protected processes rather than products. Under this system, Japanese firms could use a different process to produce a drug similar to one developed by another Japanese company or a foreign firm. With such a process-based patent—as opposed to one based on the chemical compound—the firms could avoid some of the initial exploratory work on new drugs and use a new process to introduce their version of a drug developed by another firm. This situation changed in 1976 when Japan revised its patent laws to protect products. With patents now based on the chemical compounds, firms had to increase either their R&D efforts or their dependence on licensed-in products, many of which were licensed from foreign companies.

The second major change involved the Ministry of Health and Welfare's (MHW) payment policies for prescription drugs. In Japan, doctors prescribe and fill most prescriptions, taking a margin as part of their compensation under the country's universal medical care system. All pharmaceuticals are sold to customers at the price decided on and reimbursed by the MHW under the Japanese National Health Insurance system. Doctors buy the drugs from pharmaceutical firms at a discount that they or their hospital negotiate with the firm. This margin is an important revenue source for the doctors, giving them an incentive to prescribe pharmaceuticals in order to increase their income. Because the prescription process is very decentralized, the system has encouraged pharmaceutical firms to deploy large ranks of medical representatives to encourage doctors to use the pharmaceuticals manufactured by their firm.

Traditionally, drug prices were set by the MHW following approval of the product, with manufacturers suggesting a price based on the efficacy and prices of comparable products. Prices then remained at their initial level during the market life of the drugs, declining only slowly over time. This policy provided incentives for manufacturers to maintain full lines of pharmaceutical products. To maintain product portfolios, most established Japanese pharmaceutical companies licensed many products from foreign-owned pharmaceutical companies.

In 1981, the MHW changed its pricing policy and began to reduce its payments for pharmaceuticals. Prices for established drugs declined substantially as the MHW conducted periodic reviews of National Health Insurance drug prices (which almost always resulted in lower prices) after introduction of the product and set lower initial prices for drugs that were not judged to be significantly different from existing products in the market. Drugs judged to be innovative received favorable treatment under the changed rules. Eight rounds of price reductions took place between June

1981 and April 1992, with the reductions in each round averaging from about 5 percent to almost 19 percent.

The new pricing policies had significant effects on the characteristics of the stream of returns from drug innovation. With patent protection, it is ordinarily assumed that a firm has monopoly power that will be fully exercised via higher prices throughout the patent period (Comanor, 1986). In the Japanese case, the pricing policies conflict with this assumption. After prices began to be reduced in the 1980s, a drug that had been on the market for more than 10 years often had a reimbursement price that was less than half its initial level. The more new drugs that are introduced in a product class, the steeper the decline will be in the price of older products. The newer, innovative drugs and those produced locally are favored, because of both their higher initial price and their slower rate of price reduction. Yet even for these drugs, the principle remains the same, and the price paid begins to fall almost immediately after the drug's introduction. Only by generating a consistent stream of innovative drugs can a firm avoid the profit pressure that the new regulations have imposed. The shrinking profit stream from existing products makes a strong incentive for the continuous introduction of drugs via research and development.

Changes in the Competitive Environment

During the 1980s, the Japanese pharmaceutical firms faced new competitive challenges by both international and domestic firms. Until the early 1980s, foreign pharmaceutical firms found it difficult to set up independent operations in Japan, because of restrictions on ownership, capital transfers, and regulatory approval to sell pharmaceutical products. Only in 1975 were foreign firms permitted to establish 100 percent−owned subsidiaries in Japan. By the early 1980s, the new Foreign Exchange Control Law essentially freed foreign exchange, and new foreign investment regulations eliminated other formal barriers. After 1983, foreign firms were no longer obliged to apply through their Japanese firm representative for drug approval from the MHW.

Although establishing contacts with doctors was and is a significant barrier, requiring a large number of medical representatives, many European and North American pharmaceutical companies began or were preparing to distribute products directly in Japan during the mid-1980s. Slattery (1992) identified 11 American and European firms that eliminated or reduced (or were about to do so) their distribution ties with Japanese-owned pharmaceutical companies in Japan after 1984. New and innovative drugs are important competitive weapons in gaining the entry for a foreign firm, so these drugs are now much less likely to be licensed to a Japanese firm. With the increasing penetration of foreign competitors, both the number and quality of the drugs available to Japanese firms from abroad will decline over time.

New domestic players also appeared in the competitive arena during the 1980s. Several large Japanese firms with extensive experience in the food, chemicals, and fermentation sectors entered the industry, often to commercialize biotechnology-based pharmaceutical products. The new Japanese entrants could prove to be strong competitors and, at the very least, increase the number of drugs on the market, thereby allowing the ministry to reduce further the prices of existing drugs. With the entry of foreign firms and new domestic competitors, established Japanese pharmaceutical manufacturers face significant threats to their existing positions in the marketplace.

The Rising Cost of R&D

The cost of developing new drugs has risen since the 1960s. This is a worldwide phenomenon, but one from which Japanese firms initially were partially sheltered because of the closed market during the early 1970s. As the regulatory and competitive changes took effect during the late 1970s and early 1980s, however, Japanese firms were under greater pressure to develop drugs internally and thereby encountered the higher costs of R&D. The average R&D expenditure per new product reached $154.5 million for Japan's 10 leading pharmaceutical manufacturers between 1982 and 1989, close to the average for other pharmaceutical markets. With both per-product development costs going up and the number of internally generated drugs increasing, Japanese firms raised their R&D expenditures substantially. To obtain a return from these increased expenditures, the firms had to expand beyond the local market to gain more sales.

The Responses by Industries and Companies to R&D Activities

The companies had two main responses to the environmental changes. One was to begin to establish marketing organizations outside Japan. The Japan Pharma report stated that at least 15 Japanese pharmaceutical companies have opened clinical trials and distribution centers in the United States and Europe. These foreign ventures usually have begun as partnerships with local firms, but several Japanese companies have acquired majority ownership of local sales organizations. The companies' second response was to change the intensity and focus of their research and development activity. Elements of the R&D changes have been reported in other research, but the extent of the intertwined financial and organizational changes in R&D has not been addressed.

To investigate the firms' financial and organizational R&D response to the environmental changes, we obtained public-source information for 35 major companies in the industry, together comprising more than 50 percent of drug production and sales in Japan during 1990. Table 3.1 illustrates several trends in Japanese pharmaceutical sales and R&D. We gathered data for 1975, 1976, 1982, 1983, 1989, and 1990. (Some information could not be obtained for privately held and smaller companies.) The dates represent a relatively stable initial period during the mid-1970s (1975/76), the point when firms might have begun to respond to new trends in gov-

Table 3.1. Japanese Pharmaceutical Manufacturers' Sales and R&D Trends, 1975–90

	Pharmaceutical Sales			R&D/Sales Ratios (Corporate) (%)			R&D Expenditures (Corporate)		
	Total 1990 (¥ bill.)	CAGR 1982/83, 1990 (%)	CAGR 1975/76– 1982/83 (%)	1990	1982/83	1975/76	Total 1990 (¥ bill.)	CAGR 1982/83, 1990 (%)	CAGR 1975/76– 1982/83 (%)
Takeda	355	3	7	9	6	5	49	7	11
Sankyo	277	6	21	8	6	6	26	9	15
Yamanouchi	204	12	22	12	10	7	26	14	15
Fujisawa	189	1	12	13	8	6	28	7	18
Eisai	183	7	20	14	11	8	29	10	17
Shionogi	182	2	10	11	8	7	25	8	11
Daiichi	173	11	20	12	11	7	21	13	15
Taisho	161	8	23	9	6	4	15	13	19
Tanabe	154	4	10	10	6	5	21	12	10
Chugai	119	6	21	16	10	7	20	11	20
Banyu	100	5	13	6	4	5	6	10	7
Tsumura	91	15		11	6		12	23	
Dainippon	87	6	16	9	8	7	9	7	13
Meiji Seika	85	1	8	5	2		12	16	
Kyowa Hakko	85	7	12	6	4		16	10	
Taiho	77	7		11	6		9	19	20
Ono	66	10	24	15	8	3	11	19	21

Green Cross	58	−3	17	11	6	5	8	6	28
Yoshitomi	51	2	12	13	10	8	10	6	16
Kaken	47	8	27	10	11	9	5	5	17
SS Pharm.	46	7	18	5	4		3	16	
Toyama	44	2	11	12	8	4	6	10	19
Nippon Shiny	41	3	10	13	11	6	6	6	16
Mochida	40	−1	13	14	10	4	7	5	30
Fuso	34	5		4			2		
Santen	32	11		7	6		3	16	
Hisamitsu	29	11	18	8			2		
Kissei	29	10		14	10		4	14	
Nikken	28	3		6	3		2	10	
Tokyo Tanabe	27	3	9	10	3		3	16	
Terumo	25	12		6	1		7	30	
Hokuriku	16	8		16			2		
Rohto	15	2	9	4	5		1	0	
Wakamoto	10	0		6	5		1	0	
Fujirebio	8			18			3		
Sample average		6	15	10	7	6	6	11	17
Sample total	3,168						410		

Sources: Oriental Economist, 1970, 1976, 1983, 1992; Japan Pharmaceutical Manufacturers' Association, 1991; Yano Research Institute, 1991; Nikko Research Center, 1991.

Notes: The 1975/76 and 1982/83 figures are two-year averages (when two years of data were available), and the 1975 and 1976 pharmaceutical sales required some estimates of pharmaceutical share of corporate sales.

ernment policy (1982/83), and the most recent data available that might reflect learning and experience in the new environment (1989/90). The research-expenditure figures must be treated cautiously because companies vary in how they define R&D and some companies' statistics include substantial expenditures for clinical human trials that take place before drugs are introduced to the market, but the trends are reasonably clear.

Several patterns stand out in the table. The first three columns of Table 3.1 report sales trends. Column 1 lists the pharmaceutical sales of the 35 Japanese pharmaceutical companies during 1990 as reported by the Japan Pharmaceutical Manufacturers Association (1991). The five largest companies accounted for about 20 percent of industry sales, down somewhat from the 25 percent share of the top five during the early 1970s. (The Japanese market is slightly more concentrated than the U.S. market, in which the largest firm had less than 5 percent of sales in 1990.) Columns 4 through 6 detail the changes in corporate R&D/sales ratios. (Pharmaceutical businesses' R&D expenditures are not available for the companies. The proportion of company sales derived from the pharmaceutical industry averaged about 78 percent in 1990 among the companies for which we obtained information.) The average corporate R&D/sales ratio rose slightly from 1975/76 to 1982/83 (from 6 to 7%) and then grew substantially (to 10%) during the next period. Again, there are a few exceptions among individual firms in the sample, but the trend is significant. Column 7 reports corporate R&D expenditures in 1990, which totaled ¥410 billion for the firms in the table. Total pharmaceutical R&D expenditure in 1990 amounted to about ¥500 billion (Japan Pharmaceutical Manufacturers Association, 1991, extrapolating from the 1989 figure, p. 28). The corporate R&D figure reported in Column 7 amounts to about 64 percent of the pharmaceutical industry's R&D expenditure if we assume that corporate R&D is spent in an equivalent ratio on pharmaceutical and nonpharmaceutical business (78%). This assumption is consistent with the statistical results in our study, which show no influence of the firms' pharmaceutical percentage of corporate sales on changes in R&D intensity. Columns 8 and 9 of Table 3.1 report growth in absolute corporate R&D spending during the two periods. In contrast with the corporate R&D/sales columns, absolute growth in corporate R&D dropped between 1982/83 and 1990, compared with the earlier period (11% versus 17% for the sample firms). The decline undoubtedly reflects the slower sales growth during this period. However, the average R&D/sales ratio increased substantially between 1982/83 and 1990 (from 7% to 10%), indicating that growth in R&D expenditure substantially exceeded sales growth during the period.

Overall, the trends in Table 3.1 describe an industry that grew substantially in R&D during the 1970s, which was a period of high sales growth. Most companies continued to increase their R&D/sales ratios during the 1980s, but the large reduction in sales growth that occurred during the 1980s was coupled with reduced growth in absolute R&D expenditure.

Nonetheless, there was substantial firm-based variation in the R&D compound annual growth rate (CAGR) from 1982 to 1990, with a few companies actually raising their R&D growth rate from that of the preceding seven years.

STATISTICAL ANALYSIS OF INTERFIRM VARIATION IN R&D GROWTH

The pattern of responses by different firms to these competitive challenges has varied greatly. Mitchell, Roehl, and Slattery (in press) investigated why levels of R&D expenditure levels grew more quickly for some firms. We investigated two periods. First, we chose 1975/76 to 1982/83 as the initial period because it was more stable and predictable. The later period, from 1982/83 to 1989/90, was a more turbulent era in which firms faced increasing global and health policy challenges and were experimenting with new approaches to R&D. The statistical study compared the ratio of R&D at the end of each period with that at the beginning of the period, using two-year averages to smooth minor fluctuations. The data are based on those obtained for 19 of the 25 largest firms in the industry over the 15—year period from 1975 through 1990, with the 19 firms representing about 45 percent of pharmaceutical industry sales and about 50 percent of the industry's R&D expenditure in 1990 (of about 100 Japanese firms that have R&D capabilities).

In the earlier stable period, for which we obtained a sample of 11 firms, two effects stood out: First, we found that those firms with a greater return on sales profitability at the beginning of the period increased their R&D spending at a faster rate during the period. This finding suggests that a firm's financial strength at the beginning period enabled it to spend much more on R&D. Second, by contrast, those firms that had already spent a lot on R&D at the beginning of the period spent less on it during the period. This finding indicates that large firms (size is closely correlated with R&D expenditure) were less aggressive during the first period, possibly because they were reaching the limit of their financial ability to fund R&D growth and their organizational ability to manage R&D projects.

Three other factors also affected the growth of R&D during the first period. Firms with a greater share of nonpharmaceutical products in their corporate sales expanded their R&D budgets at a faster rate, suggesting that businesses outside the pharmaceutical sector provided more research opportunities. Younger companies raised their R&D expenditure more quickly than older firms did, probably because they were attempting to build solid positions in the industry. Finally, R&D expenditure grew more rapidly in firms with larger proportions of their equity held by foreign owners. This last result might stem from the availability of financial resources provided by foreign owners, or it could indicate that foreign owners tend to invest in firms with strong research capabilities and potential.

In the more turbulent period of 1982/83 to 1989/90, for which we obtained a sample of 19 companies, greater profitability at the beginning of the period continued to lead to greater growth in R&D, but the other effects tended to weaken. Although firms with larger R&D expenditures continued to have less growth in R&D, the magnitude of the influence was smaller. This finding suggests that the potentially less available in-licensing alternative strengthened the incentive for R&D growth, even among firms that already were spending well beyond the industry average. The regulatory pressure for more breakthrough drugs also intensified the pressure for more R&D effort, regardless of firm size. Greater equity holding by foreign owners made only a marginal contribution to greater R&D growth in the turbulent period, which might stem from the greater ability of foreign firms to enter the Japanese research environment directly. Diversified corporations no longer increased their R&D spending more quickly, again indicating the pressure that pharmaceutical businesses faced for increasing their R&D. However, firms with higher growth in R&D in the stable period grew at a slower pace than did the average firm in the 1982/83 to 1989/90 period, suggesting that some firms were reaching the limits of their financial and organizational R&D capabilities. (R&D expenditures are available only for the latter period, so we cannot compare the effect of this base period variable with that of the earlier period.)

These results have important implications for firms that must continue to increase their R&D expenditures in order to compete in international pharmaceutical markets. In both periods, the larger and older the firm was, the less likely it was to raise its levels of R&D activity. Established pharmaceutical manufacturers must find ways of overcoming the limit, or they will be unable to compete effectively against larger American and European competitors.

Solutions to the limits imposed by size and age will likely entail both financial and organizational responses. Financially, greater profitability allows firms to increase their R&D programs, and the support of a foreign partner might offer access to additional financial resources. The firms also might be able to find organizational solutions that allow them to compete with larger competitors without matching their higher absolute R&D spending levels. (We investigate this challenge in the second half of the chapter, in which we report findings from our interviews during 1992 and 1993 concerning the organizational changes that the firms are making.)

A QUALITATIVE ASSESSMENT OF R&D ORGANIZATION

In the changed and more turbulent environment of the 1980s, Japanese pharmaceutical manufacturers recognized that simply allocating additional funds to R&D activities would not be sufficient to respond to the competitive challenges. Organizational changes also would be needed to discover, develop, and bring to market the new pharmaceutical products necessary to succeed in the new environment. The companies had no blueprint to follow in this endeavor. Contrary to their counterparts in the steel industry, they could not merely build world-scale "R&D production facilities" and make world-scale sales of all they could manufacture at market prices. Instead, the new R&D organization would have to be smaller than those of their foreign competitors yet still be capable of creating competitive pharmaceutical products. To do this, four themes become important: cohesive internal product-development systems, domestic laboratories for basic research and drug discovery, research activities outside Japan, and research alliances. Options within each theme could provide advantages and disadvantages for the firms.

A Cohesive Internal Product-Development System

Although the processes underlying basic research and product development differ, the activities cannot be separated neatly because the separation between basic and applied science is not as clear as the sequence of biomedical research to drug discovery to preclinical development to clinical testing suggests. Findings at each level of research feed the next level, but it is rare for a scientist to follow a compound through this whole cycle. Rather, scientists specialize in one level of research and transfer the project to the next level after having sufficiently characterized an entity at their level. Such transfers take place formally in a product-development setting or informally through scientific literature. Understanding how to apply scientific advances to specific products often requires that the people applying research results maintain contact with those carrying out the basic research. Collaboration among scientists engaged in basic research and applications is crucial to the effective transfer of knowledge through the development cycle (e.g., Finch, 1989; Jernigan, Smith, Banahan, & Juergens, 1991). Thus, a cohesive R&D system is required for the effective commercialization of new pharmaceutical products.

The use of cohesive organization has helped leading pharmaceutical manufacturers in Japan achieve world product-output levels despite their smaller size compared with major global rivals. Indeed, smaller size is sometimes an advantage. Firms seemed to consciously limit the size and growth of individual research units. For instance, one company preferred to limit a research manager's span of control to a maximum of 50 people, thereby requiring a large number of small research units for effective operation. Securities analysts told us about a firm with a small and very active research organization that lost its momentum when it tried to grow by 50 percent in a short time. An R&D staff size of 1,200 to 1,500, including researchers and support personnel, seemed to be emerging as the limit for most large companies, and some important players do not approach even these limits. The Japan Pharma report notes that only three Japanese companies had more than 1,000 R&D staff in 1987, with the largest reaching 1,600 people, whereas at least 10 major American and European firms each had more than 3,000 R&D staff members. In general, the interview information is consistent with the statistical analysis, indicating that for the foreseeable future, Japanese firms will need to rely on smaller research staffs than their foreign competitors do.

Many managers cited the ability to have a cohesive research organization as a means for them to overcome the limitations imposed by a smaller size. One smaller firm that takes research chances to make up for its relatively weaker marketing position in the industry places great emphasis on the careful integration of the different parts of its research operation and the close supervision of its development processes by senior management. Managers at another company stressed the meetings they held among researchers to make sure that everyone knew about new developments in the research laboratories.

Companies used various means to reach the cohesiveness goal. Some companies encouraged close contact among all researchers. The notion of the flexible researcher who can contribute in many ways was a frequent comment in the interviews. Rotation between laboratories early in the career was common. Firms made an effort to keep researchers in the loop as clinical trials progressed, so that they were not isolated from the uses of their research. One research manager noted that people in his company did not want to be isolated researchers and that Japanese pharmaceutical firms worked hard to develop cohesion.

It is tempting to see cohesion as a "Japanese" trait, but comments from our interviews indicated that it is not so simple. One manager told us, "Even in Japan we have a lot of trouble with coordination." Another commented how much difficulty the firm had in getting people and institutional groups to pay attention to activities outside the researchers' narrow area of expertise and interest. Nonetheless, the goal must be, as one manager put it, to find people who know the new technologies and can still "adopt to our system." Rather than a desire to be "Japanese," it was more the presence of a relatively small R&D staff that motivated this emphasis on cohesion.

Even those employees who go abroad for training, which is a career rotation given to fast-tracking future managers, were not likely to be able, immediately after their return, to initiate research projects stemming from their foreign training. One senior research manager told us about his frustration, when he returned from his study abroad, of having to wait and convince his manager of the benefits of a particular research stream. Yet his next comments were telling: He indicated that by carefully studying how his plan could fit into his unit's organizational goals, he was able to persuade his supervisor to start the project. Perhaps this is why one senior research manager reacted strongly to our question about the productivity of scientists who are hired at midcareer, asserting that they were not more productive. If one needs to understand the organization to get it to move effectively, then knowledge alone, without group cohesion, will not lead to innovation. Studies by a securities analyst suggest that the higher the percentage is of researchers in the age group around age 35 (with about 10 years of experience at their companies), the stronger the research performance of the Japanese firms will be, further evidence of the importance of cohesive organization in this market.

Advantages and Disadvantages

Cohesion creates many benefits for the companies. The presence of a common technical and market "language" across a firm tended to increase discussion and consequent innovation. Some companies have created well-organized peer review systems and have made formal attempts to integrate their marketing knowledge of their customers' demands with their research directions. At two leading companies, for instance, scientists first present research proposals to people of their own age group, the people with whom they will have to coordinate in other institutes throughout their careers. This exchange among equals has proved very successful in encouraging innovation for these two firms while not challenging organizational roles. The exchange and debate of ideas are instead supportive of the system and part of the means to develop a cohesive group of future managers. In addition, several companies used teams both to develop new products and ideas and to evaluate research plans. At one firm, the top scientist in each functional area must attend and assess the value of research projects in yearly reviews. In another, the research directors are encouraged to put researchers from varying disciplines on the research team to ensure that it has the necessary stimulus as well as the skill to be "flexible yet productive."

The cohesion also created some problems for the firms. Managers noted that the research skills available at many long-established pharmaceutical firms also restricted their ability to make drastic changes in their research focus. With midcareer hiring being uncommon in many companies, firms often are bound by the current skills and interests of the company's researchers. This is consistent with Nelson and Winter's (1982) notion of organizational routines, in which existing skills and systems influence the direction of the search for new technology. In contrast, firms that entered the pharmaceutical field more recently reported fewer such organizational limits on research direction and commented that the lack of constraints gave them competitive opportunities. Never having had the luxury of developing all the internal organization systems needed for research competitiveness, the newcomer firms could develop different routines and could investigate new product classes as they intensified their research.

If a cohesive internal organization is of major importance to a firm's R&D practices, the firm must choose its personnel carefully and integrate them into the organization quickly. Most people are hired at the master's degree level and then receive further education and training at the company. In most companies, the number of research staff with doctoral degrees has often only kept pace with overall personnel growth, and most scientists who obtained Ph.D. degrees did so after some years of experience in the company. Several managers stated that the knowledge gained from the doctoral research would contribute to the organization more quickly if the researcher first understood the firm's research directions. Although researchers were permitted to spend time away from the firm to complete their dissertation research, that time often was limited to about six months. In most such cases, doctoral degrees were awarded on the basis of work that the researchers carried out at their company.

Nonetheless, the source of training for research personnel is beginning to change in some companies. Traditionally, most Japanese pharmaceutical companies have hired research staff when they graduated from a university at the undergraduate or master's degree level. Both demand and supply conditions, however, are forcing some firms to change. A firm new to the industry or one that moves into new areas and creates new research laboratories often finds itself without researchers with appropriate skills. Research organizations are sometimes less stable at newer and more rapidly evolving companies and so perhaps are more tolerant of different ideas. On the supply side of the market for research personnel, the number of researchers going directly to doctoral training is rising, and so firms have more hiring options. This change is most apparent among those companies shifting their research focus and so are more likely to need to add staff with training outside the firm's traditional lines.

The change in the source of education has striking implications for a company's ability to change its research direction. Researchers who earn their Ph.D. while working at a company usually have very strong skills in a company's established areas of strength. The company-specific skills help researchers fit well into the firm's development system and allow them to contribute to ongoing development work that draws on the firm's traditional bases. At the same time, however, an internal training orientation might limit a firm's ability to bring in new ideas and change direction. Several people stated that researchers usually do not make major contributions to research until they are several years into their career, perhaps when they are in their mid-thirties. By this time, most of their ideas are based on their company's historical strengths. But researchers who earn their degrees in basic biomedical academic laboratories are more likely to be exposed to ideas that lie outside their firm's traditional scope. Companies that hire new researchers who have already received doctoral degrees might be better able to adapt to changing product and technological demands than would those firms that depended solely on internal training.

Although new researchers often bring new ideas into a company, hiring externally trained researchers also creates costs and difficulties. The ability to identify new chemical entities and then develop new drugs from them quickly and effectively is a competitive advantage for many Japanese pharmaceutical companies. Such ability rests on a company's having well-integrated internal systems to evaluate ideas and to transfer information among research personnel as therapeutic candidates are screened, synthesized, and tested. Bringing in people with ideas and visions that do not mesh with a company's systems often creates internal turbulence that might slow down or otherwise inhibit effective development. There is a fine balance, therefore, between bringing in new ideas and building on existing strengths. The emphasis on organizational coherence has the advantage of building on established organizational skills. Firms must, however, find ways to deal with developing new skills within that framework. As our comparative examples show, some firms have avoided becoming trapped in their existing base of skills. This challenge is particularly strong in basic research and drug discovery.

Domestic Laboratories for Basic Research and Drug Discoveries

In the early 1980s, the firms recognized that their existing research organizations could not respond adequately to the challenge of producing larger numbers of innovative drugs needed to compete in the global market. At all firms, new laboratory structures or new research systems were put in place during the 1980s. Different firms define "basic research" differently, but most of the larger companies we interviewed now carry out some investigation that is closer to basic biomedical science than to incremental product development. Although in most cases, basic-research units represent very small proportions of a firm's expenditure and personnel, the effort appears to be growing. For instance, one company recently established two new basic-research institutes with 17 people, and another firm established a unit with four people. The small size might be less of a limit than it appears, given the previous comments about closely connected research units, because an initial research success might be able to draw on development resources very quickly. For instance, managers at one firm indicated that almost one-fourth of their activity in more applied-research laboratories was in support of other laboratories closer to the basic end of the spectrum. Even from this small base, the number of units oriented toward basic research and the effort given to those units grew substantially during the mid- to late 1980s.

There is great variety also among the basic-research units as firms search for a balance between bringing in new ideas and building on existing strengths. Some laboratories concentrate on scientific function, and others focus on individual product categories. Some firms have given autonomy to their in-house efforts. One new entrant in the industry organized its basic-research functions more like those of a university and even hired a university professor to run the laboratory. Another established company symbolically gave more independence to its research effort by bringing in an outsider, a professor from the University of Tokyo, to run it. A second established firm, by contrast, has three institutes addressing fermentation, biotechnology, and new drug development but does not limit an institute to just basic research, because the company prefers a more flexible allocation of resources. And a third established company has specifically forbidden its three basic-research institutes to carry out product-development tasks. No trend now dominates, and firms report continued experimentation.

While describing their own organization, managers often mentioned that they might change their structure in the future, and several cited recent changes. One company moved from a functional approach to a product-oriented approach in 1987. Another found that its growing number of small, focused-research laboratories had led to greater operational autonomy for the laboratories within the firm's basic-research objectives, but the central research administration was concerned that it could not control that many units effectively. One manager, only half in jest, remarked that within five years, it might become centralized again. Thus, not only is there no dominant structure, but the very success of one structure will force yet additional organizational changes as research organizations become successful or face new environmental challenges.

Advantages and Disadvantages

There are clear advantages to firms if the basic-research institutes are successful. With new ideas generated in house, the firm has an edge in bringing drugs to market. In addition, the ideas from those laboratories are more likely to generate drugs that can be cross-licensed with other global players to fill a product line.

At the same time, the laboratories sometimes have two contradictory objectives: to maintain a basic-research focus and also to integrate the basic research into the firm's wider research and development organization. Firms must give sufficient independence to their basic researchers in order to protect them against being pushed into more applied research. There is constant pressure on the research organization to produce new drugs. One research manager's comments highlighted this well: "There is always too much to do to support slow-developing projects." Firms have found various ways to deal with this issue. Some isolate their research units physically, whereas others provide support from senior management. Authority is usually given to the research director to allocate resources and choose projects, subject to approval of very senior management. Although this process might seem to young researchers as limiting their ability to choose their projects, the presence of a strong research director provides an isolating mechanism that protects the basic-research organization from pressures to take on a more applied focus. Firms that use this approach usually organize forums for research staff to suggest and discuss ideas for research projects that the research director will consider. This approach requires a basic-research director who has strong credibility within the firm. One securities analyst argued that it is the ability of the senior research manager, even more than the budget that he or she controls, that decides which firms will achieve the greatest research success.

Nonetheless, integration is also important to the firm, which is evident in the earlier discussion of coherence in research organizations. Firms use several means to maintain contact among units. One company tried to maintain organizational independence for its research laboratories but required that its basic-research laboratories be located close to the rest of its research units. Some firms were more worried that the individual research teams would not share information and experience. Several firms mentioned that they used project teams, with researchers from various disciplines required to work together to address a research question. Information coming from the research project could then spread into various research units when the project ended, a rationale often used in other Japanese manufacturing industries. Other firms told of frequent research reports to senior management at the same level of management in other laboratories.

In contrast with many product-development systems in other industries in Japan, no pharmaceutical firm requires research people to follow a product into production, because the nature and purpose of basic and applied research differ so much. The Roche Institute of Molecular Biology (1990, p. 2) described the differences as follows:

> The basic researcher looks at living organisms and life processes and asks, "How do they work?" or "How did they get that way?" The applied researcher looks at living organisms and life processes and asks, "How can the process be interrupted or facilitated?" Breakthroughs in basic research establish new plateaus of scientific understanding. Breakthroughs in applied research lead to significantly safer, more effective new product.

Yet some firms do require research managers to rotate through several functional areas. In several companies, potential managers are given assignments outside research before becoming research directors, to ensure that they understand the firm's capabilities and objectives. Thus, internal cohesion on the management level retains an important place in career development for such firms.

Personnel policies also are difficult to integrate with the wider norms of the research division. Innovative researchers often prefer to concentrate on their own projects and might be unsympathetic to calls for team play to support projects that divert attention from their goal. This is especially true for people hired at midcareer who are brought in to put together a research team in a new area in which the firm has no experience. New employees with doctoral degrees expect to develop their own research streams. Some firms deal with this by providing a certain amount of time for personal research, with some companies reporting that this might amount to as much as 30 percent of a scientist's time, but the pressures for organizational conformity still make the human-resource management of the research laboratories a difficult matter for all firms.

Research Activities Outside Japan

A recent survey by the MHW showed that eight firms, all in the upper tier of the Japanese industry, were undertaking extensive research activity outside Japan. According to this MHW survey and in interviews with Japanese firms, many firms indicated an interest in following the lead of these pioneering companies. Indeed, as many as 30 firms in the industry now have some form of international research activity, ranging from sponsored projects at foreign universities to ownership of dedicated research laboratories.

We distinguish between two types of foreign research facilities: laboratories that are oriented toward basic research and early-stage drug discovery and laboratories that focus on introducing existing drugs to a foreign market. Research laboratories increasingly emphasize basic research, whereas product-introduction laboratories can be viewed as an extension of the cohesive internal product-development system theme.

Basic Research and Drug Discoveries in Foreign Facilities

Several general issues were common to the foreign research activities. Several firms initially followed relatively passive entry strategies by acquiring minority positions in foreign research-oriented companies or sponsoring research at foreign companies and universities. After gaining experience with foreign research styles, several companies then established wholly owned or majority-controlled facilities. The greater a facility's focus on basic science is, the more apt a foreign laboratory is to retain research independence, although several managers noted that their companies provided some guidance even to basic research activities. Laboratories that were directing their efforts to less basic research tended to be more integrated with the parent laboratory. Several companies found that having foreign senior managers or members of an advisory board who were familiar with the companies' systems in Japan improved the exchange of information, but the Japanese managers often mentioned the difficulty of coordination even in such cases. One firm scheduled a day for informal discussions and social interaction during research meetings, to reduce the barriers to communication between domestic and foreign researchers.

The exchange of information via research meetings was universal. All firms asked their foreign managers and researchers to make personal reports to Japanese research managers and scientists about twice a year, often rotating between the foreign facility and the Japanese laboratory. The more basic the research is, however, the harder it seems to be to evaluate the reports, and several firms expressed concerns about the evaluation process for longer term projects.

Product Introduction in Foreign Facilities

As well as undertaking basic-research and drug-discovery activities, several firms now operate product-introduction laboratories that coordinate product testing for foreign regulatory approval. One large company believes that the new drug-discovery phase of R&D is best centralized in Japan but has aggressively built the capacity to test products in the United States and

Europe. The firm has a large portfolio of products, many of which are licensed to foreign companies or have potential value in international markets. The company's goal is to strengthen its control of the development process abroad, especially the scheduling of new products, because quick approval by the regulatory agency has become an important competitive asset in all countries. Even if the costs of operating its own facilities are higher than licensing local development to local firms, control over the process has substantial value. Reputation is important to developing these new markets, in which the company is only a small player, through bulk sales, and the firm hopes that contacts with doctors at the testing stages will improve its chances of marketing success.

The firm's product-introduction ventures began almost a decade before the other companies created international research ventures. Because it had no experience and no models to draw on, the company worked with local partners that usually were firms with which it had prior licensing and marketing experience. The company is increasing its shares in the ventures, with a goal of majority ownership. But even with majority ownership, the laboratories are managed locally, with two or three Japanese nationals in support roles. Twice-yearly meetings with managers from Japan are held to address marketing and personnel issues, rather than technical questions.

The strongest appeal of company-owned laboratories is earlier access to foreign technology (in the case of basic-research laboratories) and greater breakthroughs into foreign markets (in the case of product-introduction laboratories). The foreign facilities often provide access to areas that the firms have not developed in their domestic laboratories. Some firms also hope to gain experience with research approaches different from those they use in their Japanese facilities, which in turn would stimulate researchers in their domestic laboratories.

Advantages and Disadvantages

Although the experience is still too short to make definitive judgments, some initial difficulties in achieving the goals of foreign research activities are apparent. Most managers emphasized the high cost of the foreign operations. It also is difficult for top management to judge the progress of foreign researchers, even more than in domestic basic-research laboratories, and there are difficult cross-national management problems to overcome. Especially for companies that emphasize the internal cohesion of their research operations, integrating the foreign operations is a major organizational challenge. When introducing drug candidates to market quickly requires a fast and coordinated response among the foreign research laboratories and development laboratories in Japan, then the research scientists must take time away from their own research focus to ensure the coordination. Although some companies assign Japanese managers to coordination functions, effective and speedy development also requires contact with research scientists. A partial solution might be to assign more Japanese research scientists to the foreign facilities.

Several personnel issues also might be difficult. Several people noted that the senior managers of some companies traditionally exert substantial control on the research direction of Japanese-based research facilities, but they also stated that such control is much harder to maintain when the research facilities are located outside Japan. Foreign researchers employed at the foreign laboratories might reject attempts to direct their activities, and even Japanese researchers who rotate through the foreign laboratories might receive less direction than usual, simply because of the geographic distance. Similar to the issue of where a researcher earns a doctoral degree, this situation is two edged. By establishing a foreign-based research institute, a firm can relax some of the research controls that sometimes hinder its ability to move into new areas. At the same time, though, this lack of control might lead to missed opportunities to tie in with a firm's existing strength. This creates a fine-grained issue of managerial balance.

Research Alliances

All firms reported some research alliance with other organizations. Many alliances are small individually, but the overall effect can have substantial influence for the firms. Some partners are domestic firms, often small players in the pharmaceutical industry that possess specialized capabilities not available to a leading firm. Other partners are foreign firms, often with biotechnology capabilities or other technologies that are not easily obtained in the domestic market. Alliances with domestic and foreign public-sector organizations, such as universities or hospitals, also are common. The managers with whom we spoke believed that the partnerships helped both to stretch the available internal resources and to develop internal resources further.

Domestic Alliances

The major players in the Japanese industry have formed few alliances with one another. As one manager put it, "We all are working for the same goals. Other partners [other than the major players] are much more attractive." A few partnerships among leading firms were formed when government agencies promoted and supported particular projects. Some managers stated that they would not willingly choose to enter such alliances because they were concerned that they would take people away from current projects, but they did expect tangible benefits to stem from the joint work.

The most common domestic alliances were between major firms and two types of domestic players: smaller, established firms and new entrants to the pharmaceutical industry. The smaller pharmaceutical firms sometimes can provide specialized technology in areas in which a larger firm is not strong. Many new entrants also offer specialized technology, especially skills needed to develop new biotechnology-based pharmaceuticals. From the point of view of the smaller firms and the new entrants, the alliances offer a means of gaining access to preclinical testing systems and marketing networks.

Research relationships with domestic universities are common. Firms have long-established ties to major Japanese research hospitals and university science departments. The relationships are essential to gaining regulatory approval of preclinical tests because studies that are coordinated by university professors with strong reputations are likely to receive approval more quickly. Companies also use the contacts with academic researchers to search for, as one research manager put it, "the seeds" for future in-house research. Research relationships between a company and a university professor often are long lasting and often are created through clinical trials. In addition, several firms have university advisory staffs that help them choose the direction for internal research.

At the same time, managers sometimes stated frustration with their interaction with domestic academic research. The inflexibility of the university system, the small number of medical schools with appropriate departments and adequate staff, and underfunding by the government of university research were cited as reasons for not doing more with these academic alliance partners. A conflict between corporate product-development goals and academic research interests also surfaced in several interviews, as some managers noted that they were reluctant to provide money and staff for academic research projects that did not have product-oriented goals. Those several firms with extensive activity toward the more basic end of the research spectrum seemed to be the most optimistic about the potential for future cooperation.

Foreign Alliances

The use of alliances with foreign firms varies substantially among manufacturers. Almost all domestic companies have alliances to handle marketing abroad and to bring products developed abroad to market in Japan. Yet whereas some firms have almost no foreign research alliances, others use them extensively.

Many of the strongest research-oriented alliances are with foreign biotechnology firms. The Kirin–Amgen partnership in the commercialization of EPO illustrates the attractiveness for both sides. Beginning in 1982, Kirin (a beer brewery) began a biotechnology research project as an extension of the fermentation skills that the company had developed in its traditional brewing business. When Amgen succeeded in cloning the gene required for EPO, Kirin recognized that it would not be able to catch up and so offered to form a joint venture with Amgen. Kirin offered financial support and its experience with fermentation-based production, which was critical to the product's development. The matching of Amgen's basic-research skills with Kirin's production skills made a partnership beneficial to both sides.

Although the Kirin–Amgen alliance spread over several functions, most alliances are more specific. One firm, recognizing that a foreign laboratory had the ability to use computer techniques to screen drug candidates rapidly, contracted with that firm to do specific compound screening. Many alliances involve the exchange of Japanese financing of ongoing basic research for the rights to use any output that might come from the research. The lack of distribution channels abroad also has led to another type of foreign agreement, a cross-licensing for the clinical testing of drugs by each partner in that firm's home country. The firms with few or no foreign research alliances resided on both ends of the technology spectrum. Some firms that have only started to develop extensive internal R&D capabilities are just beginning to test the waters of international research, often by sending employees to foreign universities to do doctoral or postdoctoral research. Other firms with extensive internal research capabilities also have little contact with foreign research alliances. Managers at one firm stated that they did not have the human resources to manage or evaluate foreign projects, given the substantial output of their own productive internal research staff. Thus, both an underdeveloped and a very active local R&D function in a firm might lead to relatively few international alliances.

The strong basic-research reputation of North American and European universities has encouraged a wide variety of relationships between Japanese firms and foreign academic laboratories. Several firms have endowed chairs at science departments in American and British universities, sometimes in order to obtain positions for their researchers. The relationships are sometimes seen as steps toward wider participation in international activities. For instance, one firm rented a floor at the University of Edinburgh where a small number of British and Japanese researchers work together, as an initial step toward a larger-scale research facility. One securities analyst suggested that the access issue is sometimes at least as important as the actual research. Given the discussion about a research system that values internal cohesion and depends on a faster response time to market, a worldwide system that enables a firm to search for available compounds for subsequent development is an important competitive asset.

Identifying appropriate corporate and academic partners is sometimes a problem for Japanese pharmaceutical companies. Many managers mentioned that they were besieged by requests for financial support from foreign-venture companies and universities. Many companies were struggling to draw up criteria for choosing among the offers. One criterion that is commonly suggested for finding partners in other industries, "working with partners you know," is difficult to apply in the international marketplace when alliances, whether with a firm or a university, are in an area in which a firm lacks experience. Simply choosing a partner based on its reputation might not be useful, as one firm found when it endowed a chair at a North American university in order to maintain ties with a well-known professor, only to have the person move to another job soon after. Several companies also have found that many potential partners view the alliances as being primarily financial relationships, whereas the Japanese firms understandably desire technical interchange.

Advantages and Disadvantages

The alliances have obvious advantages. By making small commitments with a wide variety of players, a firm can gain access to several research streams at a relatively low cost. By diversifying at home and abroad, the firm can be better prepared for unexpected changes as the industry develops. In addition, managing alliances sometimes is easier than managing internal facilities, at least on the surface. Because in most cases, there are explicit goals, a relatively simple contract might suffice. If the relationship does not work, there is a simple solution often voiced in interviews: "Don't continue the relationship after the initial contract expires."

At the same time, there may be serious drawbacks to depending on research alliances as a firm's primary vehicle for technology access, and managers recognize that they cannot depend on this route alone. They often mentioned the difficulties of allocating property rights. In addition, they sometimes found it difficult to control or even participate in decision making concerning the research direction of an alliance partner, a problem that most commonly arose when foreign partners were funded by multiple sources. Perhaps most important, there are many obstacles to learning from an alliance. Although management of a formal contract might appear relatively easy, an ongoing exchange of management and information is not so easy to structure within an alliance. Without participation in management by personnel in Japan, information flow is frequently limited to formal presentations, especially with the foreign alliances. Several Japanese research managers commented that they had to wait for reports of results rather than judging the process of ongoing research and consequently found it difficult to follow the progress being made. This situation conflicts with the emphasis on a cohesive research system. What is seemingly an easy solution—termination—might sometimes be too blunt an instrument, especially if the alliance partner is an important potential source of new technology or a significant point of access to information.

Implications of the Four Themes

A satisfying end to this section would be the statement that we have identified a superior pattern of R&D practices and a prescription concerning the emerging nature of competition in the pharmaceutical industry. Yet it is clear from our interviews with managers and industry security analysts that no single set of practices dominates the current trends. Firms choose elements within each of the four themes and follow different paths in their attempts to improve their positions in domestic and international markets. Although there is some diffusion of practices among firms, such as the greater emphasis on domestic basic research and the expansion of international research activities, the ways in which the activities are carried out vary widely. Even actions that are successful at one company often are not copied directly by competitors. Instead, firms usually adopt combinations that are consistent with their organization.

In many ways, these results are consistent with those in other chapters in this volume, such as Chapter 8, on set-based thinking at Toyota, and Chapter 6, on product development at Nippondenso. In the analyses of the automobile industry, the companies' wider organizational norms and accumulated experience make individual elements work in a uniquely "Toyota" or "Nippondenso" manner. Attempts by competitors simply to copy another firm's distinctive approach usually fail because of differing organizational environments. The difficulty of copying successful organizational practices is at least as strong in the pharmaceutical industry, in which firms do not have the support of major global sales networks to provide resources for organizational experiments. As each firm gains experience, it experiments with a changing and evolving combination of these elements, emphasizing those that turn out to be consistent with its internal product-development system and its wider corporate norms of building and maintaining competence.

DISCUSSION

The intensified research of the Japanese pharmaceutical industry has just begun to bear fruit. Pharmaceutical R&D is a long-term process, often taking 15 or 20 years to move from the basic investigation of a biomedical process to the commercial introduction of a particular drug. The industry undertook general increases in R&D expenditure, numbers of research staff, levels of training, and attention to basic research during the 1970s. Many companies continued to intensify their research during the 1980s. If the time and money have been spent effectively—and there is every reason to believe that they have—then the industry as a whole should show greater research output during the rest of this decade. Yet even with more research output during the 1990s, the current levels of R&D intensity might not be enough to compete effectively in world markets using the conventional internal organization.

Many Japanese pharmaceutical companies now report R&D/sales ratios that reach or surpass the levels of the major American and European pharmaceutical companies, but the absolute level of investment is much smaller because even the largest Japanese firms' sales are substantially lower than those of the major international players. Companies that do not find ways of continuing to increase their research capabilities risk becoming marginal players that cannot compete effectively in an international market. Some companies might now be approaching their limits of research intensity, and for them the challenge is to find organizational solutions that compensate for the smaller size of internal R&D staffs. We described several organizational experiments that companies use to achieve such solutions. Which, if any, of these experiments will succeed depends on more than the internal efforts of the Japanese firms. The nature of global competition in the industry will help determine the profitability of organizational innovations. A brief sketch of three possible global competition scenarios—(1) a pharmaceutical market that does not become significantly more global, (2) a marketing-oriented globalization, and (3) a technology-oriented globalization—offers useful examples. Some Japanese firms will be players in the worldwide pharmaceutical industry whatever the scenario, but some traditional leaders may not maintain their current positions. Both the uncertain developments in the world market and the uncertain returns to the variety of organizational experiments within the Japanese industry will have outcomes that no one can forecast.

Stalled Globalization

In the first scenario, there will be no significant increase in the integration of international markets for pharmaceutical products. If this occurs, then success in the Japanese market will be most important to the success of the new research organizations. If foreign firms fail to gain a larger share in Japan despite their efforts in research and marketing—and no foreign firm has yet achieved a strong market position—the main competitors will remain Japanese. Firms with cohesive internal research organizations will be able to introduce new products into the MHW pipeline most quickly. Avoiding the significant costs of foreign operations, successful firms in this scenario will tend to limit their external contacts to in-licensing and out-licensing. Some domestic and international product-development alliances will exist, given the market and regulatory differences and global span of technology development, but they will be of minor importance relative to internal laboratories.

Marketing-Oriented Globalization

The second scenario is that successful firms will need to make direct sales in all the major international markets. If this happens, Japanese firms will have to grow very quickly. This growth will require the creation of large, direct-distribution networks of medical representatives in all major markets and will require that the firms have the knowledge and organizational capabilities to win regulatory approval in all markets. This will necessitate some control, if not ownership, of the capability to conduct clinical trials in all markets. The global marketing option has been pursued since the mid-1980s: Strong attempts have been made by major American and European companies, and preliminary efforts have been made by several Japanese firms, to establish direct sales systems outside their home countries. If these efforts succeed, success in the pharmaceutical industry of the next century will come to firms with strong distribution systems in most or all major markets. These firms will be able to sell their drugs effectively and gain economies of market scale to finance their R&D. Such firms will have extremely strong bargaining positions for licensing negotiations, whereas single-country players will be in relatively weak positions. Global distributors will be able to use their size and profitability to fund larger research budgets, and they will dominate the global industry.

If this scenario came to pass, Japanese firms would have to strengthen their existing R&D base quickly so that they could establish a full line of products. A tendency to deny product access via licensing without a quid pro quo of another product might ensue, pushing the firms toward greater R&D efforts. Few corporate alliances would be possible unless the Japanese firms had desirable products to exchange, therefore domestic and foreign university alliances would predominate.

Nonetheless, there is no assurance that the global marketing option will succeed. Although forecasts of the future marketing success of international firms are often positive, sales networks owned by nationally based companies still dominate most national markets. This situation might not change much in the future. There are no obvious economies of scale in drug distribution because a new national system of medical representatives must be established in every country in which a company operates. At the same time, unquestioned costs and disadvantages are associated with operating distribution systems in several countries, including the costs of coordinating a global network and the difficulties of overcoming advantages enjoyed by local firms (Mitchell, Shaver, & Yeung, 1992). Such difficulties include attracting personnel, dealing with lingering regulatory biases, and overcoming customers' reluctance to deal with new and possibly short-lived entrants. If the advantages of direct foreign distribution do not outweigh the disadvantages, then the direct sales experiments will be toned down or rescinded. Indeed, some analysts argue that some Japanese firms that have set up foreign sales forces might be about to retreat (Maurer, 1992), whereas other analysts note that American and European firms have slowed the growth of their Japanese medical representative systems.

Technology-Oriented Globalization

Even if marketing remains local, it is possible that the pharmaceutical industry will require global technology development as firms attempt to use the global technology option as an effective means of gaining international scale. In this scenario, firms would race to develop drugs for world markets rather than race to distribute them. Those companies that can most consistently develop new products for many major markets will be in the strongest negotiating positions in licensing negotiations and, ultimately, will be the most profitable and the most likely to survive.

The global technology option is deceptively similar to the traditional practice followed in the pharmaceutical industry, in which those firms with strong, nationally based distribution systems license drugs from around the world. The critical difference from past practices, however, is that past actions have depended on national technology systems, whereas future technology practices will require that firms gain access to the international technological infrastructure. Firms that rely only on the biomedical technology developed in one country will have major disadvantages relative to those that draw on technological advances made throughout the world. Therefore, the global technology option requires that firms establish strong research bases on at least three continents in order to tap into academic and corporate research being carried out in Japan, Europe, and the United States.

In the global technology scenario, Japanese firms will need to tap into as many technological pools as possible. This will be even more important for them than for their European and U.S. counterparts because their internal pools are smaller, and it will mean a greatly expanded network of sponsored research and collaborative research with other firms and universities. Direct access through their foreign facilities will become increasingly important because in this scenario, firms will compete to control access to the knowledge base. This process might limit the deals available through contracting or at least drive up the cost of access and further reduce the degree of property rights attainable through that option. Licensing thereby becomes more attractive not just as a source of drugs in exchange but also for profitable returns on the company's drug portfolio. With the remaining marketing dominated by domestic firms, sales within Japan will still be profitable.

Just as the expansion of direct sales is expensive and difficult, the expansion of direct research will often be costly and may be difficult to coordinate. However, fruitful results already have emerged from existing international research sites. In this scenario, companies that find ways of creating effective integrated international networks of corporate and academic research sites will have major advantages in product development. These firms will then have very strong marketing positions whether the goods are sold through direct sales or through license arrangements.

CONCLUSION

The changes in the Japanese pharmaceutical industry have several implications for those seeking to understand and learn from Japanese systems of technology management. The Japanese pharmaceutical industry's market presence in international markets lags somewhat behind that of some other Japanese industries, but our study also shows that many firms in the pharmaceutical industry have developed and are continuing to improve new systems for creating research-based competitive advantages. The research systems draw on domestic strengths and international pools of technology, with many firms creating global technical presences well before they establish full-scale foreign distribution systems. As firms continue to experiment with ways of building the distribution and research systems needed in the new competitive environment, we will see further changes in the companies' relative strengths and their greater presence in the international market during the next decade.

More research is needed to address the variation of practices followed by individual firms in Japanese industries, and pharmaceuticals will provide an attractive venue for such studies. Learning from Japanese technology management practices in the 1990s will require sophisticated analysis, mixing a knowledge of "best practices" with a careful monitoring of "experimental practices" and "improving practices" in specific companies. The analysis must transcend industry and country boundaries, providing insights useful for high-technology firms as they struggle to deal with the competitive and technological challenges of the 1990s.

ACKNOWLEDGMENTS

We greatly appreciate the time and information provided by many people associated with Japanese pharmaceutical companies and the Japanese pharmaceutical industry, and we are grateful for the financial and organizational support provided by the Japan Technology Management Program and the Center for International Business Education of the University of Michigan. This chapter provided the basis for presentations prepared for the Colorado High-Technology Conference in June 1993 and the January 1993 conference of the Association of Japanese Business Studies in New York.

REFERENCES

Campbell, J. C., Mitchell, W., & Roehl, T. (1995). Trends in pharmaceutical sales, R&D, and profitability in the Japanese pharmaceutical industry before and after Ministry and Health and Welfare pharmaceutical reimbursement price adjustments, 1981–1992. In N. Ikegami & J. Campbell (Eds.), *Containing health care costs in Japan*. Ann Arbor: University of Michigan Press.

Comanor, W. (1986). The political economy of the pharmaceutical industry. *Journal of Economic Literature, 24,* 1178–1217.

Economist. (1987, February 7). *Molecules and markets: A survey of pharmaceuticals*, pp. S3–S14.

Finch, J. E. (1989). Product innovation and the process of creative destruction in the U.S. pharmaceutical industry. *Journal of Pharmaceutical Marketing and Management, 3,* 3–20.

Grabowski, H. (1990). Innovation and international competitiveness in pharmaceuticals. In A. Heertje & M. Perlman (Eds.), *Evolving technology and market structure: Studies in Schumpeterian economics,* (pp. 167–187). Ann Arbor: University of Michigan Press.

Halliday, R. G., Walker, S. R., & Lumley, C. E. (1992). R&D philosophy and management in the world's leading pharmaceutical companies. *Journal of Pharmaceutical Medicine, 2,* 139–54.

Hawkins, E. S., & Reich, M. R. (1992). Japanese originated pharmaceutical products in the United States from 1960 to 1989: An assessment of innovation. *Clinical Pharmacology and Therapeutics, 51,* 1–11.

Ikegami, N., Mitchell, W., & Penner-Hahn, J. (1994). *The contribution of pharmaceutical prices, quantities, and innovation to aggregate pharmaceutical expenditures in Japan.* Working paper, University of Michigan.

Industrial Bank of Japan. (1992). Pharmaceutical and agricultural chemical industries. *Quarterly Survey: Japanese Finance and Industry, 1,* 1–19.

James, B. (1990). *The global pharmaceutical industry in the 1990's: The challenge of change.* London: Economist Intelligence Unit.

Japan Economic Institute. (1992). *U.S.–Japan competition in pharmaceuticals: No contest?* JEI Report No. 13A. Washington, DC: Japan Economic Institute.

Japan Pharmaceutical Manufacturers Association. (1991). *Data book.* Tokyo: Japan Pharmaceutical Manufacturers Association.

Jernigan, J. M., Smith, M. C., Banahan, B. F., & Juergens, J. P. (1991). Descriptive analysis of the 15–year product life cycles of a sample of pharmaceutical products. *Journal of Pharmaceutical Marketing and Management, 6,* 3–36.

Maurer, P. R. (1992, August 3, 10). Are the Japanese Pharmaceutical Companies coming home? *Pharma Japan,* 10.

Mitchell, W., Roehl, T., & Slattery, R. (in press). R&D investment growth and organizational changes by Japanese pharmaceutical firms, 1975–1993. *Journal of High Technology Management.*

Mitchell, W., Shaver, J. M., & Yeung, B. (1992). Getting there in a global industry: Impacts on performance of changing international presence. *Strategic Management Journal, 13,* 419–32.

Nakagawa, H. (1992, July). *The Japanese pharmaceutical industry.* Unpublished company document, Morgan Stanley & Co.

Nakagawa, H. (1991). Problems in the Japanese pharmaceutical industry (in Japanese). *Capsule,* no. 37, 8–13.

Nelson, R. R., & Winter, S. J. (1982). *An evolutionary theory of economic change.* Cambridge, MA: Harvard University Press.

Nikko Research Center. (1991). *Pharmaceutical development joint venture relationships— 150 major Japanese, European and American Firms* (in Japanese). Tokyo: Nikko Research Center.

Oriental Economist. (1970, 1976, 1983, 1992). *The Japan Company Handbook.* Tokyo: Oriental Economist.

Reich, M. R. (1990, Winter). Why the Japanese don't export more pharmaceuticals: Health policy as industrial policy. *California Management Review, 32,* 124–50.

Roche Institute of Molecular Biology. (1990). *Annual Report, 1990.* Nutley, NJ: Roche Institute.

Salomon Brothers Asia Limited. (1992, July 10). *Earnings model of Japanese drug companies.* Unpublished company document.

Slattery, R. J. (1992). *Pharmaceutical and diagnostic imaging equipment technology development in Japan.* Report to the Long-Term Credit Bank of Japan, Economics Division, Tokyo.

Suguro, T. (1990). *The Japanese pharmaceutical industry* (in Japanese). Tokyo: Kyoikusha.

Yano Research Institute. (1991). *The pharmaceutical industry.* Tokyo: Yano Research Institute.

Yoshikawa, A. (1989, Winter). The other drug war: U.S.–Japan trade in pharmaceuticals. *California Management Review, 31,* 76–89.

4

Governance Structure and Technology Transfer Management in R&D Consortia in the United States and Japan

HOWARD E. ALDRICH
AND TOSHIHIRO SASAKI

Firms are no longer relying solely on their own R&D efforts (Contractor & Lorange, 1988), and they have increasingly turned to collaborative and cooperative interorganizational ties for R&D. Interorganizational arrangements, deliberately structured to promote the collective benefits of research and development, can give firms access to R&D that they could not manage on their own: joint ventures, technology licensing, subcontracting of research to private or university laboratories, and other arrangements (Auster, 1990). As Osborn and Baughn (Chapter 5 in this volume) noted, "The exchange and development of knowledge through alliances may allow firms quickly and creatively to integrate previously separate knowledge areas." Firms that use joint and cooperative R&D processes can reap economies of scale and scope beyond the reach of a single firm if they can find effective mechanisms for sharing the jointly developed knowledge (Link & Bauer, 1989).

We focus on one form of interfirm cooperation in R&D activities in the United States and Japan: consortia formed as alliances among potential competitors in the same industry. We concentrate on engineering research associations (ERAs) in Japan, registered under a 1961 law, and R&D consortia in the United States, registered under the 1984 National Cooperative Research Act. R&D consortia and ERAs are different from joint ventures and other forms of collaborative research because they involve direct competitors that pool their resources to pursue basic and applied research on long-term projects.

The goals of consortia are roughly the same in the two nations, although their governance structures differ in some respects, and thus we believe something can be learned about different national approaches to industrial policy by comparing the arrangements in each nation (Bolton, 1991). We present a comparison of the characteristics of consortia in the two nations, based on a questionnaire administered to samples of consortium managers in the United States and Japan.

A HISTORY OF INTERORGANIZATIONAL ALLIANCES IN THE UNITED STATES AND JAPAN

The United States and Japan have rather different political traditions, and this difference has shaped each nation's response to a perceived need for a more effective use of R&D expenditures. The national governments in both countries have become involved during the past few decades in interorganizational arrangements for R&D among competitors, but the Japanese government has taken a somewhat more interventionist approach than the U.S. government has (Johnson, 1982). For most of this century, the U.S. government has pursued a policy apparently focused more on controlling criminal and anticompetitive interfirm behavior than on facilitating R&D activities (Mowery, 1992). The Japanese government, by contrast, has been concerned with promoting a national goal of economic growth that often involved facilitating R&D activities via interfirm alliances (Fransman, 1990).

The United States

In 1984, the U.S. Congress passed the National Cooperative Research Act (NCRA), an act that gave substantial protection against antitrust sanctions to any R&D consortium that filed a registration form with the Justice Department (Wright, 1986). The NCRA encourages cooperative R&D among firms at the precompetitive stage, including "theoretical analysis, experimentation, or systematic study of phenomena or observable facts, the development or testing of basic engineering techniques, the experimental production and testing of models, prototypes, equipment, materials, and processes, the collection, exchange, and analysis of research information" (NCRA, sec. 2.6). Firms that file as R&D consortia are not immune to antitrust action because they can be found guilty of antitrust violations, but they can protect themselves against treble damages. No registered consortium has ever been prosecuted for any alleged antitrust violations.

The R&D consortia allowed under the 1984 NCRA, unlike most joint ventures, include direct competitors and have fairly diffuse goals for undertaking cooperative research. As such, consortia face a higher level of uncertainty than joint ventures do. The budgets of R&D consortia are usually smaller than those of joint ventures, and their administrative structures are looser and have a longer time horizon than joint ventures do.

R&D consortia have existed officially in the United States only since 1984. To qualify for protection against the awarding of treble damages in an antitrust case, a U.S. R&D consortium must register with the Department of Justice, and the process of filing a request for exemption enables a consortium to be listed in the Federal Register. In Table 4.1, we show the number of R&D consortia listed in the U.S. Federal Register, by year, beginning in 1985 and extending to the end of 1992. Consortia formed before 1985 were not created with the NCRA in mind, but some research organizations took advantage of the NCRA's protection against antitrust sanctions and registered in 1985, the year after the law went into effect. Therefore, the 50 consortia shown in Table 4.1 as having registered in 1985 include some actually formed in that year and others that were formed in previous years. (Because some consortia were formed many years before the 1984 NCRA, the column labeled "replied"—based on sample returns—shows the year that a sampled consortium was actually founded, rather than the year it registered with the Justice Department.)

Japan

In Japan, which has a very different political–legal tradition, the Ministry of International Trade and Industry (MITI), the Science and Technology Agency, and other government agencies have pursued a policy approach different from that of the United States (Fransman, 1990; Gerlach, 1987, 1992). Rather than emphasizing measures that limit anticompetitive behavior, MITI has encouraged, often in the face of substantial resistance from firms, programs that facilitate cooperative behavior among nominal competitors. Some of these programs are well known: the very large scale integrated (VLSI) semiconductor project, the optical measurement and control system project, and the fifth-generation computer project (Sakakibara, 1983).

In Japan, the organizational form most comparable to the R&D consortia formed under the U.S. NCRA of 1984 is the engineering research association (ERA). ERAs have existed as an organizational form since 1956 (although they were not formally registered until the Act on the Mining and Manufacturing Industry Technology Research Association of 1961), and they bring together firms in the same industry that are willing to cooperate on collective projects. ERAs were modeled after a British World War I program and were inaugurated in 1961 by a law providing a legal framework for the formation of cooperative research ventures (Goto & Wakasugi, 1987). British research associations (RAs) are composed of small and medium-size firms that cannot afford to fund their own R&D activities and are established primarily in traditional industries. The RAs help firms solve their technical problems, rather than carrying out specific R&D programs.

Table 4.1. Consortium Registrations and Disbandings, by Year, Number Sampled, and Number of Replies

Year of Registration or Founding	USA				Japan			
	Number Registered	Number Disbanded	Our Sample	Usable Replies[a]	Number Registered	Number Disbanded	Our Sample	Usable Replies
1950–59	—	—	0	1	—	—	—	0
1960–69	—	—	0	2	13	3	0	0
1970–79	—	1	0	0	31	8	8	5
1980–84	—	0	0	8	36	13	26	23
1985	50	5	19	5	6	4	5	3
1986	17	3	12	4	11	1	11	9
1987	27	2	10	5	6	5	6	5
1988	33	3	21	10	3	3	3	3
1989	34	2	17	4	6	3	5	3
1990	46[b]	NA	—	NA	4	2	5	3
1991	59[b]	NA	—	NA	7[b]	5	—	NA
1992	59[b]	NA	—	NA	5[b]	NA	—	NA
Total N	325	17[c]	79	39	128	47	69	4

[a] For Usable Replies, the year of founding is not necessarily the same as the year of registration. See the text for an explanation.

[b] In the United States, consortia registered in 1990, 1991, and 1992 were not included in the sample. In Japan, ERAs registered in 1991 and 1992 were not included in the sample.

[c] A total of 17 disbandings in the United States, including one consortium whose disbanding date we are not certain of.

ERAs in Japan differ in three important respects from the British RAs (Goto & Wakasugi, 1987). First, ERAs are action sets (Aldrich & Whetten, 1981) designed as temporary organizations with a limited existence and focused on a specific goal. When the project is finished, the ERA closes its doors, and the researchers who were involved go back to their original activities. Second, the member firms are large and are active in areas similar to those covered by the ERA, thus making the results easier to implement. Third, whereas the British RAs are in traditional industries, many ERAs operate in high-technology industries. Although many ERAs are in "high tech," others are not. The names of some ERAs founded during the past 35 years provide some sense of the range of industries covered: High Polymer Materials, Optical Engineering, Light Metal Composite Materials, Administrative Processing of Software Modules, Automatic Measuring Technology, Computer-Based Traffic Control System, Extrusion Cooking in Food Industries, Advanced Housing Technology, Improvement of Function in Gas Turbines, Biotechnology for Organic Fertilizers, Food Design Technology, and Waste Water Treatment Technology in Food Industries.

ERAs are can obtain government funds in two ways, through either a *research contract* (consigned payment) or a *forgivable loan* (conditional loan). In the case of a research contract, the government owns the research results, but typically it licenses patents back to the association on favorable terms. If funding is obtained through a forgivable loan, the ERA owns the technology, but it must repay the loan if the project is "successful" (Heaton, 1988).

As shown in Table 4.1, since the 1961 act went into effect, 128 Japanese ERAs have been registered. The pace of registration has increased considerably since the decade of the 1960s, when only 13 ERAs were registered. In the 1970s, 30 were registered, and in the 1980s, 72 were registered. However, the average number of foundings per year has not changed much during the past decade, especially when compared with the growth of consortia in the United States.

STUDY DESIGN

We obtained a complete list of all R&D consortia in the United States and all ERAs in Japan, from the time that the enabling legislation was passed until 1990 for the United States and until 1991 for Japan, and then we obtained information about their governance structures through a survey that was mailed to their managing directors. Table 4.1 also gives information for registrations in 1991 and 1992 for the United States and Japan, based on archival data, but our samples do not include consortia registered during those years. We also include some information on the member organizations in all consortia, which was collected from government sources.

The United States

In May 1990, we examined previous issues of the Federal Register and found the names of 161 consortia that had registered between January 1, 1985, and December 31, 1989. Our final list, however, included only 79 consortia, for a number of reasons.

First, a few consortia listed all their individual projects as separate consortia. We included each of the consortia only once in our sample, regardless of how many times it was listed in the Federal Register. We assumed that the governance structures of each separate listing would be similar, and we also believed that including each one separately would bias our sample toward very large organizations. Barnett, Mischke, and Ocasio (1993) followed the same strategy in studying consortia foundings: They labeled subsequent project listings by the same consortia as *subconsortia* rather than as new consortia.

Second, some consortia that were listed before 1990 had been disbanded, including some that never became active. Third, we could not find the address of one consortium, even after repeated phone calls and mailings to the member firms.

We prepared a mailed questionnaire that we sent in July 1990 to the managers of the 79 R&D consortia whose addresses we verified by telephone. The questionnaire asked about the consortium's history and operating characteristics and how it was governed.

We received 51 replies, including 39 completed questionnaires. Disregarding the disbanded consortia, the organizations that claimed they were no longer (or never had been) consortia, and the multiple listings for the CSMA, we estimated that 67 R&D consortia could be included in our sample. We received 39 usable replies, for a completion rate of 58 percent.

Japan

The Japanese portion of the study was carried out in 1990/91, using the same questions as in the U.S. questionnaire but translated into Japanese. The sampling list was prepared from information supplied by government agencies. Under the Act on the Mining and Manufacturing Industry Technology Research Association of 1961, regulating ERAs, 116 were established between May 1961 and September 1990. Most of them (94) were under the aegis of MITI; 20 were under the Ministry of Agriculture and Forestry (MAF); and two were under the Ministry of Transport (MT).

As in the United States, many of the ERAs had been disbanded by the time of our study, as would be expected, given their explicitly limited life span. We obtained the addresses of 69 active consortia and mailed them questionnaires in January 1991, setting a deadline of January 31 for their return. After a follow-up letter and a second mailing of the questionnaire, we received 54 usable replies, although as in the United States, not all questions were answered by every respondent. The 78 percent response rate reflects both our study's intrinsic interest to the participants and the blessing that our study received from MITI and the Japan Technology Transfer Association.

Founding Dates

In the U.S. sample, 72 percent of the consortia that replied to our questionnaire were formally established after the 1984 NCRA, as shown in Table 4.1. The rest were established before 1984; they then took advantage of the NCRA when it was enacted and registered with the Justice Department. (Because our data were collected in May 1990 and the Federal Register lags a bit behind actual foundings, we do not have any consortia founded in 1990 in our U.S. sample.) In Japan, ERAs have been legally authorized since 1961, but only five in our sample were founded before 1980, in part because many of the ERAs that were founded earlier had completed their projects and had been disbanded.

STRUCTURES OF CONSORTIA

An agreement to coordinate their research via an R&D consortium forces firms to confront three critical questions: (1) What kinds of administrative arrangements should they create? (2) How should they define their research goals? and (3) How much government involvement should they seek or allow? We used these questions to create a typology of R&D consortia forms (Aldrich & Sasaki, in press).

First, overall control varies depending on whether centralized or decentralized administrative arrangements are chosen. Firms can set up a centralized joint facility to conduct joint research whose results can be easily communicated to all members, or they can keep research projects decentralized in member firms, thus losing some of the synergies that might result from research conducted in a joint facility.

U.S. consortia are highly centralized compared with Japanese consortia. Most Japanese consortia (89%) conduct research in member firms, compared with less than half (44%) the U.S. consortia. By contrast, about half (49%) the U.S. consortia conduct research in a joint facility, compared with only 17 percent of the Japanese consortia. Japanese consortia also chose a narrower range of research arrangements than U.S. consortia did. In Japan, if a consortium conducts research in member firms, it is unlikely to conduct research also in joint facilities. By contrast, about one-fourth of U.S. consortia use both. Organizing research through member firms seems to be a barrier to using joint facilities in Japan, whereas in the United States, the two arrangements are more compatible.

Second, consortia founders may pursue a narrow or a wide range of research activities across the six stages of the technological innovation process—idea generation, technological feasibility studies, product development, prototype and pilot plant construction, interim manufacturing, and full commercialization (Felker, 1984). Almost no consortia in either nation are pursuing full commercialization (that would raise major issues of appropriability for firms that are competitors), and only a few are conducting interim manufacturing (in anticipation of full commercialization). Clearly, the choice of research focus affects a consortium's choice of administrative arrangements. For example, pilot manufacturing is very expensive and difficult to conduct in a centralized facility. Therefore, we would expect it to be conducted by member firms.

The Japanese consortia, in contrast with those in the United States, concentrate on applied product development and prototype and pilot plant development, rather than on the earlier stages of technology commercialization (Levy & Samuels, 1991). Most of the U.S. consortia say they are pursuing "idea generation," whereas very few Japanese consortia do so. Most of the U.S. consortia are examining "technical feasibility," compared with only about half in Japan. Moreover, most consortia in both nations are involved in activities that are closely linked in the R&D cycle. As the distance between phases in the research and development cycle increases, fewer consortia in either nation are involved in both.

Third, consortia managers must decide the extent to which the national government will be involved, including funding as well as coordinating projects. In this respect, most Japanese ERAs involve active government intervention in the coordination of their research arrangements, whereas there are few examples of such intervention in the United States. U.S. consortia depend heavily on members' dues, whereas Japanese consortia are heavily subsidized by the government, through either research contracts or forgivable loans. SEMATECH is a notable exception to this pattern, and for that reason it is not a very useful model for other U.S. consortia to follow. It was created with government initiative, has a huge budget, and, in its early years, received most of its funding from the government.

Thus there are some substantial differences in the overall structure of consortia in the United States and Japan. Japanese ERAs follow a strategy of using their administrative arrangements as coordinating committees, carrying out their research in member firms. U.S. consortia, by contrast, are much more likely to have joint facilities, and they may conduct their research in universities, independent laboratories, and member firms. Consortia in both nations are fairly focused, but Japanese ERAs stand out as being extremely specialized. Finally, U.S. consortia depend heavily on members' dues, whereas Japanese ERAs depend on government support.

THREE INTERNAL MANAGEMENT ISSUES FACING CONSORTIA

Consortia managers face three central issues in managing the internal affairs of their organizations: (1) membership management, including recruiting and retaining member firms; (2) conflict management, including coordinating and resolving differing interests of member firms; and (3) technology transfer management, including information exchange. We discuss each of these issues, showing differences in the ways they have been resolved in both the United States and Japan.

Membership Management

Membership management involves recruiting members, hiring staff, and creating a governance structure to manage relations among the members. In a study of only U.S. consortia, Evan and Olk (1990) concluded that U.S. consortia managers were very concerned with increasing their members' involvement in consortia activities; these managers believed that greater participation meant a more effective transfer of technology. Because members occasionally drop out of consortia, managers must find ways both to minimize dropouts and to recruit new members if they want to maintain their organization's viability.

We found that the distribution of consortia by number of sponsors or members is fairly similar in the United States and Japan, as shown in Table 4.2.[1] About 53 percent of the U.S. consortia have fewer than 20 members, compared with 65 percent of the Japanese ERAs. Size distributions for the two nations differ at the upper ends of the distributions: Two of the 54 Japanese consortia have 50 or more members, whereas seven of the 39 U.S. consortia have 50 or more members. Given the sizable spread of consortia sizes in Table 4.2, means and medians would be misleading.

Membership in Japanese consortia has been highly stable: Once a firm joins, it rarely leaves. Only four of the 114 Japanese consortia for which we have membership data over time from government sources have had any dropouts. By contrast, 16 of the 94 U.S. consortia for which we have membership data over time have had dropouts. We believe that the greater stability of membership in Japanese consortia gives them an advantage in building their governance structures, because their members are more committed to the collective effort than are members in U.S. firms. Thus, greater trust or loyalty may reduce the need for elaborate monitoring mechanisms. Several observers at our conference noted that as the board members of a U.S. consortium changed, its strategy also changed, thereby disrupting the organization's activities.

Norms regarding the membership of foreign firms in consortia have produced a great difference in the composition of membership between the two nations. As of 1990, none of the 116 Japanese consortia had enrolled a foreign firm as a member. By contrast, by 1989, about one sixth of the memberships in all U.S. consortia were held by foreign firms. About 5 percent of the total memberships were held by Japanese firms. This difference, combined with the low dropout rate for the Japanese consortia, suggests that Japanese managing directors faced both a more stable and a more homogeneous membership than U.S. managing directors did.

Table 4.2. Numbers of Members and Sizes of Staffs of Consortia

Size	Number of Members (%)		Number of Administrative Staff (%)		Number of Technical Staff (%)	
	United States	Japan	United States	Japan	United States	Japan
0–4	13	6	54	74	36	72
5–9	20	26	15	22	10	7
10–19	20	33	10	2	10	6
20–49	28	31	13	2	18	11
50 +	18	4	8	0	26	4
Total	99	100	100	100	100	100
(N)	(39)	(54)	(39)	(54)	(39)	(54)

Consortia in both nations have very lean administrative structures, as shown in Table 4.2. About 54 percent of the U.S. and 74 percent of the Japanese consortia have fewer than five administrative staff. Only two of the Japanese consortia have more than nine administrative staff, and none has more than 49. By contrast, about 31 percent of the U.S. consortia have more than nine administrative staff. The cross-national difference in administrative staff size reflects, in part, the different way in which research in the consortia is organized in the two nations. U.S. consortia rely heavily on joint facilities, requiring their own administrative staff, whereas Japanese consortia do most of their research in their members' companies and use their staff.

Olk's study of 33 consortia in the United States sheds more light on the staffing patterns of U.S. consortia.[2] He asked consortia managers about their employees during their first year of operation. Only 18 percent reported that all their employees were full time, and just 63 percent employed 50 percent of their staff full time. As other accounts of consortium start-up difficulties have suggested, 70 percent of the managers hired no staff from member firms, and only 18 percent hired one-quarter or more of their staff from member firms. If we include staff who were lent to the consortia from member firms, the picture changes slightly: 54 percent had no staff on loan from member firms, but 24 percent borrowed three-quarters or more of their employees. Still, 76 percent borrowed less than half their staff from member firms. These figures paint a picture of consortium managers constructing their administrative staffs using their own recruiting networks, a process that most Japanese ERA managers probably do not face, given their reliance on research in member firms. Unfortunately, we do not have data from Japanese ERAs comparable to Olk's.

Consortia in both nations employ more technical than administrative staff, as Table 4.2 makes clear. As is true of administrative staff, U.S. consortia employ more technical staff, in keeping with their greater likelihood of conducting research in a joint facility rather than in member companies. Almost three-fourths (72%) of the Japanese consortia employ fewer than five technical staff. This number may be a bit misleading, however, because it does not include the staff in the member companies who are working on projects coordinated by the consortia. (Unfortunately, we have no information regarding how many people inside the member firms are dedicated to consortium projects.)

Even though the majority of consortia in both nations is fairly small, employing fewer than 20 technical staff, the U.S. population includes a sizable minority with very large staffs. About one-quarter (26%) of the U.S. consortia employ 50 or more technical staff, in sharp contrast with Japan, where only 4 percent (two of 54) of the consortia are as large. The U.S. population thus appears much more heterogeneous than the Japanese population, another sign that U.S. consortia managers are not following a single model of organizing in building their operations.

The size of the consortia in each nation, regardless of how it is measured, is not affected by when the consortium was formed. We correlated number of members, staff size, and budget size with a consortium's age, and all correlations, in both nations, were statistically insignificant.

What types of governance structures do consortia create in order to manage relations among their members? We asked consortium managers which of the following mechanisms they used and how often they met, distinguishing between meetings of top managers and meetings of working personnel: (1) Top managers include boards of directors and councils, and (2) working personnel include committees, task forces, panels, user groups, and other mechanisms. Boards of directors and councils mainly play an institutional-level role, linking the consortium to its wider environment, whereas working personnel handle the actual interorganizational relationships needed to keep the consortium functioning.

As shown in Figure 4.1, about nine in 10 consortia in each country had a board of directors, and about one-third of these consortia had councils. The ubiquitous presence of boards of directors indicates the cross-national importance of institutional relations, regardless of the level of governmental involvement in the consortium. However, Japanese boards meet much less frequently than U.S. boards do, as shown in Figure 4.2. We suspect that the narrower focus and more lengthy institutional history of consortia in Japan, compared with that in the United States, reduces their need to meet as often as U.S. boards do. In another paper (Bolton, Aldrich, & Sasaki, 1993), we explored the effect of both greater stability in consortia and *keiretsu* memberships on governance mechanisms in Japanese consortia.

More Japanese consortia reported using committees than did U.S. consortia (88% in Japan versus 62% in the United States), but task forces were used equally in both nations (38% in the United States versus 35% in Japan). Panels and user groups were far less prevalent, as we might expect, given that the consortia focus on generic technologies, not on improvements of a specific product.

Boards of directors and councils were much less active in Japan than in

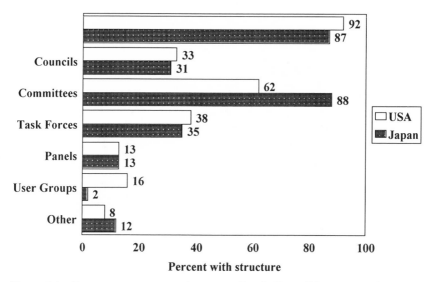

Figure 4.1. Governance structures (managers listed all possible structures).

the United States, as measured by the percentage holding two or more meetings during a six-month period, which is shown in Figure 4.2. Perhaps the higher level of board and council activity in the United States reflects the greater concern of U.S. consortia managers with control and accountability. They are under closer government scrutiny than Japanese consortia are, and their member firms are very concerned about the possible leakage of proprietary technology. Committees and task forces (which we interpret as closer to "working groups" than to boards and councils) were the most active governance structures in Japan, and their frequency of meeting closely matched the meeting of U.S. committees and task forces.

Most research in Japanese consortia is carried out in member firms, and thus we expected committees and task forces to be active because boundary-spanning mechanisms would be needed to link the members. But they are no more active than U.S. committees and task forces are, which meet in the context of highly active boards of directors. We were puzzled by this finding, and so we checked to see whether differences in the consortium's size, particularly the number of administrative staff, might account for it.

In Japan, the larger the administrative staff is, the more often the directors meet, but this is not true in the United States. Also in Japan, the size of the administrative staff is strongly associated with more committee meetings, but not in the United States, and task force meetings are not associated with administrative staff size in either nation. Apparently the role played by boards of directors, councils, committees, and task forces is different in the two countries, and further research on this question is needed.

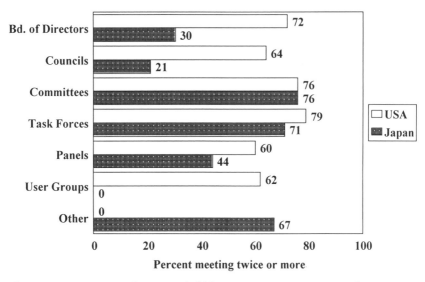

Figure 4.2. Frequency of meetings held by governance structures in the previous six months.

The administrative staff of Japanese consortia apparently play a more active role in their governance than do the staff of U.S. consortia. The managing directors of most Japanese consortia belong to an "old-boy" network along with key government employees. Indeed, most are retired bureaucrats who formerly worked for MITI. As the top boundary spanners in their organizations, they have more of an external representation function than an information-processing function (Aldrich & Herker, 1977). Nonetheless, consortia in the United States and Japan have similar structures to govern their operations, despite their differences in staff size and budget size.

Conflict Management

Consortia must manage complex interorganizational relations, especially because member firms may remain ambivalent about their participation. Managers of member firms want to know that their firms' interests are being taken into account by the consortium's managers. Similarly, consortium managers need to know what member firms' managers want from their consortium. In their 1990 study of U.S. consortia, Evans and Olk found that linkages between a consortium and its members are facilitated by boundary-spanning personnel who act as liaisons to acquire information for their firms and who represent their firms to the consortium. Conflict management is one of the keys to running an effective consortium, because member firms are concerned about obtaining a fair return on their investment in the consortium and may perceive themselves as being short-changed. We asked our respondents how their consortia ascertained their members' opinions, and the results are shown in Figure 4.3.

Mailed surveys are slightly more popular in the United States than in Japan, and members meet equally frequently. Not surprisingly, Japanese consortia, which are more likely to have committees as part of their governance structure than U.S. consortia are, rely more heavily on committees than do those in the United States. In both nations, the percentage of consortia reporting the use of committees to ascertain opinions closely parallels the percentage of consortia that actually have committees.

Member initiatives and one-to-one meetings are much more likely in the United States. Japanese consortium managers rely heavily on opinions expressed in collective gatherings, perhaps because of the different locus of research activity in Japan compared with that in the United States and the greater emphasis in Japanese organizations on group consensus in decision making. Given the Japanese structures (with research located in member firms), representatives of member firms may have a proprietary interest in keeping silent about their individual objectives, except when they can be compared with those of others in meetings.

Differences in how Japanese and U.S. consortia ascertain members' opinions are not simply a function of the tendency of U.S. consortia to use joint facilities and the tendency of the Japanese consortia to use member firms. When we controlled for how research was organized (joint facilities and member firms), cross-national differences persisted for most mechanisms. In neither the United States nor Japan is the use of mail surveys linked to whether consortia use member firms or joint facilities. In the

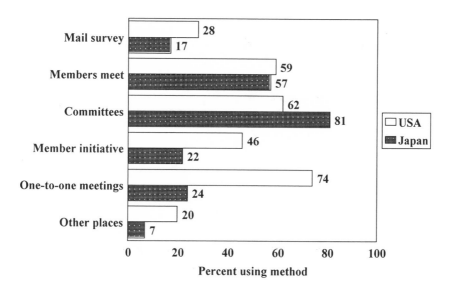

Figure 4.3. How the consortium ascertains the opinion of its members (all possible methods mentioned).

United States, consortia that use joint facilities are about twice as likely to convene meetings of their members, and the use of meetings does not depend on whether research is conducted in member firms. In Japan, research arrangements do not affect the use of member meetings. The use of committee meetings is not tied to research arrangements in either nation.

Research conducted in joint facilities does not affect member-initiated expressions of opinion in either nation. Although a member's initiative is more likely in U.S. consortia that conduct research in member firms, this is not the case in Japan. In all the comparisons we made, controlling for type of research arrangements did not eliminate the sizable national differences shown in Figure 4.3.

As another check on the results in Figure 4.3, we also asked managers where differences of opinion in their consortia were typically expressed, and the replies to this question are shown in Figure 4.4. Two generalizations stand out: (1) Differences of opinion are less likely to be expressed in any of the meetings of a Japanese consortium's governing bodies, compared with meetings in the United States, and (2) U.S. consortium boards are the single most important occasion for expressing differences, whereas only two of the 54 Japanese consortia managers reported similar behavior.

In Japan, 45 percent of the consortia managers simply stated that "differences of opinion are not expressed." Japanese organizations are well known for building consensus from the bottom up, ensuring that all interested parties have been heard before major initiatives are taken, and thus our results do not necessarily mean that differences are being suppressed. That is differences of opinion may just be settled in a different way.

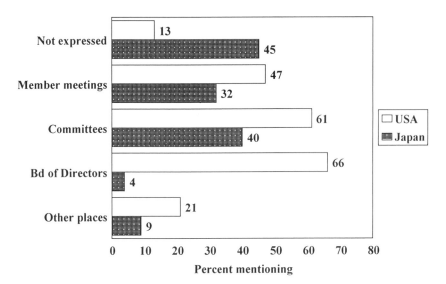

Figure 4.4. Where differences of opinion typically are expressed (managers mentioned all possible places).

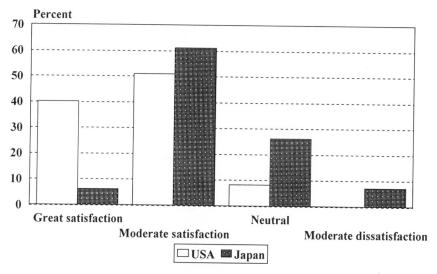

Figure 4.5. Level of satisfaction with the consortium (managers' perceptions).

Unlike board meetings in the United States, board meetings in Japan are not sites for expressing differences of opinion, according to our respondents, and this may reflect the largely symbolic role of such bodies. Our earlier results showed that Japanese boards meet less often. They may play a mainly titular role, but more research is needed on this question.

The final question we asked our respondents was, What is the current level of satisfaction or dissatisfaction with your consortium regarding technology development and technology transfer? Knowing that Japanese workers tend to express higher levels of organizational commitment but relatively lower levels of satisfaction than U.S. workers do, we expected a cross-national difference, but we were not prepared for the size of the one we found. As shown in Figure 4.5, 40 percent of the U.S. consortia managers expressed "great satisfaction," compared with only 6 percent of the Japanese managers. Neither group of managers reported "great dissatisfaction," but one-third of the Japanese managers were either neutral or moderately dissatisfied, compared with only 8 percent of the U.S. managers.

We have no objective measures of consortia performance, and so we could not determine the extent to which managers' satisfaction levels were influenced by a consortium's outputs. However, we asked managers to rank the most important internal problems they faced, and we checked to see whether Japanese consortia managers ranked some problems higher than their U.S. counterparts did. (These results are not shown in table form.) For the six specific problems that managers were asked to rank, average rankings were statistically about the same except for "recruiting/ retaining members," which U.S. managers ranked as a more difficult problem than the Japanese did. Because many managers, especially in Japan, ranked only one or two problems, the data give just a rough guide to the overall set of problems facing consortia managers.

Olk and Young (1993) studied the criteria used by both consortia managers and member firms in the United States to evaluate the consortia's effectiveness. They found higher levels of consensus on appropriate criteria within a consortium's membership than across the membership of all consortia. This consensus was not uniformly high, however, as it varied by a number of membership composition factors. Olk and Young found that having non-U.S. firms in a consortium lowered the level of consensus on appropriate evaluation criteria but that having nonbusiness organizations in a consortium had no effect. Two indicators of within-consortia heterogeneity—variation in levels of coupling between firms and variation in levels of technological uncertainty—were positively associated with consensus on evaluation criteria. They tentatively interpreted their findings as showing a "leader–follower" effect, with certain key firms taking the lead in structuring the principles governing a consortium.

Japanese consortia managers, then, rely more often on formal mechanisms of ascertaining members' opinions than do U.S. managers, and apparently they hear fewer differences of opinion expressed by members at these formal gatherings. Yet these managers also report being less satisfied with their consortia than U.S. managers are. Clearly, we need more detailed case studies from specific Japanese consortia to understand the full meaning of these results. Japanese managers may have higher expectations for their consortia, given their more limited focus, or they may simply be more realistic than U.S. managers are about what they are accomplishing.

Technology Transfer Management

The transfer of technology to member firms is the raison d'être of R&D consortia, and we were interested in whether the mechanisms they used differed by country. We gave managers a list of nine possible information-exchange mechanisms and asked them which ones they used. Our results are shown in Figure 4.6, and they suggest that U.S. and Japanese consortia managers follow different models of information transfer and diffusion. For every mechanism listed, except "other," U.S. consortia are more likely to use the procedure than Japanese consortia are. Of the 21 Japanese respondents who checked "other," 81 percent mentioned a seminar or symposium on research results (seika hokokukai). The cross-national differences are so startling that we believe they should be examined more closely in subsequent research.

U.S. consortia are more active than Japanese consortia are in promoting information exchange (all the cross-national differences in Figure 4.6 are statistically significant at the .05 level, except for "shareholder site demonstration"). We checked to see whether some of the differences could be explained for by the greater tendency of Japanese consortia to use member firms, rather than joint facilities, as their research base. We found no in-

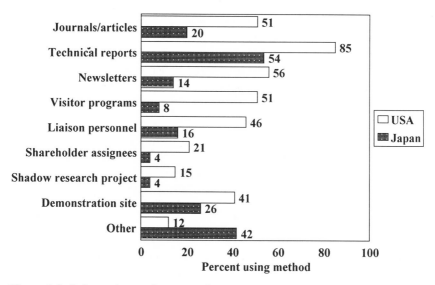

Figure 4.6. Information-exchange mechanisms used (multiple mentions possible).

stances in which joint facilities had a statistically significant association with an information-exchange mechanism in both nations, and we found two instances in which it made a difference in just the United States. We found only one instance in which research in member firms made a difference, and that was also in the United States.

In the United States, consortia that conducted research in member firms are less likely (35%) to have a visitor's program than other consortia are (64%), making them more like the Japanese consortia, only four of which have such programs (three of them are conducting research in member firms). In the United States, about 63 percent of the consortia conducting research in joint facilities use liaison personnel, compared with only 30 percent of other consortia. In Japan, by contrast, only 16 percent of the consortia use liaison personnel, and their usage is not related to where the research is being done.

Apart from these few differences linked to research arrangements, the dominant finding regarding information exchange mechanisms is that U.S. consortia are simply more active, across the board, than Japanese consortia are. The difference is not simply a consequence of the more decentralized nature of the Japanese consortia. Indeed, one might have thought that more, rather than fewer, information-exchange mechanisms would be required in Japanese consortia. Information cultures clearly differ between the two countries, as Bolton (1991) argued, and we expected to find firms in Japan more horizontally oriented in information transfer, and firms in the United States more vertically oriented. Instead, Japanese ERAs simply use all information-exchange mechanisms less often than U.S. consortia do, except for research seminars. Clearly, such seminars would carry a heavy burden of information transfer, but because ERAs are so specialized, they may well meet this challenge.

As several researchers noted at the conference, there may be many informal, day-by-day mechanisms for information exchange that are simply unknown to the consortia's managing directors. Roehl, Mitchell, and Slattery (Chapter 3 in this volume), in their study of the biomedical industry, noted:

> Although the processes underlying basic research and product development may differ, the activities cannot be separated neatly. . . . Understanding how to apply scientific advances to specific products often requires that the people applying research results maintain contact with those carrying out the basic research. Collaboration among scientists engaged in basic research and applications is crucial to the effective transfer of knowledge through the development cycle.

We need studies of the day-to-day operating activities of Japanese and U.S. consortia to understand better why U.S. consortia seem so much more active, on a formal level, than Japanese consortia do.

CONCLUSION

Comparing U.S. consortia with Japanese consortia is an extremely fruitful exercise because the enabling legislation enacted in 1961 has given the Japanese several more decades of experience with the form, compared with U.S. consortia. During that time, MITI and other Japanese governmental agencies have helped create a positive institutional environment for the creation and research activities of R&D consortia. MITI plays a subtle but important role in recruiting members for consortia, and the old-boy network supplies managing directors for many consortia. In the United States, by contrast, debate over the proper role of government in crafting "industrial policy" has meant that government has an uneven role. Government has been heavily involved in the establishment of some consortia (e.g., SEMATECH), but most consortia have been initiated by the private sector.

Japanese consortia focus on coordinating research in member firms rather than in joint facilities; therefore, they face different organizational problems than do U.S. consortia. Technology transfer is not from the center to the members but, rather, from the members to the center (and one another). U.S. consortia have liaison personnel who apparently carry a heavy burden in keeping members informed of what the center is doing. The members of Japanese consortia, on the other hand, communicate through technical reports and committee meetings. Accordingly, the managing directors of Japanese ERAs spend their time in two-way interactions with MITI rather than in internal administration.

In our comparative study of managing directors of consortia in the two nations, we found that (1) the governance structures of consortia in the two nations are fairly similar in overall composition but that U.S. consortia structures are more active; (2) Japanese consortia are much less active than U.S. consortia in managing the formal information-exchange process; and (3) that Japanese consortia managers report many fewer occasions than U.S. managers do in which differences of opinion in their consortia are expressed.

First, with respect to governance structures, the narrow focus and explicitly limited time frame of Japanese ERAs may mean that recruiting and retaining members are less of a problem in Japan than in the United States. The sizes of consortia—of members and staff—are roughly the same in the United States and Japan, and most have fewer than 20 members and fewer than five administrative staff. Administratively, consortia in both countries are extremely lean, "minimalist" organizations. In both countries, there has been no trend over time for consortia founded later to be larger on any of the dimensions we measured: members, staff, or budget size. More recent foundings are about the same size as the earliest foundings. Because our data end in 1990, we do not know whether this situation still holds for the current decade.

Consortia in both nations are governed by a board of directors in almost all cases, and about one-third also have councils. Indeed, the types of governance structures adopted are fairly similar in their frequency of adoption in each country. We discovered, however, that boards of directors and councils were much less active in Japan than in the United States, perhaps because of the narrower focus and explicitly limited time frame of the Japanese consortia, which lower the number of possibilities for conflict. At the working personnel level, committees and task forces meet equally frequently in the two nations.

Our results suggest that the administrative staff of Japanese consortia play a more influential role in governance than do U.S. administrative staff, possibly as a result of the ties that managing directors have to key government employees. Because government agencies provide the bulk of the Japanese consortia's budgets, we might expect experienced staff members to play boundary-spanning roles in their organizations.

Second, Japanese consortia managers appear to use different models of information exchange and dissemination, and U.S. consortia managers are generally more active than those in Japanese consortia. We are mindful of Mary Yoko Brannen's caution (Chapter 14 in this volume) following Westney (1987), that we should not automatically attribute national differences to "culture." The differences that we report reflect choices made in the context of different national socioeconomic and political structures. Japanese consortia are heavily assisted by government policies that encourage firms to join consortia and that heavily subsidize the consortia's activities. By contrast, the formation of U.S. consortia (with the exception of a few projects such as SEMATECH) has been spurred by the activities of trade associations, large manufacturing firms, and highly committed persons.

U.S. consortia used eight of the nine possible information-exchange routes we investigated more than the Japanese consortia did. The differences are not explained by the tendency of Japanese consortia to function as coordinating committees rather than operating entities. We speculated that the differences may reflect more subtle, informal means of communication used by Japanese consortia and their members, and between consortia and the larger research community, than our research was able to discover. In our subsequent research, we will investigate this finding by examining the characteristics of the member firms in each consortia.

Third, differences of opinion in Japanese consortia are less likely to be expressed in any of their governing bodies' meetings than they are in such meetings in the United States. Moreover, boards of directors of U.S. consortia are the sites at which differences of opinion are most likely to be aired, whereas such differences are almost never openly expressed at such meetings in Japan. Nearly one-half the managing directors of Japanese consortia reported that differences of opinion simply did not come up in their organizations.

Implications

The United States enacted the NCRA, legitimating formal cooperative precompetitive research among potential competitors, more than two decades after Japan passed similar legislation. The number of U.S. consortia founded each year is increasing, as is the total number of active consortia (because only a small number have disbanded so far). Has the United States benefited from its late start? Although concern about global technological competition with Japan clearly spurred the U.S. Congress to act and although there are many similarities between U.S. and Japanese consortia, our research has found major differences between consortia in the two nations.

The Japanese government, and in particular MITI, has played a major role in shepherding the founding of consortia and the recruitment of their members. It also provides most of the funding for the consortia, through either loans or contracts. MITI exerted strong institutional pressures on major firms to join consortia; for example, Toshiba is a member of 27 consortia. The U.S. government also has been active in promoting research leading to technological innovation, through programs at the Department of Energy, the National Science Foundation, and the Department of Defense. However, much of this research has focused on perceived national needs rather than on commercial innovations for private-sector markets. Until 1984, U.S. firms that were searching for ways to collaborate with potential competitors were always mindful of the Justice Department's mandate to prevent combinations in restraint of trade.

The U.S. consortia we studied have evolved in an era in which the legal–regulatory structure has changed, and as some have argued, the mind-set of managers in many industries has changed as well. Perhaps the higher level of governance structure activities in the U.S. consortia reflects, as meetings are held and opinions are solicited, a newfound willingness to experiment within cooperative alliances. In contrast, perhaps the activities reflect the lack of a national guiding force (the U.S. equivalent of MITI), that would provide a clear model for newly founded consortia to follow. Whatever the case, we strongly urge researchers to track the evolution of this vitally important population over time, so that the lessons learned can be codified and disseminated at future conferences on technology management.

ACKNOWLEDGMENTS

We appreciate the research assistance of Peggy Lee and the helpful suggestions of Ellen R. Auster, Christopher Baughn, Michele K. Bolton, John Ettlie, Michael Gerlach, Jeff Liker, Will Mitchell, Donald Nagle, Paul Olk, Richard N. Osborn, Thomas Roehl, and D. Eleanor Westney. Deborah Tilley designed the tables and put the manuscript into its final form.

NOTES

1. In 1989, according to figures provided by Evan and Olk (1990, p. 39), 40 of the 137 registered U.S. consortia had only two members, thus resembling typical two-parent joint ventures. However, 60 percent of the two-parent consortia that Evan and Olk found involved Bellcore, which we have included as just one consortium. If we had included Bellcore and some of the other questionable "consortia" we found in the Federal Register (which were simply just joint ventures), then a large proportion of the consortia in our sample would involve only two parties.

2. We thank Paul Olk for making his data available to us.

REFERENCES

Aldrich, H. E., & Herker, D. (1977). Boundary spanning roles and organizational structure. *Academy of Management Review, 2,* 217–30.

Aldrich, H. E., & Sasaki, T. (in press). R&D consortia in the United States and Japan. *Research Policy.*

Aldrich, H. E., & Whetten, D. A. (1981). Organization sets, action sets, and networks: Making the most of simplicity. In P. Nystrom & W. Starbuck (Eds.), *Handbook of organization design* (pp. 358–408). New York: Elsevier.

Auster, E. R. (1990). The interorganizational environment: Network theory, tools, and applications. In F. Williams & D. Gibson (Eds.), *Technology transfer* (pp. 63–89). Beverly Hills, CA: Sage.

Barnett, W. P., Mischke, G. A., & Ocasio, W. (1993). *Cooperative strategy in ecological perspective: Evidence from American R&D consortia.* Paper presented at the annual meeting of the Academy of Management, Atlanta.

Bolton, M. K. (1991, May 15–18). *U.S. and Japanese approaches to knowledge production: Internal and external information cultures.* Paper presented at the Third International

Conference on Japanese Information in Science, Technology, and Commerce, Institut de L'Information Scientifique et Technique of the Centre National de la Recherche Scientifique, Vandoeuvre-Les-Nancy.

Bolton, M. K. (1993). Organizational innovation and substandard performance: When is necessity the mother of innovation? *Organization Science, 4,* 57–75.

Bolton, M. K., Aldrich, H. E., & Sasaki, T. (1993). *Controlling and diffusing technology in U.S. and Japanese R&D consortia: An application of the organizational economics framework.* Paper presented at the annual meeting of the Academy of Management, Atlanta.

Contractor, F. J., & Lorange, P. (Eds.) (1988). *Cooperative strategies in international business.* Lexington, MA: Lexington Books.

Evan, W. M., & Olk, P. (1990, Spring). R&D consortia: A new U.S. organizational form. *Sloan Management Review, 31,* 37–46.

Felker, L. (1984, Winter). Cooperative industrial R&D: Funding the innovation gap. *Bell Atlantic Quarterly, 1,* 26–34.

Fransman, M. (1990). *The market and beyond: Cooperation and competition in information technology development in the Japanese system.* Cambridge, MA: Cambridge University Press.

Gerlach, M. (1987). Business alliances and the strategy of the Japanese firm. *California Management Review, 30,* 126–42.

Gerlach, M. (1992). *Economic organization and innovation in Japan.* Unpublished manuscript, University of California, Berkeley.

Goto, A., & Wakasugi, R. (1987). Technology policy in Japan: A short review. *Technovation, 5,* 269–79.

Heaton, G. R., Jr. (1988, Fall). The truth about Japan's cooperative R&D. *Issues in Science and Technology, 5,* 32–40.

Johnson, C. (1982). *MITI and the Japanese miracle: The growth of industrial policy, 1925–1975.* Stanford, CA: Stanford University Press.

Levy, J. D., & Samuels, R. J. (1991). Institutions and innovation: Research collaboration as technology strategy in Japan. In L. K. Mytelka (Ed.), *Strategic partnerships: States, firms, and international competition* (pp. 120–148). London: Pinter.

Link, A. N., & Bauer, L. L. (1989). *Cooperative research in U.S. manufacturing: Assessing policy initiatives and corporate strategies.* Lexington, MA: Lexington Books.

Mowery, D. C. (1992). The U.S. national innovation system: Origins and prospects for change. *Research Policy, 21,* 125–44.

Olk, P., & Young, C. (1993). *Criteria used by managers of R&D consortia to evaluate effectiveness.* Paper presented at the annual meeting of the Academy of Management, Atlanta.

Sakakibara, K. (1983). *From imitation to innovation: The very large scale integrated (VLSI) semiconductor project in Japan.* Working paper 1490–83, Massachusetts Institute of Technology.

Westney, D. E. (1987). *Imitation and innovation: The transfer of Western organizational patterns to Meiji Japan.* Cambridge, MA.: Harvard University Press.

Wright, C. (1986). The National Cooperative Research Act of 1984: A new antitrust regime for joint R&D ventures. *High Technology Law Journal, 1,* 135–93.

5

Governing United States–Japan High-Technology Alliances

RICHARD N. OSBORN
AND C. CHRISTOPHER BAUGHN

Since the mid-1980s a research team at Wayne State University has been exploring the development and evolution of corporate alliances involving U.S. and Japanese firms.[1] We were initially interested in these corporate alliances for a variety of theoretical and practical reasons. Theoretically, corporate alliances linking firms headquartered in culturally different nations appear to offer an opportunity to examine the development of new organizational forms. Furthermore, such alliances offer important outcomes, even though their survival is said to be quite problematic. Practically, however, the combination of U.S. and Japanese corporations through alliances raises a variety of questions. For instance, who will win in the competitive battles between the United States and Japan? Will the firms from one nation dominate those from another? Will alliances change both parties, and if so, how? Are there practical policy initiatives that can produce positive results for both the United States and Japan?

No one chapter could possibly cover all of these topics adequately. Rather our goal here is to provide a brief overview of the research program and its major findings. Specifically, we address the following issues: (1) Why are international alliances among leading corporations important, and what can they be used for? (2) What is the nature of the high-tech alliances between U.S. and Japanese firms? (3) How can the success of these alliances be assessed?

Our overall perspective is quite different from that of most studies of alliances. Most authors concentrate on a small number of alliances in order to derive lessons for the executives of a leading firm. In this chapter, we concentrate on a broad population of high-tech alliances formed during 1984/85 and 1988/89 to detect overall patterns of formation, evolution, and success. Of course, the two approaches complement each other. In-depth studies provide interesting anecdotes, new insights, and a real-life flavor to the study of alliances. Our work provides for empirical testing and the charting of overall trends. This work offers a different perspective in viewing alliances, stressing patterns among alliance characteristics rather than specific decisions relating to the alliances' governance form, technology transfer, or trade.

Through our research, we have identified general patterns of interaction consisting of combinations of product/knowledge flows and alliance governance form. These patterns, which we have labeled *dominance, turbulence,* and *hybridization,* appear to be related to specific technological areas. We also examine the combinations of product/knowledge flows, governance forms, and technical areas to detect patterns suggesting the relative cooperation or dominance by U.S. or Japanese firms as measured by net trade flows. The implications of firms from different nations forming alliances are anticipated to be a function of the patterns described here. As we shall note later, these patterns provide a more complex picture than simply whether U.S. or Japanese firms are winning.

WHY INTERNATIONAL ALLIANCES ARE IMPORTANT

Facing global competition, large multinationals often have orchestrated their operations across national borders with a combination of interfirm alliances (Harrigan, 1987; Perlmutter & Heenan, 1986). International firms are merging into interlocked, quasi-arm's-length networks of cooperating and competing elements. Such international alliances are becoming the key administrative elements in a global strategic competition among sets of firms. A firm in a winning network can grow and prosper with the network. Firms that attempt to go it alone or that join less successful networks simply will not grow and prosper in the 1990s.

Through alliances, multinational firms can span national boundaries to tap into a broader range of markets, products, technological expertise, and administrative systems. In high-tech areas, alliances may be a necessity. There are several important reasons for this. Technical breakthroughs are no longer the province of any single developed nation or dominant firm (De Benedetti, 1987). Alliances help establish needed institutional and interorganizational infrastructures in rapidly changing technical areas (cf. Garud & Van de Ven, 1987). They provide a mechanism for firms to specialize (e.g., Porter & Fuller, 1986) and develop unique competencies (Denekamp et al., 1993). Alliances can also be an effective mechanism for learning and exchanging technological information (Ouchi & Bolton, 1988).

The exchange and development of knowledge through alliances may allow firms quickly and creatively to integrate previously separate knowledge areas. With the current integration of products and processes—including the integration of optics and medical equipment, computers and telecommunications, and semiconductors with consumer electronics—industry distinctions are blurring, and the range of competencies required to compete may require a sustained flow of knowledge between organizations (Bahrami & Evans, 1987; Baughn & Osborn, 1989).

Firms may cooperate by sharing control, technology, management, financial resources, and markets, among other assets and competencies (Roehl & Truitt, 1987). This cooperation may take a variety of forms, including joint ventures, technology transfer or licensing agreements, original-equipment manufacture arrangements, and contractually defined joint programs or consortia (see Contractor & Lorange, 1988, for a discussion). In our work, we have defined *alliances* quite broadly to include all these forms of interorganizational relationships. Such alliances may offer firms flexibility and the ability to exploit economies of location, scale, and experience while avoiding some of the risks and costs associated with internal international expansion (see Child, 1987, for a complementary European perspective). With numerous advantages and lower risks, firms in multiple alliances can outcompete rivals that choose to go it alone.

Corporate cooperative relationships that cross-national boundaries are dramatically increasing in number and importance (e.g., Geringer, 1991; Gomes-Casseres, 1989). Our work also shows that alliances are fundamentally altering the manner in which new technical areas evolve into identifiable industries (cf. Osborn & Baughn, 1990; Osborn, Baughn, & Xiaobing, 1993). In high-tech areas, alliance development appears to be particularly important because institutional and interorganizational infrastructures appear to be poorly developed. Also, institutional settings change frequently and problematically as firms move across national boundaries (Kogut & Singh, 1988; cf. Van de Ven, Angle, & Pool, 1988). In the process of forming networks, cooperating firms change the overall developmental pattern of the industry.

Multinational Alliances in Technology-Intensive Areas: The Case of U.S. and Japanese Alliances

Shared interdependencies in technological development and transfer are readily apparent in U.S.–Japanese high-tech collaboration. Intel, for example, became involved in a three-party joint R&D project with Mitsubishi Electric and Seiko. This computer-related research (on real-time operating systems) followed Intel's establishment of a technical agreement with Oki Electric, providing for the mutual use of each other's microprocessor cells. Intel also gave Toshiba Corporation the rights to manufacture and sell its multibath system of integrated circuits. Mitsubishi Electric, Oki Electric, and Toshiba were, of course, involved in several other transactions with U.S.-based firms.

Figure 5.1 indicates some of the complexity of international, interorganizational activity involving semiconductors and computer-related and communication-related products and services for U.S. and Japanese-based firms.

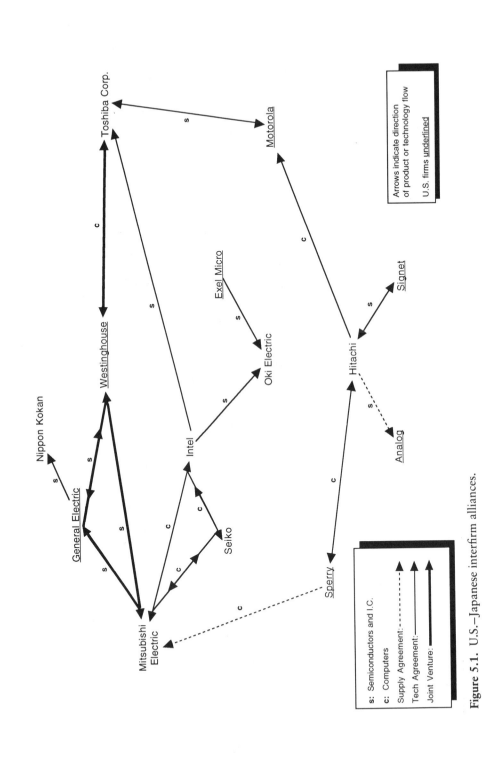

Figure 5.1. U.S.–Japanese interfirm alliances.

Legend within figure:

Arrows indicate direction of product or technology flow

U.S. firms underlined

s: Semiconductors and I.C.
c: Computers
Supply Agreement: ------
Tech Agreement: ——
Joint Venture: ——

Firms and labels: Toshiba Corp., Motorola, Westinghouse, Exel Micro, Signet, Nippon Kokan, General Electric, Intel, Oki Electric, Hitachi, Analog, Seiko, Sperry, Mitsubishi Electric

This depiction of interfirm transactions, based on listings of industrial cooperation reported by the Japan External Trade Organization (JETRO), is actually a simplified record of the interorganizational activities of the firms involved. Figure 5.1 provides examples of some of the important dimensions of interorganizational relations, including the direction of technology and product flow, the form of the linkage, and the industry. The activities of the firms listed here span traditional industry categories. Although several companies are indeed highly diversified firms, the blurring of traditional industry boundaries because of technological developments would appear to be compounded by interfirm alliances. For instance, General Electric also has established numerous linkages with Japanese firms (including Nachi–Fujikoshi in robotics and Hitachi and Sony in electronics) in other product areas.

Unfortunately, concerns about (1) developing national strengths in emerging technology-intensive areas (questions of the flow of technology across national boarders), (2) the governance patterns of alliances in emerging high-tech areas (nature of the governance forms linking firms), and (3) the emergence of specific technologies (what will happen in each) typically have been analyzed separately. But our research has shown that these factors need to be explored simultaneously.

WHO IS WINNING?

The United States, Japan, and most European nations see their economic futures relying on industries and products utilizing more research and development, high value–added services, and education (De Benedetti, 1987). Each seeks to capture the industries based on advanced technologies to ensure its future economic viability in a global economy. Although the United States once was dominant in most advanced technologies, Japan and western Europe are beginning to capture the industries and jobs in such technologies as ceramics, semiconductors, composite materials, and fiber optics.

Even though the U.S. and Japanese economies are now so closely intertwined that a failure in one would cause major problems in the other, both scholars and practitioners often ask who wins when U.S. and Japanese firms form an alliance. Individual case studies provide apparently conflicting evidence (e.g., Dreyfus, 1987; Kotkin, 1987; Perlmutter & Heenan, 1986; Reich & Mankin, 1986). From our perspective, the composition of interorganizational networks in rapidly emerging industries is expected to reflect ongoing patterns of alliance formation, dissolution, and evolution. Across a broad range and number of alliances, it is possible to estimate what types of alliances provide specific types of advantages that might be considered sufficient for "winning."

An alliance's success or failure may be assessed in terms of its contributions to its sponsors, the survival of the alliance itself, and the alliance's impact on national competitiveness (including its impact on international trade). Numerous scholars, taking an organizational perspective, have noted that multinational alliances in general and technology-intensive multinational alliances in particular, are exceedingly difficult to manage (e.g., Dunphy, 1987; Hayashi, 1987). Although an alliance's success may be assessed in terms of its net contributions to its partners in the arrangement, measurement, political, and public-relations considerations by the parent firms often make this approach problematic. For instance, we have found that comparatively few firms are willing to announce publicly that they have lost their competitive edge in an emerging technical area because they were unable to keep up with a foreign partner.

Although not to be simply equated with "success," one approach is to examine the long-term survival of the alliance itself. Some scholars expect that few alliances will survive over the long run, but there is little information on actual survival rates (see Geringer, 1991, for a review).

From a nationalistic perspective, some observers are concerned that multinational alliances will simply speed the decline of American firms as they increasingly confront globalized technologies and markets (Dreyfus, 1987; Hamel & Prahalad, 1989; Kotkin, 1987; Reich & Mankin, 1986). A decline in U.S. international competitiveness will appear in the overall trade flows among developed nations before the American economy seriously deteriorates. International alliances may intentionally or unintentionally accelerate the diffusion of technological advantage from American firms to competing Japanese firms. (Of course, just the opposite could be the case if astute U.S. firms exploited their Japanese partners.) The acceleration of diffusion to the advantage of either the United States or Japan could quickly change the balance of high-tech trade between the two countries.

What Participants Say About the Success of Alliances

In 1992 and early 1993, we consulted a list of alliances formed in 1984 and 1985, and called approximately 200 U.S. firms that had been involved in the relationships cited by the Japan External Trade Organization. To date, we have preliminary data on more than 170 of these alliances. Approximately 60 percent of the alliances formed during 1984/85 were still in existence in 1992/93.

We are now in the process of analyzing interview data concerning some 170 U.S.–Japanese alliances. Overall, our findings suggest a number of important paradoxes resulting from a longer-term association with Japanese firms. Briefly, alliance managers made such statements as the following:

"Yes, the alliance is considered successful, but I don't know what it was designed to accomplish nor can I provide any measure of its success."

"We don't trust them and they don't trust us, but we can work with them and predict their actions."

"It is very difficult to work with a Japanese firm, but at least you are working with the same individuals."

"I think I understand my Japanese counterpart, even if I don't understand his company."

"Yes, we have learned a lot from the Japanese, but I am not sure precisely what we have learned."

To understand better why U.S. or Japanese firms may or may not benefit from international alliances, it is necessary to discuss some important characteristics of alliances in greater depth. We begin with an analysis of technological flows across national boundaries.

TECHNOLOGICAL FLOWS ACROSS NATIONAL BOUNDARIES

The Japanese movement up the scale of technological development via advances in manufacturing capability has been particularly impressive. By creatively improving existing products and processes, the Japanese became global competitors in textiles and steel, then autos and consumer electronics, and now in microelectronics (Franko, 1983). In part because of a series of interfirm and government–firm alliances within Japan and across the globe, Japanese companies have emerged as a dominant force in new areas such as robotics and composite materials; for example, Naj (1989), Franko (1983), and Reich and Mankin (1986), among others, have suggested that multinational alliances between U.S. and Japanese firms have created an unbalanced technological flow. Far too often, the U.S. firms exchanged R&D and marketing for Japanese manufacturing prowess. Although they gained short-term returns, the U.S. firms lost their manufacturing expertise and eventually much of their market to their Japanese "partners." Too often the result was a significant loss of U.S. global competitiveness.

Several scholars have warned firms about the problems of technological diffusion in multinational alliances (Dreyfus, 1987; Hamel & Prahalad, 1989; Perlmutter & Heenan, 1986). For instance, too few U.S. semiconductor equipment manufacturers that were dominant in producing 16K chip equipment made the transition to the 256K chips, let alone the 1 MB chips. In 1960, firms such as Perkin-Elmer, OCA, Fairchild TS, Eaton, and Kulicke & Sofa were among the top 10 worldwide semiconductor equipment manufacturers. But by 1993, none was in the top 10, having been replaced by such firms as Tokyo Electric Limited, Nikon, Advantest, Cannon, Hitachi, and ASM International (see SEMATECH, 1992). From a national perspective, the demise of Eaton, for instance, as a top-10 equipment producer may be an important loss. However, Eaton's core competency has moved away from this highly competitive aspect of the industry toward other competencies that can continue to be profitable.

Our research implies that one must consider the potentially conflicting corporate and national interests. As we noted earlier, multinational alliances in technologically intense areas may well be beneficial for a firm, even though it loses a once-preeminent position in the industry. Alliances may permit a firm to adopt a collective strategy (e.g., Bresser, 1988) or a technology strategy (Butler, 1988; Child, 1987) that allows the firm to specialize in only one aspect of the value-added chain. As Clark and Starkey (1988) noted, such specialization may not benefit the nation as a whole, even if it is possible for a specific high-tech firm to profit from an alliance. Although a once-dominant domestic firm may well find that its core competency is no longer marketable because of a radical technological change, it might, through international alliances, still find a place elsewhere along the value-added chain that can offer adequate profits.

Given the potential gap between national and firm interests, we examined the question of flows from a strategic perspective across a wide variety of different alliances. Specifically, we examined the extent to which the proportion of product/knowledge flows moved (1) from Japan to the United States, (2) from the United States to Japan, or (3) in both directions. Rather than taking the direction of product/knowledge flows as an indicator of national success, we studied the relationship between the direction of flow and the two outcome criteria of survival and net trade flows between the two countries. Our work shows that when used alone, knowledge of the flow direction provides very little useful information about either criterion. However, in combination with other features of the alliance, it may be important.

GOVERNANCE FORMS FOR MULTINATIONAL ALLIANCES

What appears to be of considerable concern to the participating firms may be less the direction of the technological flows than the difficulty of developing a governance structure that both protects its interests and facilitates its success. Since the mid-1980s, there has been a subtle but important shift in how scholars view alliance governance. Much of this shift is based on the experience of firms with multinational alliances.

Why Governance Is Important

The obvious difficulties in integrating operations across cultural and national boundaries have led both scholars and managers to investigate alternative forms of linking firms, or what some call different governance forms (see Baughn & Osborn, 1990, and Osborn & Baughn, 1990, for extended discussions). Particularly in high-tech areas, the form of governance becomes a critical aspect of managing the flow of information among the partners (e.g., Hennart, 1988; Kogut, 1988). It becomes a primary mechanism for a mutual adjustment by sponsoring firms because the governance form typically specifies how technology, products, and processes will be administered and controlled.

There also appear to be important but subtle differences in some market-based contractual agreements. Contractual agreements to sell or provide technology, products, or services (e.g., original-equipment manufacture arrangements or licensing agreements) are common market-dominated alliance forms. The delivery to one firm by another of a finished product or component, however, should be distinguished from those arrangements that provide for the actual licensing or exchange of patents and know-how. Such technical agreements more frequently involve tacit knowledge and call on sponsors to adjust to one another in ways that are difficult to anticipate at the initial founding of the alliance.

In the mid- to late 1980s, both scholars and some practitioners urged U.S. firms to adopt governance forms that allowed maximum control and protection. More protection was often advised when exchanging knowledge and technologies. Although much technology may be transferred through supply of components and products (e.g., Ettlie, 1985), involvement through the value-added chain into R&D and technological information has profound strategic and governance implications for the alliance's sponsors (e.g., Porter & Fuller, 1986) and may have a dramatic effect on the ultimate success of the alliance and its sponsors (cf. Reich & Mankin, 1986).

Much of our work reveals that two important aspects of selecting a governance form are often neglected. There is a tendency in the literature to believe that firms select alliance forms that maximize protection from exploitation (cf. Williamson, 1985). But instead of opting simply for protection and control, we found that firms tend to select governance forms that meet the needs dominant in their industry or the technological area of the alliance's operations. Control of the learning process rather than control of the venture often is more important.

A second and often neglected factor is the actual degree of protection and control that various alliance governance forms offer sponsors. Theoretically, more equity and hierarchy should provide more control over alliance operations and more protection from exploitation (cf. Williamson, 1985). But this is not necessarily so. We found that alliance operations in technologically sensitive areas were more likely to be in the form of nonequity arrangements. Of 719 alliances tracked in 1984/85 and 1988/89, 47 percent were nonequity technological agreements; 29 percent were equity arrangements (almost all were joint ventures); and 25 percent were nonequity supply agreements.

Nonequity technical agreements may be a precursor to more elaborate alliance relationships (cf. Garud & Van De Ven, 1987; Osborn & Baughn, 1990). Moreover, we suspect that technical alliances for sharing and developing knowledge may be only one part of the process of deciding what portions of an emerging technology to keep, whom a firm will use as its suppliers, and how it will successfully market new products (cf. Garud & Van de Ven, 1987). In such arrangements, both U.S. and Japanese firms appear to mete out information and develop cooperation incrementally as each learns to predict the actions of the other. Although we discovered incidents of exploitation (by both U.S. and Japanese firms), sponsors generally reported that working through loose agreements rather than joint ventures allowed each to use its own administrative system for product–process development. Sponsors were willing to work on developing a common hierarchy through a joint venture only when both saw it as an important feature in managing their technological interface (see Osborn, Xiaobing, & Baughn, 1993).

In other words, our work suggests that the administrative system or governance form for the alliance is just one element of an overall view. Although important, it is not the most important feature and should not be examined in isolation. Furthermore, the relation of the governance form to issues of trust or exploitation appears quite uncertain. First, the core technology of the alliance appears to play an important role in the selection of a governance form. Second, protection from exploitation is not a simple function of the selection of a governance form (also see Roehl & Truitt, 1987, on this point). Yet this lack of protection does not seem to damage seriously the relationship between U.S. and Japanese firms. Instead, prediction appears more important than trust to the partners' managers (because neither one expects the other to sacrifice its long-term interests for the other party).

Flows and Governance Forms

We also would expect profound differences in the significance of national technological flows by different types of governance arrangements. Product flows from one nation to another via original-equipment manufacture and supply agreements may simply reinforce the development of a national industry and solidify the expertise of nationally based firms. However, technological flows out of the nation with market-based exchanges of technical knowledge may mean exporting more basic research and development efforts. Unless this is subsequently transformed into jobs and industries, such transfers may mean the loss of a future competitive position.

Joint ventures and equity relationships were somewhat more prominent when the sponsoring firms traded knowledge and information. In some technical areas, equity-based alliances appear to provide a better administrative system for integrating the core competencies of the sponsor firms to develop jointly new products and exploit existing or new markets. We should note, though, that many technical agreements also involved reciprocal product/knowledge exchanges. Thus there is not a clear link between flows and governance forms. Instead, our work suggests that technology must be incorporated into the picture.

TECHNOLOGICAL AREA AND MULTINATIONAL ALLIANCES

In much of the technology-based literature, it is popular either to discuss different technologies separately (as in studies focusing on a specific product or process) or to distinguish advanced technologies (typically those areas with rapid product–process developments and high R&D/sales rations) from all others. Unfortunately, these common practices hide differences among technologies (when all high technology is bundled together) or isolate analyses from one another (as in the case of technology-specific studies). We found it desirable to have a categorization scheme that allowed the integration of separate technology areas but still recognized some important differences across high-tech areas. Consequently, we turned to the concept of "industry" to develop such a scheme.

Earlier work showed that industry-specific approaches to the introduction of new products and processes, as well as differences in the attractiveness of innovation in different established industries, are important (e.g., Hitt, Ireland, & Goryunov, 1988). Indeed, Porter (1990) went so far as to argue that the industry is the key unit of analysis and that business strategy should focus on how to compete within an industry. Of course, in many high-tech areas, what we want to study is the evolution of initial firm networks that form the basis for constituting an industry.

Although it is extremely difficult to link emerging technologies to the existing industry categories, we can still use the traditional base of examining flows of products from raw materials to intermediate processing to the final consumer. Because many advanced technologies are based on information and knowledge rather than on product or process, we found it necessary to incorporate both products and services (cf. Clark & Starkey, 1988).

Essentially, we modified the typical typology of technical areas (e.g., Hitt et al., 1988) to recognize the knowledge/information components of emerging technical areas, as well as the fact that some emerging technology areas are targeted toward specific aspects of the economic value-added chain. In sum, we distinguished focused technologies from integrative ones. For the focused technologies, the area of current targeting in the economic value-added chain was a useful point of delineation.

In focused technologies, semiconductors and new materials are important raw materials. Although robotics and precision equipment may spread through the value-added chain, we found they were more focused as capital goods to be used as industrial equipment. Computers, communication equipment and services, and biotechnology, on the other hand, were rapidly emerging across a broad spectrum of economic activities, from agriculture to manufacturing to consumption (e.g., biomanufactured pharmaceuticals using computerized systems). Furthermore, we found that for computers, communication equipment and services, and biotechnology, firms commonly packaged combinations of products, services, and processes to develop a business. These industries represented more "integrated" technical areas. Thus we identified three high-tech areas: (1) high-tech materials and components, (2) integrative technologies, and (3) high-tech industrial equipment. With this last piece of the puzzle in place, we found numerous combined relationships among product/knowledge flow direction, alliance governance form, and "industry" when we examined the criteria for success.

ALLIANCE PATTERNS: DOMINANCE, TURBULENCE, AND INTERNATIONAL HYBRIDIZATION

Our studies of international alliances included collecting information about the direction of product/knowledge flows, technical area, and governance form, based on descriptions of all alliances reported to the Japanese External Trade Organization (JETRO). In 1984 and 1985 these descriptions were published in both Japanese and English, but in later years, these descriptions were not translated or routinely published. However, with the cooperation of the Michigan Department of Commerce and JETRO, we obtained photocopies of the listings for 1988 and 1989. We coded the direction of product/knowledge flow as (1) United States to Japan, (2) Japan to United States, or (3) reciprocal. The engagement form was coded as (1) original equipment manufacturer (OEM)/supply, (2) technology agreement, or (3) equity-related arrangements. (Joint ventures constituted the vast majority of the equity-related arrangements.) As we discussed earlier, the technical area of the alliance was coded as materials/components (semiconductors and new materials), integrative (computers, communications, and biotechnology), and industrial equipment (industrial robots and precision equipment). We found data for 205 announced alliances for 1984 and 1985 and more than twice as many alliances (514) for 1988 and 1989. In terms of birthrates, alliances continue to gain in popularity.

Our analyses indicated that the interpretation of relationships between any two of the alliance characteristics measured (flow, technical area, and form) must take into account the third characteristic. Configurations of the characteristics rather than simple one-to-one relationships need to be analyzed. We labeled these configural patterns as *dominance, turbulence,* and *international hybridization* and linked them to alliance trends and outcomes.

Dominance

As high-tech areas evolve, there may well be a conventional pattern of corporate and national specialization in which firms predominantly headquartered in one developed nation eventually capture much of the evolving industry for a substantial period of time (Porter, 1990). Supply alliances would be used to strengthen national capability for future development, and alliances would center on market-dominated forms. A nation's firms, through a network of competing and cooperating ties, might well be able to maintain a specialized focus on either a primary industry or a narrowly conceived secondary area.

As expected, the pattern of national dominance fits the industrial-equipment area. In 1984/85, 21 percent of the announced alliances were in the industrial-equipment area (mostly OEM/supply arrangements in which Japanese firms provided products to U.S. firms). By 1988/89, only 6 percent of the announced alliances were in the industrial-equipment area. Although the number of technical exchanges, often involving flows from the United States to Japan, remained numerically stable, the number of OEM/supply relations and flows from Japan to the United States declined substantially. It appears that nationally based specialists (here, Japanese firms) were the dominant players (relative to the United States). By 1988/89, there was apparently less need for Japanese firms to establish new supply linkages into the U.S. market.

Theoretically, the results for the industrial-equipment area fit nicely into the existing work on internalization and modes of foreign entry (cf. Anderson & Gatignon, 1986; Chi, 1990; Rugman & Vebeke, 1992). Alliances may be a useful entry mechanism into another country; but they may subsequently be replaced by direct foreign investment.

Turbulence

In the materials/components area, a pattern of national specialization and dominance is difficult to plot from the data on new alliances, even though national dominance has been both a public and a governmental policy concern in semiconductors since the mid-1980s. Technical exchanges were abundant for both study periods, making up nearly half the alliances in this technical area. Although reciprocal product/knowledge flows were important in both time periods (constituting 41 percent of the 214 alliances in the materials/components area), there was a more balanced unidirectional flow when comparing 1988/89 with 1984/85. This more balanced pattern may be partly due to the governmental interventions under discussion at the time the 1984/85 alliances were being formed and under review during 1988/89. In semiconductors, a U.S.–Japanese accord yielded controversial provisions for price floors, as well as export restrictions on the Japanese and goals for U.S. imports (e.g., Borrus, 1988). In composites, the influence of governmental action was more indirect because defense agreements allowed U.S. firms unique access to Japanese commercial expertise in composite materials (Lawrence & Litan, 1987).

The extent to which governmental initiatives altered the number of new alliances, the character of product/knowledge flows, and the forms of governance is unknown. What is known is the change in the trade flows. By 1992, the balance of trade between the two nations was moving in favor of the United States in semiconductors (U.S. Department of Commerce, 1992). It appears that governmental intervention by both the United States and Japan may have altered the developmental trajectory, making materials and components highly turbulent.

International Hybridization

The third pattern pertains to the integrative technical area, including computers, communications, and biotechnology. In these areas it is often difficult to separate products, knowledge, information, production processes, and services. Here, the potential breadth of applications offers considerable opportunities to match core competencies (Prahalad & Hamel, 1990). In the integrative technical areas, finding, developing, and nurturing productive alliances to facilitate new applications and new developments are particularly important.

In our research on integrative technical areas, we found that the product/knowledge flow was more balanced, with a higher proportion of reciprocal exchanges. In integrative areas, reciprocal product/knowledge flows characterized half of the new alliances for both 1984/85 and 1988/89. (This contrasts with 40 percent reciprocal flows for the material/components area and less than 25 percent for the industrial equipment area.) OEM/supply relationships constituted a smaller proportion of these relationships (25%), as opposed to 40 percent for the industrial equipment area. The forms of alliance governance appeared to conform to the necessity to mutually develop expertise, services, products, and processes rather than unidirectional exchanges of licenses or products for either market access or capital. Because the required skills and applications may be more diverse in alliances in this area, any one firm would be less likely to have all the skills of development expertise. Table 5.1 summarizes the character-

Table 5.1. Characteristics of Alliance Patterns

	Dominance	Turbulence	International Hybridization
Governance form	High proportion of supply arrangements; few equity arrangements.	Proportion of equity arrangements outnumbering supply agreements.	High proportion of equity and technical agreements vastly outnumbering supply agreements.
Product/ knowledge flows	Few reciprocal exchanges; one-way flows imbalanced.	Fairly high proportion of reciprocal exchanges; one-way flows imbalanced and erratic.	High proportion of reciprocal exchanges.
Technological areas	Industrial equipment (robotic, precision equipment).	Materials/ components (semiconductors, new materials).	Integrative (computers, communications, biotech).
Stability	Supply relationships diminishing as dominant firms internalize.	Not stable and may be subject to governmental intervention.	Continued pooling of information, reciprocal contributions.

istics of alliances relating to each of the dominance, turbulence, and hybridization patterns.

Stability of the Patterns

As technical areas mature and the production/service modalities for any area become more solidified, an initially hybridized pattern could well shift toward specialization and subsequent dominance. This might be starting to occur in the integrative area composed of biotechnology, computers, and telecommunications; with the shift in the pattern of product/knowledge flows to and from Japan. In 1984/85 there was a balance in the flows; but by 1988/89 the flow from the United States to Japan had grown from about 25 percent to about 38 percent. Consistent with predictions, however, reciprocal flows remained the most common.

Previously narrow technical areas might well undergo a competency-destroying, radical change and shift to a hybridized pattern or turbulent pattern (e.g., Tushman & Anderson, 1986). Or governmental intervention, alone or in combination with national firms, may tilt the developmental trajectory away from dominance. To gain a more nearly comprehensive perspective on the global evolution of emerging technical areas, it will be necessary to track the transitions in the flows and forms of these interorganizational relationships over time. It also will be necessary to expand the range of factors and variables. Some preliminary work suggests that alliance survival is significantly related to the dominance, turbulence, hybridization typology (Osborn, Xiaobing, & Baughn, 1993), with alliances in integrative technical areas showing higher survival rates. Future studies may find that international hybridization is a previously unidentified stable pattern of international technology development in other areas to which integration and breadth of applications are important.

Across the technical areas, some results were quite consistent with general characterizations of U.S. and Japanese competitive strengths. For instance, in such materials areas as semiconductors, the design skills of U.S. firms and the production–process expertise of the Japanese help explain both the outflow of knowledge from the United States and the pooling with the Japanese. The process strengths of the Japanese are clearly seen in their outflow of products in industrial equipment. Conversely, in the integrative areas, pooling is predominant. Such a pattern appears consistent with the notion that firms are "hybridizing" as these areas expand throughout both economies.

In integrative technical areas, the product/knowledge flow was more balanced, and the linkage forms appeared to reflect the necessity of hybridizing the expertise, products, and processes of the partners into a more intricately balanced reciprocal relationship. The form of the relationship appears influenced by both national strengths and the evolving character of the alliance's technical area.

ALLIANCES AND SUBSEQUENT INTERNATIONAL TRADE

Newly announced international alliances can be regarded as experiments in interfirm combinations of competency that may have an impact on the evolution of a business area. If particular combinations have a greater impact, they are more likely to be replicated and form a basis for future industry structures. One measure of impact "success" for alliances in globalized areas is whether they generate trade (cf. Porter, 1990). Specific combinations of alliance features that are related to future trade may be used to derive strategic approaches that firms can use to develop and operate international alliances.

There can be little doubt as to the importance of U.S.–Japanese trade. In 1990, for the United States, the total volume of trade with Japan was second only to that with Canada, comprising more than $138 billion. In addressing this issue, we examined U.S.–Japanese trade balances in business areas covered by more than 100 newly announced U.S.–Japanese alliances formed in 1988 and 1989. To provide specificity, we tracked imports and exports of particular commodities—products in their most basic form, often at the subproduct or component level.

We expected that the alliance patterns described previously (combinations of technological area, form, and product/knowledge flow associated with dominant, turbulent, and hybridization patterns) would be linked to trade volume. Indeed, we found that the three-way interaction among the technical area, flow direction, and administrative form of the alliances was significant when predicting subsequent U.S.–Japanese trade in the business areas covered by the alliance. Treatment of the data and analyses underlying this presentation are provided by Osborn, Denekamp, Zhang, and Baughn (1993).

In the computer and information systems area (exhibiting a hybridized pattern), equity relationships appeared to yield a more balanced pattern of trade, regardless of the intended product/knowledge flows. Although the firms in these alliances may be in a race to learn (cf. Hamel, 1991), the relatively balanced trade flows suggest that combinations of competencies governed by the joint venture in this technical area can be used to promote the development of an international business that cuts across U.S. and Japanese borders. Conversely, when a nonequity governance form is used (either OEM/supply or technical exchange), subsequent trade balances appear quite sensitive to the intended product/knowledge flows.

We predict that in technical areas in which packages of engineering design, manufacturing, and services need to be configured for global markets, hybridized combinations of competency may be a preferred long-term alliance strategy. For instance, packaging hardware, software, and service in computers or information systems calls for the linkage of at least three highly specialized technical competencies, all of which are developing rapidly. Although global excellence in one competency seems difficult, excellence in all three may be virtually impossible to sustain. From the trade data and the interviews, we noted a race to learn but not necessarily a race against the alliance partner. Rather, the race was an effort to coordinate knowledge and to develop packages that yield viable, popular products with the advanced technical features possible only with sustained inputs from each partner.

Unlike the area of computers and information systems, no particular combination of flow direction and governance form appeared more prevalent for semiconductors. The resulting findings in this "turbulent" area suggested the impact of dual sourcing. Interestingly, technical agreements flowing from the United States to Japan were associated with trade flows in the opposite direction (and vice versa).

Overall, the results of our study were consistent with the view that international interfirm alliances of firms headquartered in the United States and Japan may be important entities when analyzing subsequent trade flows.

CONCLUSIONS

Since the inception of this research program in the mid-1980s, our view and the view in the literature of international alliances in general, and alliances of U.S. and Japanese firms in particular, have changed substantially. Initially, alliances were viewed with suspicion. Firms needed to be wary of exploitation. Alliances were necessary evils that could be used for short-term tactical purposes. If these children of the alliance's parents were to succeed, the governance form was critical. Now, however, we are beginning to see alliances in a different light.

Although the possibility of exploitation is certainly a concern, the general fear of some massive exploitation by the Japanese through alliances in high technology may need to be reinterpreted. If there is a race to learn, it is not so much to learn faster than an alliance partner does, but to learn at least as fast as the technology and industry are evolving. This is particularly evident in the hybridization pattern.

U.S.–Japanese alliances are far from rare, but their commonness does not automatically translate into a greater understanding of Japanese or U.S. firms. In fact, most U.S. and Japanese firms involved in high technology appear to be quite complex entities. Futhermore, although an association with a U.S. or Japanese firm may not breed trust or understanding, this does not necessarily translate into poor relationships or death for the alliance.

Above all, the survival rates of these alliances and their relationship to trade suggest that U.S.–Japanese alliances, particularly in high technology, can be long-lasting strategic entities with important implications for the sponsors, evolution of the industry, and the national competitiveness of the two nations.

Who will win in the competitive battles between the United States and Japan, and will the firms from one nation dominate those from another? The answer appears to vary substantially depending on the technical area being discussed. There was evidence of dominance in areas in which the Japanese have had a national competitive advantage. There also was evidence that governmental policy in conjunction with industry initiatives (as in semiconductors) can block an emerging pattern of dominance. In integrative areas, such as computers and biotechnology, it appears that both U.S. and Japanese firms can benefit from alliances without dominating them. In such global technologies in which radically different core competencies involving engineering and design, manufacturing, and service need to be combined, international alliances can benefit all parties.

Will alliances change both parties, and if so, how? Overall, it appears that there are fewer direct changes resulting from a specific alliance with a U.S. or a Japanese firm than from the manner in which alliances are altering the developmental trajectory of the emerging industries in which both U.S. and Japanese firms choose to compete. Successfully operating international alliances appear to be important to the survival and success of high-tech firms in such global industries as computers, biotechnology, and semiconductors.

Are there practical policy initiatives that can produce positive results for both the United States and Japan? It appears from our research that far too much of the policy debate over U.S.–Japanese relationships is outmoded, overly simplistic, and too ideological. The future of both the United States and Japan lies in the emerging high-tech industries. Our work suggests that in these areas the old arguments for or against managed trade do not always hold. Different technical areas appear to call for different levels of governmental involvement. No single ideology covers the complex areas often labeled high technology.

Firms from both countries alone and in combination with each other can become important global players in high technology. The nature of the trading relationships in different technical areas and the nature of the alliances in these areas should be studied in much greater detail. Future joint prosperity appears to rest on nurturing the turbulent areas, such as semiconductors, to prevent destructive national trade wars in some vain attempt to dominate an emergent industry. In the hybridized areas, such as computers and biotechnology, and reciprocally linked patterns of specialization coordinated though alliances appear to be emerging as a viable developmental strategy both within developed nations and between them.

NOTE

1. The research projects for this chapter were in part funded by the National Science Foundation, ANR Pipeline Corporation, and the Hewlett Foundation.

REFERENCES

Anderson, E., & Gatignon, H. A. (1986). Modes of foreign entry: A transaction cost analysis and propositions. *Journal of International Business Studies, 17*, 1–25.

Bahrami, H., & Evans, S. (1987). Stratocracy in high-technology firms. *California Management Review, 30*, 51–66.

Baughn, C. C., & Osborn, R. N. (1989). Strategies for successful technological development. *Journal of Technology Transfer, 14*, 5–13.

Baughn, C. C., & Osborn R. N. (1990). The role of technology in the formation and form of multinational cooperative arrangements. *Journal of High Technology Management Research, 1*, 181–92.

Borrus, M. (1988). Chip wars: Can the U.S. regain its advantage in microelectronics? *California Management Review, 30*, 54–79.

Bresser, R. (1988). Matching collective and competititive strategies. *Strategic Management Journal, 9*, 375–85.

Butler, J. (1988). Theories of technological innovation as useful tools for corporate strategy. *Strategic Management Journal, 9*, 15–29.

Chi, T. (1990). *The effects of transaction costs on the choice of the institutional structure in international collaborative ventures.* Paper presented at the annual meeting of the Academy of International Business, Toronto.

Child, J. (1987). Information technology, organization, and response to strategic challenges. *California Management Review, 30*, 33–50.

Clark, P., & Starkey, K. (1988). *Organizational transitions and innovation-design.* London: Pinter.

Contractor, F. L., & Lorange, P. (1988). Why should firms cooperate? The strategy and economics basis for cooperative ventures. In F. L. Contractor & P. Lorange (Eds.), *Cooperative strategies in international business* (pp. 12–30). Lexington, MA: Lexington Books.

De Benedetti, C. (1987). Europe's new role in the global market. In A. J. Pierre (Ed.), *A high technology gap? Europe, America, and Japan* (pp. 67–87). New York: Council on Foreign Relations.

Denekamp, J., Osborn, R. N., Baughn, C., Xiaobing, X., Dasgupta, S., & Zhang, M. (1993). *Combinations of core competencies in international high tech alliances: tracing of success through bilateral trade.* Working paper, Wayne State University.

Dreyfus, J. (1987, December 21). How Japan picks America's brains. *Fortune*, pp. 79–89.

Dunphy, D. (1987). Convergence/divergence: A temporal review of the Japanese enterprise and its management. *Academy of Management Review, 12*, 445–59.

Ettlie, J. E. (1985). The impact of interorganizational manpower flows on the innovation process. *Management Science, 31*, 1055–71.

Franko, L. G. (1983). *The threat of Japanese multinationals: How the West can respond.* New York: Wiley.

Garud, R., & Van de Ven, A. H. (1987). *Innovation and the emergence of industries.* Paper presented at the annual meeting of the Academy of Management, New Orleans.

Geringer, J. M. (1991). Strategic determinants of partner selection criteria in international joint ventures. *Journal of International Business Studies, 21*, 41–62.

Gomes-Casseres, B. (1989). Joint ventures in the face of global competition. *Sloan Management Review, 30*, 17–26.

Hamel, G. (1991). Competition for competence and inter-partner learning within international strategic alliances. *Strategic Management Journal, 12*, 83–103.

Hamel, G., & Prahalad, C. K. (1989). Strategic intent. *Harvard Business Review, 67*, 63–76.

Harrigan, K. R. (1987). Strategic alliances: Their new role in global competition. *Columbia Journal of World Business, 22*, 67–70.

Hayashi, K. (1987). The internationalization of Japanese-style management. *Japan Update, 5*, 20–24.

Hennart, J. (1988). A transaction costs theory of equity joint ventures. *Strategic Management Journal, 9,* 361–74.

Hitt, M., Ireland, D., & Goryunov, I. (1988). The context of innovation: Investment in R&D and firm performance. In E. Gattiker & L. Larwood (Eds.), *Managing technological development: Strategic and human resources issues* (pp. 232–50). New York: de Gruyter.

Japan External Trade Organization (JETRO). (1984, 1985). *Cases of industrial cooperation.* Tokyo: JETRO.

Kogut, B. (1988). Joint ventures: Theoretical and empirical perspectives. *Strategic Management Journal, 9,* 319–32.

Kogut, B., & Singh, H. (1988). The effect of national culture on the choice of entry mode. *Journal of International Business Studies, 19,* 411–32.

Kotkin, J. (1987, March). Do the Japanese make good partners? *Inc.,* pp. 27–39.

Lawrence, R., & Litan, R. E. (1987). Why protectionism doesn't pay. *Harvard Business Review, 65,* 60–67.

Naj, J. (1989, December 26). U.S. loses edge in composite materials. *Wall Street Journal,* p. B2.

Osborn, R. N., & Baughn, C. C. (1990). Forms of interorganizational governance for multinational alliances. *Academy of Management Journal, 33,* 503–19.

Osborn, R. N., Baughn, C. C., & Xiaobing, X. (1993). *Identifying a new technology development configuration from analyses of U.S./Japanese alliances.* Paper presented at the annual conference of the Academy of International Business, Maui, HI.

Osborn, R. N., Denekamp, J. G., Zhang, M., & Baughn, C. (1993). *Networks of interfirm alliances in high-tech: Implications for international trade.* Paper presented at the European Science Foundation Conference, Berlin.

Osborn, R. N., Xiaobing, X., & Baughn, C. (1993). *The survival of U.S./Japanese high-tech alliances: Messages from the firing lines.* Paper presented at the annual conference of the Academy of Management, Atlanta.

Ouchi, W., & Bolton, M. (1988). The logic of joint research and development. *California Management Review, 30,* 9–33.

Perlmutter, H., & Heenan, D. (1986). Cooperate to compete globally. *Harvard Business Review, 64,* 136–62.

Porter, M. (1990). The competitive advantage of nations. *Harvard Business Review, 64,* 73–93.

Porter, M., & Fuller, M. (1986). Coalitions and global strategy. In M. Porter (Ed.), *Competition in global industries* (pp. 316–43). Boston: Harvard Business School Press.

Prahalad, C. K., & Hamel, G. (1990). The core competence of the corporation. *Harvard Business Review, 68,* 79–91.

Reich, R., & Mankin, R. (1986). Joint ventures with Japan give away our future. *Harvard Business Review, 64,* 78–86.

Roehl, T. W., & Truitt, J. F. (1987). Stormy open marriages are better: Evidence from U.S., Japanese and French cooperative ventures in commercial aircraft. *Columbia Journal of World Business, 22,* 87–95.

Rugman, A. M., & Vebeke, A. (1992). A note on the transnational solution and the transaction cost theory of multinational strategic management. *Journal of International Business Studies, 23,* 761–72.

SEMATECH. (1992). *Partnering for total quality.* Austin, TX: SEMATECH.

Tushman, M., & Anderson, P. (1986). Technological discontinuities and organizational environments. *Administrative Science Quarterly, 31,* 439–65.

U.S. Department of Commerce. (1992, July). National Trade Data Bank: CD ROM. Washington, DC: Bureau of Economic Analysis.

Van de Ven, A. H., Angle, H., & Poole, M. S. (1988). *Research on the management of innovation.* Cambridge, MA: Ballinger.

Williamson, O. E. (1985). *The economic institutions of capitalism: Firms, markets and relational contracting.* New York: Free Press.

II

PRODUCT–PROCESS
DEVELOPMENT PRACTICES

6

Nippondenso Co. Ltd.: A Case Study of Strategic Product Design

DANIEL E. WHITNEY

Nippondenso Co. Ltd. (NDCL) is Japan's foremost manufacturer of automotive components. It faces the challenge of manufacturing mass production–volume products in an unpredictable model mix to meet the high-variety just-in-time (JIT) production requirements of its customers, notably Toyota. Over the past 25 years, it has increased its ability to meet this challenge and, indeed, has made conquering variety a prime corporate goal. Although flexible manufacturing of this type is usually attacked as a problem involving factory floor operations, NDCL has defined and solved it mainly as a problem of product design. For the most part, production is made flexible by manipulating the assembly process, which in most cases is highly automated. The close coordination of top management objectives, product design, and production technology is required to carry out this approach. As a result, NDCL has taken concurrent engineering well beyond the goal of improving fabrication or assembly. Instead, NDCL has learned how to use design to achieve the essentially strategic goal of meeting the demands of its dominant customer.

In pursuit of this approach, NDCL categorized the problems of assembly automation into distinct classes, identified applicable solutions for each class, and successively attacked and solved increasingly difficult problems. In this chapter I describe this approach, give examples of its evolution, and indicate how NDCL has managed its production technology, principally robots, as part of the overall attack. I also discuss NDCL's approaches to concurrent engineering (CE) and new-product risk management. My research is based on seven personal visits to NDCL during 1974 to 1991, including extensive interviews with NDCL engineers and managers, tours of the plant, and papers published by NDCL and interviews with their authors.

BACKGROUND

Nippondenso Co. Ltd. (NDCL) is one of the world's great manufacturing companies. It makes automotive components for Toyota and other Japanese and foreign car companies. Its main challenge is to manufacture high-volume products in an unpredictable variety in a just-in-time (JIT) environment and to do so efficiently. NDCL sells to other manufacturers, and to stay in business, it must manufacture economically to meet their product-performance specifications, cost targets, and ordering patterns. This is a *strategic business challenge,* which NDCL has met by raising product design and manufacturing engineering to the company's strategic level.

The core of NDCL's response has been to design its products so that it can automate their production to a high degree while at the same time maintaining flexibility, an extremely difficult combination. Because the *fabrication* of individual parts must be automated in the car industry because of high production rates and can be achieved in many proven ways, the innovation here has focused on automating the *assembly* of such items.

Although this challenge is normally considered a problem of designing and operating factory-floor facilities, NDCL's approach is totally different. Its solution is in the product design office. NDCL has learned how to design products so that it is relatively easy to manufacture them in high production volumes, in a JIT environment, and with little or no change-over time. Furthermore, the product and its parts are designed "intelligently" so that their assembly is flexible. Often the assembly technology is very ordinary and not robotic or high tech. A technique that I call *assembly-driven manufacturing* has emerged. It is essential to recognize the holistic nature of NDCL's response. Many companies see the need to implement product design using computer-aided design (CAD) or to improve their ability to assemble products efficiently using design for assembly (DFA). Fewer see the need to be able to manufacture their products in unique ways, much less to be able to build in house the specialized equipment necessary to do so. Fewer yet are those who see the need to write their own CAD software to tie together their own carefully groomed product–process design methodology. Fewest of all are those who see the need to do all of these. I wrote earlier (July/Sept. 1992) that the majority of the last-mentioned companies are Japanese. NDCL is one of the most advanced in understanding that all these actions must be taken together systematically. This combination of skills gives NDCL the ability to use the design of its products and processes strategically, that is, so that it can meet the needs of its customers in ways that other companies cannot.

Venkatesan (1992) discussed core competencies in terms of make–buy decisions, indicating that firms should buy when they can find others who can do portions of their business better than they can in house. NDCL drew up the following list of core competencies of a responsive, innovative, high volume–high variety manufacturer:

1. Knowing how to use engineering design to create products that can easily be made in many models and, as a result, can often be made efficiently in high variety by less sophisticated manufacturing equipment than is commonly believed necessary to achieve this capability.
2. Being conscious of the need to learn over many years how to create this kind of design and of the need to develop a step-by-step procedure for learning and developing the skill.
3. Being willing to take responsibility for simultaneously learning to make key manufacturing equipment and design software in house and to integrate those skilled in their development with those skilled in product design, including supporting advanced production engineering and CAD development at the corporate level.

Researchers currently have no adequate theories of the "value of knowledge" or the value of combining many "islands of knowledge" into one system. Many of NDCL's make–buy choices in technology (as well as those of other large Japanese firms) often seem uneconomical or indicative of a not-invented-here attitude. An engineer at another Japanese firm put it bluntly: "You learn by trying, not by buying." This statement indicates that *learning* is the valued commodity, rather than any individual skills, and that this commodity is considered almost beyond conventional economic measure in such companies.

NDCL's approach was driven by its main customer, Toyota, which developed JIT in the late 1940s and extended it to its suppliers in the early 1950s. As Japanese car makers broadened their product offerings in the 1980s and as NDCL began selling to more customers, its problems with high-variety model mix production grew, making automated, flexible production even harder. But NDCL's systematic approach and its experience with simpler problems in simpler circumstances helped it with the more difficult problems.

An important feature of this approach is avoiding complex assembly technology such as "intelligent dexterous" robots. Instead, NDCL put as much as possible of the "intelligence" into the product itself, by focusing the *design process* on supporting high-volume mixed-model JIT automated assembly. Large numbers of robots are indeed used at NDCL, some quite innovatively, but they and other complex technology are not the core of the approach. This fact should interest managers of technology as well as academic researchers interested in concurrent engineering (CE), production automation, and product design.

The difficulty of achieving high-volume model-mix JIT automated production can be put in the context of a generic, long-standing conflict in manufacturing: the *flexibility–efficiency trade-off*. Efficiency can be defined as low unit cost, high-percentage utilization, or any other congenial metric that benefits from eliminating waste. Flexibility is also loosely defined as the ability to alter important operating characteristics of the equipment or features of the item being made. It is commonly assumed that flexibility and efficiency are basically counteracting characteristics in manufacturing, inasmuch as efficiency in the past has been achieved by using rigid, simple, and fast manufacturing equipment coupled tightly to parts transfer equipment. In this way, neither time nor motion is wasted. However, making the equipment do something else, in either the short term or the long term, is difficult or impossible. Rigid equipment avoids "wasters" that normally accompany flexibility, such as changing tools, dies, or fixtures; making adjustments to accommodate different product models; or making measurements and decisions. In addition to requiring some of these "wasters," typical flexible equipment such as robots also tends to be slower and more expensive than simpler, more rigid machines, further lowering its efficiency by most measures.

Although the flexibility–efficiency trade-off appears alive and well in most factories, it can be beaten in two basic ways: by designing equipment so that "wasters" are small (see Shingo, 1986) and by designing products so that "wasters" are not needed. NDCL has used the second method: embedding flexibility in the product during the design process and, with notable exceptions, using substantially traditional factory equipment.

NDCL focuses on one aspect of flexibility, the ability to respond to a mostly known set of possible operating conditions. Other authors and companies have sought in "flexibility" an antidote to the consequences of making a wrong decision, such as failing to guess the future course of the market. This may be a vain hope. Some of NDCL's methods indeed provide some cushion against unpredictable events, but most are planned actions against fairly well anticipated ensembles of challenges. Indeed, some designs deliberately make efforts to eliminate unpredictable events so that no "flexibility" to meet them is needed at all.

Another way to view what NDCL has done is to recognize that it achieves its flexibility goals by designing rather ordinary parts and then employing unusual methods to assemble them. That is, model mix and JIT can be addressed much more easily and economically during assembly than during fabrication. In fact, only one of the items described in this chapter requires novel fabrication techniques. (In some cases, however, more than usual attention to tolerances may be required.) The ability to manufacture flexibly and efficiently is starting to be more widely recognized as a strategic competitive strength. Because assembly has a particularly strong power to address these goals, it is receiving more attention earlier in the product design process than it did in the past (Whitney, 1988).

RELEVANT LITERATURE

The fact that manufacturing can be a competitive weapon when wielded strategically has been known for a long time. A typical analysis of the potential may be found in Skinner, 1985, although this study and most others lack detail and usually cite the same factors but ascribe them to different companies. The literature on Japanese manufacturing methods in particular is extensive, and focuses on management approaches such as CE; the implementation of project-management methods; and the introduction of computer-aided design (CAD), computer-aided engineering (CAE), and factory automation (FA). Most of these studies are general in the sense that they highlight the use of one or more practices at several "successful" companies but contain little detail concerning the specific engineering or design actions taken by each company in response to particular circumstances.

The special class of literature known as case studies typically concentrates on one company and circumstance and is found exclusively in the management literature. With some exceptions, the topics covered are strictly oriented toward management. The engineering design literature, on the other hand, tends to focus on technical issues exclusively and rarely notes the relation between the way a product is designed and such management issues as marketing strategy or the dominant customers' ordering patterns. An interesting exception is Mather (1987), who presents the idea of "design for logistics." An example is arranging the design and production sequence of a complex product so that customer-unique or long-lead items can be identified early in the building sequence but are not needed until late. Similarly, the product, its subassembly boundaries, and its assembly sequence might be designed so that customer-unique parts are attached last, or on the outside, thereby enabling most of the process to be the same (and thus less error prone), regardless of any special features.

Many authors deal with the general product deployment strategies of Japanese manufacturing companies. Abegglen and Stalk (1985) observe that the most successful companies limited the variety of their product lines, thereby saving money and reducing complexity. They also note the emergence of wider ranges of offerings in the mid-1980s; presumably cost and complexity should have risen. But they do not describe the methods employed to achieve more product variety or how associated costs and complexities were avoided.

Other authors have discussed design-process management and improvement in general. Toyota's project-management methods are described by Meyer (1992) and Clark and Fujimoto (1989). The methods these authors outline comprise overlapped tasks during design, involvement of suppliers in the design and engineering processes, incremental rather than revolutionary progress from one design to the next, and close communication among the designers, engineers, and manufacturers. The aim is to shorten the product-development cycle, an important competitive weapon. From Sasaki (1991), we learn about the importance of analyzing the various stages of the design process in order to improve it, especially by finding computer tools that speed up a particular stage. Various authors (e.g., Hayes, 1981; Perry, 1990; Robb, 1992; Shina, 1991) stress CE in one form or another, the goal being to combine project management with close communication between design and manufacturing so that problems are discovered during design rather than on the shop floor. Other authors recommend specific technologies or approaches, including statistical quality control (SQC) (Box et al., 1988; Modarress & Ansari, 1990), flexible manufacturing systems (FMS) (Attaran, 1992; Huang & Sakurai, 1990), forward cost predictions (Worthy, 1991), CAD/CAE (von Hassell, 1991), just-in-time manufacturing (Zipkin, 1991), or some combination of them (Atkinson, 1990). Whitney (1986) discussed the fact that attention to design can reduce the complexity of assembly technology.

Business school case studies of manufacturing usually deal with management issues and rarely with design. For example, internal debates at Sony regarding the advisability of setting up a separate manufacturing engineering division are described by Wheelwright and Gill (HBS Case Cat. No. 9-690-031). They also analyze the operation of the well-regarded Motorola Bandit Pager manufacturing system, which can make individual pagers to order, at the same unit cost regardless of batch size (Wheelwright & Gill, cat. 9-690-043). The only HBS case studies that center on the relationship between what happens on the factory floor and how the product is designed are by Jaikumar (cat. 0-686-083). For example, he describes the design strategies of Yamazaki Mazak Machine Tool company to ensure that its flexible manufacturing systems (FMS) operate efficiently. The most important of these is the "defined tool method," under which product designers must assume the availability of a limited set of cutting tools and must design each part so that this set will be sufficient to make it. Similar techniques are common in the electronics industry, in which a limited set of standard, quality-certified, easy-to-insert parts must be used by designers to the exclusion of all others.

Two gaps appear in the literature: With the exceptions noted, there is little detail on the actions taken within the recommended policy frameworks. "Form teams, involve suppliers, communicate with manufacturing, employ CAD," and so on are general prescriptions. Second, there is little to indicate that design practices (CE, CAD) and manufacturing practices (JIT, SQC) are related or that the former can affect the ability to accomplish the latter. Instead, they are treated as separate worthy practices whose aims are narrow and only technical: Avoid or find problems early; make processes more efficient; reduce cost; and so on.

NDCL linked these two sets of practices to achieve a specific strategic corporate goal. But no specific study of Nippondenso has come to my attention, except for those published by NDCL itself, such as the article by Kawai (1984), which explains the need for automating assembly for quality, cost, and speed and shows how product redesign is used for this purpose. The difficulty of doing this in the face of increasing product variety and model mix is made clear. Kawai also indicates that NDCL recognizes the importance of automating not only "the flow of things" but also "the flow of information." Both tend to be discrete, but the objective is to make them "flow as smoothly as if they were fluids." Thus, NDCL found it important to develop an in-house ability to create both product designs and factory automation systems, combined with the required information systems.

NDCL is a first-tier supplier to Toyota and other car makers. Although Toyota has heavily influenced the way that NDCL manages its day-to-day manufacturing, which in turn influences design, Toyota apparently has little other influence on the way that NDCL designs or makes its products. NDCL is a good example of the subsystem engineering supplier, as identified in Chapter 7 by Liker, Kamath, Wasti, and Nagamachi: It is given the overall requirements for a system and left alone to design it.

THE HISTORY OF NDCL AND THE EVOLUTION OF ITS APPROACH TO DESIGN AND MANUFACTURING

NDCL began as the electrical and radiator department of Toyota in 1937. It was spun off as an independent but partly owned affiliate of Toyota in 1949. A strategic alliance with Bosch in 1953 gave NDCL access to Bosch's fuel injection patents and brought Bosch an equity stake in NDCL. Toyota and Bosch still own stakes in NDCL but they are smaller than they once were. NDCL moved rapidly into international markets, opening its first U.S. operations in 1971 and its first European operations in 1973. It now operates 20 plants in 15 foreign countries in addition to 10 plants in Japan. With 43,000 employees worldwide (1991), it is almost half Toyota's size and the largest company in Toyota's supplier group. NDCL itself has 18 domestic affiliates and subsidiaries with another 18,000 employees (1991). In 1989, its total sales were ¥1230 billion (more than U.S. $10 billion at 1992 exchange rates).

NDCL's products are those automotive parts not considered part of the drive train, chassis, body, interior, or trim. This leaves air conditioners and heaters (more than 35% of sales), electrical equipment (approximately 25%), entertainment (15%), plus meters, radiators, diesel components, filters, brake systems and controls, and so on. In air conditioning and most electrical equipment, NDCL is the market leader, often dominating market share, technology, and/or price. Practically speaking, NDCL often takes higher-technology approaches to both products and production methods than does its main customer, Toyota. This is an exception to the usual *keiretsu* pattern in Japan, in which the upper strata of the supply chain teach the lower strata. Here the exchange is more equal, with Toyota supplying the JIT methods and NDCL providing the product design and production technology. For example, Toyota buys nearly all its robots, whereas NDCL makes nearly all of its robots in house (and sells none).

Many companies make excellent use of manufacturing technology or have innovative product designs. However, NDCL is interesting because,

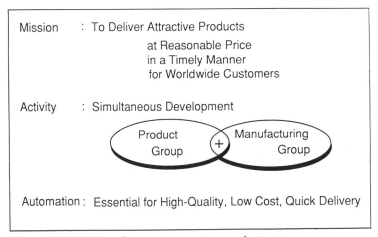

Figure 6.1. Mission of auto-component manufacturers.

as an original equipment manufacturer (OEM), its large industrial customers rely on objective criteria when evaluating its products: performance,
delivery, price, reliability, and service. These characteristics (except for service) are driven totally by design, engineering, and manufacturing. Therefore, NDCL is a "pure play" on factors that are objective and easy to
evaluate, unmixed with any that can be capricious, such as product aes-
thetics, advertising, or consumer tastes. The result is that one can concentrate on a facet of the company that has clear cause-and-effect properties
and learn a great deal. NDCL's reliance on its engineering design and production capability to stay in business is shown in Figure 6.1.

NDCL's approach to product design and manufacturing has evolved toward greater interaction between the design/engineering and manufacturing functions, primarily because of the influence of Katsuo Aoki, who retired in 1984. At that time, he was a nationally recognized figure and vice
president of engineering (including product, process, field service, plant
construction, and maintenance engineering), having moved up through the
ranks of the firm's production side. He was responsible for NDCL's technology strategy, including the decision in 1968 to begin building robots in
house. Because few companies have made this decision (and none at all in
the United States), the robot story is important and is sketched in a later
section of this chapter.

The main feature of NDCL's approach to manufacturing can only be
described as relentless and pervasive automation. Much of this automation
is quite conventional, although in places it is very innovative, even compared with some university research efforts. Advanced and complex automation has been applied only selectively, however.

In almost every case, the nontraditional or groundbreaking automation (robotics, plant communication systems, automated guided vehicles, top–down factory control) has been implemented by in-house teams using in-house technology. More conventional automation is also often designed and built in house, owing to claimed cost advantages, quality limitations of outside vendors, or (at least in the high-growth 1980s) the outright unavailability of outside vendors (Koichi Fukaya, assistant general manager, NDCL production engineering department, personal communication, August 1990).

Support for this activity comes from the Production Engineering Department and the Machinery and Tools Department. Both are part of the central corporate structure and report directly to the board of directors (see Figure 6.2). These departments provide expertise, equipment designs, and equipment to the product groups and their factories. The product groups provide product engineering and production engineering. This arrangement permits corporate support for costly innovations, retains and develops a corporate reservoir of skills, and keeps the partnership going. Neither the corporate headquarters nor the divisions can provide the products or factories by themselves. These corporate functions do not sell equipment outside NDCL and, as far as I know, are not considered as profit

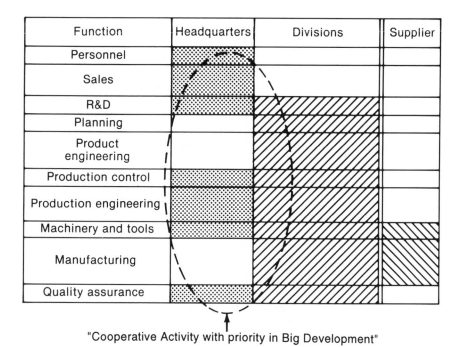

Function	Headquarters	Divisions	Supplier
Personnel			
Sales			
R&D			
Planning			
Product engineering			
Production control			
Production engineering			
Machinery and tools			
Manufacturing			
Quality assurance			

"Cooperative Activity with priority in Big Development"

Figure 6.2. Organizational structure of Nippondenso: Distribution of staff between headquarters and divisions in each function.

centers. But I do have anecdotal evidence that NDCL sometimes sells auto-mation system design and installation services. It apparently helped General Electric with its breakthrough dishwasher plant in the early 1980s.

Toyota's forceful role in this evolution also must be recognized. Imagine the phone ringing each day at NDCL and a voice from Toyota demanding, "We want 4,316 of meter type A, 301 of type B, 1,633 of type C, and 4 of Type D, tomorrow morning. Thank you. Good-bye." The next day, totally different distributions might be ordered. One cannot possibly re-spond to this type of customer by order-picking from a warehouse or by adjusting fabrication patterns. This customer at one point, however, ac-counted for 90 percent of the business and still commands more than 50 percent. NDCL noted that it adopted the slogan "Conquer Diversity," but one could say that the slogan is "Never Say No to Toyota." Either way, top management recognized the required focus, and engineering re-sponded.

TECHNOLOGY AS A STRATEGIC CHOICE

Different companies might respond in different ways to the challenges posed by Toyota. Even if a technological response (rather than, say, ag-gressive pricing or creative advertising) is appropriate, most companies re-spond by trying to buy those technologies that are not in their line of products. NDCL, the pure play on technological response, decided that in order to win competitively, it must have internal control over the main hardware, software, and design technologies required to design and manu-facture its products. Only by doing so does it feel it can achieve tight product–process integration and successfully resolve difficult trade-offs (e.g., improving flexibility by means of a clever design attribute or an inno-vative piece of production equipment).

In its choice to develop and keep production technology in house, NDCL followed a strategy that is frequently found in Japan. Not only do companies like Honda and Matsushita maintain production-engineering departments with several thousands of employees, but they also have production-technology development units that create new capabilities. In a similar fashion, a number of the largest Japanese manufacturers, among them Sony, Toyota, Nissan, and Nippondenso, have spent the last 15 years developing their own CAD software and allied engineering analysis and data management programs. (Whitney, July/Sept. 1992, discusses the strat-egies of several Japanese companies regarding the in-house development of CAD capabilities and their relation to product-development methodologies in general.)

Behind both the hardware and software decisions lie several basic atti-tudes. First, the Japanese are well known for putting a high priority on pro-cess capability. Developing new manufacturing technologies along with the ability to put them into the factory are parts of this trend. Second, advanced companies also see product design as a process analogous to manufacturing, and they recognize the need to have in-house skills to support it. The design process is usually carefully cultivated and idiosyncratic to each company, and it is tightly linked to, and drives, the capabilities of the supporting software. Hence, many of these companies also have opted to develop their own design software rather than rely on outside vendors who often lack sufficient understanding of design and manufacturing in general or the particular company's design methods. The disadvantage is that the companies must devote considerable resources to software support.

U.S. and European companies take different approaches. U.S. companies are most likely to leave both manufacturing technology and design-process software to outside vendors. These decisions reflect a desire to focus on "core competencies" combined with a failure to recognize process skills (design and manufacturing) as strategically important. It was not always this way. GE had a large automation-development division that was disbanded in the early 1980s when it was unable to perform as a profit center. GM developed an industrial robot and a 3-D CAD system in the 1960s before either was commercially available, but it abandoned both because "its business is cars." Today, both Ford and GM have design software that is an uncomfortable hybrid of older in-house packages and newer commercial programs.

In Europe, many companies have adopted a mixed strategy. Having long recognized the development of manufacturing technology as strategically important, they maintain this skill in house. But they still mainly buy their software from the outside, although some companies augment it with significantly tailored add-ons that contain proprietary data or specialized programs. The main problem is to "explain to the CAD vendors what we want," a deeper problem than just maintaining software. (The status of design methodologies and strategies regarding CAD in European companies is discussed in Whitney, Dec. 2, 1992.)

A recent article by Venkatesan (1992) weighs the pros and cons of relying on suppliers, indicating rightly that the "strategic" things should be kept in house. The different decisions made in the United States, Europe, and Japan indicate that Japanese firms tend to consider more things strategic than do other firms.

In sum, NDCL has decided that the ability to manufacture in high volume and high variety is an essential core competence and that design is an essential component of this ability. It has also decided that in order to achieve a high level of this competence, it must carry in-house capability further than have most companies have.

THE ELEMENTS OF NIPPONDENSO'S APPROACH

NDCL has responded to the challenge of efficient model-mix JIT production automation in four ways, by developing

1. A focus on integrated product–process development (IPPD) capability as a strategic weapon.
2. New product design methodologies that capitalize on IPPD.
3. In-house capability for implementing these methodologies using in-house design and manufacturing equipment.
4. An intellectual framework for understanding and developing the necessary skills and methods, including the classification of problems and solutions, the simplification of designs and processes, and the use of the assembly process as the main vehicle for flexible, high-variety, high-volume production.

NEW PRODUCT-DESIGN METHODOLOGIES

The methodologies span the range from the obvious to the sophisticated. The first method is to attack product diversity directly by means of standardization. This process requires analyzing the product's requirements and functions, studying the parts lists of similar products to discover opportunities to eliminate redundancy, and negotiating with the customer to trim low-volume members of the model-mix set. In one case, a small relay, originally designed to have either three or four poles, was replaced by one with four poles. A price discount was offered as an incentive, and NDCL apparently cut off the extra wire terminals on those "fours" that its customer wanted to use as "threes."

The next method, at a greater level of sophistication, is to identify time and money wasters in product design or production methods, including barriers to assembly automation. NDCL was careful to include in these studies the impact of product diversity, the main challenge. As one interesting result, NDCL's design-for-assembly (DFA) methods now use demerit points for a design that is difficult to change over from one version to another. This is quite a departure from conventional DFA, which focuses more on reducing part counts and predicting the time and ease of manually assembling individual parts outside the context in which the product is being made.

Because NDCL needs to automate and wants to use assembly strategically, it must solve many difficult assembly technology problems. Figure 6.3 shows examples of how NDCL has used design rather than complex production technology to solve these problems. The approach starts by classifying assembly automation problems into "dexterous/intricate" and "large variation." These two are different according to NDCL, although they often are treated as the same by other companies. Once they are seen as different, the tendency to attack both with the massive application of complex technology can be replaced by more rational approaches suited to each class.

"Dexterous/intricate" implies that the capabilities of people would normally be required to perform the assembly. At NDCL, it has been attacked mostly by redesigning the products. The large plastic air-conditioner cases

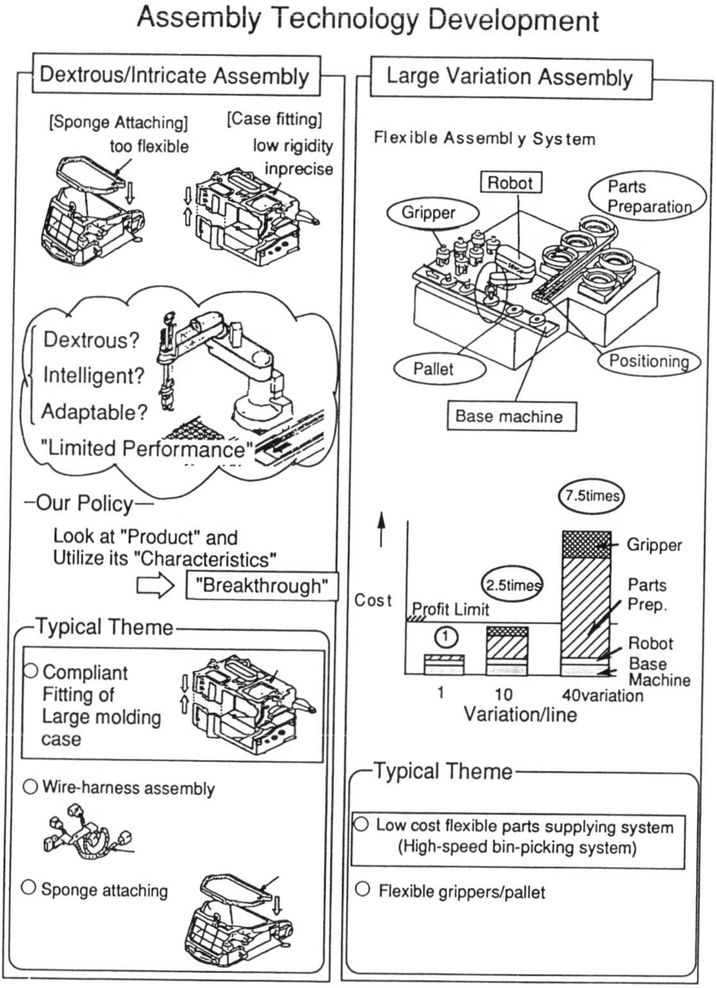

Assembly Technology Development

Figure 6.3. Development of assembly technology.

shown on the left vary too much from one "identical" case to the next to permit conventional robot assembly. (Sometimes the left sides contact first and the right sides miss, and at other times the left sides contact and the right sides miss.) Instead of applying robot vision sensing, for example, NDCL redesigned the shape of the interface between the uppercase and lowercase halves so that for a given robot trajectory, one side of the top half always contacts the lower half first, regardless of how the cases' shapes vary from normal. A deterministic robot trajectory can then be used, thus removing the need for sensing. On the other hand, the method for attaching seals between air-conditioner case halves (called *sponges* in Figure 6.3) required the development of a novel but deterministic articulated robot gripper; when the models change, the robot changes grippers.

"Large variation" is normally thought of as a natural target for robots because they can change from one product to another, "just by switching software." However, NDCL's time/cost study showed that feeding and preparing parts are the cost driver in high-variety situations. Having a robot at the workstation had little effect on the cost and little to contribute to the solution. Several attacks on this problem are now under way, in addition to extending DFA. These attack strategies include quick-change pallets loaded with different kinds of parts, plus robot grippers that can be changed quickly to permit the different kinds of parts to be gripped. This approach is similar to Sony's APOS vibratory pallet-filling technique (Nevins & Whitney, 1989).

The next product-design method used by NDCL to make feasible an efficient model-mix production is to design deliberately the product for a quick changeover from one version to another. Two common barriers to changeover are the logistics of the parts themselves and the logistics of the jigs and fixtures unique to each version. Fixtures can sometimes be the larger challenge. They are costly, so the investment in fixtures rises with the number of versions supported. The number of fixtures also rises with the production rate; it is not uncommon for 300 or more identical fixtures to fill the pipeline of a high-volume assembly process. Second, when a changeover is required, all the old fixtures must be swept out of the production line and new ones swept in, a procedure that can take a long time and encourage "economic lot size mentality." Third, fixtures can be a psychological barrier to process improvement because they represent a large investment. In the manufacture of radiators, described in the following paragraphs, fixtures have largely been removed from the process through redesign of the product. There is no such thing as an economic order quantity (EOQ) anymore, and any quantity or mix ordered can be made at the same unit cost as any other can.

The last and possibly most sophisticated approach I have labeled the *combinatoric method*. Product variety is created by having several versions of each part in the product. The product is designed so that the parts' physical and functional interfaces are the same for all versions of each part. The result is that any combination of part versions can be assembled into a working unit. The interfaces between the parts and the assembly equipment are similarly standardized so that differences among part versions are transparent to the automated equipment. The dashboard-panel meters described in the following paragraphs are a good example of this strategy.

In a larger sense, the combinatoric strategy reflects the advantage of using assembly rather than fabrication to make things different. Relying on fabrication to express model differences means producing complex parts with different features that express the differences. Complex parts are harder to make; they are more costly, require more inspection, and fail more often in test or use. Fabrication also has a longer lead time than assembly does, by one to two orders of magnitude (hours to days versus seconds to minutes). Therefore, changing from one model to another can take a long time. By contrast, the combinatoric method uses simpler parts but possibly more of them per product unit to achieve the same function. Assembling a larger quantity of simpler parts presents its own problems, mainly logistical, but it is easier to change models quickly and, on an individual step basis, is simpler and faster than fabrication. NDCL most often has employed assembly to express model differences. Figure 6.4 sketches these ideas, which are discussed in more detail in the example of the panel meter.

In-House Capability for Implementing These Methodologies

In-house capability has been established in three areas: the methodology for forming and operating product–process design teams and the associated risk-management methods; the engineers and shops that build and maintain automation machinery; and the system-integration area in which chains of machines are linked and the necessary local and wide area networks, computer control, scheduling, communication, quality monitoring, and display technologies are brought together. Both model-mix JIT production and on-line quality control are intensely information driven as well as design driven. Thus all three are considered strategic and tightly linked. Kawai (1984) made it clear that NDCL was acutely aware of these issues more than a decade ago. Product–process design teams are composed of high-level representatives from corporate production engineering, machinery and tools, and divisional product-engineering departments. Teams are small at the beginning of a project and are chaired by top managers from those departments. As the project matures from the concept to the detail design stage, the teams are enlarged. They follow the development and risk-management plan worked out at the concept stage. An important feature is the willingness of NDCL's top management to step in if a serious problem arises. When a quick crucial decision is needed, top management is there to make it.

Several methods have been adopted to shorten the design cycle. As illustrated in Figure 6.5, a parallel approach is used to overlap some design steps, both between the two major activities of product design and production design as well as within each. To aid the overlapping of adjacent tasks, "early sourcing" is used to feed forward to the next task advanced information about the coming information before it is finalized. Each downstream task provides "front loading" back to the ongoing previous task in the form of commentary and suggestions based on the advance information (see Whitney, July/Sept. 1992, for a description of Toyota's overlapping-task method of product development). Whenever possible, computers have been introduced to shorten each design task. Finally, hav-

a. **FABRICATION-DRIVEN MANUFACTURING**

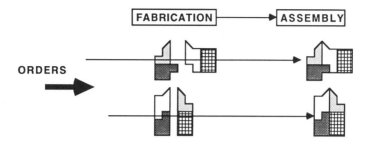

ORDERS

RELIES ON FABRICATION TO EXPRESS MODEL
MIX AND ACHIEVE FLEXIBILITY:

IN RESPONSE TO ORDERS, COMPLEX
PARTS ARE MADE AND THEN ASSEMBLED
INTO FINAL ITEMS.

THIS IS A LOW BANDWIDTH METHOD BECAUSE
FABRICATION TAKES SO LONG.

b. **ASSEMBLY-DRIVEN MANUFACTURING**

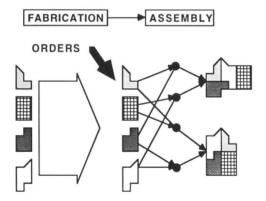

RELIES ON ASSEMBLY TO EXPRESS MODEL MIX
AND ACHIEVE FLEXIBILITY:

SIMPLE PARTS ARE MADE TO STATISTICAL TRENDS.
IN RESPONSE TO ORDERS, ITEMS ARE ASSEMBLED.

THIS IS A HIGH BANDWIDTH METHOD BECAUSE
ASSEMBLY HAPPENS SO QUICKLY.

Figure 6.4 (a) Fabrication-driven manufacturing. (b) Assembly-driven manufacturing.

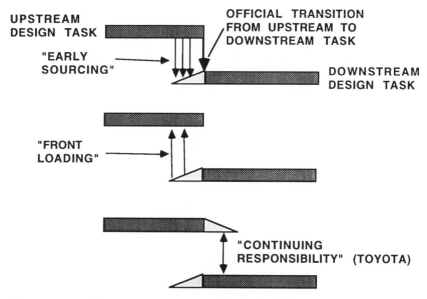

Figure 6.5. Overlapping product–process development at Toyota.

ing production-technology and system-integration skills in house shortens many crucial communication loops, contributing to faster product design and introduction. For example, when a new alternator was necessary, an in-house production-technology capability created a more tightly integrated product–process design than would likely have been possible if product and process were designed separately by different companies. This design is described later in this chapter.

An Intellectual Framework

From an academic point of view, the intellectual framework is probably the most interesting aspect, in part because many companies have followed a number of the methods described earlier. What one sees at NDCL is repeated attempts to classify problems and solutions, prioritize, find the right combination of problem and solution, and attack one problem at a time, starting with the simplest. Classification is at least as old as Aristotle and is usually found in academic environments, but NDCL has developed useful classifications of automation, flexibility, and products. The combination of these classes and the selection of items from each class drive the implementation of the strategy. Each kind of flexibility and product demands a different response, and each kind of automation represents a different level of difficulty.

One can see these points, for example, if one reconsiders Figure 6.3.

Barriers to economical *assembly automation* are shown here as falling into two classes normally lumped together simply as suitable targets for "flexible robots." However, NDCL considers these two separate problems distinguishable as two different kinds of flexibility. On the left is what might be called *within-task flexibility*, arising from the apparent need to adjust the robot's action because the progress of a task cannot be predicted in advance because of tolerances or part differences. On the right is what might be called *between-task flexibility*, arising from the need to redirect the robot to a new product model, an entirely predictable event. The former cannot be anticipated, and so NDCL decided to eliminate it at the source by redesigning the product so that unpredictable events do not occur. The latter can be anticipated and so is attacked, as shown in Figure 6.3, by economic analysis that leads NDCL to focus on designing better means of part preparation, which is not a function of the robot at all.

Within-task and *between-task* are two types of flexibility that occur at a single automated workstation. NDCL has identified three broad classes of flexibility in Figure 6.6. Within each are several subclasses representing different levels of difficulty. Volume change and product variation are day-to-day issues imposed by the customers. Design change in the past meant minor improvements but now addresses the most difficult challenge, namely, how to avoid a total factory reinvestment when the next-generation product arrives. Examples later in the chapter show how NDCL responded to volume and product-size changes and uncertainties.

Automation systems and products are classified in Figure 6.7, which gives a 40–year snapshot of NDCL's evolution in automation ambitions and achievements. The various terms (e.g., spot, line, FMS-0, FMS-I) are

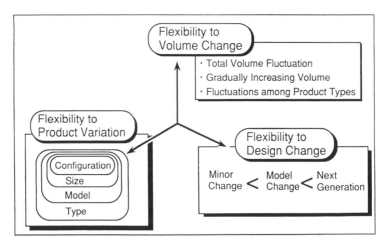

Figure 6.6. Three characteristics of flexibility.

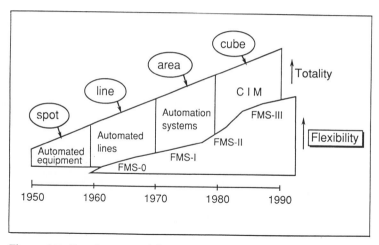

Figure 6.7. Development of the automated manufacturing system.

NDCL's names for successively more complex levels of automation. *Spot* refers to a single automated workstation, and *line* refers to a series of such stations integrated into a line. *FMS-0* is an integrated set of stations in a single machine, complete with a limited ability to make a variety of models; *FMS-I* is such an integrated system with a much wider ability to achieve model-mix assembly using the combinatoric method; *FMS-II* can use the combinatoric method even when different models have different parts complements; and *FMS-III* can do so even when the different models are of somewhat different size. These differences are associated with product examples in a similar time-line presentation in Figure 6.8.

The categorization of automation systems indicates not only the systems' greater size and sophistication but also their ability to respond to more difficult levels of flexibility, as defined in Figure 6.6. The products in Figure 6.8 may be classified according to Table 6.1.

It is well known that the easiest items to assemble automatically are small and have the same number of parts in each model. The difficulty and cost rise with the product's size, and providing the option to omit or include parts based on the model type adds even more difficulty. The most difficult among those in this table is the provision for different-size items on the same assembly equipment. Thus Table 6.1, whose downward order corresponds to the history of automation at NDCL, is in order of increasing difficulty, indicating that NDCL picked its targets systematically. Production and assembly equipment is typically 100 to 1,000 times the size of the product itself, with equipment cost being a strong function of size. Accordingly, a carefully combined product and production-system design becomes more crucial as the product's size increases.

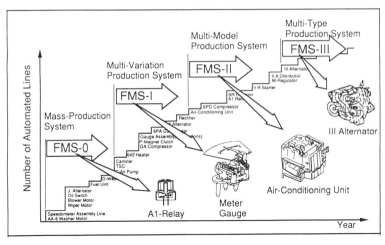

Figure 6.8. History of FMS at Nippondenso.

EXAMPLES OF NDCL'S METHODS

NDCL's methods provide important examples of

1. Technology management as exemplified by in-house robot development.
2. Several strategically designed products that attack different kinds of flexibility problems, such as
   a. Panel meters (flexible production of a small product with the same part count and part type in each model).

Table 6.1.   Classification and Properties of Several Products Whose Model-Mix Assembly Was Totally or Mostly Automated at NDCL

Product	Size and Size Ratio: Model Relationship	Part Count and Model Relationship	Period When Assembly Was Automated
Relay	Very small and same for each model	Same for each model	Early 1970s
Meter gauge	Small and same for each model	Same for each model	Mid-1970s
Radiator	Large and same for each model	Same for each model	Early 1980s
A/C unit	Large and same for each model	Different for some models	Early to mid-1980s
Alternator	Large and different for each model	Same for each model	Mid- to late 1980s

Note: The radiator does not appear in Figure 6.8, but it is shown schematically in Figure 6.10.

  b. Radiators (flexible jigless production of a large product with the same part count and part type in each model).
  c. Alternators (flexible production of a large product with the same part count but a different size for different models).

These examples illustrate aspects of NDCL's general approach in technology management, make–buy decisions, application of classification, and use of assembly to express model variety during production.

Robots at NDCL

In the mid-1960s, Aoki purchased a Versatran robot from the United States. After some testing, it appeared to lack sufficient reliability, so in 1967 Aoki assigned a new employee, Masayuki Hattori, to redesign it. Hattori used a new technology, the powerful electrohydraulic stepper motors from Fujitsu-Fanuc, to drive this large robot. The robots were therefore more costly than desired but they were strong, fast, and reliable. By 1974, 40 of these robots were being used in a shop unloading die-casting machines.

In 1977, Aoki introduced me to Hattori, who showed me an assembly machine for building dashboard-panel meters. (The panel meter is shown in Figure 6.9.) He called my attention to the simple "robot" at the first workstation of this machine, whose task was to choose among several types of casing or base plate and load the casing into the machine. He also pointed out that the machine could make several varieties of panel meter. I did not understand the significance of this for the company's business

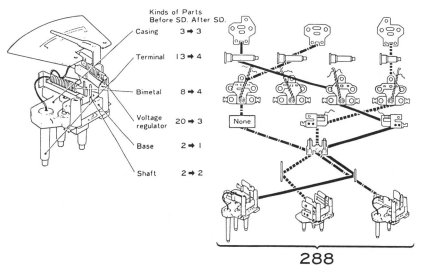

Figure 6.9. The combinatoric method applied to panel meters.

until 1980. In that year, NDCL used about 200 robots, all designed by Hattori and built in his department. Several of the types commonly used in industry were represented. (As the years went by, Hattori built all the types in common use.) Just before my 1980 visit, I listened to one of the first public descriptions in English of Toyota's production system (including JIT). NDCL's production engineers gave me a very lucid explanation of how they implemented JIT, noting that trucks full of alternators and panel meters left for Toyota plants (about 10 to 20 miles away at most) "every hour." I also showed a film to a large audience of engineers illustrating a research demonstration of the robot assembly of alternators executed in our laboratory (Nevins & Whitney, 1978).

In 1983, NDCL used about 500 robots, all designed and built in house.

In 1986, NDCL's robots with tool changers were assembling the cases and some simple internal parts of air conditioners.

In 1987, NDCL used about 1,500 robots, among which were several involved in the assembly of alternators. Other robots assembled the more difficult plumbing parts of air conditioners, resulting in a complete end-to-end automated assembly system. This system included both robot vision to help the robot locate threaded pipe ends relative to each other and to join them, and the articulated "sponge" attachment robots discussed earlier. In 1991, NDCL had 2,500 robots, and the number was planned to increase at about 1,000 per year for the next year or two.

Between 1974 and 1991, Hattori was my host, discussing problems of robot technology as he rose in responsibility. His constant concerns were cost and speed. Conventional economic considerations were always taken into account, just as they are in U.S. companies, when deciding whether to automate. But the required payback periods were much longer, typically three to four years. Even so, robots were not economical compared with manual assembly unless quite large production volumes were anticipated, usually more than 500,000 per year. "Forget low-volume applications for robots," Hattori told me in 1986.

An important reason that robots were economical at all was that in the early 1980s there was a breakthrough in electric actuators: direct drives. These powerful motors were less expensive than the early electrohydraulic steppers. Whereas in the 1970s, most assembly robots supported cycle times no less than about six seconds, by the early to mid-1980s, cycle times of two seconds were realistic for robots with less than a one-meter reach. The combination of lower cost and higher speed was a powerful impetus, and robot assembly applications multiplied. The fastest such robots employed a configuration known as SCARA, which provided only horizontal motions (except for the vertical motion of a light gripper at the end) (see Makino, 1980, for a full description of SCARA). This arrangement relieved the motors of the task of supporting the arm against gravity, thereby permitting more torque to be used to generate speed. Today, nearly all assembly robots are of this configuration, and the race for a one-second cycle time is on.

This configuration, however, can make only XYZ moves, requiring that the product be designed so that this limited repertoire is sufficient. Although most NDCL products can be designed in this way, it takes some discipline and understanding. Sony's products, by contrast, are much more complex, so it must augment its SCARAs with innovative grippers and tools. (Photos of these tools and a description of how Sony uses SCARAs may be found in Nevins & Whitney, 1989.)

In choosing to make its own robots, NDCL offered three justifications. First, it would have control over the technology and could create what it needed to match the requirements of its products. Second, it claimed that it could produce robots for a lower cost than it could buy them, quoting in 1991 an effective in-house cost of about $30,000, versus a price of nearly $80,000 for a similar U.S.-made SCARA, both equipped with a vision system. Third, it could keep control over maintenance and repair and could muster service personnel 24 hours per day, something unavailable from outside vendors during the 1980s, when every company was stretched very thin.

Of these justifications, the ability to retain control over the technology undoubtedly is the most important. Not only can NDCL integrate product design and robot-assembly system design, but it also can leverage its other corporate technologies, such as microelectronics, software, and sensors, into advancing the state of the art of the robots it makes, which are as fast, accurate, and reliable as any on the market.

EXAMPLES OF PRODUCTS DESIGNED FOR HIGH-VOLUME/ HIGH-VARIETY MANUFACTURING

Three products illustrate how they were designed for manufacturability to meet the OEM-JIT selling environment imposed by Toyota. In each case, design for manufacture (DFM) and design for assembly (DFA) were not used conventionally, that is, to make fabrication and assembly easier or faster. On the contrary, they were used as enablers for the larger strategy of using design to meet customers' varying demands. Additional technical details about these products and their production equipment are discussed by Kawai (1984).

Panel Meters

The panel meters shown in Figure 6.9 were manufactured by the combinatoric method. A meter has six parts (in rare cases, only five). Before the combinatoric method was implemented, some varieties of each part were eliminated. Then each type of each part was redesigned so that its mating features to its neighbors were identical for all parts of that type. Similarly, the surfaces where the assembly machine's feeder tracks or grippers touched each type were also made the same. The result was that any combination of the six parts would fit together and function as a meter, and the machine could assemble any of the 288 types. (The panel-meter machine and NDCL's quality strategy are described by Aoki, 1980. Kawai, 1984, discusses the small relays at length and indicates that they are made in eight varieties using a restricted version of the combinatoric strategy. Before product simplification, 114 varieties were needed to meet all customer requirements.)

The assembly machine functions as follows: The machine's control panel has thumbwheels into which the foreman can dial the required quantity for each of up to 40 types of meter. The machine is a serial system consisting of a conveyor that runs past several workstations. The stations operate simultaneously, and each cycle of the machine produces a finished meter. At the first station, a robot picks up the correct casing and places it on the conveyor. This casing serves as the assembly base during subsequent steps. Casings follow one another along the conveyor with no empty space between them. When a case reaches the workstation where terminals are installed, a feeder track delivers a terminal to a simple gripper, which installs it. The casing visits each subsequent workstation and receives the remaining parts, one at each station.

The machine builds one type of meter in this way until the counter on the control panel indicates that the day's (or shift's) need for that type has been filled. The robot then places a dummy casing on the conveyor. This casing acts as a signal beacon, tripping a sensor as it enters each workstation. The gripper at the station does nothing, but the feeder track is moved by a simple air piston so that it feeds another type of part. The next casing after the dummy is a real one, so the station resumes operation after losing one cycle as the dummy passes through. Following this pattern, the machine builds solid batches of each type ordered until the orders are all filled.

Radiators

Because radiators are many times larger than panel meters, the "machine" is in fact an entire factory. In a conventional radiator factory, the radiators are carried around in fixtures that hang from an overhead conveyor. The fixtures hold several metal items together (see Figure 6.10); these are the core, two end plates, and two headers. The cores are quite springy and would pop apart if not securely held by the fixtures. The parts are soldered together in a large oven, through which the conveyor travels. Then the radiators are removed from the fixtures and placed in a crimping machine where the plastic inlet and outlet tanks are crimped securely into place. Typically this is done with a large press die shaped to conform to the tank. When a new type of radiator is to be made, the factory must switch over. Depending on the EOQ, this switch may occur every few hours. A lot of time is lost while one kind of fixture and press die is exchanged for another. Possibly hundreds of fixtures are involved in the switch.

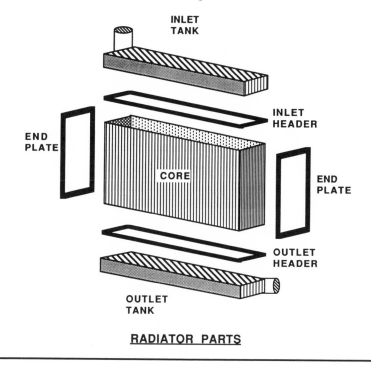

RADIATOR PARTS

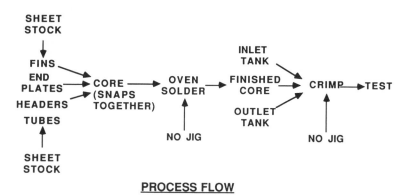

PROCESS FLOW

Figure 6.10. The process flow for radiator manufacture.

The new design, created in the early 1980s, dispenses with these fixtures because the parts snap together securely enough to be soldered, after which the assembly is quite rigid (Ohta & Hanai, 1986). Any correctly shaped combination of core, end plate, and header easily snap together into a valid unit. Thus this is a version of the combinatoric method being used here. The redesigned press die consists of several pressure points rather than one continuous press face. Each pressure point looks like a piano key and is inserted by its own air piston. Inserted keys cause a tab to be crimped when the machine presses. A bar code on the tank tells the press die which pistons to activate. In this way, the system conforms to the shape of the tank. Consequently, each tank can be different, and the machine can crimp it.

Unlike the panel-meter machine, this factory can make a batch size of one as easily as 100. When I first heard Kazuhiro Ohta describe this factory in public in 1986, he was asked, "How much did this factory cost?" "Strictly speaking," he said, "you have to include the cost of redesigning the product." That is, it is not simply a factory unless the product has been designed correctly.

Alternators

Alternators, like radiators, are not glamorous items. Therefore, to radically change one's market share for such a product, one must do something dramatic in price or performance. In the early 1980s, NDCL chose to attack price, which meant not only automating but also doing so for much less cost than before. The fact that alternators are made in about 250 varieties, in three different outside diameters, complicates the problem because typically automation works on items of only one size. Different sizes are made on different machines. In this case, as with radiators, "machine" really means factory, and each additional factory means hundreds of millions of dollars of additional investment.

Here again, NDCL divided the problem into different challenges of different levels of difficulty. Some of those pertaining to individual parts are shown in Figure 6.11. Dealing with different-size stators was judged the most difficult challenge.

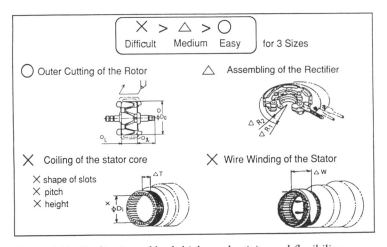

Figure 6.11. Realization of both high-productivity and flexibility.

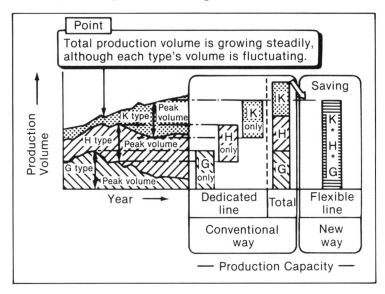

Figure 6.12. New FMS concept: FMS-III.

Figure 6.12 shows the capital-investment problem. Not only is total volume growing (one type of flexibility shown in Figure 6.6), but the relative volume share of each of the three sizes also is not known (another type of flexibility). To accommodate the worst case, the demand for each size would result in considerable overinvestment. This is especially bad in Japan, where land is expensive and, in many areas, earthquakes preclude multistory factories.

One way of dealing with different sizes is shown in Figure 6.13, where the typical method is shown on the left. Stator laminations are typically built by stacking rings that have been stamped from flat sheet stock. The inside of each ring and the four outside corners are scrap. When a different diameter is needed, different stamping and assembly machines are used. The new continuous-coiling method, by contrast, starts with straight strip stock, cuts (almost) rectangular holes in it, slits it longitudinally, and coils it into a stator. By comparison there is much less waste. When a different diameter is also needed, the size and spacing of the punched holes are changed, and the coiling diameter also is changed, each by means of quickly substituting one punch die or coiling spindle for another. One machine can thus make any size needed. Different sizes elsewhere in the assembly process are relatively easy to accomodate, resulting in a system that can switch on demand from one size to another.

One must respect the degree to which the method on the right in Figure 6.13 differs from conventional alternator or motor manufacture. This alternator, as a business concept, exists basically because of the manufacturing process. Like very large scale integration (VLSI) but totally unlike con-

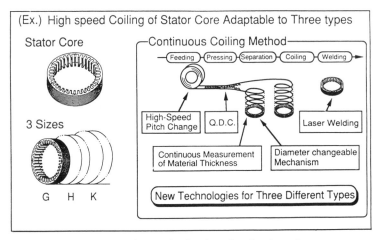

Figure 6.13. Example of a newly developed technology for stator cores.

ventionally made alternators, this product is the child of its process. It is unlikely that a conventional product-design process, in which manufacturing skills are purchased from outside vendors, would have come up with this method.

NEW PRODUCT-DEVELOPMENT PROCESS

These interesting products emerged from a concurrent engineering process aimed at creating breakthroughs in an existing product line. Again, a classification has been made, this time of product-development methods, as shown in Figure 6.14. The process used on the alternator is the *jikigata* (meaning "strategic new product") type. It is aimed at creating major improvements in performance, as opposed to minor tweakings. *Jikigata* is used on products that are deemed to be the mainstays of a product division but that face or might face severe competition. To ensure technical, budget, and schedule success, a systematic approach is used. This approach is applied from the beginning of the design project and involves the tight integration of product planning and development along with the implementation of process development and manufacturing.

The *jikigata* process shown in Figure 6.15 indicates two teams, one focused on product design and the other on production-system design. In fact, the agendas of these two teams are established at the beginning of the project by the Strategic New Product Development Council, which coordinates the subsequent activities. Although the figure indicates two separate teams, in fact they are closely coordinated, and the distinction between the teams may not, in fact, be very strong.

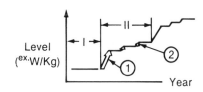

Class	Definition	Examples
1 Strategic new product, *Jikigata*	• Big improvement in existing main product (Lightweight, high–efficiency, etc.)	• Type III alternator • SR radiator • H–38 fuel pump, etc.
2 Seminew product	• Minor change in existing product	• Speedometer for ◯◯ model • Cooling unit for △△ model, etc.
3 Innovative new product	• Completely new product that does not exist on current lineup	• CRT display system • Suspension control, etc.

Figure 6.14. Classification of new-product development at Nippondenso.

What is more important is the degree of advanced joint planning and setting of objectives. The first step in this process is to create an "image of the new product," which means defining the specifications and performance of both the product and its production process. In the case of the alternator, this step means requiring the production process to accommodate several sizes. Once this image is complete, the process expands to two larger teams that create action agendas for achieving this image plus other objectives for production. As indicated in Figure 6.16, each objective is given specifications and two classifications according to desirability and

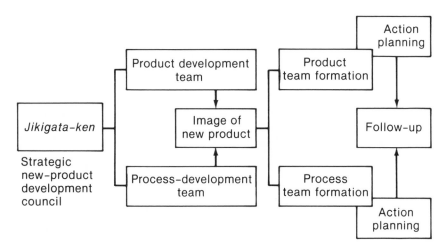

Figure 6.15. Role of *Jikigata-ken*.

Prod. Eng. Team

Theme	Person	Goal	Seriousness	Difficulty	Schedule	Alternative Plan
New-resin application	Section 4-2 Mr. A	Weight $-$ 30% Cost $-$ 20%	W_1	B	B — A▽	Al material
Soldering-free	Section 3-1 Mr. B	Life span $+$ 50% Cost $-$ 30%	M	B	B ¬ A▽ — A	—
Laser welding	Section 3-1 Mr. G Machinery Div. Mr. J	Flexibility up High-speed $+$ 50%	W_1	B	B — A▽	Spot welding
High-speed cutting	Section 2-6 Mr. E	Cutting speed $+$200%	W_2	C	C ¬ B — A▽	Several machines
Precision machine	Machinery Div. Mr. D	Precision $+$100%	M	B	B ¬ A▽ — A	—
High-speed assembly line	Section 1-1 Mr. M	Productivity $+$300% lead time $-$ 50%	M	B	B ¬ A▽ — A	—

⊙ Classified Management

⊙ Trigger Point

▽ Decision timing of the technical feasibility.
Some alternatives are ready in advance.

Seriousness

M	Must
W_1	Want 1
W_2	Want 2

Difficulty

A	Feasible as of today
B	Under examination for mass production
C	Under basic examination

Figure 6.16. Action plan of XX product development.

risk. The action plan specifies a schedule and identifies fallbacks in case the more risky objectives cannot be achieved by their due dates (called *trigger points*). This process, its pursuit, and the follow-up, constitute the product–process design and risk management. To shorten the overall time, process development begins along with product design and, in the case of the alternator, fundamentally affects the design.

The vice president of engineering at Polaroid once called the setting of trigger dates *scheduling inventions,* a dangerous practice (Hugh MacKenzie, personal communication). The difference here is that each invention can be abandoned without abandoning the entire product, although it will miss some of its goals. In addition, management has agreed not to let the trigger dates slip and has blessed the difficulty classifications, making it easier for everyone to give up when necessary.

A young design engineer at Apple Computer recently described his company's shift in product-development imperatives in this way: In the quite recent past, product development took too long because the philosophy was still that of Steve Jobs, namely, to keep working until it is "insanely great." Now the philosophy is "Ship it!" meaning get it going and out the door (Levy, 1992).

COMPARING HOW OTHER COMPANIES MEET SIMILAR CHALLENGES

Hitachi

Hitachi makes a wide variety of products, among them automotive parts similar to NDCL's. It uses methods similar to NDCL's to manufacture video cameras and VCRs. Among Hitachi's innovative practices is a model-mix assembly method I call *station lockout*. In this method, each assembly arrives on a pallet bearing an identification tag that indicates which parts are to be assembled to it. Each assembly station contains a robot or machine capable of adding one part in one variety. If a station is equipped for a part that a model does not require, that station simply remains idle while that assembly passes through. This method is simple but probably requires more stations and floor space than NDCL's combinatoric method does. Like NDCL, Hitachi designs and makes its own robots and many of its manufacturing and assembly systems. Thus, it is well positioned to try various approaches to model-mix assembly.

Sony

Sony is a consumer electronics company with an unusual ability to sense the needs and desires of its customers. An important component of its product strategy is to switch models or to expand their features at a rapid pace. Products may appear on the market and disappear in 18 months. In contrast with NDCL, Sony is its own Toyota, providing the stress on variety manufacturing from within. Indeed, the pace became so hectic in the late 1970s that the production-engineering department could not keep up using conventional fixed automation. Sony's response was to launch a series of robot developments (Nevins & Whitney, 1989). Initially, an XYZ robot was used to assemble the first Walkman models. These units had about 30 parts, 15 on each side of a chassis. The XYZ robots soon proved too slow and expensive and so were replaced by a four-axis, jointed robot that could attach a part every two seconds.

Today, Sony assembles VCRs containing 100 parts using these robots with five-gripper tools attached permanently to a turret on the robot's wrist. Each tool assembles a different part, and typically five parts are added by one robot before the VCR moves to the next robot. The parts are in pallets, and the robot gets and inserts each one before picking up the next. The parts and assembly actions often are much more complex than those typically encountered by NDCL. Short-term model mix is probably limited in the Sony system because the tools and insertion routines are so intricate that they are quite specialized to particular parts and take a long time to teach and debug. Sony likely exploits the modularity of these robot stations (which it designs and builds in house) to handle long-term model evolution; new stations are prepared off line and brought to the line ready to run when needed. They all are the same size and plug in physically, electrically, and electronically, making them easy to swing in and out.

Sony sells these robot modules to other manufacturers. One manufacturer in the United States reports that it can switch a line of 15 to 20 robots from one product design to a totally new one in about eight weeks. Some of its Sony robots have been in the factory for five years and have built a different product each year.

Yamazaki Mazak

Yamazaki is a somewhat paradoxical company: It uses world-class unattended flexible manufacturing methods to make otherwise fairly ordinary machine tools. Its business success is based largely on a few important design innovations plus low cost, high reliability, and attentive service. Among its manufacturing innovations is the "defined tool method" for machining parts. (The defined tool method was explained to me by Hiroshi Awane of Yamazaki Mazak in 1991; see Whitney, July/Sept. 1992. The discussion here also draws on Jaikumar, cat. 0-686-083.) This method requires designers to create sets of different parts that can be machined using the same fixed (and not very large) repertoire of cutting tools. Compared with the typical machine design, this method has several large advantages, especially when programmable flexible machining systems (FMS) are used for production. Two of these advantages concern scheduling the FMS.

Typical FMSs are plagued by two kinds of scheduling problems: the logistics of parts and the logistics of tools. Because in typical designs a limited set of part features might require 10 different tools, the flow rate of tools through an FMS can exceed the flow rate of parts by a factor of 10. The number of tool storage sockets on each machine is therefore often insufficient. One remedy is to provide ever larger tool storage magazines. Another is to limit the range of parts that the FMS can handle to that small set whose required tools can be stored on the machines in any given segment of the system's operation. Another is to route the part through several machines that among them hold all the required tools. Scheduling such a system is a constant battle to find a consistent set of parts and routings that will reasonably use the system and not overflow the tool storage. One company even sells quick-change tool magazines.

The defined tool method restricts the number of tools so that the storage magazines do not overflow. A part can therefore get most of the necessary machining operations for one set of features by visiting one machine. Yamazaki's FMSs are therefore small, consisting typically of four machines, each equipped with identical tools. The parts visit these FMSs in series in order to obtain all the required machining. Scheduling each FMS is a breeze: "The next available part goes to the next available machine." While guiding some visiting American dignitaries around the shop, one of the Yamazaki brothers pointed out two sets of machines awaiting shipment. "The ones with 60 tool storage sockets are for Japanese customers. Those with 120 are for the USA. Americans always want more tool storage" (personal communications to author from Clinton Kelly, 1988).

Telemechanique

Telemechanique makes a wide variety of electrical, hydraulic, and pneumatic control devices, among a large range of industrial products. It faces many of the same problems that NDCL does, except that it receives small orders worldwide from thousands of customers rather than from one or two dominant customers. As Telemechanique strives to improve its order response and approach true JIT, it has begun to systematize its product design in ways similar to NDCL's. (This description is based on discussions with Albert Morelli, director of research at Telemechanique; see Whitney, Sept./Oct. 1992.) A typical problem is that of designing and producing a family of products, whose family members usually differ by size and other measures of "capacity," such as electrical power. Larger members of the family are not simple scale-ups of smaller ones but may differ qualitatively or quantitatively. Efforts are under way to gain control over part proliferation, part-naming conventions, consistency of approach to the design and redesign of different members of the same family, systematic ways of transferring design changes from one member to others, and so on.

One fascinating challenge is to design modular products. A *module* is an element chosen by the customer; buyers can design their own item by choosing base modules and adding feature modules to suit their requirements. *Buying* amounts to searching through a catalog for the needed modules. A successful product line is likely to be one that is "easy to buy" in some sense. Designing such a product requires placing oneself in the customers' shoes and emulating their thought processes as they consider their needs and the modular ways of meeting them. One must visualize how the customers might analyze their problem and then prepare module options that fit that analysis. Then one designs a "buying process" around that analysis and implements it in a design for the catalog, exploiting the process by creating modules that perform easily identifiable options and fit into recognizable classes. Only then does one design the modules, using the parts' commonality when possible, taking care that tolerances do not build up too much as the modules are stuck together to make systems, and deciding how to divide the product into subassemblies (not the same as modules, and so on). Like NDCL's products, Telemechanique's modules are good examples of products whose engineering is driven by the conditions under which the items will be sold or, equivalently, by the customer's behavior while buying.

REMARKS

Although each company described here has responded creatively to the challenge of high-variety manufacturing, only NDCL has adopted all the techniques identified in this chapter. For example, both Hitachi and Yamazaki Mazak appear to focus on fabrication and assembly methods rather than an overall design strategy. Only Telemechanique among these companies appears to be thinking about design and assembly in ways similar to NDCL's methods. Telemechanique also makes some of its manufacturing equipment, but nothing as sophisticated as either NDCL's robots or the coiling method of making alternator stators.

SUMMARY AND CONCLUSIONS

NDCL has spent the last 30 years becoming smart about developing products for the high-volume JIT model-mix business environment. The trend has not been so much increasing the *quantitative* variety or reducing the *quantitative* batch size as much as increasing the *qualitative* variety that can be accommodated while reducing short-term (changeover, tool change) or long-term (reinvestment) waste. It has done this mainly by exploiting the design process and the assembly process of each product. In this way it has succeeded in largely decoupling flexibility from efficiency while increasing the former without sacrificing the latter.

In general, NDCL's approach has depended on creating new product-design methodologies, developing in-house capabilities for realizing and making these designs, pursuing an intellectual classification of problems and solutions, and identifying a sequence of harder and harder problems to pursue.

From these examples, one can see a number of principles, only some of which are applicable to each situation or product:

1. Use the least complex approach available (e.g., try to get the customer to reduce the variety in its orders or to accept more standard items; use conventional automation where possible or conventional automation with minor enhancements).
2. Increase the standardization of its own designs (e.g., by finding ways to carry out more functions with the same parts or by eliminating variations in design that the customer does not want).
3. Build the capability for variety into the product rather than depending on the manufacturing system to be flexible or reconfigurable (e.g., by using different combinations of the same parts assembled by simple automation, rather than assemblies of different parts created by programmable robots that access different part supplies).
4. Express the variety during the assembly process rather than during the fabrication process. (Each model is made of several different but simple parts rather than one complex part unique to each model. Assembly is more complex this way, but fabrication is less complex. Also, JIT is better supported because the lead time for assembly is seconds to minutes, whereas the lead time for fabrication can be minutes to hours or more.)
5. Identify the sources of model/variety changeover time or cost, and seek ways to eliminate them through product design if possible. Otherwise, identify places where fixed tooling with a long changeover time and a high first cost can be replaced by reconfigurable tooling, and design the product to use that tooling.

Each of these ideas alone can be found at many companies. What sets NDCL apart is that these ideas not only are used together but also are part of a larger intellectualizing of product–process design. This intellectualizing sees product–process design and automation as an organically growing set of capabilities divided into distinct problem and solution classes and maturing into more and more difficult solutions. NDCL recognizes the importance of this organic process and supports it from the top by means of organization, corporate support for generic activities, and intervention to solve problems.

The circumstances in which such approaches can be successful are not present in every industry. NDCL's products are technologically rather stable. Redesigns are made every three to five years, providing temporal stability as well. Under this stable umbrella, NDCL has met a number of demands that shift more rapidly, such as the pattern of types or sizes needed within a defined set. The same methods that NDCL uses to respond to pattern shifts that occur every few seconds can be used, without modification, for responding to shifts that occur over hours, days, or weeks. Only a totally new design (a shift that comes once in three years or so) currently requires a new approach, and NDCL has targeted that challenge, too.

REFERENCES

Aoki, K. (1980). Speed and flexible automated assembly line—Why has automation successfully advanced in Japan? *Proceedings of the Fourth International Conference on Production Engineering.* (pp. 1–6). Tokyo: Japan Society of Precision Engineering.

Abegglen, J. C., & Stalk, G., Jr. (1985). Kaisha, *the Japanese corporation.* New York: Basic Books.

Atkinson, W. (1990, May). The customer-responsive manufacturing organization. *Manufacturing Systems, 8,* 59–61.

Attaran, M. (1992, Spring). Flexible manufacturing systems: Implementing an automated factory. *Information Systems Management, 9,* 44–47.

Box, G. E., Kacker, R. N., Nair, V. N., Phadke, M., & Shoemaker, A. C. (1988, March). Quality practices in Japan. *Quality Progress, 21,* 37–41.

Clark, K., & Fujimoto, T. (1989, September). Lead time in automobile product development: Explaining the Japanese advantage. *Journal of Engineering & Technology Management, 6.* 25–58.

Dierdonck, R. (1990, July). The manufacturing–design interface. *R&D Management, 20,* 203–9.

Hayes, R. H. (1981, July–August). Why Japanese factories work. *Harvard Business Review,* 56–66.

Huang, P. V., & Sakurai, M. (1990, May). Factory automation: The Japanese experience. *IEEE Transactions on Engineering Management, 37,* 102–9.

Jaikumar, R. *Yamazaki Mazak (A).* HBS Case Cat. No 0-686-083.

Kawai, M. (1984, September). *An example of FA for the assembly of electronic equipment.* Paper presented at a Machines Society Seminar on Recent Trends of Factory Automation in Assembly Operations.

Levy, D. (1992, October). *Apple-eyed engineering at Apple.* Seminar presented at the Massachusetts Institute of Technology.

Makino, H. (1980). Research and development of the SCARA robot. *Proceedings of the Fourth International Conference on Production Engineering.* (pp. 885–90). Tokyo: Society of Precision Engineering.

Mather, H. (1987, November). Logistics in manufacturing: A way to beat the competition. *Assembly Automation, 7,* 175–78.

Meyer, R. (1992, April). Systems integration: Toyota. *Financial World, 161,* 4.

Modarress, B., & Ansari, A. (1990). Two strategies for regaining US manufacturing dominance. *International Journal of Quality and Reliability Management, 7,* 59–77.

Nevins, J. L., & Whitney, D. E. (1978, February). Computer controlled assembly. *Scientific American,* pp. 62–74.

Nevins, J. L., & Whitney, D. E., (Eds.) (1989). *Concurrent design of products and processes.* New York: McGraw-Hill.

Ohta, K., & Hanai, M. (1986). Flexible automated production system for automotive radiators. *Proceedings of the First International Japan–USA Symposium on Flexible Automation,* (pp. 553–58). Osaka, Japan Association of Automatic Control Engineers.

Perry, T. S. (1990, October). Teamwork plus technology cuts development time. *IEEE Spectrum, 27,* 61–67.

Robb, W. L. (1992, March–April). Don't change the engineers—Change the process. *Research-Technology Management, 35,* 8–9.

Sasaki, T. (1991, February). How the Japanese accelerated new car development. *Long Range Planning, 24,* 15–25.

Shina, S. G. (1991, July). New rules for world-class companies. *IEEE Spectrum, 28*, 23–26.

Shingo, S. (1986). *The single minute exchange of dies system.* Kempston, Bedford, IFS Publications.

Skinner, W. (1985). *Manufacturing: The formidable competitive weapon.* New York: Wiley.

Venkatesan, R. (1992, November–December). Strategic sourcing: To make or not to make. *Harvard Business Review, 70,* 98–107.

von Hassell, A. (1991, September). Nissan redefines CAD/CAE with novel design system. *Plastics World, 49,* 60–61.

Wheelwright, S. C., & Gill, G. K. Motorola bandit pager. HBS Case Cat. No 9-690-043.

Wheelwright, S. C., & Gill, G. K. Sony Corp. Workstation Division. HBS Case Cat. No 9-690-031.

Whitney, D. E. (1986, May–June). Real robots do need jigs. *Harvard Business Review,* 110–116.

Whitney, D. E. (1988, July–August). Manufacturing by design. *Harvard Business Review, 66,* 83–91.

Whitney, D. E. (1992, July-September). State of the art in Japanese CAD methodologies for mechanical products—Reports on individual visits to companies and universities. *Office of Naval Research Asia Scientific Information Bulletin, 17,* 83–172.

Whitney, D. E. (1992, September–October). State of the art in Japanese CAD methodologies. Appendix 1: Detailed company visit reports. *Office of Naval Research Asia Scientific Information Bulletin,* 83–172.

Whitney, D. E. (1992, December). Design research practice in electro-mechanical product design in Europe. C. S. Draper Laboratory Paper P-3226.

Worthy, F. S. (1991, August 12). Japan's smart secret weapon. *Fortune,* pp. 72–75.

Zipkin, P. M. (1991, January–February). Does manufacturing need a JIT revolution? *Harvard Business Review, 59,* 0–50.

7

Integrating Suppliers into Fast-Cycle Product Development

JEFFREY K. LIKER, RAJAN R. KAMATH, S. NAZLI WASTI, AND MITSUO NAGAMACHI

Japanese companies are frequently cited as world-class models of effective manufacturer–supplier relationships (Clark & Fujimoto, 1991; Cusumano & Takeishi, 1991; Helper, 1991; Smitka, 1991; Womack, Jones, & Roos, 1990). The Japanese approach includes such features as a high percentage of outsourced (as opposed to internally produced) parts, long-term relationships with a small number of dedicated suppliers, and the early involvement of suppliers in the design process (Clark & Fujimoto, 1991). The close working relationship with outside suppliers in product development is cited as one way that Japanese auto manufacturers have reduced their product development time from approved concept to production to under three years, whereas U.S. auto companies usually take four or more years to develop new vehicles. An automobile consists of 10,000 to 20,000 separate parts, and in Japan about 70 percent of these parts are purchased from outside suppliers (Smitka, 1991). Therefore, any serious attempt to engage in concurrent engineering and reduce product-development time must provide a role for parts suppliers.

Historically, U.S. automakers have taken a much different approach to supplier relationships (Clark & Fujimoto, 1991). The traditional U.S. approach has been characterized by large in-house component operations, which have a major role in product development. A relatively small percentage of parts are purchased from outside suppliers, which generally lack the capability to engineer their own parts. U.S. automakers traditionally have been much more likely than their Japanese counterparts to hand blueprints to suppliers and ask them to build to print, whereas Japanese companies are more likely to give general requirements to suppliers, which then design and build the parts. U.S. automakers generally have used a variety of different suppliers for the same part, and purchasing departments award business to the lowest bidder; that is, they consider cost above quality, delivery capability, and engineering capability. This tradition has led to adversarial relationships between automakers and outside suppliers in the United States. Automakers try to get the lowest-priced parts, and the suppliers often bid low and then claim they need price increases after the part is in production and the automaker is dependent on them. Outside suppliers are reluctant to share information about their manufacturing processes with their customers for fear that their customers will appropriate this knowledge and give it to their own in-house components divisions (Liker & Kamath, 1994).

U.S. automakers have long been aware of Japan's success with manufacturer–supplier relations as well as their own limitations and tradition of adversarial relations. During the 1980s, the Big Three made major changes regarding how they manage their supply base. For example, they instituted quality awards focusing on the use of statistical quality-control methods in the factory, which were inspired by leaders such as W. Edwards Deming. The Cadillac Motor Division won the Malcolm Baldrige Award in 1988, which was based in part on its aggressive design for a manufacturing program that had a strong role for suppliers. Ford, in its development of the successful Taurus/Sable line, had the unprecedented involvement of its suppliers as early as the product-planning stage, and Ford cites this as a major factor in its success (Mitchell, 1986). Saturn Corporation viewed its suppliers as "partners" in the development of its hot-selling vehicle line. More recently, Chrysler was able to develop the LH platform (e.g., Concorde), including a new six-cylinder engine, in 37 months. It claims that an important factor in its success was the involvement of key suppliers early in the product-development process (Lavin, 1993). Several comparative surveys of automotive suppliers in the United States and Japan have concluded that U.S. companies are adopting many aspects of the Japanese model (Cusumano & Takeishi, 1991; Helper, 1991).

Unfortunately, although much has been written about the importance of the early involvement of suppliers in the design process, with Japanese companies as the model, little has been written about how this is done beyond general admonitions to involve suppliers early in product development and to develop close, long-term relationships between suppliers and manufacturers. Although these are perhaps good things to do, in this chapter we argue that there is much more to effectively integrating suppliers into the product-development process. Our analysis is based on a combination of two different data sources: in-depth interviews with managers and engineers in three Japanese automotive companies and seven of these companies' first-tier suppliers, and a mail survey of approximately 150 Japanese and 200 U.S. automotive component suppliers. Our focus is on two dyadic relationships—the relationship between Japanese component suppliers in Japan and their largest Japanese automotive customer and the relationship between U.S. component suppliers in the United States and their largest Big-Three customer.

Our findings from the survey provide two surprising results. First, the "Japanese model" actually does not apply uniformly to Japanese component suppliers. In fact, the model applies mainly to a small group of large, first-tier suppliers of complete subsystems (e.g., exhaust systems, air-conditioning systems, automatic transmissions). Second, we find that U.S. companies have developed, perhaps through attempts to copy and catch up, levels of supplier involvement in product development rivaling those of Japanese companies. However, as might be expected given that U.S. companies are new to this game, they seem to be having some problems managing the underlying processes that contribute to the Japanese automakers' success.

In this chapter, we first define the characteristics of *black-box sourcing*, a name used to describe the practice of handing over the general specifications of a component to suppliers and asking them to design and manufacture a component to meet those specifications. Then we discuss why it is important to study black-box sourcing in order to understand the Japanese supplier management model. Next, we describe the research methods used for this study. Finally, we distill and organize our interview and survey findings according to the following two dimensions: (1) how the Japanese companies manage what seem to be highly complex information flows associated with distributing design responsibility among so many outside suppliers (referred to as the *system-integration problem*) and (2) how such companies manage the potential risks associated with this process. We conclude by discussing the implications of our findings for manufacturers that seek to use their suppliers more effectively in product development and for suppliers that seek to expand their business with Japanese manufacturers and their transplants across the globe.

WHAT IS BLACK-BOX SOURCING?

In world-class manufacturing organizations, it is commonly accepted that suppliers must become involved in product development. Today, several labels are commonly used to refer to the role of suppliers in product development. *Black-box sourcing* is a common American term that is now increasingly being used in Japan. This label refers to the practice of treating a purchased part or subassembly as a black box; that is, the supplier is given the functional and interface requirements of the subassembly and is expected to design the rest. *Design-in* is a term coined by Toyota in 1990 to describe the same phenomenon in Japan, although the practice began in Japan far earlier, probably in the 1960s. Cusumano (1985) documented the history of Toyota's rise in productivity which, in fact, exceeded that of U.S. companies in the mid-1960s.

The emergence of black-box sourcing has been well documented. For example, Womack, Jones, and Roos (1990) reported, based on data collected in the mid-1980s, that in the U.S. automotive industry as much as

16 percent of the suppliers' activities could be described as black-box activities, whereas in the Japanese automotive industry the corresponding figure was 62 percent. Not surprisingly, 14 percent of the total engineering hours spent on designing a car in the United States represented the suppliers' design activities, whereas the corresponding figure in Japan was 51 percent.

The use of black-box sourcing by world-class organizations and the emerging evidence of this phenomenon's competitive significance raises many questions about how this process is managed. How do world-class organizations design and manage the organizational processes that support the black-box approach to sourcing? Even a moderately complex end product requires more than 100 suppliers engaged in the design. How can this creative frenzy be orchestrated into a high-quality vehicle that has integrity as a total system? What are the organizational conditions that make black-box sourcing feasible? What are the capabilities or competencies that are associated with black-box sourcing?

Black-box sourcing, as we observed it, has three characteristics: early involvement of suppliers, clear communication of the customer's design-related requirements, and extensive design-related responsibility assumed by the suppliers.

Early involvement by the supplier helps communicate the customer's design-related requirements. A precise articulation of these requirements is critical because it constrains the supplier's design with respect to performance, space, interface requirements, timing, and so on. These communications can be formal or informal, verbal, or computer based. World-class organizations develop a complex interface with each of their suppliers. This interface is not restricted to the customer's purchasing function. In the concept stage, the supplier may interact with several functional areas in the organization. Finally, early involvement makes it possible for the supplier to assume extensive design responsibility. Essentially, the customer relies on the supplier to (1) produce a high-quality design, (2) test the design, and (3) build the prototype, all within a time frame that is stipulated well in advance.

These characteristics outline a complex process that is rife with potential risks, both commercial and technical. These risks, for customers and suppliers, reflect the problems associated with extreme dependence on an outside organization. Imagine anywhere between 100 and 500 suppliers with design autonomy over subsystems that must (of necessity) interface smoothly and come together in a high-quality end product. For example, in a given car model, how does the manufacturer ensure that the climate-control system will dovetail with the engine-performance characteristics, the instrument panel, and the under-the-hood space available when the engine designer, the air-conditioner designer, and the styling designer design their subsystems independently? How can the car assembler share critical strategic plans related to the launch of the model with hundreds of suppliers, as much as four years before the beginning of production, and not suffer a competitive setback? Why would a supplier invest in the development of a subsystem years before production with no concrete assurance that the supply contract will be forthcoming?

CAN ECONOMIC OR MANAGEMENT THEORY EXPLAIN BLACK-BOX SOURCING?

The kinds of problems identified earlier have been addressed by a highly respected part of modern management theory known as the *transaction costs paradigm* (Williamson, 1975, 1981, 1991). This paradigm explains the make–buy decision in terms of the firm's efficient use of either market mechanisms or bureaucratic control to complete the transaction. That is, should the firm buy a product in the open market, rely on market mechanisms to set a competitive price, and relinquish the control inherent in a management hierarchy? Or should the firm rely on its internal manufacturing capability, use its management hierarchy to control the production, and relinquish the efficiencies of the market mechanism? According to the transaction costs model, a manufacturer should generally not buy something as intangible and difficult to monitor as the design of a product. The supplier's idiosyncratic investments in the design process would raise the potential costs of monitoring and policing the transactions to the point that it would make more sense to bring the activity in house. In other words, customers should not delegate design activities to their parts suppliers.

Another relevant and highly respected management theory is *agency theory* (Eisenhardt, 1989; Fama, 1980; Jenson & Meckling, 1976). Proponents of this theory suggest that there is a "moral hazard" (i.e., a chance of being taken advantage of) inherent in every principal–agent situation. The agent (in this case the supplier) could always pursue his or her own agenda to the detriment of the principal (in this case the customer). The delegation of design responsibilities to the supplier presents the supplier with just such an opportunity. In other words, the supplier, acting as the customer's agent while engaging in design, would seem to be likely to behave in such a way that improves the supplier's lot and hurts the customer in the long run.

Despite the intellectual appeal of these theories, it seems clear that the emergence of black-box sourcing simply does not fit neatly into these theoretical paradigms. In addition, the attempt to reconcile the success of Japanese supplier management with the tenets of these theories has given rise to a plethora of myths. For example, the common explanations for the ability of Japanese firms to overcome the moral-hazard problem predicted by agency theory can be classified under two headings: (1) the emergence of trust in a long-term customer–supplier relationship and (2) the extreme dominance of small, weak suppliers by large, predatory organizations. What we observed in our case studies simply cannot be explained by notions of trust in the conventional sense. We also did not observe customers dominating their suppliers and taking advantage of them. In order to understand the reality behind some of these myths, it is important to look deeper into black-box sourcing and find out how Japanese suppliers really work.

RESEARCH METHODS

In 1992, we conducted extensive interviews regarding product development with the top management in the technical administration and purchasing departments of three Japanese automobile companies and with a large number of managers, in both line positions and executive ranks, at seven Japanese first-tier suppliers. By *first-tier suppliers* we mean those that directly supply their automotive customers and that are, in turn, supplied by second-, third-, and lower-tier suppliers. We intentionally focused on large, first-tier suppliers because we expected that they would handle the largest portion of black-box design. For the survey, we concentrated mainly on the first tier, although it was difficult to identify first-tier suppliers based on publicly available sources, and so some lower-tier suppliers entered our sample. For our purposes, we defined first-tier as those that work directly with and ship parts to the assembly or engine divisions of the automaker. Suppliers to internal component divisions of automakers or suppliers that primarily supplied other outside suppliers were considered to be second tier or lower.

We do not claim that our description of black-box sourcing applies to all Japanese suppliers, or even to all Japanese first-tier suppliers. Rather, we are characterizing the approach used by some of the most successful automakers in the world to manage a small, elite group of large, first-tier suppliers.

Our interviews and survey also were restricted to suppliers of manufactured automotive components. Inputs excluded from the study were raw materials and chemicals, assembly and processing equipment, indirect materials (e.g., oils, tapes, sealants), tooling and dies, computers and software, and consulting services. The types of automotive vehicles are limited to passenger cars, light trucks, utility vehicles, and minivans. The respondent population is defined as automotive suppliers who supply the following parts.

1. Individual parts: generic individual components or groups of nonassembled components (e.g., batteries, belts, gears, hinges, pistons, pumps, locks, seals, tires, fasteners, cables, bolts).
2. Assembled units: generally parts of a larger subsystem (e.g., air bags, disc brake calipers, seat frames, small motors, windshield wipers, fans, lamps).
3. Completed subsystems: more complete assemblies that can be installed intact in the vehicle (e.g., audio systems, fuel and emission systems, window systems, ignition systems, heating and air-conditioning systems, transmissions).

For the survey, we used mailed, self-administered questionnaires. Before being mailed, the questionnaire was pretested in several sites in both the

United States and Japan, to eliminate ambiguities and errors. Respondents were asked to answer the questions regarding a particular product referred to as Product X. *Product X* is defined as the vehicle component or component group that accounted for the largest dollar sales volume for the supplier. The questions were also to be answered with a specific automotive customer in mind, referred to as Customer A. *Customer A* is defined as the largest automotive customer for Product X in dollar sales volume and could be either a car or a truck maker or one of its suppliers.

The questionnaire was translated into Japanese by Mitsuo Nagamachi and then was translated back into English by a Japanese MBA student at the University of Michigan. After differences in the questionnaire were reconciled, it was edited further by Nagamachi and several engineers at the Toyota Motor Company, and we believe we now have a faithful translation. Fortunately, enough of the concepts in the auto industry are used in both the United States and Japan that there is considerable common engineering terminology for product development. To reduce the bias that comes with interpretation across countries, whenever possible we used concrete events and activities and avoided subjective ratings on scales.

As a final check on our data, we presented simple mean comparisons to groups of engineers, purchasing managers, and supplier representatives at Nissan and Toyota for their comments. They offered interpretations of counterintuitive results and also checked the translation of these questions to make sure that we were asking the same questions in both English and Japanese. These sessions indicated that the translation was faithful to our original questionnaire.

Although our primary interest was in first-tier suppliers, publicly available mailing lists do not indicate whether a supplier is first tier, and in the United States the tier structure is not as clear-cut as it is in Japan. Thus we selected companies as best as we could that seemed to be first-tier suppliers. The initial mailing lists for the United States and Japan were compiled using existing supplier lists in *Chilton's Automotive Industries* for the U.S. sample and the Japan Auto Parts Industry Association (JAPIA) list and the Dodwell Associates' list for the Japanese sample. Using the information in these guides, we chose those suppliers that satisfied our population criteria. We dropped any supplier whose main customer was clearly another supplier rather than an automaker. We also dropped companies with fewer than 500 employees because first-tier suppliers are generally larger than lower-tier suppliers. We telephoned the companies in order to obtain the name of the proper respondent, a chief or head engineer or engineering manager overseeing product design and development for a given product or division. In some cases, we found that certain companies had discontinued their automotive business or had merged with other companies. After we had made all these changes in the mailing lists, we mailed the questionnaire to 475 U.S. companies and 570 Japanese companies. The Japanese mailing and phone calls were made from Hiroshima University.

In the United States, we later discovered that the Chilton's list was limited and that a more comprehensive list could be found in the ELM Consultants' publications. Accordingly, we supplemented the U.S. sample with additional suppliers that met our criteria from the ELM publication. This change led to an additional 336 U.S. companies, which we contacted through a second mailing in March. In all, 811 U.S. suppliers received questionnaires. Attempts to enhance the response rate were made through follow-up telephone calls and repeat mailings to nonrespondents. The final response rate was 26 percent in the United States and 27 percent in Japan.

The statistics presented in this chapter are based on those responses received by June 13, 1993. In all, 210 responses were received in the United States, and 155 came from Japanese suppliers. From these responses, 11 cases in the U.S. sample and 13 cases in the Japanese sample were eliminated from the study because of an unspecified or not applicable Product X (i.e., the product did not satisfy the previous product/vehicle criteria). Furthermore, in order to eliminate relationships with transplant auto manufacturers, one Japanese supplier supplying to an American company and 10 U.S. suppliers supplying to Japanese auto manufacturers or suppliers were removed from the sample. Thus, the total usable sample was reduced to 189 U.S. cases and 142 Japanese cases. Finally, for the purposes of this chapter, we dropped second- or lower-tier suppliers that were still in our sample, leaving a total of 128 suppliers in the United States and 107 suppliers in Japan.

The survey data we present here are separated both by U.S. respondents and Japan respondents and by what we call *subsystem suppliers* and *first-tier nonsystem suppliers*. This distinction is an important one. All the first-tier suppliers we interviewed face-to-face in Japan were supplying complete subsystems to their customers (e.g., exhaust systems). We discovered from our survey that these system suppliers were a minority of the first-tier suppliers, many of which supplied smaller assemblies or individual parts. In order to have a subgroup that was most comparable to the interview data, we separated out the subsystem suppliers from the nonsystem suppliers. This variable was a major factor in the degree and nature of supplier involvement in design.

For this chapter we present only means (after the elimination of outliers) for certain variables of interest. We show the means separately for first-tier suppliers providing complete subsystems and first-tier nonsystem suppliers (suppliers providing individual parts and assembled units). The number of cases in each category is as follows.

Category	Number of Cases
U.S. subsystem supplier	38
U.S. first-tier nonsystem suppliers	90
Japan subsystem suppliers	37
Japan first-tier nonsystem suppliers	70

RESULTS

How Much Are Suppliers Involved in Design?

According to Clark and Fujimoto's (1991) data, there is far more supplier involvement in Japan than in the United States. For example, they
report that 62 percent of Japanese suppliers provide black-box parts and
that only 30 percent of such suppliers build according to blueprints provided by customers (which they call *detail-controlled parts*). In contrast,
only 16 percent of U.S. suppliers provide black-box parts, and 81 percent
of such suppliers build according to their customers' prints. However,
Clark and Fujimoto's data on this topic are limited in a number of respects.

First, the data are old, gathered in the mid-1980s. In the late 1980s and
early 1990s, there was a great deal of effort to increase suppliers' involvement in design in the United States. Second, the data came from the auto
companies, not from a survey of suppliers. It is not clear whether auto
companies keep a reliable, running tab of how many suppliers are involved
in design. Third, there may be a problem in the definition of *detail-
controlled parts* in the United States. In a separate article, we describe the
conventional practice among U.S. automakers of soliciting designs from
outside suppliers and then redrawing the components according to the automaker's blueprints (Liker & Kamath, 1994). Although the automaker
assigns engineers to each component, often the engineers lack the in-depth
knowledge necessary for developing the part from scratch and so must rely
on outside suppliers to provide the designs as part of their bid package. In
this case, is the drawing the customer's blueprint or the outside supplier's?
We have seen cases in which both the auto company and the supplier
claimed that they designed the parts.

The results of our survey of first-tier suppliers were in striking contrast
to Clark and Fujimoto's (1991). Shown in Table 7.1 are the answers to
two questions. First, we asked whether the supplier had any product-
development capability at all for any of its automotive components. Although the numbers are high for all categories, they actually are higher in
the United States. Most of the U.S. subsystem and nonsystem first-tier suppliers (97–98%) reported that they had some design capability, whereas
in Japan this number was slightly smaller (91–92%).

We also asked specifically about their design capability (1) for their
largest dollar volume product, Product X, and (2) for their largest customer, Customer A. We asked the suppliers whether the usual situation
during the last five years was for Customer A to provide completed designs
for them to manufacture, whether they jointly designed the parts with Customer A, or whether they took responsibility for designing the parts according to Customer A's specifications.

The results in Table 7.1 show that it was relatively uncommon in both

Table 7.1. How Much Are Suppliers Involved in Product X Design?

	Japanese Suppliers		U.S. Suppliers	
	Subsystem Supplier ($n=37$)	First-Tier Nonsystem Supplier ($n=70$)	Subsystem Supplier ($n=38$)	First-Tier Nonsystem Supplier ($n=90$)
Any design capability?	94.4%	91.3%	97.4%	97.8%
Design for last car program:				
Customer A designed	0	11.9	2.9	13.6
Jointly designed	21.6	41.8	40	39.8
Supplier designed	<u>78.4</u>	<u>46.3</u>	<u>57.1</u>	<u>46.6</u>
	100%	100%	100%	100%

countries for the customer to design the parts and then hand the blueprints to the supplier. In 97 percent of the cases of subsystem suppliers and in more than 85 percent of the cases of nonsystem suppliers, the supplier was involved in the design process. There is evidence that Japanese subsystem suppliers were more likely to take complete responsibility for the design. In all, 76 percent of the subsystem suppliers in Japan, compared with 57 percent in the United States, said they took responsibility for the design. Fewer than half of the nonsystem suppliers in both countries said they took the major responsibility for design, but even these differences are relatively small compared with Clark and Fujimoto's (1991) estimate of about a 4-to-1 ratio between Japanese and U.S. suppliers that handle black-box design.

MANAGING INFORMATION COMPLEXITY

The question of how the Japanese manage information complexity may appear to be a technical issue, but it is solved through a combination of engineering and management practices. The technical issue is coordinating the inputs of separate designers into a single vehicle that has high product integrity. The Japanese have been able to achieve high vehicle integrity (see, for example, the discussion of world-class body stamping in Chapter 10 of this book).

The brief answer to the question is that Japanese automakers have become highly skilled at systems engineering. By *systems engineering,* we do not mean the highly mathematical body of theory in engineering textbooks on this subject. Rather, we are referring to more intuitive ways of thinking about the design. One central problem in systems engineering is dividing the system into subsystems and then assembling the subsystems into a complete system in which all of the pieces fit together properly. Part of the solution is deciding how to break the system into relatively autonomous pieces. We discuss this solution in the following paragraphs as the task of sourcing *self-contained chunks*. Another part of the systems engineering solution is to think through the performance and spatial requirements for each subsystem before designing the subsystems. That is, the Japanese automakers must carefully think through the specifications they will give to suppliers as inputs to their subsystem development so that the end result will be a subsystem that mates well with other subsystems. We call this process *developing clear and stable interface requirements*. Even highly skilled systems engineers are not omniscient and cannot anticipate all of the complex interactions between parts and subsystems up front; therefore, it is important that they communicate early and often with suppliers about system-interface issues as the subsystems are being developed. Ultimately, the only way really to understand how the system functions as a whole is to build and test it. Thus, fully functional prototypes should be developed early in the design process in order to test the total system. Finally, the systems-engineering problem also applies at the subsystem level. That is, suppliers of subsystems must consider the integration of the parts that make up their subsystem and have the technical capabilities to design, build, and test their smaller systems of parts. One way to simplify the problem of integration into subsystems is for the suppliers to have all the capabilities they need to develop the subsystem in house, that is, to have "full-service technological capabilities." We will discuss each of these systems-engineering issues.

Sourcing Self-Contained Chunks

It is well known that Japanese manufacturing firms have developed a supplier infrastructure that is best described as a multitier hierarchy. For example, Clark and Fujimoto (1991) provide typical comparisons of the traditional, U.S.-style supplier infrastructure with the Japanese-style alternative in the automotive industry. The authors depict the U.S. approach as a flat hierarchy in which outside suppliers directly supply parts to the automaker and have little responsibility for their design. By contrast, the Japanese structure looks more like a traditional organization chart. First-tier suppliers, which make up only a small percentage of the total suppliers, report directly to the automotive companies. They deal directly with the auto company on design issues and send the components directly to the auto companies' assembly plants. First-tier suppliers then are responsible for managing a second tier of suppliers, which ship intermediate products to the first tier. Second-tier suppliers manage third-tier suppliers, and so on. The development of an infrastructure that looks "Japanese" in terms of the multiple layers and the total number of suppliers does not, however, necessarily reflect the logic of the underlying processes at work.

One of the keys to black-box sourcing is how the automaker breaks the end product into pieces to distribute to suppliers. From a systems-engineering perspective, the goal is to divide the total system into relatively self-contained pieces, which we call *self-contained chunks*.[1] By *self-*

contained we mean that all the complicated interactions among parts are inside the subsystem and that there are relatively few interactions across subsystems. (The statistical methods of factor analysis and cluster analysis accomplish an analogous process for sets of measured variables.)

These self-contained chunks are then outsourced using the tier structure. For example, Calsonic, one of Nissan's first-tier suppliers, takes responsibility for entire exhaust systems and air-conditioning units. Hirotech, a first-tier supplier for Mazda, designs, manufactures, and ships entire doors to that company. Aisin Seiki, a first-tier supplier for Toyota, designs and ships complete transmissions (among other products) to Toyota. In fact, managers at Aisin Seiki explained to us that Toyota is moving toward appointing some suppliers as system integrators for entire electromechanical systems. Although Aisin Seiki previously focused on mechanical components and Nippondenso focused on electrical systems, Aisin Seiki finds itself competing with Nippondenso to be Toyota's electromechanical systems integrator. The creation of self-contained design tasks reduces the complexity of information processing faced by the customer, because it allows the customer to concentrate on the overall design of the end product and on the integration of the outsourced subsystems. It also allows the first-tier supplier to take on independent design responsibilities and "parcels" out to the first-tier supplier the task of coordinating the activities of the second-tier suppliers. Thus many first-tier suppliers assume the responsibility for systems engineering at the level of automotive subsystems, as explained to us by one first-tier supplier: "In Japan we consider ourselves systems suppliers. For example, the HVAC consists of the compressor, the exchanger, and other parts. In the United States, suppliers consider themselves component suppliers. . . . If the integration is weak, even a high-quality component is useless."

This quotation is an excellent example of the kind of systems thinking we heard during our visits to Japanese automakers and suppliers, who recognized that the whole is indeed greater than the sum of its parts. At least based on his limited experience, this Japanese executive felt that U.S. companies were devoting too much attention to individual components rather than to system integration. This sentiment was also echoed by Thomas Gale, Chrysler's vice president for design, who criticized the past functional orientation of Chrysler: "We were building great components but not great cars" (Smith, 1992, p. 38).

The statistical prevalence of sourcing in chunks in the United States and Japan was measured in our questionnaire by two questions (see Table 7.2). Is Product X a set of individual parts, an assembled unit, or a complete subsystem? If it is an assembled unit or a complete subsystem, how many unique part numbers are in the assembly?[2] We asked the second question to get a measure of the complexity of the assembled unit or subsystem delegated to the supplier. In general, we expected that the more distinct parts that are involved, the more likely the supplier is truly being asked to provide a complete subsystem or "chunk."

Table 7.2. Extent of "Sourcing in Chunks"

	Japanese Suppliers ($n = 107$)	U.S. Suppliers ($n = 128$)
Product X type (%)		
(1) Individual parts[a]	29.6	33.6
(2) Assembled components	35.2	36.7
(3) Subsystems	35.2	29.7
Number of parts if (2) or (3) for		
Subsystem suppliers	165.7[b]	70.5[b]
First-tier nonsystem suppliers	35.8[b]	15.7

[a] Single parts or group of nonassembled parts.

[b] After the elimination of one outlier.

The Japanese car companies are slightly more likely to source complete subsystems from their first-tier suppliers—35 percent in Japan compared with 30 percent in the United States. These represent what we call *subsystem suppliers*. There also is evidence that considerably more complex assembled units are being sourced from outside suppliers in Japan than in the United States. On average, the Japanese suppliers' assembled units have more than twice as many distinct part numbers than do units made in the United States. The Japanese subsystem suppliers are responsible for the most complex assemblies, with 166 part numbers compared with 71 for U.S. subsystem suppliers. Nonsystem suppliers are responsible for much simpler components, though these are still more complex in Japan than they are in the United States. Although there are numerous explanations for these differences (e.g., U.S. automakers have reduced part counts through design for assembly, or U.S. and Japan automakers use different ways of classifying part numbers), these results are consistent with the hypothesis that Japanese automakers are outsourcing more complete subsystems than do automakers in the United States.

Even if U.S. companies were as likely to buy complete subsystems from suppliers, this would be only one part of the picture. There are various other requirements for successful systems engineering, such as how subsystem specifications are determined and communicated.

Developing Clear and Stable Interface Requirements

Japanese automotive customers often initiate the design process by giving the supplier a general conceptual description of the part or subsystem. This general description is followed by intense joint activity by the customer's and the supplier's engineering staff. Such interaction gives the supplier an opportunity to participate in the development of the part's specifications. Finally, there is a formal release of the design specifications to the supplier. The supplier then has a relatively short amount of time to design and build the first prototype. Changes in the basic design after the first prototype are rare. Several suppliers told us that as much as 80 percent of the design was determined by the first prototype.

The customers' requirements generally include little about the design of the components but, rather, focus on critical performance requirements and space constraints. For example, one supplier described the specifications for cooling fans in engines as follows: "They [the customer] usually give us objectives on performance, packaging constraints, etc. For example, in the case of the cooling fan, they give us the airflow volume, the current consumption, the size or diameter, and the weight. These are major characteristics. It is not like they give us drawings."

Even though the three Japanese companies we visited provided only the critical performance and space requirements, there was variation in the degree to which supplier input was incorporated into the setting of the specifications. As described in Chapter 8 in this book, Toyota stood out: It allowed suppliers far more influence over setting the specifications, compared with the other two Japanese automakers, and it kept the specifications flexible for a longer period of time. Toyota's suppliers, knowing that their input was expected, invested in exploring the trade-offs among performance requirements, space requirements, and cost, and they gave Toyota that information in order to help in setting the specifications. To aid its suppliers in this effort, Toyota provided a drawing of the layout of parts surrounding those of the suppliers' so that they could understand the reason for the spatial constraints and perhaps suggest alternative layouts to reduce the cost of the overall system. In other words, at Toyota, systems-engineering issues were worked out through joint problem solving between Toyota engineers and supplier engineers.

The survey data in Table 7.3 indicate that almost all the subsystem suppliers in Japan receive early concept information from their customers and have influence over setting the specifications for their subsystems, with the

Table 7.3. Learning About Customers' Specifications

	Japanese Suppliers		U.S. Suppliers	
	Subsystem Supplier ($n=37$)	First-Tier Nonsystem Supplier ($n=70$)	Subsystem Supplier ($n=38$)	First-Tier Nonsystem Supplier ($n=90$)
Customers shared vehicle concept.	91.9%	69.1%	75.7%	62.5%
Suppliers influenced specifications in concept stage.	90.5	76.7	86.7	88.5
Customers made big change in specifications after first prototype.	30.6	21.7	37.8	36.8

United States rapidly catching up. For example, 92 percent of Japanese subsystem suppliers reported that their customer shared the vehicle concept with them, whereas 76 percent of U.S. suppliers said that this was true. Nonsystem suppliers in both countries were less likely to be given vehicle-concept information early on.

Regarding the issue of the stability of specifications, Japanese companies were somewhat less likely to change the specifications after the first prototype was built. We were surprised to find that the difference was small among subsystem suppliers. Thirty-one percent in Japan, compared with 38 percent in the United States, reported that the automaker changed its specifications significantly after the first prototype. Interestingly, Japanese nonsystem suppliers were the least likely to report that their customers made big changes in the specifications after the first prototype (only 22 percent), compared with 37 percent of U.S. nonsystem suppliers. We suspect that this difference in Japan between the stability of specifications for subsystem and nonsystem suppliers is due to the relative complexity of setting specifications for subsystems as opposed to smaller components. There are likely to be more unanticipated interactions among subsystems, which will show up in the prototyping process and lead to changes in specifications. As noted in Chapter 8, Toyota intentionally keeps specifications flexible early in the development process and uses a set-narrowing process to settle on a final set of specifications.

Communicating Early and Often About System-Interface Issues

When we first began our interviews, we were struck by the short time that suppliers had to design and build the first prototype after formally being given the specifications by their customers. They might have as little as two or three months to design and build their first prototype. As we explained earlier, Japanese suppliers actually receive partial information about the specifications informally before being given the complete specifications for the first prototype.

All the Japanese automakers and suppliers that we studied discussed the practice of using "guest" or "resident" engineers. These are design engineers from the supplier firm who spend time in the customer's design department during the concept-development stage. It does not mean frequent visits to the customer; rather, the supplier engineers take up residence at their customer's development engineering offices for months or, in some cases, years. Toyota stood out: Nippondenso reported that its guest engineers would stay from two to three years in Toyota's design office. During this time, the guest engineer constantly relayed information to the supplier. The engineers of Mazda's first-tier suppliers stayed for a shorter period of time at their customer's offices (a few months), but these engineers also had permanent mailboxes at Mazda's engineering center where they could daily receive mail about the progress of the design.

The guest engineer serves as a two-way conduit of information flow between the customer and the supplier. One critical role of such a person is monitoring product-development activities at the customer's office while the vehicle concepts take shape and immediately relaying any new developments to the home supplier. This communication gives the supplier an opportunity to examine the subsystem's specifications while they evolve during a critical period when the customer is continuously making design decisions that affect the supplier's job. In fact, as we pointed out earlier, the supplier may be able to influence the specifications for the subsystems that it will at a later time design and make. The guest engineer is in a position to work on a daily basis with the automaker's engineers to help shape the specifications. This process brings in-depth knowledge about the supplier's parts into the system-engineering process, and it also allows the supplier to influence design decisions so that the parts can be manufactured at low cost in the supplier's facilities. For example, Nippondenso explained that in the packaging of a radiator it may be considerably cheaper to route the pipes to one side rather than the other side of the radiator because of the way that the existing dies have been designed. Company engineers may make suggestions to Toyota about redesigning part of the engine to make the pipe routing more favorable for the radiator manufacture. Both the customer and the supplier considered these interchanges vital to the success of black-box sourcing and fast-cycle product development.

Our survey data show a determined effort by U.S. companies to establish early and frequent communication with their suppliers. In both countries, there was more frequent design-related communication among subsystem suppliers than among nonsystem suppliers. For both categories of suppliers, there was more frequent communication in the United States. Table 7.4 gives the percentage of suppliers that communicated at least weekly during the vehicle-concept stage and during the stage of designing and building the first prototype. During the vehicle-concept stage, only 31

Table 7.4. Customer/Supplier Design Communication

	Japanese Suppliers		U.S. Suppliers	
	Subsystem Supplier $(n=37)$	First-Tier Nonsystem Supplier $(n=70)$	Subsystem Supplier $(n=38)$	First-Tier Nonsystem Supplier $(n=90)$
Percentage communicating at least weekly				
Vehicle-concept stage	31.4%	10.6%	64.9%	42.0%
First-prototype stage	59.5	31.8	83.8	63.6
Percentage of supplier's engineers spending > 15 days with Customer A before first prototype	61.1	29.9	54.1	31.0

percent of Japanese subsystem suppliers reported communicating weekly, compared with 65 percent of U.S. subsystem suppliers. During the first-prototype stage, 60 percent of Japanese subsystem suppliers and 84 percent of U.S. subsystem suppliers reported communicating at least weekly.

Even more surprising, suppliers in the United States were almost as likely to have their engineers pay an extended visit to their main customers. More than half the subsystem suppliers in both countries had the engineers stay for at least 15 days at the design offices of their Customer A. Of course, the Japanese practice of guest engineers often involves a considerably longer stay, lasting months or even years.

The *frequency* of the communication does not necessarily reflect the *quality* of the communication. When we presented the survey results showing more frequent communication in the United States to managers of engineering and purchasing at Toyota and Nissan, both companies offered the same explanation. On the one hand, they noted that they communicated at different frequencies with different suppliers. Obviously, they are communicating constantly with suppliers that have guest engineers on the premises. But it is not necessary to communicate weekly with all suppliers that are designing parts. They also explained that because they have such a long history of relationships with their suppliers, they can very quickly and easily communicate their needs to them. By contrast, the U.S. auto companies only recently have involved their suppliers in design, and so more frequent communication is needed. We should also note that effective systems engineering also may reduce the need for frequent communication. If suppliers are developing self-contained "chunks" and have clear specifications, communication requirements are substantially reduced.

An earlier study shed some light on the issue of the quantity and the quality of communication between customers and suppliers. As part of that study, we visited the U.S. operations of a Japanese supplier that supplies major outer-body stampings to a U.S. automaker. The head of engineering, who had been transferred from Japan, explained that when dealing with the supplier's main Japanese customer, the supplier was used to communicating with one design section and knew the engineers in that section well. Its customer's engineers had a great deal of technical knowledge about the supplier's component. The supplier was usually able to call one engineer and quickly receive answers to questions or to explain the need for engineering changes and get an immediate response. The supplier complained, however, that when dealing with its largest U.S. auto customer, it spent much more time communicating with its engineers, and it found this process very inefficient. Apparently, the U.S. customer is trying to involve its suppliers earlier and more often in product-development decisions. Therefore, the supplier must frequently send engineers to the customer's offices for meetings. But because these engineers often are recent college graduates who know little about the component, the supplier must spend time educating them in order to receive a sound technical decision. The supplier also found that no one person has the authority or informa-

Table 7.5. Problems Getting Design Information from Customers[a]

	Japanese Suppliers		U.S. Suppliers	
	Subsystem Supplier ($n=37$)	First-Tier Nonsystem Supplier ($n=70$)	Subsystem Supplier ($n=38$)	First-Tier Nonsystem Supplier ($n=90$)
Design responsibility dispersed within Customer A	11.1%	7.5%	31.6%	24.4%
Contacts in Customer A new on job	8.6	7.6	35.1	14.6
Contacts in Customer A lacking knowledge	8.6	10.1	21.6	13.5

[a] Percentage of suppliers responding "4" or "5" on a 5-point scale ranging from "Never" to "All the Time."

tion to make engineering decisions; therefore, the supplier must talk with engineers in several divisions and departments and "integrate design information from the outside." The Japanese supplier found this process very disturbing because it wasted the time of expensive engineers in communications with its customer's engineers, and they did not receive extra compensation for this time.

The survey data support these qualitative impressions. Based on the experience of this supplier, we included in our survey some questions about various problems that suppliers might have in obtaining product-design information from their main auto customers. The results, shown in Table 7.5, indicate that communication difficulties are far more prevalent in the United States than in Japan. In the United States, about one-third of the suppliers said that design responsibility is widely dispersed within Customer A and that they must call around to find out information, as opposed to 13 percent in Japan. One-third of the suppliers in the United States also complained that their design-engineering contacts at Customer A were new to the job and lacked in-depth knowledge of the products they supplied. The U.S. practice of rotating young engineers across different components, with as little as one year spent on a particular component, has been documented elsewhere (Liker & Fleischer, 1992; Liker & Hancock, 1986). We should note that there were differences in Japan in the prevalence of these practices. In particular, only about 5 percent of Toyota's suppliers mentioned any of these problems in dealing with Toyota's engineers, who were generally regarded as very knowledgeable and responsive.

Using a Stable, Well-Understood Development Process with Early Prototype Testing

All three Japanese manufacturers use a highly stable and widely understood product-development process centered on prototype testing. When the supplier gets word that the concept session for a specific model is being scheduled, there is no ambiguity about (1) what the milestone events in the development process are, (2) roughly when these events will occur, and (3) what the customer's expectations are. Figure 7.1 shows a typical chart of the various milestones and the roles of the customer and the supplier in the development process. With a few minor variations, all the manufacturers gave us similar charts. At first glance, these charts seem so simple as to be trivial; their significance is the precision and the consistency with which any first-tier supplier can explain the milestone events, their timing, and the customer's expectations.

This knowledge orchestrates the activities of the first-tier suppliers and greatly reduces their complexity. For example, the supplier knows that there is a clear, though small, window of opportunity when it can suggest new technology and attempt to introduce new methods. Outside that time period (see Figure 7.2), the overall effort is focused on incremental cost-saving improvements that do not involve the redesign of mating parts and subsystems. Therefore, if the supplier's technical efforts result in a major breakthrough at a time that does not coincide with one of these windows, the supplier will simply wait until the next such window comes along before suggesting a major design change. In other words, the widespread and consistent adoption of a simple and clear process allows the suppliers the flexibility to be creative without being disruptive.

U.S. car makers have worked hard recently at creating structured design

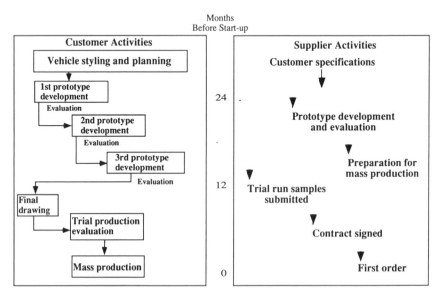

(Source: Revised from the 1992 Japan Auto Manufacturers Association Guidebook)

Figure 7.1. The product development cycle of Japanese automakers. (Revised from the 1992 *Japan Auto Manufacturers Association Guidebook*.)

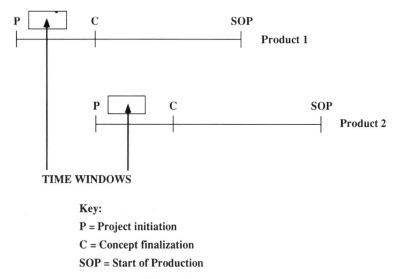

TIME WINDOWS

Key:
P = Project initiation
C = Concept finalization
SOP = Start of Production

Figure 7.2. Time windows for introducing new technology.

processes, but along very different lines. The process description at Toyota and Nissan fits a single 11-in.-by-17-in. page, which is prepared by the project leader. At General Motors, the "four-phase process" is documented by a bookshelf of thick notebooks prepared by an office staff. There is a similar level of documentation for Ford's world-class timing program. Ironically, these processes were developed in response to Japan's fast-cycle development. Yet the U.S. response to Japanese competition seems to be based on detailed documentation almost as an end onto itself; that is, U.S. companies seem to have lost sight of the purpose. By contrast, the Japanese companies maintain only that level of documentation necessary to ensure an effective design process.

Prototypes are an integral part of the Japanese automaker's development process depicted in Figure 7.1. Prototype testing and evaluation are the main methods used by the customer to test for overall vehicle integrity; they also provide a way of monitoring the suppliers' activities. Complex processes such as design are almost impossible to track. Instead, each prototype stage provides an opportunity for appraising the supplier's performance. Missing a prototype delivery deadline is a serious problem that can result in severe sanctions, such as the award of the next contract to a competitor. Performance problems with the prototype are not in themselves considered as serious. But the failure to work quickly and effectively to correct such problems based on the customer's suggestions may well lead to the loss of future business.

In our conversations with executives in the United States, we gained the impression that sophisticated engineering analysis and the use of computer-aided design (CAD) have reduced the importance of prototypes in the development process. Conversely, although the Japanese companies were making sophisticated use of CAD, every Japanese supplier firm that we studied emphasized the central role of the prototyping activity, and we saw no evidence that computer simulations were replacing physical prototypes. Prototypes are still the primary mechanism used to fine-tune the design. In fact, suppliers stressed that they could learn little by testing their own prototypes in isolation and that some of the most valuable data came from their customers' tests of the prototypes in the context of the entire assembled prototype vehicle. There was simply no way that a supplier could anticipate all the complex interactions of variables between their prototype and the total system without physical tests of the total assembly.

It was also clear that the Japanese companies placed greater emphasis on the *first* prototype than we saw in U.S. companies. In Japan, because the first prototype is built and tested several years before production begins, one might think of it as an opportunity to experiment with new ideas and to use crudely crafted versions of the final design for functional testing only. U.S. car companies have traditionally done this, and in fact, for some components not yet designed, they may use older parts from earlier models in the first prototype. Japanese car manufacturers emphasize that the first prototype should be fully functional and complete in appearance, down to surface finishes. This emphasis means that all suppliers must get their completed prototype to the customer by the deadline required to assemble the prototype vehicle. Tests on the prototype vehicle are viewed as a test of the overall integrity of the vehicle, not as a test of the freestanding individual parts.

The Japanese suppliers are expected to respond rapidly to the data from the full-vehicle-prototype tests with appropriate design changes, regardless of whether the fault lies with the original specifications given to the supplier or with the supplier's approach to the design. The suppliers made it clear that often the part meets their own tests yet does not work as expected when installed in the completed vehicle. According to an HVAC subsystem supplier:

> Performance evaluation is based on the car data, not our data. For example, if the HVAC, when fitted in a car, does not meet their [the customer's] requirements, it does not matter that it meets our specifications. They may ask us to change it. If the engine's heat characteristics are different from the original estimates, they may ask us to change it.

Expecting Suppliers to Develop Full-Service Technological Capabilities

We have seen that Japanese automakers give their subsystem suppliers responsibility for critical subsystems. To deliver these subsystems within the tight time constraints of the rapid development cycles in Japan and to adhere to the performance requirements and severe cost targets established for them, Japanese subsystem suppliers must have extensive product-development capability. In our visits to Japanese suppliers, we saw what we came to call *full-service technological capabilities*. Subsystem suppliers were able to develop completely and test their designs with little outside help from either the customer or outside suppliers. For example, Sangyo (a supplier of exhaust systems for Toyota) has an entire plant used as a prototype shop. Calsonic (a supplier of exhaust systems and air-conditioning units for Nissan) has 5,500 employees worldwide, of which 1,200 (i.e., 22%), are technical personnel involved in some aspect of product development (including prototyping and testing). More striking is that Calsonic in Japan has 1,700 employees, of which 1,000 (i.e., 59%) work on product development.

We originally assumed that the large subsystem suppliers in Japan were, in turn, coordinating the product-development activities of the lower-tier suppliers that designed smaller component systems. But executives from both firms pointed out that they literally "threw their designs over the wall" to most of their second-tier suppliers. According to these sources, by and large, second-tier suppliers engage in relatively minor design activities.

The pressure to develop strong internal product-development capability comes directly from the automakers. Just as ambitious people in any hierarchical organization try to work their way up the hierarchy, ambitious suppliers want to move up the tier structure. It is well known that the purchasing function in large Japanese companies uses elaborate rating systems to grade its suppliers (Fruin, 1993), including their technological capability and performance. Suppliers who really want to get ahead must prove time and time again that they can develop products on time that meet the specifications of their customers and then ruthlessly cut costs through value-engineering activities (discussed in another section of this chapter). Suppliers also made it clear to us that if they wanted additional business with new automotive customers, they obtained it through their technological capabilities. They knew that their competitors were continuously improving the product's cost and quality, and strong manufacturing capability was simply the price of entry into the competition. In order to win a new customer, a supplier needed to demonstrate that its product was technologically superior to that of its competitors. As Whitney describes in Chapter 6, Nippondenso has a superb ability to create breakthrough product and process technologies that will make it a performance and price leader for as much as 10 years into the future.

One indicator of technological capability is the number of technical personnel devoted to product development. Table 7.6 presents these numbers divided into technical administration, product designing and engineering, engineering analysis and simulation, prototype making and testing, and other technical staff. The question asked for total numbers of technical staff whose jobs are related to design for "all products." Overall, Japanese

Table 7.6. Suppliers' Product-Development Resources

	Japanese Suppliers		U.S. Suppliers	
	Subsystem Supplier (n = 37)	First-Tier Nonsystem Supplier (n = 70)	Subsystem Supplier (n = 38)	First-Tier Nonsystem Supplier (n = 90)
Number of design staff in				
Technical administration	19	18	13	8
Product designers and engineers	93	66	70	30
Engineering analysis and simulation	40	21	16	15
Prototype making	29	21	31	12
Prototype testing	15	14	21	13
Other technical staff	11	5	3	5
Total design staff	207	145	154	83
Total worldwide personnel	1,718	2,833	11,965	14,463
Total worldwide sales ($ U.S. million)[a]	508	730	1,281	2,070
Percentage of technical staff with four-year degrees	58	57	66	60

[a] U.S. $1 = ¥ 120 at the time of the survey.

suppliers had significantly greater numbers of design staff, even though the Japanese suppliers were far smaller than the U.S. suppliers in terms of worldwide personnel and sales. For example, Japanese subsystem suppliers had only 1,718 employees on average, compared with almost 12,000 employees of U.S. subsystem suppliers. We are hesitant to divide the number of design staff by the numbers of employees worldwide because the respondents seemed to be somewhat confused about the appropriate unit of analysis. We believe that in multidivisional companies—particularly common in the United States—some respondents may have been thinking only about their own division when reporting on numbers of design staff and about all divisions when reporting the total number of employees worldwide. In any case, the evidence strongly suggests that much larger portions of the Japanese employee base are technical personnel involved in product development.

In summary, one can step back from a description of the techniques for reducing information complexity and notice a distinct pattern. This pattern is illustrated through the analogy of semiautonomous work groups. Today, many manufacturing plants are moving toward the formation of semiautonomous or self-managing work groups. Davis (1982) suggests that in order to create a self-maintaining or semiautonomous work group, we need to (1) separate the group's task from the rest of the process, (2) give the group the appropriate resources, and (3) give the group the autonomy to make decisions and evaluate its own output.

In a similar way, the logic of sourcing in chunks grows out of the need to break the end product into a set of separate subsystems. Each subsystem is reasonably complete in terms of information-processing needs and can be designed independently to a great extent. This decoupling of the supplier's design task is shaped as much by the internal logic of the subsystem as it is by the customer's skill and experience in specifying the performance requirements in a way that accounts for the interfaces with the other subsystems. The sharing of information in early design-concept sessions and the use of guest engineers give the suppliers the information they need to complete the subsystem design. Even though the subsystem suppliers can design their systems relatively autonomously, they can perform only limited tests on their own. Therefore, it becomes important for the suppliers to deliver their subsystems according to schedule to the customer, so that the customer can test them with the complete vehicle. The suppliers must then be able to react quickly to the complete vehicle test data so that they can deliver revised designs and prototypes in time for the next rounds of prototype testing. If the prototypes are significantly different from products that would be built by a mass-production system, these tests are meaningless. Thus even the first prototype must approximate mass-production conditions as much as possible. The full-service technical capabilities of suppliers contribute to the effective decoupling of the suppliers' design task while they guarantee the appropriate technical resources to carry it out.

Most of our observations of the techniques for managing information complexity can be cast in the framework of rational methods for solving complex problems and are simply good systems engineering. There is nothing specifically Japanese about these methods. What is striking is the execution—how well these joint activities are coordinated between the customer and the supplier. In the process, both the customer and the supplier seem to be exposing themselves to serious risk.

MANAGING RISK

Whenever multiple companies work together, they must take certain risks. Because each company wants to make a profit, there are bound to be times when it is in the short-term interest of one partner to exploit the relationship for its own gain. For example, suppliers who are privy to sensitive information about their customers' long-term development plans could exploit that information by revealing it to competitors. Suppliers who are given significant developmental responsibility could design a product that only they could build, thus gaining an effective monopoly on the customers' purchases for that product and using this position of power to force price increases on their customers. For their part, customers could use proprietary technical information that they learn from their "open" communications with suppliers to make large-volume parts in house, or they could go outside and find firms that have not invested in development capability (and therefore could make the parts more cheaply)—a practice that has been all too common historically in the U.S. auto industry (Liker & Kamath, 1994).

The easiest way to reduce these risks is to avoid passing on sensitive competitive information to one's partner. Customers should give only absolutely essential information to their suppliers, and suppliers should give only enough information to their customers so that the customers can know the suppliers have something worth buying. This process prevents true collaboration between customers and suppliers. The systems-engineering process that we have described thus far would not be possible without close cooperation and the open sharing of information between customers and suppliers. What we observed is that Japanese companies have evolved into a system by which they freely share highly sensitive technical and cost information, yet neither party seems to exploit the other. Let us consider some of the ways in which Japanese auto companies manage the risks of black-box sourcing.

Using the Target-Price Method and Value Engineering

Japanese manufacturers use target pricing effectively to control some of the risks associated with black-box sourcing. Along with the specifications that are handed out at the concept stage, the supplier receives a target price. This is the appropriate price of the subsystem that has been calculated by working backward from the target selling price of the end product. For example, Toyota might use market-research data to estimate the appropriate selling price of a particular model of car and then use this estimate, combined with historical experience, to calculate the target price for that model for its exhaust-system supplier. Thus although U.S. suppliers typically compute their costs, add in a profit margin, and quote that price, Japanese automakers begin with the target selling price of the vehicle and arrive at the necessary target price for each subsystem to meet that vehicle's price. The supplier's profit is then the difference between the target price and the supplier's cost for making the product. Often the target price is lower than the previous purchase price of the component, and so the suppliers must reduce the cost or lose money.

The target price is open to only limited negotiation. If the target price in a specific situation squeezes the supplier's profit margin too hard, the supplier can explain why and request a price increase. But unless something is drastically wrong, neither side would expect a price adjustment until the next supply contract. As a supplier of stamped parts explained to us, "We cannot surpass the target price. We have to do research and lower the price until we meet the target. . . . We always try to produce using the least resources. . . . We can use value engineering to meet the target price."

The targets that are set generally are very aggressive, leaving little room for profit unless the supplier can be equally aggressive in reducing its costs, and this is where value engineering and value analysis come in. *Value engineering* (VE) refers to the process of making cost reductions during the development process before the start of production. *Value analysis* (VA) refers to cost reductions made after the product is in production. Suppliers recognize that they have the most leverage in reducing costs during the development cycle. Therefore they work intensively on any design change that can reduce costs through VE. When we asked suppliers what methods they used for VE, none described any particular methodology or tool. Rather, they talked about cross-functional teams, such as product engineering, manufacturing engineering, and purchasing, that come together for meetings to discuss ways to reduce the cost of the product. Such cross-functional teamwork is often thought to be an almost innate Japanese ability. But in this case, the motivation for working together is clear. With the target-pricing method, if the team cannot reduce costs, its company will not make a profit.

The survey data in Table 7.7 support the more widespread use of target pricing in Japan and the greater prevalence of competitive bidding in the United States, but again, practices are converging. Although virtually all the Japanese subsystem suppliers reported prices set through target pricing, over 60 percent of U.S. subsystem suppliers also reported the use of target pricing. Almost 60 percent of the U.S. suppliers reported that the use of competitive bids was a major way prices were set, but 51 percent of Japanese subsystem suppliers also noted that competitive bidding was used.

Table 7.7. Pricing Mechanisms for Suppliers' Components and Value-Engineering Activities

	Japanese Suppliers		U.S. Suppliers	
	Subsystem Supplier ($n = 37$)	First-Tier Nonsystem Supplier ($n = 70$)	Subsystem Supplier ($n = 38$)	First-Tier Nonsystem Supplier ($n = 90$)
Pricing mechanisms[a]				
Target pricing	94.4%	86.6%	61.8%	39.3%
Competitive bids	51.5	35.8	57.1	65.1
Negotiations	70.3	68.1	75.7	71.3
Value engineering/analysis				
Percentage using VA/VE process	92	87	70	54
Those using VA/VE				
Percentage preproduction cost reduction	17	13	15	10
Percentage cost reduction in first year of production	6	7	7	4
Percentage using VE/VA teams	68	49	62	47

[a] Percentage of suppliers responding "4" or "5" on a 5-point scale ranging from "No Influence" to "Major Influence."

The data in Table 7.7 also indicate a more widespread use of VA/VE. Almost all Japanese subsystem suppliers (92%) reported using some kind of VA/VE process, and this generally meant using cross-functional teams (68%). A surprisingly large number of U.S. suppliers, a total of 70 percent of subsystem suppliers, reported using VA/VE, which is another indication that U.S. suppliers are adopting the "Japanese" model. Value engineering in the preproduction stage led to substantial cost reductions, particularly among subsystem suppliers that generally would have a greater opportunity for cost savings through design decisions, compared with nonsystem suppliers. Subsystem suppliers cited an average of 17 percent cost savings in Japan and 15 percent in the United States through VE activities.

Giving Key Suppliers Long-Term Contracts and Portfolios of Jobs

From the customer's perspective, it is very expensive and time-consuming to evaluate a supplier's capability. By the same token, the supplier spends time and energy understanding the customer's specific needs. Moreover, suppliers invest a great deal of resources, with little direct compensation, in developing specific versions of their products for their customers. In the vocabulary of the economist, both parties make substantial *relationship-specific investments*, investments that are of little or no value outside the specific buyer–supplier relationship. This process is tolerable only because both the customer and the suppliers view their interactions in the context of long-term contracts. This helps the supplier amortize the design costs of a specific model over the life cycle of that model and perhaps other models as well. Take one Japanese supplier that was aggressively trying to expand its U.S. business:

> When we do business in the United States we always fear the contract length. Our investment is always at risk. Long-term relationships are vital to cost control, good design, etc. . . . Once GM and a supplier developed a part jointly. GM did not give the supplier the contract. This is a bad experience [for the supplier]. When "design-in" involves joint work, mutual trust is most important. Based on trust, the relationship in Japan is long term.

The long-term customer–supplier relationship has its roots in the post-war reconstruction era, when manufacturers rebuilt their supply base by financing, helping, and sometimes managing their own suppliers (Smitka, 1991). There also are contemporary reasons, however, for preferring long-term relationships with suppliers. Among these, one must appreciate that the technical resources that go into evaluating and monitoring a supplier's capabilities are scarce. In the words of a Toyota executive, "One more supplier on the list is more work. Unless the supplier adds value, why do it?"

For their part, suppliers have invested substantial resources in developing a product for which they have no written guarantee of producing. But once a part is ordered, a Japanese customer tends to continue its association with a particular supplier for the duration of the product's life. We were surprised to learn that "long-term contracts" were not, in fact, formal written contracts. In fact, suppliers explained that they typically worked on the product-development program for two or three years before receiving a written contract for the first batch of production, which might be for only one year, although there were strong expectations of continued business. As one supplier explained, to change (suppliers) before the product's life is over is "outside the dictionary." In addition to giving suppliers long-term contracts, Japanese automakers give their key suppliers portfolios of different jobs, a practice that allows for remarkable degrees of maneuverability. It permits the supplier to make money on an overall relationship rather than on every individual contract or episode. Although some of these contracts are lucrative for the supplier, others are not. Some deadlines and cost-reduction targets are easily met, whereas others involve considerable effort. Some design-related investments that the supplier makes can be recovered almost instantly in the next contract, but some must simply be written off as the cost of doing business. We found that in most cases the customer directly pays some of the design costs, for example, for the design and manufacture of the prototype. Seldom, however, are all the costs of product development paid immediately by the customer.

After the component is in production, Japanese automakers expect yearly price reductions, assuming that their suppliers will use value analysis to continuously reduce costs. Here again, the portfolio approach adds flexibility. Targets for price reductions are given for the portfolio of jobs carried out by the supplier, so that even if the supplier cannot cut the costs for one product, it can make up for this by making larger than average cost reductions for another product. The portfolio approach also allows the customer some flexibility in meeting its target vehicle prices: If it has to price one vehicle aggressively for strategic purposes, company executives can negotiate lower prices with its suppliers and then make that up on other vehicles that have more "breathing room."

The combined effect of a long-term relationship and the portfolio of different jobs is that there is room for the relationship to work itself out over a series of transactions over a long period of time, rather than have each transaction pay for itself. This approach lowers the overall risk associated with the relationship because individual events or episodes do not become make-or-break or win–lose situations. As one supplier explained when asked how this company deals with contracts in which it loses money: "But over the whole relationship if we can make money, it is OK."

Again, the survey data show differences in the expected direction, but not nearly as great as we expected. Table 7.8 measures the degree to which suppliers have a long-term dedicated relationship with their largest customer. In the conventional image of *keiretsu* relations, we expected long-term relationships in which the largest customer is the dominant customer for the supplier that has only a small number of automotive customers.

Table 7.8. Extent of Long-Term, Dedicated Relationships

	Japanese Suppliers		U.S. Suppliers	
	Subsystem Supplier (n = 37)	First-Tier Nonsystem Supplier (n = 70)	Subsystem Supplier (n = 38)	First-Tier Nonsystem Supplier (n = 90)
Number of years supplying largest customer	20.8	24.4	18.4	19.3
Percentage of total sales to largest customer	60.9%	49.4%	36.8%	26.4%
Number of automotive customers	5.7	7.5	11.2	11.7[a]
Percentage of supplier owned by largest customer	17.5%	9.8%	2.7%	0%

[a] After the elimination of two outliers.

Many researchers have observed that Japanese customers own a major share of equity in their first-tier suppliers and that therefore they can exercise control directly.

The results show that the total number of years spent supplying the largest customer is only slightly longer in Japan than in the United States: 21 and 24 years for Japanese subsystem and nonsystem suppliers, as opposed to 18 and 19 years for U.S. subsystem and nonsystem suppliers. But Japanese suppliers are considerably more dependent on their largest customer. The percentage of total sales that go to Customer A is highest among Japanese subsystem suppliers, at 61 percent versus 37 percent for U.S. subsystem suppliers. U.S. suppliers, on average, have about twice as many different automotive customers as do Japanese suppliers. Finally, equity ownership is more prevalent in Japan, 17.5 percent for subsystem suppliers and 10 percent for nonsystem first-tier suppliers, compared with 2.7 and 0 percent, respectively, in the United States. Note that equity ownership is the highest among subsystem suppliers.

Using Parallel Sourcing for Controlled Competition

Contrary to the popular notion of sole sourcing of components by Japanese manufacturers, we found controlled competition to be consistent in all the relationships that we studied. All suppliers were quick to point out that a competitor with superior technology could take business away from them, regardless of their long-standing relationship with the customer. Most Japanese suppliers face one or more competitors at the design stage of the contract. The recognition that technological strength is the only way to retain the customer's business in the long term keeps the supplier striving to be at the cutting edge of technology.

At first glance, this seems to counteract any effects of long-term relationships. However, if one reexamines the steps in the development process, the only point at which a proposal from a competing supplier with superior technology would be entertained would be before the concept stage. Japanese supplier firms that bid for business with new potential customers with whom they do not have a prior contract expect that they will have to enter with technology presentations at the preconcept stage for two to five new models. If they are able to make a favorable impression based on their technological capability, they can expect a trickle of test orders that should increase slowly in size if their performance is consistently superior. Clearly, at this stage, existing suppliers have a major competitive advantage.

Apart from the "competition" faced by the supplier at the design stage, the simple fact is that each customer has at least one alternative supplier for each subsystem. This alternative supplier—in rare cases an internal division of the customer—usually supplies a similar part for a different family of products or for different markets. But each supplier knows that the customer can, relatively easily, find an alternative source for a part. As a result, suppliers are fiercely competitive, and they see advanced technology as the main route to increasing their market share. Because suppliers' competitors generally have strong product-development and manufacturing capabilities, innovative design concepts are often the tiebreaker. If the supplier can introduce these innovative design concepts in the concept stage, the chances are good that it will get the job.

The survey data in Table 7.9 illustrate the strong presence of competi-

Table 7.9.   Degree of Competition Among Suppliers for Design and Production

	Japanese Suppliers		U.S. Suppliers	
	Subsystem Supplier ($n = 37$)	First-Tier Nonsystem Supplier ($n = 70$)	Subsystem Supplier ($n = 38$)	First-Tier Nonsystem Supplier ($n = 90$)
Percentage of suppliers competing for last manufacturing contract with				
One competitor	44%	26%	24%	25%
Two competitors	25	28	21	27
≥ Three competitors	14	20	47	39
Percentage of suppliers competing for last design contract with				
One competitor	58	34	24	30
Two competitors	22	29	29	33
≥ Three competitors	6	13	26	23
Percentage of suppliers competing with an internal division of largest customer[a]	0	4	8	22

[a]Percentage of suppliers responding "4" or "5" on a 5-point scale ranging from "Never" to "Always."

tion in Japan. In both the United States and Japan, the great majority of suppliers reported that for their last contract they had at least one competitor for both the design contract and the manufacturing contract. In Japan, there were more likely to be one (or perhaps two) competitor(s). More than three competitors for the design contract were reported by 47 percent of the U.S. subsystem supplier cases, versus only 14 of the Japanese subsystem suppliers. It was also more common in the United States for a competitor to be an internal division of the automotive company.

Richardson (1993) uses the term *parallel sourcing* to describe the Japanese approach. He noted that with the large amount of relationship-specific investment in the Japanese manufacturer–supplier relationship, sole sourcing would be very dangerous indeed for the manufacturer. For their part, suppliers would not be willing to invest the amount required, give in to the customers' demands for aggressive target prices, and respond to the pressures of aggressive development cycles if the customers could choose from a large group of competitors at any time. Richardson uses game theory and mathematical modeling to show that parallel sourcing provides incentives for suppliers' performance associated with multiple sourcing while at the same time providing many of the claimed benefits of sole sourcing.

Redefining Trust as a Form of Mutual Dependence

The inherent complexity and risk associated with involving suppliers in fast-cycle product development demand the establishment of mutual trust in the customer–supplier relationship. The notions of trust expressed in our study are far removed, however, from the traditional concept of trust. Almost uniformly we found no expression of blind faith and mutual loyalty. Rather, trust was always articulated as a form of mutual dependence (Smitka, 1991). As Campbell argues in Chapter 13, it is not necessary to explain the kind of "trust" we are talking about as a cultural feature that naturally leads to cooperation and a feeling of obligation in Japan. There are plenty of structural forces leading to a "trusting relationship" between manufacturer and supplier.

Japanese suppliers made it clear that they trusted their customers not to reveal proprietary information to competitors or to exploit their design capability and then give their business to a competitor, but mainly because they realized that the customers have too much to lose by violating their trust. Automotive companies made it clear that they trusted their suppliers, but only as long as they had an alternative supplier that they could use in a pinch.

"Trust" as mutual dependence suggests that each party realizes that it has much to lose by endangering the relationship. The process of engendering mutual dependence might ultimately mean the elimination of any redundant design or production capability in the customer's organization: At this point the delegation of the design responsibility to the supplier is complete. Similarly, the supplier invests in dedicated prototyping and test-ing facilities as well as personnel who have specialized knowledge regard-ing the customer's needs. At this stage, the supplier has gained admission to the inner circle, a select subset of first-tier suppliers. The benefits of the inner circle include access to strategic plans and information, the support of the customer in times of trouble, and long-term profitability linked with the customer's success. The price of admission is the complete subordina-tion of the supplier's design and production activities to the demands of the customer's development cycle.

Both the customer and the supplier could do each other grievous harm, but any move in that direction would threaten the core business of each party, and it could end a profitable relationship that has taken years to build. First-tier suppliers and their customers are on the same boat; they will either sink or swim together. This is not to say they have equal levels of power and influence. Clearly, this is a hierarchical relationship in which the customer has the greater power. With a few exceptions, such as Nip-pondenso, suppliers realize that they need their largest customer more than their customer needs them.

The bottom line in a parallel-sourcing relationship is that if things go well, the accumulated investments in the relationship on either side will be enormous (Richardson, 1993). From a transaction cost economics perspec-tive, there is such a heavy investment in relationship-specific assets (e.g., specific product knowledge, investments in organizational routines, invest-ments in specific tooling and equipment) that it is in the interests of both parties to keep the relationship healthy. In fact, these sunk costs are delib-erately allowed to build up so that a feeling of joint destiny is created on both sides of the relationship. To use an old cold-war military term, invest-ments are made to the point of *mutually assured destruction*. Both parties have enough invested in the relationship, financially, organizationally, and technologically, that one could virtually sink the other party, or at least do severe damage.

CONCLUSIONS AND IMPLICATIONS

We began this chapter discussing world-class practice in managing the sup-pliers' role in product development. We used a model of Japanese practice that appeared to be uniformly applied across suppliers. The basis of differ-entiation was thought to be tier structure: First-tier suppliers are the main participants in "design-in" activities, and they are involved from the begin-ning of the design cycle, and so on. In reality, what we uncovered looks more like a differentiated network of suppliers surrounding the automotive customer, with the suppliers occupying different niches depending on their capabilities and products. Among first-tier suppliers, we distinguished sub-system suppliers from nonsystem suppliers. The subsystem suppliers most closely fit the models of black-box sourcing described in sources like Clark and Fujimoto (1991). In retrospect, we realize that the large subsystem suppliers that we visited for our interviews (e.g., Nippondenso, Aisin Seiki, and Calsonic) are an elite group, even among subsystem suppliers, and that each one has particularly close ties and access to its parent company. The majority of first-tier suppliers design and build simpler component systems or individual parts and are far less integrated into their customers' product-development cycle—they are less involved in early concept development, communicate less, are less likely to have a guest engineer on site, have smaller product-development staffs, are less dependent on their largest customers, and are less likely to be partly owned by their largest customers.

This variation across suppliers does not occur by chance. Japanese automakers give their suppliers responsibility based on close monitoring and systematic ratings of their capabilities. To become a true subsystem supplier requires major investments in the human and technical infrastructure of product development. These suppliers must stay at the cutting edge of technology while also ruthlessly controlling costs and adhering strictly to their customers' aggressive development schedule.

We organized our arguments around two major tasks that face customers practicing black-box sourcing on a broad scale. First is the technical problem of reintegrating what has been split apart, which we call *managing complexity*. Second is the business problem of managing risk. Our findings are summarized in Figure 7.3, which suggests that underlying many of the observed characteristics of the Japanese model of supplier involvement in product development are two factors: excellence in systems engineering and mutual dependence.

Excellence in systems engineering is at the core of the Japanese auto-

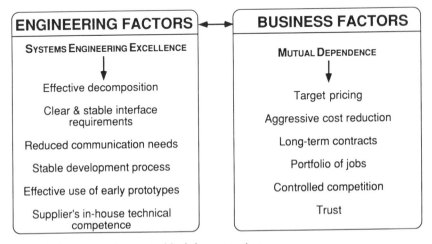

Figure 7.3. Success factors in black-box sourcing.

makers' ability to manage what would seem to be overwhelming complexity. Excellence in systems engineering means developing the competencies needed to divide the automobile into relatively autonomous subsystems as well as being able to identify critical spatial and performance specifications early and being able to communicate these clearly to the supplier. Excellent systems engineering significantly reduces information complexity and leads to less need for frequent communication, particularly late in the development cycle. In order for the process of systems engineering to work, each supplier must do its part in a tightly scheduled system. To coordinate numerous suppliers' activities requires a stable, predictable development process. Prototypes play a central role because not all interactions across components can be anticipated. The supplier must have excellent in-house technical competence to (1) suggest new technology, (2) participate in developing the specifications, (3) rapidly design and build prototypes, (4) interpret and respond to test data, and (5) identify ways to reduce costs during the development process.

This systems-engineering process can take place only in the context of stable, trusting, long-term relationships. We argue that underlying such a relationship is not blind faith but, rather, a mutual dependence created over many years. Customers and suppliers have such high levels of relationship-specific investments that the consequences of violating this trust far exceed any possible short-term gains. As suppliers move up the hierarchy toward becoming first-tier subsystem suppliers, the benefits and costs of high levels of mutual dependence increase. The benefits include being privy to their customers' long-term product-development plans and even being able to influence those plans so that products are designed to optimize use of the suppliers' manufacturing system. The costs are a high level of dependence on a single customer and the need to subordinate development capabilities and pricing flexibility to that customer's specific demands.

In our model in Figure 7.3, we show that mutual dependence—a sense of joint destiny—is necessary to enable the other factors that are part of what we call *managing risk*. For example, suppliers are not likely to accept a target price below their current costs unless they see their fate closely tied to the fate of their customer. Long-term contracts are rarely formally written, and they are meaningful only if the supplier sees itself as an integral part of the customer's value chain. Customers have no need to limit competition to only two or three suppliers unless there is a sense of a long-term joint dependence. Thus, we contend that trust is a result of mutual dependence rather than a cause.

We should note that there is a broader institutional context that supports this mutual dependence. This context includes the equity ownership that the auto companies hold, particularly in their key subsystem suppliers, as well as such institutional arrangements as supplier associations, which have been much discussed in recent literature (e.g., Fruin, 1993; Smitka,

1991). In Japan, suppliers' associations are company based (e.g., the Toyota supplier association), and suppliers attend regular association meetings and get to know one another. Perhaps the most important feature of suppliers' associations is the informal camaraderie and information sharing that ensue. If Toyota were to mistreat a supplier, this would quickly become known among other Toyota suppliers. This closeness reinforces the special community of customers and suppliers that feel a sense of shared destiny.

What was most surprising about the survey data was the similarity in results across the U.S. and Japanese data. It seems that in recent years, U.S. automakers have broadly adopted "Japanese" approaches such as the early involvement of suppliers in product development. We were able to measure mainly surface structural features that may or may not reflect systems-engineering excellence and mutual dependence. It is possible to imitate surface features such as early involvement, intense communications, and early sourcing without developing the underlying disciplines of systems engineering. Also, offering suppliers a guarantee of business if they participate in product development does not automatically engender the kind of deep sense of shared destiny that is part of the broader institutional structure of the Japanese supply system.

After evaluating some of the patterns that emerged over the course of our study, we drew up a series of recommendations for, first, suppliers wanting to obtain first-tier positions with Japanese customers and Japanese transplants across the globe and, second, manufacturers seeking to increase their suppliers' role in product development.

Implications for U.S. Suppliers

It is important to reiterate that there is a great deal of variation in the way that a given Japanese automotive customer deals with its suppliers. First-tier suppliers are dealt with much differently than lower-tier suppliers are, and subsystem suppliers are dealt with differently than nonsystem suppliers are. Thus there is no one strategy for a U.S. supplier that wishes to sell to the Japanese. How it is chosen will depend greatly on the strategic niche it occupies in the customer's supplier network. We can suggest the following paths for supplier firms that wish to establish themselves as first-tier suppliers.

Invest in Research, Development, Engineering, and Prototyping Capabilities

These characteristics are vital to accomplishing the targets set by the customer. Ideally, suppliers should be able to make prototypes in house. In addition, the supplier firm's top management should provide the resources and the attention to ensure that problems are resolved quickly during the prototype stage.

Make Up-Front Investments in Product Development

Top management must recognize that development costs are investments in a long-term relationship. Sometimes, especially relatively early in the relationship, these investments fall primarily on the shoulders of the supplier. This lesson is especially hard to learn if top management insists that the profitability of a transaction is more important than the profitability of a long-term relationship.

Reduce Cycle Time

U.S. suppliers must focus their resources on reducing the development cycle time. This is essential because the supplier must often scramble to implement an innovation in time to showcase it during the critical time window in the customer's development cycle. In addition, the support systems and the mind-set associated with reducing cycle time are essential to achieving the quick response expected during the prototype stage.

Accept Reduced Control over Pricing

Suppliers usually adopt the perspective that there is a price range over which the business is attractive and a price below which they are willing to walk away from the business. Our research suggests that an alternative approach is to begin with a price that allows the customer to manufacture a competitive end product and to work at ways to make this price commercially viable for the supplier. This target-price approach means that there is usually very little up-front assurance of profitability. It also means that commercial viability is an ongoing effort. Finally, it means that the supplier's top management must enter the relationship convinced that this relationship represents long-term value for the firm. This conviction depends on top management's assessment of the customer's overall competitive position as well as top management's confidence in its own capability.

Develop VE/VA Processes

The determination to make the target price commercially viable grows out of the supplier firm's confidence in its value-engineering and value-analysis programs. These programs are synonymous with a commitment to continuous improvement, along with all the incentive systems, management systems, and information-management systems that are the building blocks of any continuous improvement effort.

Build a Relationship with the Customer

Perhaps most important, the supplier must see the value of building a relationship with the customer. Many of the mechanisms that we have described simply cannot be implemented outside an ongoing relationship. In advocating this shift to a relationship orientation (as opposed to a transaction orientation), we are not suggesting that the supplier rely on notions such as loyalty and blind faith. Rather, we recommend that the supplier view its long-term relationships as a deliberate, alert, and conscious move toward mutual dependence. Suppliers should steer clear of unilateral acts of faith and should remember that no customer, Japanese or otherwise, will tolerate inefficiency or technological sloppiness. Within these constraints, suppliers should expect to make an up-front investment of time and energy to develop technology presentations and samples that will, over time, help them gain entry into their customers' files. The rejection of the initial samples does not necessarily mean that the contract is lost. It is the ability to respond quickly by implementing suggestions and coming back with improved samples that will help the supplier get its first order, which is likely to be a small one until the supplier has demonstrated its capabilities.

Implications for U.S. Manufacturers

U.S. manufacturing firms that wish to enlarge their roles as suppliers in product development must achieve excellence in systems engineering. This means that systems engineers must carefully decide how to divide the product into relatively autonomous subsystems. They must also identify the critical performance specifications, with the supplier's input, which will guide the supplier's developmental process. The following are some of the aspects of successful systems engineering:

Invest in a Stable, World-Class Design Process

Every Japanese manufacturer that we studied had invested considerably in developing a clear and stable design process. The steps in this process do not change over time or across product families. The milestones in the process and the events related to these milestones are clearly identified.

Educate Suppliers About the Design Process

Suppliers must be given consistent instructions about the design process over a long period of time. Every Japanese supplier firm that we studied could give us an unambiguous description of its major customer's design process. There were variations across customers, but by and large, it was clear that the suppliers had been briefed very carefully about events, expectations, and responsibilities related to the process.

Involve Key Suppliers Early in the Design Process

Key suppliers are brought in relatively early in the design process. These suppliers are given their first briefing at the concept stage. They remain intensely involved in the customer's design activities and help draw up the specifications for the subsystems. This early involvement helps take care of most design-related problems before they become too expensive to fix.

Source in "Chunks"

Suppliers should be given the responsibility for designing and manufacturing subsystems that are significant chunks of the end product. The chunks are defined in terms of self-contained design tasks. These chunks are then outsourced to key suppliers, which in turn assume the responsibility of managing and coordinating the activities of all the second-tier and third-tier suppliers that supply parts for the subsystem.

Exploit Prototypes to Achieve High-Quality, Manufacturable Designs

Prototypes are far from an anachronism, and it is unlikely that they will be replaced by engineering-analysis models any time soon. It is simply too difficult to model all the complex interactions that contribute to the function and feel of a complex assembly. Each prototype, including the first, should be tested as thoroughly as if it were the final product, and test data from the trials should be promptly fed back to the individual suppliers to begin the next improvement cycle. Prototype manufacturing conditions should approximate mass-production conditions as early as possible.

Develop Long-Term Relationships

Finally, manufacturers should try to create a network of long-term, codependent relationships with first-tier suppliers. This approach means being able to evaluate the technological and competitive capability of each supplier. It also requires a delicate balancing act between too much and too little dependence on a given supplier.

Once again, we should emphasize that it is possible to imitate many of the superficial features of the Japanese system, such as black-box sourcing and long-term contracts, without mastering the underlying systems that make black-box sourcing work. Certainly, imitating the surface features of a system that Japanese companies have evolved over decades will not enable U.S. companies to catch up and reap the benefits they desire. Excellence in systems engineering, the development of a cadre of technically capable first-tier suppliers, the creation of an atmosphere of controlled competition, and the creation of a sense of codestiny will undoubtedly take a firm many years, and such a route may violate American sensibilities about the free market. Japanese automakers have demonstrated that this approach to supplier management can work to produce high-quality, manufacturable, low-cost designs in short periods of time. It is not the only system, but it certainly bears a close look.

ACKNOWLEDGMENTS

This research was sponsored by the Air Force Office for Scientific Research through the Japan Technology Management program at the University of Michigan. We are grateful to John Campbell, for his support as director of JTM, and to Toyota, Mazda, and Nissan, who opened their doors to us and helped us gain access to some of their key suppliers in Japan. We also thank Daniel Whitney, Mark Fruin, and Allen Ward for their insightful suggestions on an earlier draft.

NOTES

1. We first heard the term *sourcing in chunks* from Eugene Goodson in 1984. At that time, he was a vice president for Hoover Universal. He used the term to refer to the way that Nissan was sourcing entire seats from Hoover, as compared with U.S. companies, which typically purchased parts of seats from different suppliers and assembled them in house.

2. We asked about *part numbers* rather than parts, to avoid multiple counting of simple parts used repeatedly in the assembly. For example, by our accounting, 25 of the same washers would count as one part number.

REFERENCES

Clark, K. B., & Fujimoto, T. (1991). *Product development performance.* Boston: Harvard Business School Press.

Cusumano, M. A. (1985). *The Japanese automobile industry.* Cambridge, MA: Harvard University Press.

Cusumano, M. A. (1988, Fall). Manufacturing innovation: Lessons from the Japanese auto industry. *Sloan Management Review*, 29–39.

Cusumano, M. A., & Takeishi, A. (1991). Supplier relations and management: A survey of Japanese, Japanese-transplant, and U.S. auto plants. *Strategic Management Journal, 12*, 563–88.

Davis, L. E. (1982). Organization Design. In G. Salvendy (Ed.), *Handbook of industrial engineering*, (pp. 2.1.1–2.1.29). New York: John Wiley & Sons.

Eisenhardt, K. (1989). Agency theory: An assessment and a review. *Academy of Management Review, 14*, 57–74.

Fama, E. (1980). Agency problems and the theory of the firm. *Journal of Political Economy, 88*, 288–307.

Fruin, W. M. (1993, September). *The visible hand and invisible assets: Network organization and supplier relations in the electronics industry in Japan.* Paper presented at the Vancouver Network Conference, Vancouver and Whistler, BC.

Helper, S. (1991, Summer). How much has really changed between U.S. automakers and their suppliers? *Sloan Management Review*, 15–28.

Japan Automobile Manufacturers Association (JAMA). (1991, June). *Supplier involvement in vehicle development in the Japanese auto industry: A guidebook for U.S. suppliers.* Tokyo: Japan Automobile Manufacturers Association and the Motor & Equipment Manufacturers Association.

Jenson, M. C., & Meckling, W. (1976). Theory of the firm: Managerial behavior, agency cost and ownership structure. *Journal of Financial Economics, 3*, 305–60.

Kamath, R. R., & Liker, J. K. (1990). Supplier dependence and innovation: A contingency model of suppliers' innovative activities. *Journal of Engineering and Technology Management, 7*, 111–27.

Kamath, R. R., & Wilson, R. C. (1983). *Characteristics of the United States automotive supplier industry.* Working Paper Series No. 10. Ann Arbor: Joint U.S.–Japan Automotive Study, Center for Japanese Studies, University of Michigan.

Lavin, D. (1993, May 14). Chrysler's man of many parts cut costs. *Wall Street Journal*, pp. B1, B9.

Liker, J. K., & Fleischer, M. (1992). *Organizational context barriers to DFM in large U.S. corporations.* Chapter 13 in G. Susman & J. Dean (Eds.), *Integrating design and manufacturing for competitive advantage* (pp. 228–264). New York: Oxford University Press.

Liker, J. K., & Hancock, W. M. (1986, May). Organizational systems barriers to engineering effectiveness. *IEEE Transactions on Engineering Management, 33*, 82–91.

Liker, J. K., & Kamath, R. R. (1994). Manufacturer–supplier relations and product design in U.S. and Japan auto industries. Unpublished manuscript, University of Michigan, Ann Arbor.

Mitchell, R. (1986, June 30). How Ford hit the bull's eye with Taurus. *Business Week*, pp. 69–70.

Richardson, J. (1993). Parallel sourcing and supplier performance in the Japanese automobile industry. *Strategic Management Journal, 14*, 339–50.

Smitka, M. (1991). *Competitive ties: Subcontracting in the Japanese automotive industry.* New York: Columbia University Press.

Smith, D. C. (1992, March). Chrysler's LH Team. *Ward's Auto World*, pp. 38–39.

Williamson, O. E. (1975). *Markets and hierarchies: Analysis and antitrust implications.* New York: Free Press.

Williamson, O. E. (1981). The economics of organization: The transaction cost approach. *American Journal of Sociology, 87*, 548–74.

Williamson, O. E. (1991). Comparative economic organization: The analysis of discrete structural alternatives. *Administrative Science Quarterly, 36*, 269–96.

Womack, J. P., Jones, D. T., & Roos, D. (1990). *The machine that changed the world.* New York: MacMillan.

8

Toyota, Concurrent Engineering, and Set-Based Design

ALLEN WARD, DURWARD K. SOBEK II,
JOHN J. CRISTIANO, AND JEFFREY K. LIKER

Concurrent engineering, the practice of simultaneously designing a product and its manufacturing system, is generally viewed as a major source of Japanese competitive advantage (Clark & Fujimoto, 1991). U.S. companies have rushed to construct structured design processes and multifunctional, often colocated teams in order to compete (Nevins & Whitney, 1989). Ironically, however, we discovered in our research that most managers at Japanese auto companies are fairly new to concurrent engineering, which many regard as a Toyota invention. Equally paradoxical, our research found that managers at Toyota, which has long experience with concurrent engineering, made little use of many commonly touted "crucial elements" of successful concurrent engineering. Toyota uses neither colocated nor dedicated multidisciplinary teams, and significant portions of the development process remain relatively unstructured. The approach that Toyota does use is almost counterintuitive—a totally different development paradigm, which we have named *set-based design*. This process on the surface appears grossly inefficient, even irrational—but is, in fact, as we point out, extremely effective and efficient.

Our method for learning about the design approach of the U.S. and Japanese automotive manufacturers (original-equipment manufacturers, or OEMs) and their suppliers was through interviews in both countries. In Japan, we interviewed managers and engineers at Toyota, Nissan, and Mazda, as well as a number of their key first-tier suppliers. The Toyota suppliers we visited, who worked mostly with Toyota, were from Sango, Aisin Seiki, Nippondenso, Atsugi Unisia, Toyoda Machine Works, Tsuda Industries, and Cataler Industrial Company. In the United States, we interviewed engineers and managers at Ford, Chrysler, and GM, as well as five U.S. suppliers.

We do not claim to have matched pairs of case examples in the United States and Japan. For example, we tried to interview body engineers at the auto companies to learn about this central development process, but this was not possible in all cases. We also asked managers and all the auto companies how they set specifications for suppliers, which is an important and externally visible part of the design below. The suppliers we visited produce a wide range of products, for example, fan blades and fan clutches, exhaust systems, radiators, piston bearings, exhaust manifolds, plastic injection parts, and fuel rails. Despite the heterogeneous mix of suppliers, we found that Toyota's suppliers had far more in common with one another than they did with the suppliers to other automobile companies.

We characterize Toyota's approach to product development as *set-based design*. This term was not used by Toyota; it was developed by Ward and Seering (1989a,b). It is an approach to design problems in which designers think and reason about sets of design alternatives. Over time, these sets are gradually narrowed as the designers eliminate inferior alternatives until they find a final solution. This approach differs from the common practice of making iterations (i.e., making several modifications or improvements in series) of one alternative until a satisfactory solution emerges.

We hypothesized that Japanese auto companies are more set based in their design approach than U.S. automakers are and that this difference helps account for their rapid development cycles and high-quality results. We also assumed that Japanese companies were more advanced in their use of concurrent engineering. Our working hypothesis proved false: Toyota appeared far more advanced than Nissan, Mazda, or the U.S. companies with regard to concurrent engineering, and only Toyota really fit our concept of set-based design.

Our interviews were conducted primarily in English, although we had a Japanese translator with us at all times. Because the Japanese companies sent only English-speaking managers and engineers to be interviewed, Japanese translation was usually not necessary. We arrived with a set of questions designed to determine the extent to which the companies were using a set-based approach, but we did not use the questions in a rigid, structured way. Rather, we asked the respondents to describe their development process from the early conceptual stages through the production processes, and then we probed at appropriate points in order to find out whether they were using a set-based approach. In fact, we were so surprised by what we heard from Toyota and its suppliers during our first set of interviews in the summer of 1992 that we returned in the spring of 1993. Two of the three interviewers on the second visit had not been at the previous visit. Moreover, two of the researchers made a third trip to Toyota and its suppliers in the summer of 1993. In addition to Toyota, we interviewed engineers at Nissan during our second and third visits. The follow-up interviews confirmed the apparent paradoxes that we heard in the first interviews.

In the following pages, we briefly summarize Toyota's contributions and approach to concurrent engineering, and we outline the paradoxical conflict between Toyota's highly efficient overall process and the seemingly inefficient steps in that process. We then describe the basic theory of set-based design and explain the advantages of using it; these advantages, in turn, provide a rationale for Toyota's use of the process (although this is not necessarily Toyota's rationale). Finally, we provide a series of case studies that demonstrate how Toyota and its suppliers implement the set-based design model compared with companies that follow a more conventional paradigm.

TOYOTA AND CONCURRENT ENGINEERING

Concurrent engineering (CE) refers by definition to the simultaneous design of aspects of a system that traditionally have been developed sequen-

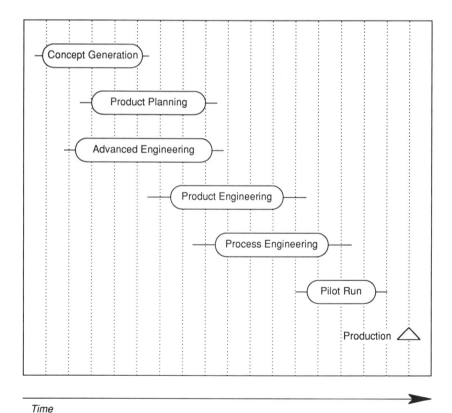

Time

Figure 8.1. Overlapping concurrent engineering. (From Clark & Fujimoto, 1991.)

tially; most important, it is the simultaneous development of products and their manufacturing systems (Chapman, Bahill, & Wymore 1992; Nevins & Whitney, 1989). Like the overall lean production paradigm of which it is a part, CE is often regarded as a Japanese phenomenon, which is being copied with some difficulty by American companies (Clark & Fujimoto, 1991; Womack, Jones, & Roos, 1990). In fact, like lean production, CE is mainly an invention of the Toyota Motor Company.

Toyota began moving to concurrent development in the 1960s; Mazda in the late 1970s; and Nissan not until the mid-1980s. Furthermore, Toyota's process continues to be far more concurrent than those of other companies. For example, Toyota begins the design process by not only designing but also building body-stamping dies before the body-part drawings are finished; neither Nissan nor Mazda follows suit. Clark and Fujimoto (1991) portrayed concurrent engineering as *overlapping problem solving*, as shown in Figure 8.1. Toyota, however, described its own process, as shown in Figure 8.2, as one in which the emphasis placed on different tasks may change over time. Tasks begin whenever the groups responsible for the task think they should begin. In other words, each group starts whenever it needs to in order to meet deadlines.

Toyota's concurrent engineering practice seems extraordinarily effective. For example, of the eight cars at the top of the 1993 *Consumer Reports* reliability study, Toyota has five. Toyota's world market share has grown by 25 percent in the last decade. The process is also extraordinarily efficient. *Concept approval*, the formal start of a car program in most companies, is given at Toyota 27 months before the start of production. The development process takes a little more time at Nissan, about 29 months. Development at Toyota is much faster than the best U.S. examples—the Chrysler LH team took 37 months. In addition, a Toyota team employs about 500 people, as opposed to approximately 750 on the Chrysler LH team. Thus, Toyota's development practice requires at least 50 percent

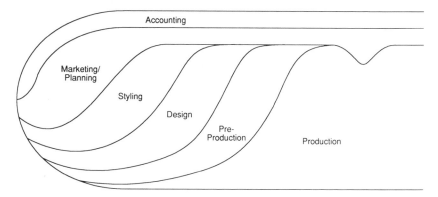

Figure 8.2. Toyota's process, as reported by Toyota.

fewer (people–person) years than Chrysler's recent record-breaking (for Chrysler) performance. This efficiency is key in allowing Toyota to produce about 45 different models.

Ironically, Toyota's success cannot be attributed to many of the mechanisms considered in the United States to be "essential" to concurrent engineering—specifically, colocated cross-functional teams and a highly structured development process.

First, Toyota does not use colocated or dedicated teams. Most personnel are organized in the traditional "chimney" functional structure, and the ideal load for an engineer is considered to be two projects (suggesting that many have more than two). There are usually only about six people assigned specifically to each project. When we interviewed managers at Chrysler, they explained with unswerving certainty that the key to successful concurrent engineering is the dedicated colocated team. They have reorganized around a platform-team approach for large cars, small cars, and light trucks and minivans. Each team has a high-level general manager (who reports to a vice president), and most of the development staff report solely to one platform-team head and have one project to work on at a time. The common opinion at Chrysler LH was that dedicated platform teams are essential to its success and that matrix management approaches that combine program managers with functional organizations cannot work. But Toyota is able to combine a widely reported emphasis on teamwork, communication, and consensus with its functional organizational structure.

Toyota's designers also seem to have an attitude toward the head designer that has been much less imitated in the United States. An old tradition in U.S. engineering glorified the Kelly Johnson or Henry Ford who understood every aspect of the product and the manufacturing process and provided the integrating force to make the design work. Toyota has institutionalized the development of such people: They are carefully selected and groomed outstanding design engineers who also have the required leadership potential. This *"shusa"* acts as a vehicle program head and is responsible for a program's development from start to finish. *Shusa* are on the same level as the general managers of functional groups, but the *shusa* has only a limited dedicated staff, and he or she must borrow staff from the functions, which is a matrix organization approach. *Shusa* are often called *heavy-weight project managers* in the U.S. literature (Clark & Fujimoto, 1991), but this name understates their real roles as design leaders. Toyota employees translate the term as *chief engineer*, and they refer to the vehicle under development as *the shusa's car*. They assured us that the *shusa* has final, absolute authority over every aspect of vehicle development.

Such powerful engineering leaders have fallen from favor in the United States, in part because several of them made large, company-threatening errors. For example, Henry Ford insisted on retaining the Model-T design long after the market had passed it by. Yet despite the power and prestige awarded to *shusa,* Toyota seems to avoid such idiosyncratic decisions. Rather, these *shusa* seem to act as a spur to consensus: The Toyota general managers for body engineering and styling told us that they had never failed to reach agreement with a *shusa.*

Second, despite its well-earned reputation for short and rigidly enforced development schedules, Toyota does not use a highly structured, thoroughly planned development process in the early stages of vehicle development. Instead, as in the *kanban* system on the factory floor, subteams are responsible for deciding when they need to start work. Suppliers and manufacturing teams, for example, are given major deadlines such as the start of full production or the first vehicle prototype. As long as these groups can meet the deadline while satisfying the customer, Toyota does not care, or keep track of, when these groups begin their work. It is up to the suppliers' (or manufacturing's) initiative to find out the information they need to meet the deadline. Some use a "guest engineer" at Toyota; others use faxes and phone calls. The wall charts and thick process manuals so popular in the United States seem much simplified at Toyota and its suppliers.

Advocates of concurrent engineering also emphasize frequent meetings with suppliers, who assume a major role in the development of parts. Again, ironically, although Toyota is widely and, it seems, correctly regarded as having superb communications between the parent company and its suppliers, Liker and his colleagues' data (see Chapter 7) show that a smaller percentage of Toyota suppliers reported communicating at least weekly with Toyota about design, compared with other Japanese or U.S. companies. That is, Toyota suppliers spend *less* time communicating with the parent company. Furthermore, Toyota's suppliers are (by their own testimony) significantly less likely to design their parts "jointly" with Toyota—Toyota either designs the parts and provides blueprints, or it uses its "design-in" process to give suppliers the autonomy to handle their own design subject to Toyota's specifications and constraints.

These contrasts between Toyota's ability to achieve best-in-class quality in concurrent engineering and its pursuit of practices rather at variance with the U.S. perspectives on concurrent engineering require explanation. In the next section we intensify the contrasts by summarizing practices that appear astoundingly wasteful. This paradox, in turn, points the way to a plausible explanation of all the idiosyncrasies in the Toyota process.

THE TOYOTA PARADOX

The central paradox of Toyota's development process is this: Despite its obvious effectiveness as a system, the individual steps in it appear extraordinarily inefficient. The evidence is summarized in Table 8.1, and selected case studies are provided in detail later in this chapter.

Toyota and its suppliers, as opposed to their competition, appear to:

Table 8.1. Comparison of Toyota with Other U.S. and Japanese Companies

Area	Other Companies	Toyota and Suppliers
Number of one-fourth- or one-fifth-scale clay models developed.	Japanese OEM: 3 to 5.	Toyota: 5 to 20.
Body hard points made.	U.S. OEM: fix before full-sized clay model—avoid changes.	Toyota: 2–4 cm "design tolerance" at first stage of full-sized clay model, fixed at second stage.
Exhaust-system specifications made.	Japanese supplier: receive hard specifications and test data; can argue if impossible to meet.	Toyota and Sango: specifications are targets or *gurai* (about) until the second prototype.
Number of exhaust-system designs prototyped.	Japanese supplier: 1.	Sango: 10 to 50.
Cooling-fan specifications determined.	Japanese OEM: provide hard specification for full-sized clay model.	Aisin Seiki: "design tolerance" = 30 percent at first prototype; 5 percent at second prototype.
Number of fans for prototypes made.	Japanese OEM (about supplier): 2 or 3.	Aisin Seiki: average = 4–5, maximum = 30.

1. Explore a far larger number of possible concepts at a one-fourth- or one-fifth-scale clay-model level.
2. Delay fixing body hard points (the key dimensions that determine the body's shape), thereby increasing the uncertainty faced by the design team and decreasing the time available to the stamping die designers after the body shape is fully determined. In the words of Toyota's manager of body engineering, "The manager's job is to prevent people from making decisions too quickly." We use the phrase *design tolerance* to refer to the amount of flexibility remaining in the design (e.g., this dimension may be $x \pm 20$ percent).
3. Delay releasing hard specifications to suppliers until very late in the design process. This is a conscious decision: Toyota managers report that for their more capable suppliers, they either provide approximate specifications or state targets. The suppliers are expected to try to improve their products to meet the targets. Hard specifications are chosen according to the results of these efforts.
4. Prototype an extraordinary number of different designs for subsystems.

Engineers at one of Toyota's leading Japanese competitors reacted to these data with polite incredulity. Their own process, it seemed to them, must be more efficient. They could not imagine that the strongest automaker in the world would waste so much effort. The data suggest a slow and wasteful process, a management that has difficulty making decisions, and a breadth of exploration that seems completely inconsistent with the known effectiveness of the Toyota process.

Of course, on first reading, the lean production process, with its effort to force batch sizes far below the "minimum economic order quantity," its emphasis on general-purpose machinery and flexibility, and its obsessive attention to quality and variation reduction, also seems highly inefficient. As with lean production, the Toyota design process would be inefficient if Toyota were following the conventional paradigm. But Toyota is not, and its practices make perfect sense according to the paradigm that it follows.

EXPLAINING THE PARADOX: THE SET-BASED DESIGN MODEL

In this section, we summarize the conventional model of the design process and offer a new model that explains Toyota's practices.

The Conventional Model

The most widely used engineering design text in the United States is Shigley's *Mechanical Engineering Design,* from which Figure 8.3 is taken. It prescribes a process that repeatedly iterates through a sequence of steps, in which a problem is first understood and a solution is synthesized. The solution is then analyzed and evaluated. Based on the analysis, a new solution may be tried (and the problem definition may even be modified). The principal point is that a single solution is synthesized first and then analyzed and changed accordingly. This is often described as a *hill-climbing process:* Each successive solution is another step toward the best possible design at the top of the hill. Because the process moves from point to point in the space of possible designs, we refer to it as *point-based design.* Optimization theory provides a rich mathematical description of the process.

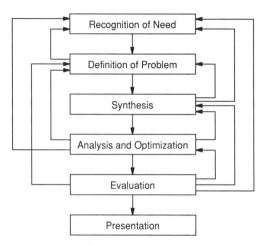

Figure 8.3. Shigley's model of the design process.

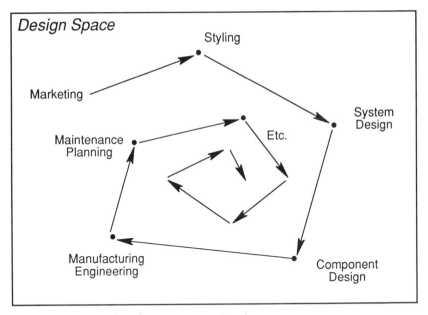

Figure 8.4. A point-based concurrent engineering process.

This view of engineering design is so widely accepted that it is almost invisible and pervades engineers' thinking. Hence, it is not surprising that the U.S. picture of the CE process simply adds multiple actors to this basic model. A typical point-based design process begins with the generation of many design ideas, or alternatives, which are evaluated based on currently available information to determine the best alternative. An iteration process on the perceived best alternative begins in one part of the organization, where the design is analyzed and refined. It is passed on to other parts of the company for criticism and modification (Figure 8.4). The design "moves up the hill" toward total optimality until a satisfactory solution to the design problem is found. Modifications attempt to eliminate conflicts among different functional areas of the organization (e.g., product design and manufacturing).

Much of the university CE research conducted in the United States is focused on using computers to accelerate communication concerning designs. In U.S. industry, locating the members of the team close together (so that they can communicate easily) is heavily emphasized. But the process still remains one of point-based design.

In comparison, Toyota's process appears inefficient. Why, an outside observer could reasonably ask, does Toyota need to go through the iteration so many times, generating different designs? Why does it take Toyota so long to synthesize the first solution, providing the starting point for modifications?

Toyota's Model

Toyota's development process appears expensive, clumsy, and inefficient to outsiders (including other Japanese companies) because they view it as a badly run version of their own point-to-point search. But Toyota does not intend to conduct a point-to-point search. Rather, as suggested in Fig-

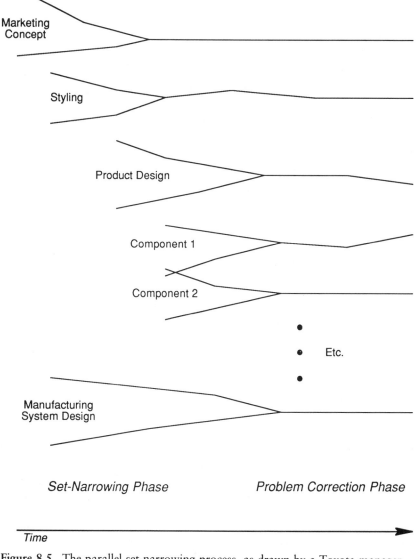

Figure 8.5. The parallel set-narrowing process, as drawn by a Toyota manager.

ure 8.5 (made from a sketch by Toyota's general manager of body engineering), Toyota follows this general approach:

1. The team defines a set of solutions, rather than a single solution, at the system
   level.
2. They define sets of possible solutions for various subsystems.
3. They explore these possible subsystems in parallel, using analysis, design rules,
   and experiments to characterize those parts of the design space.
4. They use this analysis to gradually narrow the sets of solutions, converging
   slowly toward a single solution. In particular, they analyze the possibilities for
   the subsystems to determine the appropriate specifications. Both Toyota's engineers and Toyota's suppliers described an extensive negotiation process.
5. Once they have established the single solution for any part of the design, it is
   not changed unless absolutely necessary. In particular, the single solution is not
   changed to gain improvements (i.e., to climb the optimality hill).

This process may, in fact, add to the costs of development in the earliest
stages, but its advantages are enormous, making it clear why Toyota's
development costs are lower overall.

THE ADVANTAGES OF SET-BASED DESIGN

This section shows how Toyota's use of a different paradigm explains the
central paradox of the previous section and the contrast of apparently inefficient steps with a highly efficient overall process.

1. Set-Based Design Enables Reliable, Efficient Communications

In conventional, point-to-point search, every change made by part of the
organization may invalidate all previous communications and decisions.
Because designs are highly interconnected in ways that may not be obvious, it is generally impossible to know whether a particular change will
invalidate previous decisions or facts. Nor is there any reason to suppose
that the changes will necessarily converge. Often, teams simply run out
of time to make more changes and so hastily patch together something
that fits.

Most of us have experienced this phenomenon in the simplest of all
concurrent engineering problems—selecting a meeting time. To establish
a meeting time for three or more participants, the organizer of the meeting
selects a time and date that seem convenient and starts inviting people.
When this person checks with the first person invited, it is not unusual for
a conflict to arise between the selected time and that person's availability.
This can be resolved in conversation by selecting a new time and date that
is good for both parties. But when the organizer invites the third person,
the meeting time may need to be changed again, often to a date and time
at which the first person invited might have been able to attend originally

but, because of the delay, now has another commitment. With a group of any significant size, agreement on a meeting time satisfactory to all parties requires a long period of time and intense communication. This is the dilemma of a point-to-point search.

Conversely, in a set-based approach, all communications describe the whole set of possible solutions. As the set narrows, the surviving solutions remain true (a fact that can be demonstrated using formal logic).

A set-based approach to planning a meeting would be for all the participants to submit the times that they would be available to meet within the desired time frame. Each person agrees not to schedule any additional commitments until an agreement on the meeting time has been reached. Once all participants have submitted a set of possible times, a time that is convenient for all can be determined (or the intersection of all the specified sets). By taking the time to understand all the constraints on meeting time (i.e., the design space) early in the process, the meeting organizer saves time in the end by avoiding a runaround.

This difference between point-based and set-based communications has a number of consequences. Most obviously, it eliminates work wasted on solutions that later must be changed (e.g., scheduling and rescheduling meetings). Second, it reduces the number and length of the meetings required for communication. In the conventional approach, every change requires a new meeting. Furthermore, because the consequences of the decisions are unclear, several decisions must be made collectively, which can result in relatively prolonged meetings. Conversely, Toyota's engineers and suppliers can work mostly independently, because each meeting communicates information about an entire space of designs. These arguments are consistent with Liker and his colleagues' finding that Toyota suppliers report having the best communications with the parent company of any surveyed, and they also report spending less time communicating than others do. These suppliers also are significantly less likely to "share" design activity between their design engineers and the Toyota design engineers; that is, they are more likely to work independently.

A third consequence of set-based design regards the reliability of information. With a point-based approach, members of the team have strong incentives to delay getting started if the information on which they must rely is subject to change. This incentive is much reduced if people can count on their information's being correct. As long as the participants in our meeting example agree not to schedule any other commitments until this time is set, we can be sure that they will be available during the set of possible meeting times they submitted. This may be a major reason that Toyota can allow the parts of the team to get started when they think they need to, rather than having to force them to follow a rigid schedule.

A fourth and final consequence is that the set-based design process promotes a harmonious and trusting working relationship. If I tell you early in the process that I am planning a particular solution, before I really have enough data to make those decisions, you will know that I cannot be trusted to stick with this solution and that I am likely to make changes late in the game. Conversely, if I merely describe the set of solutions, I can give you a lot of information early on, without deceiving you.

This effective, efficient communication process may be the reason that Toyota, with all its experience with concurrent engineering, does not find it necessary to use colocated dedicated development teams.

2. Set-Based Design Allows Much Greater Parallelism in the Process, with Much More Effective Use of Subteams Early in the Process

It makes little sense, in terms of the conventional paradigm, to start planning the manufacturing process before the product is defined. If the design is still in the iteration loop, it will be subject to further modifications that are neither bounded nor predictable and that could nullify significant portions of process planning, thereby discouraging early process design. Conversely, in the set-based paradigm, it makes perfect sense to think about, early in the design, the set of manufacturing processes that might apply to a set of possible products. Thus, innovation in the manufacturing process may drive innovation in the product design, as described in Whitney's discussion of Nippondenso's *jikigata* designs (see Chapter 6). That is, the manufacturing team is free to focus on a new part of the product design space, to assume that the product will be designed just as much to fit the new manufacturing system, as they will have to fit the manufacturing system to the new product.

3. Set-Based Design Allows the Most Critical, Early Decisions to Be Based on Data

It is widely (and, we think, correctly) believed that the earliest decisions about designs have the largest impact on the ultimate quality and cost but that such decisions also are made with the smallest amount of data. Powerful engineering analysis tools, such as finite element analysis, are difficult to apply until the design has been detailed. In consequence, major changes often must be made late in the design process. Engineering change orders are expensive, and many organizations try to reduce them by "doing it right the first time." But this solution is equivalent to telling members of the organization to try harder and be more careful, usually not particularly useful advice. Toyota has a specific mechanism for "doing it right": Explore the space of possible designs before making the important decisions.

That is, before Toyota's managers establish specifications for subsystems, they already have seen a variety of subsystems being designed and tested. They therefore can optimize their specification decisions in order to determine the best fit between subsystems and the best overall system.

This emphasis on set-based exploration and the use of data has a more subtle effect on relationships among personnel. Powerful design leaders seem to have been associated with the most truly outstanding designs, playing key roles in enabling tightly integrated, highly advanced designs. Such leaders are also frequently associated with catastrophic mistakes, such as the large and unsuccessful instant motion picture effort at Polaroid, or Henry Ford's insistence on keeping the Model T essentially unchanged long after the market had passed it by. Toyota, more than any other major company, seems to emphasize developing and empowering design leaders. It seems likely that it can afford to do so because these leaders make their decisions much more on the basis of data, rather than on intuition, than in other companies. Hence, Toyota gains the benefits of the leaders' experience, imagination, and integrating leadership, without the costs of their mistakes.

4. The Set-Based Process Promotes Institutional Learning

Designers are notoriously resistant to documenting their work. One reason may be the sense that documentation is generally useless. Describing the process of changes by which a design arrived at its final configuration is equivalent to providing a set of directions to where you are now—but the next design will use the current one as a starting point, and the directions will be useful only if the team is tempted to backtrack.

Conversely, the Toyota process helps the members of the team form mental "maps of the design space," because a larger fraction of the space is systematically explored. As an example, Toyota's suppliers usually give Toyota their test data, analysis results, and trade-offs between different factors on several design alternatives—valuable information on which sound decisions can be made for the current vehicle. This knowledge is useful in the future, too; for example, the cooling-fan design that was too large for the current car may be perfectly suited to the next one. Hence, members of the Toyota team start with a far better picture of what they want than other designers do, and then they refine that picture more deeply by further exploring of the design space.

This is consistent with another of Liker and his colleagues' (Chapter 7) findings based on Toyota's supplier data. Although Toyota's engineers have about the same average experience as do engineers in other companies, Toyota suppliers were far less likely than were suppliers of other OEMs to report that Toyota's engineers did not know as much as they should. Only about 5 percent of Toyota's first-tier suppliers reported problems created by the lack of knowledge on Toyota's part, compared with 22 percent for other Japanese companies and over 50 percent for U.S. OEMs.

It is therefore reasonable that these four advantages—efficient and effective communications, increased concurrency in the process, important early decisions based on data, and flexibility to customer demands—far outweigh the costs of exploring more alternatives.

CASE STUDIES

As we have seen, our interviews with many employees in companies in the auto industry found that Toyota differs sharply from other companies in its approach to product development. Top managers and engineers from this company consistently spoke of a process that narrows a set of alternatives over time and that during this time much work is poured into understanding constraints, trade-offs, and other environmental factors associated with motor-vehicle design.

In this section, we present three different groups of case examples that contrast point-based with set-based approaches to product development. All the point-based approaches are drawn from U.S. OEMs and their suppliers, although Mazda and Nissan and their suppliers also seemed to take relatively point-based approaches to design, compared with Toyota. We did not include all examples from our interviews but only a few select cases to illustrate the point-based approach. The set-based examples come from Toyota and its suppliers. It should be noted here that there is variation in the data. In each company, different departments take different approaches to design. Even if the underlying philosophy is the same, the techniques and tools can differ tremendously. Also, different persons in a department may have differing opinions on why a certain technique or aspect of the approach is important, or even what the basic design philosophy is or ought to be. Our investigation required that we interview people, and so the information we gathered is colored by these people's perceptions. The case examples, therefore, serve to illustrate contrasting approaches with real-world, hard examples and not to generalize across vast conglomerates.

First, we contrast approaches to body design and die engineering. Then we describe in detail the process of establishing suppliers' specifications, from both Toyota's perspective and some suppliers' perspectives in the United States and Japan. Third, we examine a special case of innovation management at Nippondenso, one of Toyota's biggest suppliers, that incorporates many set-based principles.

Point-Based Body Design and Die Engineering at a U.S. OEM

A U.S. automotive manufacturer, in a recent interview, described to us a point-based design and development process for the body design of an advanced vehicle. This OEM has less than five years' experience with CE and has lost significant world market share in the past 10 years. The manufacturer's design and development process consists of concept development, prototype, production tooling, and production phases. Although the information included in this example represents only the specific experiences of the people we interviewed in one large division of this company, their descriptions are consistent with what we have heard from other areas of the company.

Very early in the concept-development phase, a small group of project designers work with a number of different sketches representing different body-design alternatives. From these sketches, the designers evaluate each alternative and choose the best. The vehicle architecture is then laid out based on this design. This process is typically completed four to five months into the concept-development phase, approximately 43 months before production. Although some of the designers had had a variety of experiences in product development, there is no manufacturing representative on the team. Manufacturing is brought into the development loop only after the "base design" has been defined. Manufacturing recently was colocated with the product-design team for the purpose of bringing manufacturing considerations into the design.

A scaled plastic model of the base design is created to facilitate evaluation. Members of manufacturing and other functional areas evaluate the design and propose changes in terms of the plastic model. Whenever possible, these changes are incorporated into the design, and a second scaled plastic model is constructed for further evaluation. After a total of three to four plastic models, this iterative process results in a final body architecture that is completed 36 months before production. Subsystems and components are "optimized" using a similar strategy: Establish one basic design and "iterate like mad" to improve it.

This is an example of classic point-based design. A single design solution was selected (in this case from one functional perspective, namely, body design) very early in the development cycle, and then it was modified from different functional perspectives (such as body manufacturing) to achieve an acceptable result.

Set-Based Body Design and Die Engineering at Toyota

We interviewed a body-design engineer and a general manager of body engineering at Toyota who described a development process in stark contrast with the one we just described.

After many sketches and drawings of possible design ideas, this company typically makes from five to 20 $1/5$ scale clay models, each decidedly different (of course, 20 would be an extreme case). The drawings and the clay models are studied by both the marketing department to help determine customer satisfaction and the production engineers to determine the feasibility of the design and the cost of production.

Body designers of other auto companies told us that for the full-size clay model, the hard points are set and will not vary by more than 1 to 2 mm. (Hard points are critical dimensions on the body.) Toyota has two stages of full-size clay models. At the first stage (about 27 months before production), typically two full-size clay models are created. Toyota designers maintain as much as 2 to 4 cm of flexibility on the critical design points at this stage. This flexibility explicitly represents a range, or a set, of different design alternatives. Meanwhile, employees continue to collect marketability and manufacturability data. Eventually, these "design tolerances" on the hard points are narrowed until specifications are set (i.e., the hard points are fixed). A final full-size clay model is created using these specifications, typically at about 24 months before production.

The ultimate criterion for setting hard points is 100 percent customer satisfaction. According to the general manager, delaying the decision to set the hard points until the latest possible moment is necessary to ensure that customers' expectations are fully understood, that they will be satisfied by the body design, and that the body design also can be manufactured.

Typically, the final theme or concept is not chosen until 27 months before production (i.e., the first full-size clay stage), leaving just a little over two years to get from concept approval to full-volume production. Toyota's ability to do this hinges on early development of the manufacturing process, that is, die design and production. Die design begins long before the hard points are fixed. In some cases, castings are ordered and die production begins while "design tolerances" are still being maintained on the hard points. Process engineers are able to perform preliminary work on the dies because of the high level of confidence that the ultimate body design will not exceed the design tolerances communicated to them. Thus, process engineers can do all the work they desire as long as they maintain enough flexibility to accommodate all possibilities within the design tolerances. As these tolerances narrow, process engineers can continue to develop the dies.

Notice the set-based nature of this approach and how such an approach facilitates simultaneous product and process development. The sketches and drawings are a means of exploring the feasible design region. Toyota further develops a significant number of these alternatives by creating scaled clay models. Throughout each stage, Toyota continues to compile information on the environment, the market, and various constraints and trade-offs among different alternatives. Even through the full-scale model stage, flexibility, often in the form of explicit ranges, is maintained on the body's hard points until the final clay model. These ranges can be seen as representing sets of design alternatives, as a method of managing uncertainty, or both. Process engineers are able to get an early start on die development because such ranges on the hard points place bounds on anticipated changes downstream in the design process.

Point-Based Approach to Supplier Specifications

The example we chose to illustrate a point-based approach to setting supplier specifications is that of a restraint system (i.e., seat-belt design) designed by a U.S. supplier for a U.S. OEM. The OEM has had less than five years' experience with CE and until 1985 maintained internal responsibility for designing restraint systems for passenger vehicles. Before that time, suppliers were contracted solely for the purpose of manufacturing the product. Currently, the development and procurement of restraints means providing specifications to the supplier for basic requirements such as the size, shape, and location of the attachment as well as specific feature requirements for the latch type, spring rates, and sensitivities. The supplier maintains sole responsibility for designing and developing the system, with the exception of dynamic testing. The basic components of a restraint system are the internal retractor hardware, the webbing, the latch, and the interior styling trim.

The supplier's involvement is initiated early in the design process through a letter from the OEM describing the high-level requirements for the upcoming vehicle-development program. This is typically the first step in a competitive selection process, and the letter gives the high-level requirements for the retractor, the webbing, the system friction components, and the guideloops. The supplier is requested to present a proposal in response to these requirements within 30 days of the invitation and is "encouraged" to bring sample parts to demonstrate the concepts of its proposed design. To be responsive to the customer's request requires that the supplier converge to a specific design solution within 30 days, based on very general requirements. As a result, the initial step of a typical development cycle for the supplier consists of rapidly developing a solution based on off-the-shelf technology.

If the supplier is selected as a potential source for the vehicle program, the OEM employees develop detailed specifications. During the development of the detailed specifications, the restraint release group in the OEM communicates the supplier's proposed design to the sheet metal and interior trim groups. If any changes are required owing to location or packaging, the restraint release group will communicate these back to the supplier, who will make the necessary changes to the initial proposed solution. As additional details of the vehicle design are defined, this process is repeated until all functional, spatial, and packaging requirements are satisfied.

In this example, the OEM and supplier are using a point-based design and development process. A single solution is rapidly selected early in the program, with all downstream changes being described as deviations to the baseline design. To support this, a serial-communication process is used, in which the members of each function make decisions and communicate them to the next in line. A possible explanation for using a point-based design process for the passenger restraints is the maturity of the technology used in the system. However, the stories we heard from five different U.S. suppliers all were variants of this point-based design approach.

Set-Based Approach to Supplier Specifications

We interviewed parties on both sides of Toyota's specification-setting process. In this section we first discuss our interviews with Toyota representatives, and then we present what we learned at the Toyota suppliers we visited. The stories coincided well.

Toyota's View

From our interviews with top managers, we found that Toyota has no formal means of integrating the supplier's development of a part or for initiating up-front involvement with a supplier. When suppliers feel they need information, they come to Toyota and ask for it. Toyota will tell suppliers what it knows at the time. This initial information often is in the form of approximate "targets," and it is usually communicated with a "rationale" for the targets. Targets differ from specifications in being only approximations, designed to express Toyota's intent.

The supplier is allowed to suggest alternatives to the initial targets. Toyota considers these suggestions in conjunction with suggestions from the suppliers of other related parts and then begins the process of refining the targets. At first a sizable range may be given for the targets and then these ranges are narrowed very gradually. The nominal dimension also may change. Toyota does not guarantee that the final specification will stay within these ranges, and so the supplier does take some risk, but generally the supplier can judge the confidence of the Toyota engineers based on experience gained through a long-term relationship and through consistent and meaningful communication.

An example will help illustrate the process. One Toyota manager discussed air-conditioner design, noting that initially a target may be expressed as *gurai* 2,000 kcal/hr. *Gurai* is roughly translated "about," and although no range is explicitly communicated, the use of *gurai* implies an anticipated deviation from that target of up to 20 or 25 percent. Later, after receiving suggestions and data from the supplier, a range may be explicitly shown on the target, such as 2,000 kcal/hr ± 100, although generally the range is simply implied. Eventually the range is narrowed further, and the nominal target may change until specifications are set (e.g., 1,900 kcal/hr ±10).

Usually targets are expressed in sets that include performance, space, and cost. For example, Toyota would like an air conditioner for ¥100,000 with such and such performance characteristics that can fit into a specified space. Suppliers can make suggestions using these targets as guides, such as "We can give you an air conditioner ¥10,000 cheaper with a slight degradation in performance." The suppliers can use the information that Toyota gives them about the environment to help make intelligent suggestions. For example, Toyota may give its suppliers a layout showing adjacent parts that enables them to understand the spatial constraints and to make intelligent suggestions for possible changes. Clearly, if suppliers can make suggestions that improve performance or other requirements at the same or less cost, this will be greatly appreciated. Toyota considers this information in making its design decisions, which are made in a range-narrowing way. Toyota claims that this narrowing process takes place every day and that it is necessary for suppliers to come to Toyota often in order to·keep abreast of the design's progress. This allows Toyota's suppliers to design their component at the same time that Toyota is determining the specifications. Otherwise they would have to wait for Toyota to establish final, concrete specifications before they could begin.

Cooling-Fan Supplier's View

This example is based on discussions with a Japanese supplier of both cooling-fan blades and clutches for automobiles. The supplier is a large company with approximately 10,000 employees. The diverse company product line consists of more than 20,000 products, of which 94 percent are automotive related. The company has full design, development, and manufacturing capabilities for high-volume production and more than 25 years' experience with CE.

In the early stages of the automobile-development process, Toyota establishes specifications for cooling-fan parameters such as space available and cubic feet per minute (CFM), with an understanding from the OEM that there is a 20 to 30 percent "design tolerance" for each of these parameters; that is, each of the specified parameters (including spatial requirements) may increase or decrease up to 30 percent. This gives the supplier the bounds necessary to explore the feasible design space through the development and testing of approximately 15 fan prototypes. From these prototypes, the design tolerance is temporarily narrowed in order to produce the first engine prototype, four years before production. The 20 to 30 percent design tolerance is maintained, however, during the development of the second engine prototype (three years before production) as the supplier develops approximately 10 additional fan prototypes to explore the set of possible designs. The tolerance on design parameters is narrowed to 5 percent for the development of the third prototype, and it will remain in place until approximately one year before production, at which time the supplier will produce a drawing for the final fan design and specifications for the OEM to approve. During the design process, the supplier may coordinate directly with other suppliers independent of the OEM. During one such development cycle, an extreme case, this supplier produced a total of approximately 30 cooling-fan prototypes.

The design and development process that the supplier employs in conjunction with the OEM clearly sets boundaries on the parameters for cooling-fan designs, and it allows the supplier to explore the feasible designs, as opposed to selecting a single design alternative. The gradual narrowing of the design tolerance as more information becomes available from both fan and car prototypes is representative of a set-based design process.

Exhaust-System Supplier's View

We also talked to managers at a large supplier of exhaust systems for Toyota. This supplier receives approximate figures for basic requirements about 30 months before production. These figures are vague and may change by as much as 20 percent. During the next three months, the supplier is busy exploring different designs, building prototypes, and testing them. Typically it generates about 10, and sometimes as many as 50, different designs (generally minor variants on a basic design).

The knowledge that the supplier accumulates through testing the various prototypes is used to help Toyota establish the targets for the exhaust-system requirements. This supplier claimed that Toyota demands a great deal of test data to quantify the trade-offs associated with all the various constraints (e.g., noise level versus back pressure, cost versus performance). Targets are established around 27 months before production, but even at this point the targets are flexible, up to 5 percent. Sometimes intervals are given with the targets. The supplier continues to develop alternatives that explore the design space in these interval ranges, and it feeds the test data back to Toyota.

The design is released nine months before production begins. If the manufacturing process already exists, there is no need for CE (because much of the process has been designed), and so the process design begins at this time. If a new manufacturing process is needed, design of the manufacturing process will start much earlier, at roughly 20 months before production starts, which is often even before the customer has set specifications. However, the manufacturing people are involved even earlier in the design process, to comment on the product design, 24 months, at the latest, before production.

Both the exhaust-system and cooling-fan suppliers expend a tremendous amount of energy in order to understand the design space and the environment. The suppliers' results are then communicated to the customer so that the customer can better understand the implications of each design alternative and make wise decisions.

An obvious question now arises: How do Toyota engineers use this information to make decisions? In fact, we asked this question on several occasions, and inevitably the reply was, "It's case by case." Toyota engineers could not describe a general process for making these kinds of decisions. It became clear that Toyota does not have a standardized procedure for analyzing the data and making decisions. Individual decisions are made based on the engineers' professional judgment and experience. Toyota has a significant advantage over many other auto companies in this area because it keeps engineers in the same function for many years. It is clear that Toyota engineers know their cars, and they know how to make good decisions, even if they cannot describe a standardized decision-making process.

Tying It Together

As mentioned in the discussion on body design, typically the final style is not chosen until 27 months before production starts. Thus the exhaust-system supplier has already done a great deal of design work in helping the customer establish targets even before the concept is approved. Notice the set-based nature of the entire development system: It seems that every major component of the vehicle is explored using many different design alternatives simultaneously. These different design groups are communicating the constraints and characteristics of their respective designs to one another and to the OEM. Decisions are made only when enough is understood about the design space, the constraints, the dependencies, and the environment (e.g., the market). Sets of design alternatives are gradually narrowed until a final solution is reached that strikes the appropriate balance of constraints.

Planning for Breakthroughs at Nippondenso

We also interviewed product engineers and manufacturing-process engineers from the radiator-development division of Nippondenso, the major radiator supplier for Toyota. A similar process was described to us by the alternator engineers at Nippondenso. These engineers told us that radiators could be broken into two parts: the core, which includes the fins and coolant tubing inside the radiator (the core is the actual cooling mechanism), and the periphery parts, which include intake and outlet hoses, mounting devices, and so on. Nippondenso essentially split the design of all their radiators into these two parts.

In the mid-1970s, the radiator designers at Nippondenso decided that it was time for a breakthrough in radiator design. Before getting started, these designers mapped out the history of radiator design, graphing the progress of core weight versus cooling effect over time. Nippondenso's designers projected the trend line 10 years from the most advanced in the industry. They set a target for their upcoming product-development program at the 10–year projection, which happened to be a 50 percent reduction in weight with no sacrifice in cooling effect.

During the next two years, designers developed a single-row radiator design that had the same performance as the previous year's double-row radiator design. An additional year of in-vehicle testing verified this. Nippondenso achieved its objective by placing itself more than 10 years ahead of its competitors.

Nippondenso now had tremendous bargaining power. Automakers like Toyota clearly wanted this new technology because weight is at a premium in vehicle design. Nippondenso did not stop here, however, because weight is not the only consideration—cost also is important. But there was a problem. The savings in standardization can be tremendous—we all know that it is much cheaper to produce 1 million parts of a single design than to produce 200,000 parts each of five designs—but customers like to maintain design flexibility. Another way of putting it is that customers are best satisfied with custom designs for each order, but it is much cheaper to offer only a limited number of standardized designs.

Nippondenso approached the cost/flexibility problem in core design with a philosophy that it termed *standardized variety*. Nippondenso engineers talked to customers (primarily Toyota) to find out what their needs were at the present time and what they anticipated their needs would be in the future. The supplier mapped this information in terms of combinations of core dimensions. It then determined discrete combinations of dimensions that would meet all its customers' needs and standardized these combinations. The key to Nippondenso's ability to offer a large number of combinations was its development of a manufacturing process that could make different-size cores. When customers want to order radiators, they simply determine their needs and then choose the standardized core that best satisfies these needs.

Toyota places high value on customized design. Toyota likes its suppliers to expend great efforts to meet or exceed its needs and expectations rather than simply purchasing a part off the shelf. But because Nippondenso made great efforts to understand Toyota's needs and planned its standardization around those needs, Toyota was willing to accept this method. In addition, Toyota realized great cost savings owing to standardization, plus it wanted this state-of-the-art (single-row) radiator technology in its cars.

The core is only one part of the radiator design, however; the radiator periphery connects the core to the rest of the car. Although the core could be the same from model to model, the periphery is always different because it must be customized to that particular model's packaging. For each new radiator, during the development cycle, Nippondenso generally creates three different designs with 20 to 30 variations on each and builds prototypes for each of these variations and tests them. The customer communicates not only its product requirements but also information about the surrounding and connecting parts so that the supplier better understands the environment in which the radiator will operate.

Nippondenso builds many prototypes in order to help deal with the uncertainty of the car design in its earlier stages. The supplier is able to test its prototypes and feed back the test data to the customer. This process helps Toyota's employees understand the uncertainties they face so that they can make some decisions. As this uncertainty decreases, the number of radiator designs under consideration also decreases. This narrowing procedure continues until finally a single solution is achieved, sometimes by the first vehicle prototype but often between the first and second vehicle prototypes.

There are clear signs of set-based approaches in this example. The supplier spends much time and effort understanding its customers' needs, and it has devised a system to help meet many constraints. We offered two examples: anticipating/predicting breakthroughs in technology that defy previous constraints and striking a proper balance between standardization and customization. All of this developmental work that is done even before the supplier receives an order helps it better understand the design space, and this knowledge can be passed on to the customer to help make good decisions. Regarding the peripheral parts, the supplier explores the design space with the help of many design varieties and prototypes. This set of possibilities is gradually narrowed over time until a final solution is reached.

CONCLUSIONS

Toyota has long understood that its manufacturing practices are unusual: Books on the Toyota production system are common. That system has a well-understood genesis in the work of Taiichi Ohno, a vice president of Toyota. The differences between Toyota's development practices and the world's standard development processes are also fairly clear to Toyota's employees, who regard them as part of the "Toyota way." Toyota did not give much thought to its theoretical underpinnings; rather, they simply evolved.

We went to Toyota looking for indications of a set-based approach, because one of us (Ward) had begun developing a theory of set-based design in the context of design automation. The theory suggested that experience with concurrent engineering should lead to a set-based approach. What we found far exceeded our expectations. Toyota and its suppliers have created a new way of thinking about design, as unique and important as its new way of thinking about manufacturing.

These startling differences suggest that much of the conventional wisdom about concurrent engineering is misguided, that many of the perceived trade-offs can be avoided or ameliorated. CE does not necessarily require dedicated, colocated teams (with the concomitant risk of loss of specialized expertise), nor does it need a highly structured (and rigid) development process. CE communications can be both very effective and quite efficient, and most work can be done independently. Consensus-oriented, highly reliable decisions can be combined with powerful, creative design leadership. A thorough exploration of the design space, leading to highly optimized designs, can be combined with a very fast and efficient process: You *can* have it "cheap, good, and fast," but you must change the conceptual paradigm under which you conduct the development process.

ACKNOWLEDGMENTS

We would like to acknowledge the generous cooperation of all the U.S. and Japanese companies we interviewed for this study. We would especially like to thank Toyota Motor Company, which opened its doors three times and helped us gain entry to some of its key suppliers. What we say in this chapter about Toyota's practices reflect our views, not the official views of Toyota. In fact, we were warned by Toyota against holding up its design process as exemplary because it was not convinced that it had the best design approach.

REFERENCES

Clark, K. B., & Fujimoto, T. (1991). *Product development performance.* Boston: Harvard Business School Press.

Chapman, W. L., Bahill, A. T., & Wymore, A. W. (1992). *Engineering modeling and design.* Boca Raton, FL: CRC Press.

Chrysler LH team struts its stuff. (1992, March). *Ward's Auto World, 28,* 37–62.

Concurrent engineering. (1991, July). *IEEE Spectrum,* 22–38.

Nevins, J. L., & Whitney, D. E. (1989). *Concurrent design of products and processes.* New York: McGraw-Hill.

Ward, A., & Seering, W. (1989a). The performance of a mechanical design compiler. *Proceedings of the 1989 International Conference on Engineering Design* (pp. 142–148). London.

Ward, A., & Seering, W. (1989b). Quantitative inference in a mechanical design compiler. *Proceedings of the First International ASME Conference on Design Theory and Methodology,* (pp. 89–98). Montreal.

Womack, J. P., Jones, D. T., & Roos, D. (1990). *The machine that changed the world.* New York: Macmillan.

9

Competing in the Old-Fashioned Way: Localizing and Integrating Knowledge Resources in Fast-to-Market Competition

W. MARK FRUIN

Although the basic ingredients for market success in manufacturing have not changed exceptionally in the last 50 years—price, quality, and availability fairly well cover all the bases—time to market has changed remarkably. Being first to market or, at least, fast to market in rapidly changing, technically driven industries is increasingly critical as product life cycles are shortening and consumer preferences are multiplying. In these circumstances "late to market" all too often means "dead in the market."

Even as time-to-market capabilities become more and more important to competitive survival and success, all firms are not created equal in their technology-management capabilities or in the speed with which these can be mobilized; price, quality, and availability, that is, the conditions of today's globalized competition, are roughly comparable, the winning firms are fast to market. Time-based competition is critical even when proprietary know-how and property rights are important, because of a general upgrading and standardization of product development and the R&D capabilities of large firms around the world.

Historically, Japanese firms were not time-based competitors. Rather, they industrialized on the basis of what was already known elsewhere. Knowledge was bought, borrowed, and begged from abroad, reverse engineered, adapted, and modified to local circumstances. For the first five or six decades of the twentieth century, as a result, Japanese products were competitive only when there were no product substitutes and Western products were lacking with regard to price, quality, and availability. Being first to market or fast to market was not important.

Now all of that has changed. Beginning in the 1960s and certainly by the 1970s, not only were the price, quality, and availability of Japanese products often superior to those of Western competitors, but by the 1980s, they appeared more quickly and were updated more often. By the 1990s, Japanese firms secured a worldwide reputation as fearsome time-based competitors brandishing well-executed, fast-to-market strategies and banishing more and more would-be competitors to less demanding markets (Clark & Fujimoto, 1991; Womack, Jones, & Roos, 1990).

Timing has a lot to do with how Japanese firms can do it faster. Global time-based competition in the 1980s emerged shortly after Japanese industrials had met price, quality, and availability conditions, as seen in their mastery of scale and scope economies in manufacturing. That mastery was related to the localization and integration of knowledge resources at the factory level of organization. Japanese firms simply continued to do what they already did well, only they did so more quickly and more economically, thus competing in the old-fashioned way.

In this chapter, we offer an organizational explanation for how Japanese firms accomplished this transformation. How did relatively small and generally outclassed firms that could only be called historical and technical laggards transform themselves into world-class, time-based technology leaders and managers? A supreme sleight of hand, an Ultraman's (Urutoraman) *henshin?* (Urutoraman, a popular Japanese sci-fi character, modifies his functional capabilities by changing his appearance.) My answer mimics John Houseman's television advertisements for Paine Webber. "How do they do it?" he asks (meaning How does Paine Webber make money for you?) "The old-fashioned way," he rasps, "They earn it." They do it themselves.

THE S-CURVE AND TIME-BASED COMPETITION

An S-curve describes the basic elements in technology-based competition. The S-curve depicts an upward-sloping, curvilinear relationship between the costs and requirements for technology development (the vertical axis) and product–process applications (the horizontal axis). Essentially, the more useful and appropriable a technology is, the larger the sunk costs in technology acquisition, adaptation, and application will be.

Historically, Japanese firms jumped on the technology bandwagon somewhere along the steeply rising midsection to the top end of the S-curve. That is, they acquired well-developed, existing technology and modified it to fit Japanese circumstances. Noguchi Jun's role in the founding and development of Nichitsu, one of the largest chemical companies of the prewar period, offers a perfect case in point. Nichitsu was the first firm in Japan to produce ammonium sulfates from calcium cyanamides. The ammonium sulfates technology in question was imported lock, stock, and barrel from Germany. Although Noguchi must be given his due, his role was more entrepreneurial than technical. The same could be said of Toyoda Kiichiro, the founder of the Toyota Motor Company (see Molony, 1989, on Noguchi, and Fruin, 1992, on Toyoda).

In addition to Noguchi and Toyoda, the list of technology entrepreneurs, as opposed to technology pioneers, could be extended almost indefinitely until, of course, Japanese firms caught up with their Western counterparts and technology acquisition had to be replaced by technology generation. Depending on the industry in question, this happened sometime during the 1960s in the case of textiles, shipbuilding, cameras, and most other optical goods; the 1970s for structural ceramics, consumer electronics, and motor vehicles; and the 1980s for memory chips, electronic controls, and information-processing devices.

S-curve competition is not confined to how fast one can move up the curve. Moving across the curve also becomes critical once firms realize the state of the art with regard to a particular technology. State of the art really means a kind of plateau, a maturation or leveling off in the process of technology development and a standardization of technique across many firms. Competitively speaking, once large numbers of firms reach a technology plateau, they are forced to do something better, quicker, and decidedly different in order to distinguish themselves from equally endowed competitors (Abernathy & Utterback, 1975).

Better, quicker, and decidedly different often means moving across the S-curve, bringing out new versions of products and combinations with existing technology but doing it faster and cheaper and in more interesting ways than rival firms do. Intergenerational product competition becomes the norm. For example, little distinguishes mainstream Ford, Chevrolet, and Nissan products except that Nissan hits the street with the same technology well before Ford and Chevy do. Nissan's Maxima four-door sedan was essentially a family sports car with a high-revving V-6 engine, McPherson struts, and full wishbone suspension. Maxima dominated the family sports car market in the mid-1980s until Ford and Chevy responded with their own versions, such as the four-door Sable and Grand Prix models, a full-model cycle later. Even then, it may be argued that the Sable and Grand Prix models never quite lived up to the market niche created by Nissan's Maxima. In motor vehicles as in electronics, fast-to-market product strategies carry the day, forcing rival firms to fit their products to the dominant firm's preemptive definition of the market.

Whether one is moving up or across the S-curve, the speed with which functional, organizational, and informational requirements for rapid technology transfer are met is crucial. Localizing and integrating knowledge resources speed up the technology transfer process. Localization and integration refer to the consolidation of technical, organizational, and informational resources; all required resources for research, design, development, engineering, prototyping, scaled-up production, and even marketing are juxtaposed in the same facility or in closely aligned facilities. Multiple functions and activities are unified and integrated by means of iterative, interactive, and positive feedback loops.

The degree to which resources may be (and should be) consolidated and integrated varies by product strategy and by industry. The general rule is simple enough, however. The more important that time to market is as a competitive factor, the more important that the localizing and integrating efforts will be. In contemporary Japan, product life cycles of three to six months are typical in low-end consumer electronics and optical goods, handheld and laptop information processors, and fashion garments. But even in less extreme cases, an ability to cut 10 or 20 percent from product development and scaled-up production cycles can make all the difference. Witness Toyota's unparalleled success in upstaging rival firms in the motor vehicle industry (Clark & Fujimoto, 1991).

No matter what the industry, when time to market is critical, there is a generic strategy for localizing and integrating knowledge resources. In this chapter, I describe the strategy. Although most detailed facts and figures are based on my fieldwork observations at and internal documentation from the Toshiba Corporation and one of its main factories, the Yanagi-cho Works, I am confident that the general model can be applied throughout the electronics industry and even more generally to technology-driven industries in which being first to market and fast to market are decisive.

The Long March to Time-Based Competiveness

The Yanagicho Works' long march to fast-to-market competitiveness began 25 years ago. By the late 1960s, Yanagicho was already producing electromechanical typewriters, mail-sorting equipment with optical character recognition (OCR) capabilities, and lots of desktop and handheld calculators. Freezers, refrigerators, and food display cabinets were also manufactured at Yanagicho, but they had little in common with information and office products like typewriters, sorters, and calculators. In the early 1970s, most refrigeration products were moved to Toshiba's Nagoya Works.

The intense developmental activities that were focused on the manufacture of photocopiers, automatic mail sorting, railroad ticket equipment, and other precision, paper-handling, labor-saving devices at Yanagicho during the late 1960s and 1970s transformed the factory into a knowledge works, a factory where the generation and accumulation of knowledge and know-how were as important as the output and throughput of products. A shorthand for this learning orientation is multifunction and multiproduct organizational competence.

Multifunction, multiproduct organizational competence was and is a long time coming. The key point is that Yanagicho was not established as a knowledge works. Rather, it became one by combining large-scale manufacturing experience (mostly for calculators and household appliances) with intense design, development, and engineering activities (mostly for photocopiers and automatic mail-sorting equipment). Markets for high-tech products—products that typically require multifunctional capabilities—are characteristically volatile, often treacherously so. Thus a decision to concentrate design, development, and engineering resources for the manufacture of technically demanding products is a high-risk, high-cost decision.

In this regard, how much easier it is to have built up competence and capabilities during the scale-oriented manufacturing era of the 1960s and 1970s than to take the plunge during the 1980s and 1990s, when scope economies appear to have displaced scale economies as the primary drivers of manufacturing strategy! (My argument here diverges from that of Piore and Sabel, 1984.) By the end of the 1980s, 80 percent of Toshiba's 27 factories in Japan had adopted some form of the knowledge works architecture. Clearly, general notions of how to calibrate and balance product scale and scope are being developed at Toshiba.

KNOWLEDGE WORKS: THE BASIC ARCHITECTURE

The knowledge-works architecture ultimately consolidates six distinct industrial functions—research and development, design, engineering, production, product management, and marketing—into one operational structure. That is, anything and everything from applied research, prototyping, testing, quality assurance, production, market planning, evaluation, and feedback may be done on site.

Saying so, simply and straightforwardly, conceals the long developmental cycle that precedes the organizational architecture; rather, it is the art and wisdom and the strategy behind it. For organizations as well as for people, experience is an expensive but good teacher. A long period of trial, error, and experimentation in adapting, adjusting, and modifying different organizational forms and technical and managerial functions precedes the successful localization and integration of knowledge resources. That history is crucial. Without it, fast-to-market factories cannot identify what works best in any given production setup or market situation. With it, "what works best" confers competitive advantage, something hard to appropriate and even harder to emulate.

Fast-to-market factories typically encompass multiple functions and multiple products in integrated sites unified around the centrality of production and the proximity of technical and organizational resources. Instead of discrete, essentially disconnected steps in a long process of R&D, design, product development, engineering, manufacturing, and marketing, the entire process, from beginning to end, is accomplished neatly and nearly continuously within well-organized and managed boundaries. This is the linked-chain or multiple-functions model, as seen in Figure 9.1.

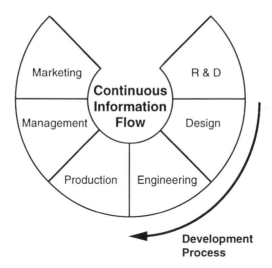

Figure 9.1. The linked-chain or multiple-functions model.

Site Specificity

Multifunctionality is site specific insofar as the multiple functions refer to the design, engineering, testing, manufacture, and marketing of particular products and product families. Site specificity for a computer maker, as an example, might be knowing how to interlace sophisticated hardware requirements with well-specified sales engineering detail and when to train, motivate, and involve employees in these activities. Such details require hands-on management and front-line decision making because only those directly involved—the planners, designers, developers, and operators familiar with the product and the production process—are able to accurately and quickly alter product specifications, process requirements, and marketing guidelines.

Capabilities of this sort represent aesthetic acts in some sense, at once both site and relation specific. That is, each new generation of products demands ever higher levels of design, development, processing know-how, information sharing, and sense making from workers, engineers, and managers. In rapidly changing technical fields, design, development, and processing know-how are really arts in the making. This is equally true of such fields as solid-state physics, molecular biology, genetic engineering, and advanced structural ceramics, any field in which leading-edge knowledge is as much art as science.

But art is not borne in nothingness. Workmanship, intuition, feel, discipline, practice, and style make a difference, not once in a while but all along the value chain of product design and development. Because these qualities are tied to particular products and processes and to particular persons who manage product and process flow, a rich, sticky, textured culture always characterizes factories with high levels of intangible asset specificity. What holds together this asset specificity or art in the making is the technical, organizational, managerial, and strategic know-how that is embodied in a particular knowledge-works form.

Obviously, employees are the transforming force underlying knowledge works. Hence, employees with the "right" knowledge, know-how, and knack are found more often in production sites charged with accelerating specific product design and development cycles in technically intensive industries. The strategic importance of site specificity and knowledge intensivity cannot be exaggerated in these industries, and the search for these qualities recommends the intentional localization and integration of functions and activities at one site and the training, motivating, and managing of human-specific resources there.

Relation Specificity

Site specificity and knowledge intensivity create a countervailing need for focus, specialization, and a reasonable division of labor. These factors are realized by situating multiple functions and multiple products in single "factory" sites and, at the same time, nurturing a network of supporting organizations that are tied relationally to developmental and production cycles at core sites (Asanuma, 1989). In other words, multiple functions and products are a combination of on-site, factory-specific resources and off-site, relation-specific networks of suppliers. The interrelation of these, made possible by the permeability of interorganizational boundaries, is the strategic core of the knowledge-works architecture.

Multifunction, multiproduct capabilities are relation specific; that is, they are tied to a set of on-site/off-site interorganizational relations. A basic tenet of relation specificity is that knowledge and practice are inseparable. Their connection and fusion may be reworked, even strengthened, through annealing processes of repeated knowledge acquisition and application. The intense, dense, and durable interorganizational transactions binding core suppliers and assemblers in Japan often result in ever tighter orchestrations of mutually beneficial economic activities (Fruin, 1992).

Note the differences between knowledge works and traditional models of manufacturing organization. Knowledge works are neither a functional organization with appended product departments nor a matrix structure with intersecting functional and product nodes. Functional capabilities are subsumed under product departments for the most part, as shown in Figure 9.2; more general technical and operational decisions are the responsibility of factory management.

Organizing for Multiple Functions and Products

Multiple products may range from numerous models of the same product, such as Toyota's full line of motor vehicles—sport coupes, two- and four-

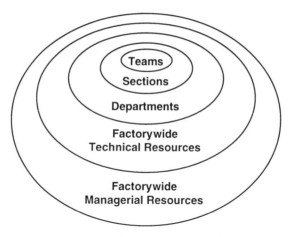

Figure 9.2. The Doughnut-ring or multiple-products model.

door sedans, luxury GTOs, light utility vehicles—to products that are rather different in form, function, and features but happen nevertheless to be manufactured at the same site, such as Yanagicho's SuperSmart cards, photocopiers, ATMs, automatic railroad validation, and mail-sorting equipment. Yanagicho's diverse product line is representative of Toshiba's manufacturing organization and strategy. Hitachi's production is organized similarly to Toshiba's, whereas Matsushita Electric Industrial's (MEI) is less factory focused (Fruin, 1992). Most of MEI's product is sourced from organizationally independent but financially dependent original-equipment manufacturers (OEMs).

In fact, an examination of 16 Toshiba factories (60% of the domestic total) reveals that during the 1990/91 fiscal year, half had 12 or more distinct product lines (and dozens of different product models). In some cases, an incredible 19, 20, 21, or 23 different product lines per site may be found (Toshiba factory brochures, 1990–92). The more product lines there are, the more likely a factory is serving two or more corporate divisions. Less obviously, the more product lines and corporate divisions that are served by a single site, the more authority it wields, the more responsibility it shoulders, and the more strategic its role is in determining corporate performance and market success (Fruin, In Press).

As illustrated in Figure 9.3, the linked-chain or multiple-functions model is actually embedded in the doughnut-ring or multiple-products model. This means that functionality is subsumed under department organization in multiproduct manufacturing sites. However, when products are similar—actually model variations on a single theme—whole factories may be geared toward making a family of products. Toyota Motor is a prime example of focusing design, engineering, and marketing around a single production function. In such cases, cross-functional collaboration is really a question of the effectiveness of interdepartmental coordination.

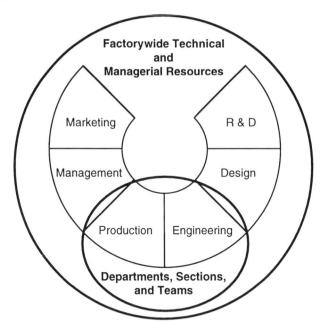

Figure 9.3. The multiple-functions model overlaid by the multiple-products model.

When products are not so similar, however, cross-functional collaboration is realized by product departments dedicated to the design, development, manufacture, and marketing of particular products. *Intramural* rather than interdepartmental coordination becomes key. Electrical/electronic assembly operations are much more of this sort, as shown by the product line count in Toshiba factories (Toshiba factory brochures, 1990–92). Synthetic fibers, memory chips, nonelectric machinery, measuring and calculating instruments, telecommunications products, and certain biotechnology applications mirror Toshiba's product diversity and product department robustness at the factory level of organization. Given the pervasiveness of multiple product factories in Japan, single product models of manufacturing organization and strategy seriously underrepresent the complexity of the contemporary situation (Imai, Nonaka, & Takeuchi, 1985).

In multifunction, multiproduct sites, when intramural resources prove inadequate, extramural yet within-factory resources may be called upon. Additional design, testing, or manufacturing engineers, for example, may be temporarily transferred from one factory department to another or from staff offices of functional specialists for as long as more focus, specialization, and product-specific know-how are needed. These are temporary resources, however, on loan until production runs fully and steadily again. Once this happens, engineers and technicians are returned to home departments or reassigned according to need.

Product department managers, therefore, are concerned primarily with the effectiveness of intramural, cross-functional, information-sharing processes at the local level. At the same time, department walls are open to "outsiders," both managerial and technical, and regular factorywide activities ensure the permeability of internal organizational boundaries. Factory managers are mainly free to concern themselves with the overall balance of factorywide resources.

Like nested yet interconnected (permeated) doughnut rings, tasks are demarcated by organizational boundaries separating shop-floor teams from technical support sections; product departments from factorywide research, design, and development departments; and technical units from managerial units. From shop-floor workers to factory managers, as many as six or seven levels of organizaton may be found in multiproduct plants because of the functional and managerial complexities associated with so many different product lines. Yet in the final analysis, teams, sections, and departments are enveloped and nourished by a factory's centrality, complementary resources, and wide-ranging capabilities. The linked-chain model of functional integration is embedded in the doughnut-ring model of multiple-product organization.

Fast-to-Market Contingencies

To reiterate the argument so far, richly endowed, well-bounded, and managed knowledge works attempt to contain market uncertainty and technical demands by balancing the push and pull of multiple functions—R&D, design, engineering, manufacturing, management, and marketing activities—with multiple products. Localizing and integrating so much at single sites creates the following three sources of operational diversity and managerial complexity.

Market Pull

The length of production runs of products' life cycles varies considerably. For example, product life cycles may be as brutally short as six months (radio cassettes) or as long as 10 years (power generators) in the same electrical equipment/electronics industry. Given such rate differences, a factor of 20 to 1 in these two cases, a proper mix of products and an appropriate balance among them at single manufacturing sites are hard to find and harder to hold onto.

Product–Process Complexity

Design and systems-engineering requirements vary enormously from product to product, despite apparent similarities in appearance, form, and function. One- and four-megabyte chips look a lot alike, but in fact they are not. Standardizing design, parts supply, and process know-how is critical to minimizing these differences, in finding and maintaining balance in operations, and thus in maximizing site-specific scale, scope, and learning economies.

Complexity may be measured in various ways: by the parts count per final unit of assembly, by the degree of parts similarity among models of the same product family, by the kind and amount of supplier value-added contributions to manufacturing costs, and by the level of automation and systems engineering in the design and manufacturing processes.

Technology Push

The strength of association between near-term and intermediate-term R&D and current production is an important indicator of how much technical continuity exists in upstream and downstream functions. Technology push depends on industry maturation, length of product life cycles, frequency of innovation, and whether innovations are induced from inside or outside the industry. There is far more continuity in the motor vehicle industry than in microelectronics, for example, and the technology push is comparatively less as a result.

Conceptually speaking, markets, product–process complexity, and technology generate cycle or rate differences. Obviously, formal points of balance in synchronizing many different technical, functional, and product cycles and in replenishing rate-dependent resources are difficult to find and just as likely to be lost. Toshiba's day-to-day answer for this high-wire balancing act is to group products that are sufficiently similar in technical aspects and engineering, so that one product's wobble and axis resonance—market gain or slip, manufacturing triumph or snafu—does not bring down the rest. Knowledge works spread risk across families of products, quite unlike a single-product factory's solution to the problem of dynamic balance.

The combination of multiple functions (linked-chain model) and multiple products (doughnut-ring model) yields production sites that are organizationally complex, technically versatile, functionally robust, and managerially and strategically integrated. This synthesis, so simple in concept, so widespread in Japan, is unrivaled worldwide because it reflects country-specific patterns of organizational and strategic evolution: the later industrialization of Japan, the unprecedented economic growth of the postwar years, and an extraordinary concentration of wealth and consumption in the urban corridor joining Tokyo and Osaka. Comparable manufacturing sites and programs to Toshiba's knowledge works, such as 3M's prototype plant in St. Paul or Dow Chemical's overall manufacturing strategy may be found in the West, but the issue is really one of pervasiveness. How widely and how well is the knowledge-works model of localization and integration followed? It is a general model in Japan but not elsewhere. The coincidence of environmental factors, as outlined earlier in regard to the evolution of large Japanese industrials, has inspired a widespread adoption of the knowledge-works form as a means of surviving and succeeding in fast-to-market competition.

INNOVATION ARCHITECTURES: VARIATIONS ON A THEME

Champion-Line Model

The balance of functions and products is not a midpoint, a mean, or an average of everything attempted. Thus, in knowledge works, not all products and processes are created equal. Indeed, some are clearly more equal than others. Although equality or importance may be measured in various ways, such as by the value that a product contributes to a factory's output, the amount of floor space dedicated to different products, or the number of employees assigned to different sections, importance in fast-to-market factories is more directly related to the degree that knowledge resources are localized and integrated. The question of degree is not often visible to the naked eye.

It may be argued that certain products or processes have had more significance than others in the evolution of a particular plant's engineering and manufacturing capabilities. For example, during the 1960s and 1970s, televisions, refrigerators, washing machines, calculators, pocket radios, and cassette players were produced in huge volumes in Japan. To run fully and steadily with very little slack, high quality and reliability, design and engineering resources were concentrated and dedicated to particular products. Hence, scale-oriented manufacturing gave certain products and processes more significance and weight than others. As a result of making a few products in high volume and in especially demanding ways, these products assumed unusual importance in the evolution of a factory's manufacturing know-how and capabilities.

In other words, organizational learning is not an abstract activity but a concrete one. Yanagicho's plain-paper copiers (PPC) reflect this kind of importance; in the fast-to-market genre of manufacturing, this kind of importance is more the rule than the exception. That is, a factory's asset endowment, technology-management system, and product–process mix are rooted in a particular manufacturing experience. The value of PPC manufactures in the overall factory output, accounting for approximately 50 percent of Yanagicho's total production value during the 1980s, underscores the weightiness for Yanagicho of making photocopiers.

For knowledge spillover to nourish related products, scale-oriented manufacturing experiences with *particular* products and processes are necessary. That is, a threshold of multifunctional activity must be realized in *one* product area before other products can benefit from the experience. In Yanagicho's case, photocopier manufacture was the scale-oriented experience that allowed the factory to garner and enhance technical capabilities and organizational resources as a multifunction production site. PPC manufacture paid the freight for the rest of the delivery. Toshiba photocopiers have to contend with the likes of Canon, Mita, Minolta, Ricoh, Sharp, and Fuji Xerox in this market segment, all companies that are more dependent on photocopier sales than Toshiba is. Even so, Toshiba has to be as good or nearly as good as they are in photocopier design, development, and manufacture. This competitive reality translates into a necessity or, rather, a strategy of creating knowledge works–like capabilities.

The centrality of PPC production also indicates some practical difficulties of balancing organizational resources across a spectrum of many products and functions. What it takes to make a topflight PPC is not really what it takes to produce a high-quality laser beam printer (LBP), for example, in spite of the obvious similarities, technical and otherwise, of the two products. Although it seems possible, even desirable, to link the design, development, and manufacture of PPCs and LBPs, in fact it is not at all desirable to do so.

The key components and product strategies for PPCs and LBPs diverge dramatically. Selenium drums are key for high-performance PPCs, laser diodes for LBPs. Also, printed circuit board layout, design, and function are different for the two products. PPCs product life cycles are about six months in Japan; that is, within half a year, rival firms will bring out similar products that compete favorably on price and features. LBPs product life cycles are two or three times longer despite relatively greater intergenerational product differences (as compared with PPCs) and a relatively less mature market for laser beam office equipment (Fruin, 1994). Given these rate differences in development and production cycles for PPCs and LBPs, separate product-development and manufacturing departments are called for, even if they are located in the same factory. Hence, the champion-line product for conferring a focus and direction to a factory's technical and organizational evolution is important. The centrality of the PPC's multifunctionality to an overall mix of functional and technical resource is indicated by the shaded areas in Figure 9.4.

Yanagicho's PPC line—its champion line—guarantees a scale of activities in development, design, engineering, tool and die making, and manufacture that enriches and nourishes the development and manufacture of many related products, including LBPs. In this example and many others, scale and volume, pure and simple, count because a certain level of activity has to be realized, sustained, and reflected on (*kaizen*-ed) in order for cross-product knowledge to be transferred and to spill over. Ultimately, the assembly of PPCs became a platform for the design and manufacture of numerous other products, including laser beam printers, railroad ticket validation equipment, ATM machines, and cash-handling devices.

Balanced-Line Model

Aside from the champion-line architecture, in which a single product dominates the overall product mix and resource endowment, another architecture, the balanced-line model, spreads resources and capabilities across an entire landscape of products and departments. Toshiba's Hino Works, at which a variety of telephones, small telecommunication devices, and pri-

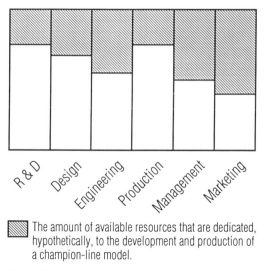

The amount of available resources that are dedicated, hypothetically, to the development and production of a champion-line model.

Figure 9.4. The champion-line model.

vate branch exchanges are manufactured, is a balanced-line factory. The process–product requirements associated with any particular product line does not dominate the asset endowment and technical development activities of a knowledge-oriented factory.

At first glance, this architecture may appear similar to the "focused-factory" concept of product shops, sometimes referred to as the *plant-within-plants* (PWP) genre of manufacturing organization. Although some integration of activities, such as purchasing, transport, and administrative information processing, may be sought in the PWP model, the focused-factory concept does not capture the boundary-spanning mechanisms, the knowledge centrality and intensity, and thus the full-function capabilities of the knowledge-works model (Aguren & Edgren, 1980; Harmon & Peterson, 1990; Skinner, 1974). Instead, limited resources are decentralized around organizational subunits according to specific product and process manufacturing requirements.

To review the knowledge-works thesis, product department boundaries are central even while a dialectic of unit-specific and factorywide activities keeps boundaries open and permeable, as illustrated by the numerous productivity, safety, and quality assurance campaigns that cut across product, R&D, and management departments in Toshiba's factories (Fruin, 1994). The factorywide mandate in favor of multiple functions and products distinguishes the knowledge works from PWP models.

In the balanced-line model, as in the champion-line model, stabililty and symmetry are essential, only more so. Product and functional requirements are more or less in balance at any single time, relative to their contributions to and demands against the allocation of resources (as seen in Figure 9.5). Yet balancing multiple-product resource allocations is never easy.

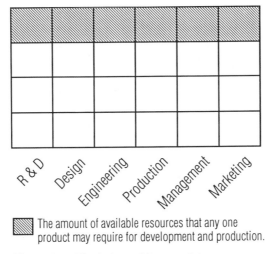

R & D   Design   Engineering   Production   Management   Marketing

▨ The amount of available resources that any one
product may require for development and production.

Figure 9.5. The balanced-line model.

One department may request more funds for researching media substrates for optical disk drives, for example, whereas another wants more testing of an engineering sample of selenium drums, and still another seeks training in application software for its sales engineers. All along the way, departments are competing for resources, and it becomes extremely difficult to maintain stability and symmetry in such circumstances.

Ironically enough, in the long run, the champion-line architecture is more stable than the balanced-line architecture. In champion-line factories, resources and capabilities are more obviously weighed in favor of particular products and processes; such priorities free both department and factory managers from the troubling tasks of always trying to balance resources, prioritize demands, and negotiate budgets. Most important, champion-line dominance is negotiated, not imposed.

In the extremely long run, however, both champion-line and balanced-line models are inherently unstable because of the unpredictability of markets, technological discontinuity, and product obsolescence. So a regular oscillation between the two is likely. Yet it is easier to have an identifiable focus or fulcrum for planning and coordination, and hence, in most instances, the champion-line model predominates. This preference does not appear to eliminate the need for regular change and reorientation, but it does lengthen the cycle after which a major organizational renewal is required.

CLOSING THOUGHTS

Competing in the old-fashioned way means just that. Before science- and technology-based competition became preeminent and thus before geographical, organizational, and informational research and development were separated from production and marketing, corporate resources were localized and integrated in one or a few sites (Graham & Pruett, 1991). Localization and integration, classical processes in U-form or unitary firms, merged corporate activities around the provision of a single dominant product or, at best, a few related product lines. A limited product range coupled with a consolidation of resources to support them meant that the firms did it themselves. They added value in the old-fashioned way, as intoned by John Houseman.

The rise of large industrial firms making and selling multiple product lines killed the unitary or U-firm approach to management. M-form or multidivisional firms advanced by creating internal but separate divisional organizations for managing different product lines. Such a specialization and separation of functions through the creation of product divisions happened nearly three-quarters of a century ago for major Western firms but considerably more recently for large Japanese ones.

DuPont, General Motors, and General Electric, the leading advocates of the M-form transformation, pioneered divisional forms of organization and management during the interwar years between World Wars I and II. Asahi Chemical, Toyota Motor, and Hitachi, their Japanese counterparts, did not adopt M-form-like structures until the 1960s and 1970s. More pointedly, some argue that large Japanese firms are not truly M-form, even today (Chandler, 1962, 1977, 1990; Fruin, 1992).

Whenever and wherever M-form firms are the norm, research labs, product-testing facilities, engineering services, design centers, quality-assurance programs, and one after another value-adding operations are separated from the corporate core for each product division. A specialization of tasks and a division of labor prosper even as the speed with which corporate resources may be mobilized suffers. But Japanese industrial firms have not pursued a division of labor to the same degree as comparable American and European industrials have, and as a result, they are not as skewed toward the M-firm end of the U-firm/M-firm continuum.

Histories of organizational change and development are important because time-based competition has changed the strategic basis for and importance of technology management. Today the race is to the quick and bold, assuming, of course, that price, quality, and availability are acceptable. Japanese firms met price, quality, and availability conditions by the third quarter of the twentieth century, and subsequently they plunged ahead and shaped the conditions under which first-to-market and fast-to-market competition made sense.

These conditions are the localization and integration of a firm's knowledge resources, especially when engineering and technical progress are intimately tied to manufacturing practice. In Japan, the maturation of manufacturing practice coincided with the globalization of markets in such a way that industrial firms moved directly to time-based competition without adopting full-fledged vertical integration and product-diversification strategies, as in M-form firms.

Toshiba's technology-management strategy fits the general Japanese model of localizing and integrating knowledge resources by aligning full-function capabilities in multiproduct plants and by delegating sufficient managerial authority at the factory level of organization to wield those capabilities quickly, decisively, and well. This is competing in the old-fashioned way, closer to a U-form than an M-form firm strategy. Without a successful consolidation of knowledge resources in time-based competition, as in Toshiba's knowledge works, one might as well run with the hares and hunt with the hounds. In other words, one might as well attempt the impossible.

REFERENCES

Abernathy, W. J., & Utterback, J. M. (1975). A dynamic model of process and product innovation. *Omega, 3*, 3–6, 639–56.

Aguren, S., & Edgren, J. (1980). *New factories.* Stockholm: Swedish Employers' Confederation.

Asanuma, B. (1989). Manufacturer–supplier relationships in Japan and the concept of relation-specific skill. *Journal of Japanese and International Economies, 3*, 1–30.

Chandler, A. D., Jr. (1962). *Strategy and structure.* Cambridge, MA: MIT Press.

Chandler, A. D., Jr. (1977). *The visible hand.* Cambridge, MA: Harvard University Press.

Chandler, A. D., Jr. (1990). *Scale and scope.* Cambridge, MA: Harvard University Press.

Clark, K., & Fujimoto, T. (1991). *Product development performance.* Boston: Harvard Business School Press.

Fruin, W. M. (1992). *The Japanese enterprise system.* New York: Oxford University Press.

Fruin, W. M. (1994). Good fences make good neighbors—Organizational property rights and permeability in product development strategies in Japan. In Y. Doz (Ed.), *Managing technology and innovation for corporate renewal.* New York: Oxford University Press.

Fruin, W. M. (In Press). *Knowledge works.* New York: Oxford University Press.

Graham, M. W. B., & Pruett, B. (1991). *R&D for industry.* Cambridge: Cambridge University Press.

Harmon, R. L., & Peterson, L. D. (1990). *Reinventing the factory.* New York: Basic Books.

Imai, K., Nonaka, I., & Takeuchi, H. (1985). Managing the new product development process: How Japanese companies learn and unlearn. In K. B. Clark, R. H. Hayes, & C. Lorenz (Eds.), *The uneasy alliance.* (pp. 337–375). Boston: Harvard Business School Press.

Molony, B. (1989). Innovation and strategy in the prewar chemical industry. In K. Nakagawa & T. Yui (Eds.), *Japanese management in historical perspective.* (pp. 141–166). Tokyo: University of Tokyo Press.

Piore, M., & Sabel, C. (1984). *The second industrial divide.* New York: Basic Books.

Skinner, W. (1974, May–June). The focused factory. *Harvard Business Review*, 113–21.

Toshiba Corporation. (1990/91). Toshiba factory product brochures and catalogues.

Womack, J., Jones, D. T., & Roos, D. (1990). *The machine that changed the world.* New York: Macmillan.

III

MANUFACTURING METHODS
AND MANAGEMENT

10

Producing a World-Class Automotive Body

PATRICK C. HAMMETT,
WALTON M. HANCOCK,
AND JAY S. BARON

As competition in the automotive industry increases, more car production subsystems are being analyzed for potential advantages in cost, quality, and lead time. One subsystem that is being studied is the production of the automotive body, or the body-in-white. Body-in-white fabrication includes all the manufacturing processes required to produce a steel car body before the painting operation. Three major body-in-white processes are die development (planning, designing, building and trying out dies), part fabrication (stamping), and the assembly (welding) of stamped components. In this chapter, we briefly discuss the manufacturing methods and management practices used in each of these processes.

The importance of car-body quality to the customer is reflected by its inclusion in the automotive marketing strategy. For example, in a commercial for Lexus, a ball bearing is rolled between the car's exterior body components (e.g., hood, doors, fenders, trunk), implying a high-quality automotive body with tight, consistent body gaps. (A car-body gap is the space between two exterior components, such as a door and fender.) Nissan responded with a similar commercial emphasizing a high-quality car body on a lower-end vehicle, the Altima. These advertisements highlight two body-in-white quality indicators, body gap flushness and parallelism. In another body-in-white–related advertisement, Chrysler emphasized the noise that the driver does *not* hear inside the cab of a Jeep Cherokee. In this commercial, a Cherokee owner is sitting inside a truck cab in complete silence. The owner then opens the door and hears loud sounds from nature and a waterfall, suggesting that the car body is sealed so well that the driver is isolated from outside noise.

Competitive assessments of car body quality for different manufacturers and models are reported in *Consumer Reports* and publications of J. D. Power & Associates. These publications, in addition to the television commercials, are raising customers' expectations of car body quality. Customers are now requiring cars with tighter, more consistent body gaps and without squeaks, rattles, wind noise, or water leaks.

Perhaps even more significant than customers' perceptions of subtle differences in body gaps is the impact of dimensional variation on manufacturing performance. The data in Table 10.1 illustrate the disparity in body-in-white–related costs and the productivity of leading manufacturers over typical U.S. producers in the mid- to late 1980s. At the time of these studies, the leading manufacturers were primarily Japanese producers (e.g., Toyota, Nissan, Honda, Mazda). However, the data in Table 10.1 are at least eight years old, and since that time, the U.S. manufacturers have significantly improved their body-in-white processes. In fact, the question of which are better, U.S. or Japanese companies, is less important than an understanding of world-class practices.

The purpose of this study is to identify the leading manufacturing practices in automotive-body production, regardless of which company implemented them. Specific references to Japanese or U.S. companies have been included mainly to assign credit for a world-class management or manufacturing practice. Thus, the figures presented in Table 10.1 are not intended as the basis of a comparative study of Japanese and U.S. auto companies but are used to suggest that the adoption and/or improvement of key manufacturing practices will result in competitive advantages in time to market, manufacturing costs, and productivity. Formally establishing causal relationships between practices and performance is beyond the scope of this chapter. Numerous factors have an impact on performance, including a company's culture, resources, and production volumes. But we hypothesize that differences in quality and economic performance can be traced, to an important degree, to a set of engineering and manufacturing practices applied systematically.

Table 10.1. Cost and Productivity Comparisons for a Typical Mass-Production Vehicle

Performance Category	World Leaders' Performance, Mid- to Late 1980s	Typical U.S. Performance, Mid- to Late 1980s
Tooling costs per car[a]	$250 million	$700 million
Tooling lead time[b]	14 months	25 months
Stamping production uptime[a]	80–90%	50–60%

Sources: Adapted from Baron, 1992, p. 4.

[a] Based on research by the Industrial Development Division at the University of Michigan, 1990. This cost figure assumes that new car models are using existing engines and transmissions.

[b] From Clark & Fujimoto, 1991.

STUDY METHODS

In addition to a review of the available literature on body-in-white practices, this chapter is based on interviews and visits by University of Michigan researchers to U.S. and Japanese automotive plants (both stamping and assembly). We visited several Japanese companies at both their main plants in Japan and their U.S. satellites. The satellites included Toyota in Georgetown, Kentucky; Nissan in Smyrna, Tennessee; Mazda in Flat Rock, Michigan; and NUMMI (a joint venture of Toyota and General Motors) in Fremont, California. Many body-in-white operations were also observed at General Motors, Ford, and Chrysler plants throughout North America.

A few manufacturers also provided dimensional data from several body-in-white processes, including die tryout, stamping, door subassemblies, and final body assembly. Based on the analysis of these data, the literature, and plant visits, we believe that certain key engineering, management, and manufacturing practices have allowed some producers to achieve a competitive advantage in the automotive body. In the following sections, we explore many of these practices in each of the three major body-in-white processes: die development, part fabrication, and body assembly.

DIE DEVELOPMENT

Die development can be considered a four-phase process: plan, design, build, and tryout. This complex sequence traditionally begins with making clay models and line drawings and ends with constructing and testing the stamping dies relative to the clay model. Two critical measures of a company's die-development performance are tooling costs and lead time. Reductions in these measures are often the result of fewer and less costly engineering changes (usually a result of changes made early in the development process), more manufacturing-driven designs, a limited number of dies, and simplified die standards so that dies are lighter and easier to produce (see Industrial Development Division, 1991, for additional information). Leading development companies have been able to implement these cost-saving practices by disseminating design experience, integrating manufacturing and design, and taking a more systematic approach to constructing the car body.

Disseminating Design Experience

In an interview in which a Japanese manager at a leading company was asked how the company set specifications on part dimensions, he replied, "We determined them from experience." This was a common response to many questions directed at engineers in this company. Design experience has been gained over the years by identifying and documenting design concerns, paying attention to detail, and instilling discipline into the systems. For instance, one leading Japanese company produced a manual (150 pages) of acceptable design practices for body components. Interestingly, many of the sketches in this book were hand drawn. Die engineers at this company and their suppliers are required to follow these established design guidelines. Any changes require a thorough explanation and justification to other engineers as to why a new design practice or standard is needed. Clearly, this practice has helped the company maintain design continuity between car models and disseminate experience throughout the body-in-white development process.

A problem at some North American manufacturers is that their designers can introduce any changes they desire. This process interrupts continuity, and when an effective design is found, it may not be documented and passed on to future programs. The simple, empirical design manual is an effective means of standardizing practices and preventing a regression to earlier mistakes. A well-known philosophy developed by Henry Ford was to standardize complex manufacturing tasks in order to make them routine and predictable. The Japanese design manual carries that principle into engineering.

Companies Lacking Die-Engineering Experience

Unfortunately, many companies trying to improve their die designs lack the required experience or have conflicting expert opinions. In such situations, design decisions can be resolved quickly by using modern data-collection methods, coupled with analytical techniques such as time series analysis, variation simulation, analysis of variance, and finite element analysis. These techniques help engineers find cause-and-effect relationships among die designs, component-part features, and finished-product quality. To our knowledge, Japanese companies have not made extensive use of these analytical tools. Several North American companies are turning to outside resources to help them apply these techniques. When new methodologies are applied and knowledge about systems is accumulated, it is important to establish standards and to disseminate the findings throughout the areas of design and manufacturing engineering. This is difficult without established standards or practices and a simple dissemination vehicle.

Integrating the Development Process

A high-quality, minimal-cost automotive body is also dependent on the degree of integration of the development process with other body-in-white processes. Upstream groups like styling, product engineering, and die design must take into account the concerns of the manufacturing (process) engineers and production personnel. This practice helps avoid more costly engineering changes later, by identifying potential or known manufacturing problems earlier in the development process when they are less expensive to correct. In addition, integrating the development process allows more parallel activity during the development phases: planning, designing, building, and die tryout. Parallel activity is critical to reducing the tooling lead time and, subsequently, the total time required to bring a new car to market. Parallel activities, however, require design and process standardization so that different functions will know what to expect from one another (see Clark & Fujimoto, 1991, or Industrial Development Division, 1991, for additional information).

Relationship with Die Suppliers

By establishing close relationships with fewer suppliers (which perform larger portions of development), leading manufacturers can complete more steps in the die-development process in parallel, because communication and coordination are much simpler. Suppliers also have indicated that when entire submodules are assigned to them, they often can find improvements or make adjustments to interrelated parts. Another consequence of reducing the number of suppliers is that they become specialists on certain body components. For example, when a supplier becomes proficient at designing and making dies for door subassemblies, it can more easily standardize and carry over this expertise to the next door–development project. These benefits would not be possible if the parts were scattered among several locations as a result of low-cost bidding as the prevailing decision rule.

The close relationship of the leading companies with their suppliers also supports the integration of technology. For instance, Toyota has a fully integrated system, Caelum, which unifies computer-aided design, engineering, manufacturing, and testing functions into a single database (Toyota, 1992). Toyota has worked diligently to link its major suppliers to the Caelum system, and this approach has advanced the technological capabilities of its suppliers and helped shorten the overall development cycle. Toyota's Caelum system, however, is only one example of the integration of information. Other car-body manufacturers, in both North America and Japan, are also heading in this direction. Further discussion of integrating suppliers into development work can be found in Chapter 7 of this book.

Manufacturing Process-Driven Designs

When dies are designed to produce automotive body parts, an important concept is interchangeability. The idea can be traced back to Henry Ford and his moving assembly line. Ford wanted to select at random any part from a batch so that the one selected could be assembled and would function satisfactorily without adjustment by the operator. Interchangeability can be measured in terms of the repeatability of a process to produce acceptable parts. Although most companies agree that interchangeability is desirable, this target is often difficult to achieve in automotive-body production because of the large variation in stamped parts and welding processes.

When interchangeability is difficult to achieve, companies use more manufacturing process–driven designs. By this, we mean designs that take into account the inherent variation and limitations of various stamping and body-assembly processes, which require engineers to know the capability of existing operations. Although this point seems obvious, many companies routinely specify tolerances on part or subassembly dimensions that cannot be achieved or, in some cases, are unnecessary. When unnecessary tolerances are assigned, they almost always result in additional cost and lead time as manufacturing tries to achieve them. As we will see later, a technique referred to as *functional build* can help avoid the problem of setting unrealistic or unnecessary tolerances. This problem also can be addressed by institutionalizing standardized design practices.

Springback Considerations

One recurring problem in die design is *springback*, the extent to which metal shifts back to its original position after a forming process (see Figure 10.1). Whenever metal is formed, some springback is inevitable. The die design can compensate for springback by overbending (overcrowning) parts, in the hope that after springback they will be at their desired shape. For body panels such as hoods, doors, and fenders, springback has always been extremely difficult to predict and control. Manufacturing can make subtle process adjustments to control springback, but the impact is minor, making them useful only for fine-tuning. An effective approach for dealing with springback is to make accommodations in the body's styling and design. For example, by introducing a "character line" (a small bend in the panel sometimes covered with an outer trim part), the amount of springback can be reduced. Springback also can be minimized on flanges (Figure 10.1) by decreasing the radius of the bend. This, however, may require steel with higher formability

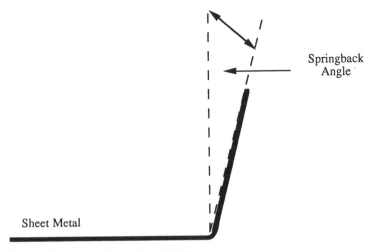

Figure 10.1. Springback for a 90° flange.

and lower strength so that it does not split. Another way to accommodate springback on light panels (outer surfaces) is to assemble it to a more rigid inner panel in order to force the springback out of the part (light panels tend to conform to the shape of heavier ones when attached). There are several ways to address springback, and many of the simpler options must be decided during design. If springback is still a problem after the dies are made, the number of options decreases while the cost of their implementation increases. The leading manufacturers try to lower their manufacturing costs by using better designs to predict and compensate for springback before the manufacturing phase.

Design for Manufacturability

When a car body is produced, the components should be designed so that they are both easy to fabricate and easy to assemble within the required functional specifications. For instance, the more successful companies have improved the manufacturability of their designs through consistent dimensional control of stamping, subassembly, and assembly. One specific action has been to use the same reference or datum points (i.e., locating pin holes and surfaces) throughout all these processes. By changing reference points for different processes, companies add another source of variation. Inconsistent reference points reveals a company's poor communication among engineering groups and a lack of systems approach among their various body-in-white functions.

Integrated and Double-Attached Parts

Some leading manufacturers have also improved manufacturability by combining several stamped components into larger, integrated parts, such as a one-piece side aperture (side frame of a car's body). Although this large component requires a more complex die and may waste additional metal, fewer dies are needed to produce the aperture because it has fewer components. Assembly also is a much simpler operation because fewer parts need to be welded together, and there is less variation because the assembly process is eliminated.

Another practice that is sometimes used by different manufacturers to cut die costs, stamping time, and lead time is the double attaching of parts. This is done when components (usually right and left ones such as fenders or doors) pass through a series of presses attached as one part and are then separated into two individual components in the last press operation. Although the design complexity of the one set of dies increases with double-attached parts, companies can significantly save on their overall tooling and production costs by limiting the number of dies to just one set rather than two. In an example presented in a University of Michigan study, double-attached dies for body panels resulted in a 20 percent cost saving over parts that were not double attached (Industrial Development Division, 1991).

The practices of double-attaching and integrating parts are steadily increasing in automotive-body production because they can greatly reduce the number of dies needed to produce the car body and, therefore, the manufacturing and development costs. Although these practices have been recognized by the U.S. car companies for several years, Japanese manufacturers have more actively pursued their implementation. Honda, for example, traditionally has used many small, simple parts to produce its car bodies, so double attaching was a logical option. Honda reduced its overall costs without increasing its die complexity beyond a manageable level. The U.S. companies have followed with major programs aimed at lowering the number of dies used to make their car bodies. Two recent car models that have benefited from these programs are Chrysler's Neon and General Motors' Camaro. Chrysler reduced by 60 percent the number of dies needed to produce the Neon from its predecessor, the Sundance/Shadow, (Ingrassia & Lavin, 1993). General Motors reported similar reductions with the Camaro. Although several factors have had an impact on the reduction of dies, the practices of integrating and double-attaching parts have been recognized as major contributors.

Die Tryout

Approving a die for production in the body-development phase is usually a two-stage process: primary tryout (where the die is made) and secondary tryout (at the stamping plant where the die will be run). Some companies have additional die tryouts to fine-tune their processes or to test a part's specifications (dimensions) when they have been changed. To evaluate the dies during tryout, manufacturers measure several features of a stamped component and then compute the mean, standard deviation, and process capability of each feature. Process capability measures the ability of a process to produce parts within the specified tolerance. During tryout, if the mean, standard deviation, or process-capability indices are not acceptable, the dies are reworked. Unfortunately, these indices often are unreliable (Baron, 1992). There are two problems. First, these indices often have a poor correlation between the primary and the secondary tryout, resulting in unnecessary rework and lead time during the primary tryout. Second, even when the indices show a high level of quality, there is no guarantee that a high level of interchangeability will be achieved. This problem stems from the fact that the variation in stamping and assembly is difficult to predict. Some manufacturers, especially in Japan, de-emphasize these indices during die tryout. Rather, their approach is to get the dies quickly into production and then evaluate them through prototype builds.

Relationship of Die Tryout to Production Performance

Table 10.2 correlates some common evaluation criteria between primary and secondary die tryouts at a typical manufacturer. These data suggest that the results of the primary die tryout are often inconsistent with the

Table 10.2. Comparison of Evaluation Criteria for Primary and Secondary Die Tryouts

Evaluation Criteria	Correlation Between Primary and Secondary Tryout (R^2)
Mean	0.6
Process capability, Cp	0.2
Standard deviation	0.2

Sources: J. S. Baron, Body-in-white dimensional process control, lecture presented at University of Michigan: Management Briefing Seminar, Traverse City, MI, 1992.

secondary tryout figures. Although this is only one study, we believe that the extraordinary results warrant further investigation.

Based on the data from this study, only the means of individual dimensions of a part show a significant correlation (an adjusted $R^2 > 0.5$) between the two tryouts. The process standard deviation experienced at the die source does not appear to be a good predictor of the variation that occurs in the stamping plant. Because process capability includes the standard deviation in its calculation, this evaluation criterion also is inconsistent between tryouts. Some possible explanations for the lack of correlation in these two criteria are that the stamping plants use different presses than the die manufacturer does to try out the dies, and in many cases, they change the operating conditions or process variables. Thus, grinding and reworking dies at the primary tryout to reduce variation on some features may have little or no effect on solving die-design or construction problems in production. In fact, making unnecessary changes during the primary die tryout not only wastes additional tooling costs and lead time, but it can also adversely affect the dies. Of course, the converse also is true. Important features that may appear acceptable in the primary tryout later require more work on the dies once they are on the production equipment.

Two ways in which a company can increase its process capability are by reducing the standard deviation of the process or by widening the tolerances. When traditional automotive companies find that they cannot meet the original process-capability requirements even after extensive die rework, they often increase the tolerances. According to Baron (1992), this occurs in approximately 20 percent of the cases, thus indicating that the tolerances were not meaningfully assigned in the first place.

Two commonly used process-capability indices are Cp and Cpk. (Cp is the total tolerance for a dimension divided by 6 * standard deviation.) Cp differs from Cpk because it assumes that the process mean is at the center of the tolerances or at the specification nominal. But for most stamping operations, the process means for individual dimensions of a part are rarely at their specification nominals because of springback and other factors, making the Cp index a poor indicator of process capability or quality. For most machining operations, a mean of an individual dimension can be shifted toward its specification nominal simply by adjusting a tool, by turning a knob. However, in stamping, shifting the mean to the specification nominal often requires die rework or extensive maintenance repair and may not be possible at all!

To improve the correlation and repeatability of the die tryout, many companies record critical process variables like shut height (the distance from the bottom of the press slide to the top of the press bed [bolster] with the slide down), tonnage (force applied as the upper and the lower die are squeezed together), and press speed at the primary tryout, and then they set up the presses on the home line (at the secondary tryout) with these same conditions. Although this approach seems to be one of common sense, interviews with key stamping personnel at many plants admit that this practice has just recently been adopted in their tryouts.

Functional Build Versus Net Build

Many U.S. and European automotive manufacturers traditionally have used a tryout approach referred to as *net build*. This approach simply means that dies are built to meet original print specifications. The net-build philosophy assumes that if all components meet their original print specifications, then the final assembly of these body components also should meet its specifications (at least more than 99% of the time). Under net build, if a die produces parts in which the mean of an individual dimension is not at the specification nominal (desired target), it is reworked until the specifications are met. This often results in major changes to the dies, because they rarely produce parts whose means are at the specification nominal. In some instances, these changes are wasted effort because later print specifications are found to be incorrect or are not important. As a result, some dies are modified to correct certain dimensions, even though these dimensions may not adversely affect the quality of the finished car body. In reality, companies that use the net-build approach recognize that they cannot correct every dimensional bias. Instead, they often accept a dimensional bias and try to correct for it in the assembly process.

Although trying to manufacture parts that match their original print specifications may seem like a good engineering practice, another approach, referred to as *functional build*, has proved to be effective. Under functional build, the original print specifications are treated as "targets" rather than absolute goals. During the tryout, the various body components being produced by the dies are assembled into a prototype car body, or *screw body*. Each component is then evaluated based on its relation to the other parts of the car body instead of to its print specification. If a part deviates from its print specification but assembles into an acceptable car body, the die is not modified. In other words, car bodies are refined around the dimensions produced by the dies, rather than trying to make the parts conform to specifications that under the traditional net-build approach are often flawed.

The functional-build approach helps avoid specifying features that do not have an impact on the final quality. Part drawings developed for use with functional build often specify fewer dimensions than under the net-build approach. In other words, more dimensions can be left to chance, because the screw-body process will identify any flaws before the start of production. Of course, the specifications on the part drawings do identify those features that are important to the standardized design guidelines. This process is preferred by many die makers because the "loosening" of requirements allows them more freedom in designing and building the dies. By waiting until prototypes are evaluated, the functional-build approach tends to reduce the total number of changes that must be made during the die tryouts, thereby decreasing development costs and lead time.

The Screw-Body Prototype

The functional-build process usually consists of assembling die-tryout parts that are representative of those being produced by the stamping process into a screw-body prototype (usually one or two per car model). As the name suggests, the screw-body prototype is assembled with screws, as opposed to the normal welding operations. This minimizes the distortion of components caused by welding in assembly. The screw-body prototypes are evaluated to determine which parts (i.e., dies) need to be modified to improve the appearance and quality of the car body. A part may be considered acceptable even if it does not meet its original print specification. The important considerations are whether the part assembles properly with the other parts and if the car body is of sufficient quality. When deviations in the car-body design must be made, engineers search for the least costly rational-quality alternative. This could even result in modifying a feature that is within the specifications. For example, if the quality of the body is poor because an overall dimension of several parts in a subassembly is too large, perhaps only one die may need to be reworked to produce a satisfactory car body. In many cases, the die scheduled to be reworked is the cheapest die. (Under the net-build approach, each part is evaluated independently against the specification, and more than one die may end up being modified.)

Once an acceptable car body is produced, the dimensions of the individual components of the screw body become the manufacturing specifications, essentially replacing the original print specifications. Under functional build, the screw body displaces the original clay model as the new master for the dimensional objectives.

Implementing Functional Build

Screw-body techniques were developed in the United States in the 1970s, but their original objectives were primarily to check part interference in subassemblies. This process, generally known as *screw and scribe,* evaluated major subassemblies and did not produce a full screw body. One

Japanese manufacturer benchmarked this U.S. technique and developed the functional-build and screw-body approaches. So far, several Japanese manufacturers have succeeded in implementing functional build, but not all to the same degree.

Several non-Japanese companies (at least two in North America) are adopting aspects of the functional-build approach. A precursor to success with functional build is well-controlled stamping and assembly processes. Processes that fluctuate with large part-to-part or run-to-run variations will cause many problems for companies that attempt functional build. Baron (1992) showed that some of these processes in North America are not well controlled and recommended that gaining control be a top priority before attempting functional build.

To be successful at functional build, companies must be able to predict the long-term process means of part dimensions during the secondary die tryout. In other words, the sample means of the part dimensions computed at the tryout must be similar to those that will occur during regular production, and the variation about the mean cannot be large. At all stamping plants, the means of individual part dimensions routinely shift from run to run during regular production. For example, Figure 10.2 shows a shifting mean for a part dimension. The mean for this dimension varies from 0.1 mm to 1.0 mm. This difference makes it difficult to choose representative parts for the screw body (i.e., to know whether the parts being used for functional-build prototypes are at the process mean dimension). Figure 10.2 also illustrates a process with a long-term stable mean. Companies with this level of dimensional control can use the sample means computed

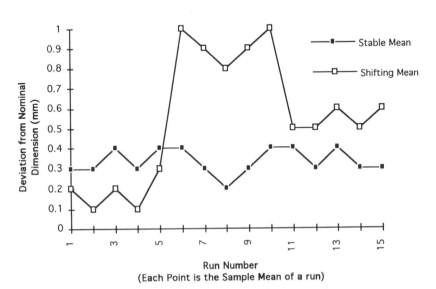

Figure 10.2. Comparison from run to run of a stable versus shifting process mean on a finished-part dimension.

during the die tryout (e.g., run 1 of Figure 10.2) to predict the long-term expected mean, because there is minimal variation in the mean (see the section entitled "Sources of Stamping Variation"). Thus companies trying to implement functional build will be more successful if they can control significant shifts in the process mean, because their screw-body prototypes will more accurately predict the dimensional characteristics of the car bodies being produced by their manufacturing processes.

The timing of the die-build phase is also important to achieving functional build. Japanese companies that use functional build emphasize the importance of getting the dies to the home stamping plants as quickly as possible for tryout. Time must be budgeted at the home stamping plants to produce prototype parts, assemble the screw body, and make changes very close to the start of production. Typically, in North America, there would not be sufficient press time available to stamp prototype parts or time to evaluate and rework the dies because they arrive too close to the start of production. To resolve this problem, die designs should be released sooner to the die makers; fewer changes should be requested of them while the die is being built; less time should be spent on the primary tryout; and resources (press time and engineering expertise) in the production stamping plants should be budgeted.

Potential Use of Computer Simulation

Many companies that have traditionally used the net-build approach are currently using, or planning to use, some aspects of the functional-build process. We feel that all car companies can further improve net-build and functional-build approaches by using analytical methods. To our knowledge, Japanese companies have not been as aggressive as North American companies have in applying certain analytical techniques. Computers can show variation simulations on the stack-up of component parts to predict the final dimensions on the car bodies.

In our opinion, current efforts to use these simulation techniques have not been effective because critical features of the stamping and assembly processes have been omitted. For example, many simulation models do not consider variation because of shifts in the process mean and/or wrongly assume that the long-term process mean will be at the nominal specification, particularly when operating under a net-build approach. Many models also incorrectly assume that the variances of two component parts will add when assembled. In many cases, when a stamped part with low rigidity is fastened to a stiff component, the variances do not add. Instead, the variation of their assembly tends to resemble the stiffer component (Takezawa, 1980). Standardizing the part and process designs (similar to standardized design practices) can help to establish a knowledge base from which necessary component and assembly variations can be predicted. Computer models can be updated (fine-tuned) with actual production data during a functional-build tryout, and the long-term variation performance can be predicted.

PART FABRICATION (STAMPING)

Another major body-in-white process is part fabrication, or stamping. The stamping process transforms sheet metal into stamped components. The stamping process is similar for most body panels. Sheet metal is first cut into blanks (rough shapes larger than the actual part) from steel rolls on fast-blanking presses. The blanks are sent through a series of presses, which transforms them into stamped components. A typical press series might be draw, trim, flange, and pierce. A press series may have more or fewer dies depending on the complexity of the part (complicated parts may have as many as nine dies). A press series or line can run an assortment of body panels if its dies are changed.

Two important performance measures of a stamping line are uptime (the percentage of time that the press is producing acceptable parts) and dimensional control. World-class stampers have reported 20 to 30 percent higher uptimes than non-world-class manufacturers have (see Table 10.1). A major factor of stamping uptime is the amount of time required to change dies for different parts. Another factor is the ability to keep the parts coming off the press within an acceptable variation. Some lower uptimes can be explained by less control of the stamping processes. For example, dimensional shifts in stamped parts because of changes in the characteristics of the material or changes in the process variables can cause companies to shut down their presses to make adjustments. Thus, dimensional control and uptime are closely related.

Dimensional Control of Stamped Components

In most facilities, producing parts on stamping presses has long been considered an art as much as a science. These facilities have difficulty controlling their stamping processes because they operate their presses without knowing the sources of variation, the critical process variables, or their acceptable operating ranges. In some cases, companies cannot even obtain information on process variables like tonnage because they have not yet installed measuring devices to collect the appropriate data. In other instances, companies measure some input variables but do not relate them to the final part dimensions. These companies simply check the final part dimensions on checking fixtures or coordinate measuring machines (CMM) and then alter the dies (e.g., put a shim in a die) if a part is unacceptable, often without understanding the root cause of the process shift. This method can account for a large part of the variation from run to run identified by Baron (1992).

A problem with checking only the finished dimensions on a CMM is that the feedback system can be quite slow. The parts that must be measured often are backlogged until the following day. As a result, a stamping plant may produce unacceptable parts for 24 hours (as much as 10,000 parts) before a problem is even detected. This type of system audits the process but does not control it. To implement a control plan, companies must understand the different sources of variation in a stamping process and institute appropriate control procedures.

Sources of Stamping Variation

Three sources of stamping variation are die-process bias, part-to-part variation, and mean shift variation (see Figure 10.3). The die-process bias is the deviation of the average part dimension (over the long run) from the print specification nominal. For example, in Figure 10.3, the die-process bias is -0.4 millimeters. One effective tool in reducing the die-process bias has been functional build because it redefines the print specification to coincide with the dimensions of the screw body.

Part-to-part variation is the random variation in the stamping process within a run or batch of parts. Stamping plants with large part-to-part variation have probably done a poor job of identifying and controlling critical process variables and their appropriate ranges of settings. A closer look at the variation data will likely show nonrandom variation, indicating an out-of-control process.

Although within-run or part-to-part variation is certainly important, the data that we and others have analyzed indicate that the principal dimensional variation in stamping is caused by mean shifts or variations from batch to batch. Mean shift variation is often the result of changing sheet metal lots or exchanging dies in a press for a new part. Although many stamping operations have been able to achieve equivalent levels of part-to-

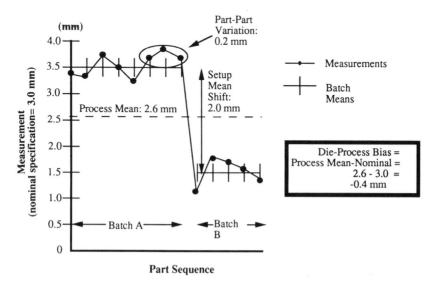

Figure 10.3. Sources of stamping variation (from two batches).

part variation, the leading companies appear to have lowered their mean shift variation, by controlling of incoming steel, rigorously maintaining their dies and presses, and meticulously developing and executing change-over procedures.

Die Preventive Maintenance Program

Most companies have implemented some form of a preventive maintenance program for their dies, although many are not effectively using these programs to monitor the condition of their dies. The leading manufacturers tend to have more rigorous maintenance procedures in which the dies are closely scrutinized for wear and deformities before they have a chance to produce defects. Several companies use detailed die maintenance check sheets that were created with input from the stamping-press operators to help tool-and-die makers maintain critical die characteristics. Whenever possible, these companies insist on repairing dies in the maintenance shop and not at the stamping presses. This policy contributes substantially to press uptime.

Die Setup

Die setup is not just the time it takes to change a die in a press; it also includes the time required to start producing good parts. A key to producing good parts quickly is standardized procedures. Leading manufacturers have detailed die-setup procedures that are strictly followed by operators and die setters. These procedures ensure that critical process variables like shut height, tonnage, and air pressures are set at their appropriate levels. For example, some companies increase their chance of quickly producing acceptable parts following a die change by automatically setting key process variables to the exact conditions that were used the last time the part was run. Equipment that can be reset is, of course, a prerequisite.

Controlling the Process Variables Before Starting Production

Most companies monitor quality by measuring the finished parts and then adjusting the process if the dimensional measurements fall outside the tolerances. Unfortunately, many of these companies do not determine the reasons that these measurements are shifting outside their tolerances in the first place.

In contrast, we have observed the following manufacturing philosophy at a few leading Japanese companies: If the process is truly efficient, quality can be monitored simply by maintaining the process variables. By identifying and controlling the critical process variables that cause variation, these companies no longer need to measure finished parts. In fact, the majority of their quality checks are made visually; that is, the parts are inspected for surface flaws as they are being unloaded from the stamping line.

These manufacturers use very few statistical process control (SPC) charts in their stamping operations. During the tryout, they establish operating ranges for their process input variables that are robust to manufacturing variation. By operating within these ranges, they are able to control the quality of the final part. Subsequently, they require less investment for dimensional measurement equipment (hard gauges, coordinate measuring machines, etc.) to check finished parts during production runs. It appears that the process at these companies is controlled before the start of production, by identifying process-influencing factors during the die tryout and controlling them in setup and maintenance procedures. Although these companies do not rely heavily on dimensional measurement or SPC, we do not advocate that companies striving to produce world-class automotive bodies eliminate their gauging and data-collection systems at the stamping and assembly plants. These systems are needed to identify and solve stamping problems, especially for companies trying to reduce variation in their processes.

Collecting Useful Data

Based on our visits to many non-world-class facilities, we believe that most of their current data-collection efforts are inefficient. For instance, the data that we observed being collected are often of limited use because there is insufficient information to identify root-cause problems. Also, as we mentioned earlier, because many dimensions specified by net build are superfluous, they can go out of control without adverse effects on the final quality. Consequently, operators ignore SPC charts showing an out-of-control condition, and they respond only when employees handling downstream processes (assembly) complain or make specific requests. Erroneous assumptions also can be made when many SPC charts are constructed in stamping. Baron (1992) showed that process-control data tend to be automatically correlated in stamping and are not random within runs or from run to run. Consequently, setting the control limits is too constrictive when the process engineers assume random data, as is often the case. Furthermore, data collection can be simplified because multiple part features often are correlated. For example, if two dimensions of a component are 90 percent correlated, then it is not necessary to collect data on both dimensions. If one dimension is known, the other can be easily predicted. Many companies could significantly cut their data collection and analysis with more careful investigation into the process data.

Changing Dies

Some companies require fewer die changes and are less likely to invest in quick die-change technology, because they have enough volume to dedicate certain press lines to relatively few component parts. Most companies, however, must change their dies more frequently, and quick die-change technology can increase the ability to run more parts in smaller batches on a particular press line. Furthermore, a quick die change forces an organization to analyze thoroughly the process-control aspects of die tryout, die setup, die maintenance, and die production, regardless of how often the dies must be changed. Not surprisingly, companies that change their dies extremely quickly (less than 15 minutes to exchange a die and begin producing acceptable parts) tend to have excellent dimensional control. One could also make the point that excellent dimensional control is a requisite for quickly changing dies.

History of Quick Die Change

Vasil Georgeff of Danly Machine in Chicago, Illinois, invented a quick die-change system in 1956 that used dual moving bolsters to exchange a large stamping die in less than 10 minutes (Smith, 1991). At this point, the United States was years ahead of the rest of the world in developing quick die-change technology. The reasons that the U.S. manufacturers did not pursue this technological advantage are not entirely clear, but one possible explanation is that their large, centralized stamping plants and long production runs "de-emphasized" the need for quick die setups.

Reducing setup time through quick die changes, however, was actively pursued by Taiichi Ohno, who is generally credited with developing the Toyota production system. Ohno considered quick die change to be an integral part of just-in-time (JIT) manufacturing. Ohno found that it actually could be cheaper to produce stamped components in small batches, compared with the large lot sizes mass-produced by some companies (Womack, Jones, & Roos, 1990). The main reasons were lower inventory costs and a system that more quickly detected stamping problems. In effect, the elimination of buffers (in-process inventory) in the JIT system forced the stamping-component suppliers to focus on first-time-through quality and increasing stamping uptime through practices like quick die change.

In his book *A Revolution in Manufacturing: The SMED System*, Shigeo Shingo retells the history of quick die change in Japan, detailing the concept of the "single-minute exchange of dies," or SMED. Shingo considers his work at a Mazda plant in 1950 as the first significant breakthrough in the development of SMED. After studying the die-change process at a Mazda plant, Shingo realized that there were two types of setup operations: internal setups (operations that can be performed only while the machine is stopped) and external setups (operations that can be performed while a machine is running). Shingo developed a standardized procedure for external setups that ensured that the die scheduled to produce the next part would be "ready" to be changed before shutting down the press. This system eliminated nuisance problems that occurred frequently during die changes (e.g., missing bolts or not having the proper part-transfer mechanisms).

Nineteen years later at the Toyota body shop, Shingo further refined his system when he and the workers were able to shorten the press setup time from four hours to three minutes. Shingo began by applying methods analysis to identify each task or operation required to perform both an internal and an external setup. By cutting out unnecessary operations, combining tasks, and installing quick-change tooling, Shingo initially reduced the setup time to 90 minutes. This was further reduced to three minutes by converting internal setup operations to external operations. Thus although the total time required to exchange a die was virtually the same, the time that the press was actually idle (i.e., running production because of internal setups) was reduced, thereby increasing the stamping uptime.

Critical Features of Stamping and Assembly Processes

The stamping process includes several characteristics that make it different from typical fabrication or machining operations. For typical companies operating under the net-build approach, even dies machined on high-precision equipment rarely stamp a part whose detail dimensions are at the specification nominal (see Figure 10.4). Shifting these dimensions back toward nominal is extremely difficult in a stamping process. For instance, grinding a die to adjust one dimensional measurement may adversely affect another point, if they are related. Because a component is stamped in a series of dies, isolating the die that caused the deviation also can be a challenging task, especially because many dies are dimensionally intercorrelated.

Many companies attempt to deal with the problems of dimensional variation of stamped components in their assembly process. Because stamped components are not rigid, they can be bent during assembly to meet body-assembly fixture requirements. In addition, the variation in a nonrigid component may not contribute to the overall variation in its subassembly

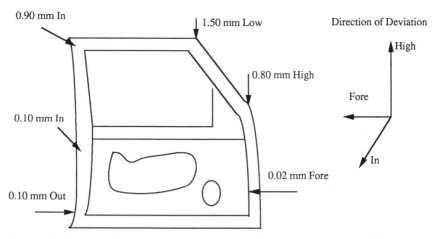

Figure 10.4. Some dimensional measurements of an inner door panel. All measurements are deviations from a nominal specification of 0.00 mm. The direction of deviation is also indicated (see Axis description).

because it will conform to the more rigid subassemblies during welding or other fastening operations. This contradicts the additive theory of variance used in tolerance analysis, according to which variation increases with additional parts. Most of the specification-tolerance analysis techniques (root-sum-squares and worst-case stacking) currently being used in industry are incorrect for these reasons, rendering the specifications and their Cp/Cpk requirements ineffective.

ASSEMBLY OF THE BODY-IN-WHITE

The traditional body-in-white assembly process consists of welding various stamped components into a car body. This process generally encompasses a number of welding lines of subassembly processes, which attach from 150 to 400 parts. In a typical body-assembly process, the major subassemblies (e.g., underbody, body sides, roof) form the car's shell, and the closure panels (e.g., hood, deck lid, doors) are added to complete the body-in-white. The trend in body assembly is toward full automation of the welding and assembly through the use of robots.

Closure panels continue to be a major obstacle to the full automation of body assembly because the large variation in these components and their positioning to others make it difficult to eliminate the people from the process. Also, the body-opening dimensions for the closure panels vary according to a complex buildup of all the component-part variations. The variation is so large that the concept of interchangeability is not currently used by any known car manufacturer. Because the present assembly technology relies heavily on the concept of interchangeability, deviations from the expected mean dimensions on a part usually result in bending or mislocation. Operators are asked to compensate for these problems through adjustments. For example, many plants constantly refit doors throughout their assembly process because of variation in the gaps, flushness, and sealing surfaces between the doors and the rest of the body.

Toyota's and Nissan's Body-Assembly Technology

Body-assembly tooling and welders require large capital expenditures and are on the "critical path" in bringing a new car to market. Because of the capital investment in body-assembly systems, manufacturing flexibility has been cited as a critical objective in product and process design. Toyota and Nissan have addressed retooling costs and flexibility issues by developing the "Toyota flexible body line," and the "intelligent body-assembly system (IBAS)," respectively. These systems reflect an overall management strategy to increase flexibility. We will use Nissan's IBAS (Nissan, 1991) as an example to illustrate the use of technology to integrate product development with assembly and gain flexibility in the global market.

IBAS allows the computer-aided design (CAD) data for a new body to be programmed into numerically controlled (NC) locators that position the components for the welding processes. Programmable robots then weld the car together. Different body styles can be produced on a single line simply by changing the welding and positioning programs.

IBAS uses laser beams to measure the body's dimensions, which are then compared with the specifications. If these body dimensions seem to be exceeding the specification tolerances, a signal is transmitted to the NC locators to make positioning corrections, if possible. By linking the body-measurement system and the NC locators, IBAS becomes a closed-loop feedback system. This closed-loop system also establishes an electronic database of dimensional variation and correction effects that can be readily analyzed at an engineering workstation.

IBAS also has reduced the body-retooling lead time for new models from 12 months to three months (Nissan, 1991). Instead of major hard-tooling changes, IBAS uses CAD simulation software to reprogram the NC locators and welding robots for a new car-body model. Under this system, the majority of changes for a new model can be made during production, which further shortens the development time.

Although the flexibility of Toyota's and Nissan's systems offers several important advantages, there are two principal disadvantages: up-front costs and the limitations placed on new product design. The general notion that flexibility is always beneficial because of future uncertainties is also true in body assembly, but flexibility always comes with a cost. Nissan has said that it takes two car programs (about eight years) to justify the investment cost of IBAS. The financial decision makers at most U.S. companies, however, insist that new systems be justified within one car program, thereby making investments for these systems unlikely. Toyota and Nissan, however, believe that the benefits of flexibility greatly offset this up-front investment. The other disadvantage of a flexible system is that it can restrict the design freedom of future-year car models. IBAS and FBL tooling, though flexible, can accommodate certain car models only within a geometric envelope. Although Toyota and Nissan claim that these restriction are minimal, U.S. companies have indicated that their manufacturing groups are not permitted to place any constraints on the designs of future car models.

Although Nissan's and Toyota's body-assembly systems offer tremendous flexibility in producing a large number of models, their plants generally produce only two to four body styles. The constraint on flexibility is largely dictated by final assembly (downstream from the body-in-white). Because of the many final-assembly options (trim, upholstery, powertrain, etc.), the inventory and complexity of final assembly appears to limit (to about four) the maximum number of body styles that can be made at one location. Thus, Nissan and Toyota do not appear to be using their flexible body-assembly systems as part of a marketing or production strategy to increase the number of models at an assembly plant. The principal benefit for Toyota and Nissan has been a quick model changeover for new car lines, which has resulted in major savings when bringing new cars to market.

Other Body-Assembly Technology

Other automotive companies also have been developing more automated body-assembly systems than in the past. One system being used in many U.S. assembly plants is Robogate. Like IBAS and FBL, Robogate uses a single framing station to weld the shell of the car. The Robogate system uses hard tooling dedicated to a car body, as in traditional framing stations. In Robogate, however, up to three sets of tooling (one set per body variation) can be quickly indexed depending on which set is required for the body being produced. Some U.S. plants have two Robogates in parallel, enabling up to six body variations. The U.S. manufacturers believe that Robogate is as good as Toyota's and Nissan's systems and easier to justify with their current accounting practices.

TAKING A SYSTEMS APPROACH: CHRYSLER'S ZJ CASE EXAMPLE

Although we have separately presented key body-in-white practices in three areas (die development, part fabrication, and assembly), manufacturers cannot improve their competitiveness by mastering only one of them. Production of a world-class automotive body requires a systems approach. One example is Chrysler's efforts to reduce the variation on its ZJ vehicle.

In 1991, a joint group from the Chrysler Jefferson North Assembly Plant, Chrysler Stamping Operations, and the University of Michigan proposed a "2 mm (6–standard deviation) program" to reduce body-in-white variation (Ceglarek, Shi, & Zhou, 1993). The group took a systematic problem-solving approach, classifying problems by area of responsibility and production stage. Under area of responsibility, the group listed four types of problems: design related, installation related, maintenance related, and supplier related. For each type, members of the group determined its contribution to dimensional variation. They further divided the problem areas into four different production stages: preproduction, production launch, first-shift full production, and second-shift full production.

By identifying the root causes of the various problems, the group focused its efforts on where substantial improvements could be made. This required a total approach, including design, stamping, and assembly. Two years later, in 1993, the Chrysler ZJ reached its world-class quality objectives for body-in-white dimensional variation when the company achieved 2 mm (6–standard deviation) variation on key product characteristics of the car's shell. In addition, the variation in the doors and lift gate reached Chrysler's goal of 1.5 mm.

To aid in identifying and analyzing problems, the group recognized the importance of measurement systems. Accurate, flexible, and readily available measurement systems are needed to provide meaningful information for data analysis of product dimensions and process variables. Earlier we mentioned that some leading Japanese companies appear to make a lot of good decisions based on "experience." In Chrysler's case, employees have applied the experience gained from their variation-reduction efforts on the ZJ to their introduction of the T300 truck. According to Chrysler, the dimensional variation on the T300 is even less than that on the ZJ.

CREATING CULTURE IN THE STAMPING PLANT

Many experts believe that U.S. manufacturers have been steadily closing the gap with their Japanese competitors in terms of cost and quality in automotive-body production, making outdated many of the statistics from studies like that by Clark and Fujimoto. Still, although Chrysler's ZJ vehicle and some other domestic success stories indicate substantial improvements in the fit of the car bodies, many plants are still lagging behind. Nevertheless, the domestic success stories and the high achievements by many Japanese satellite plants demonstrate that body-in-white engineering and management practices are not nationally culture bound, although we do believe that company culture is important to producing a world-class automotive body.

Japanese satellite plants have managed to adapt features of their parent companies' cultures, creating a new culture that is accepted and supported by the American worker. During visits to Toyota's stamping facility in Georgetown, we had an opportunity to observe this company culture and compare our observations with the numerous writings on Toyota.

Many Toyota workers described "the Toyota production system" as critical to the success of the plant, indicating that Toyota has instilled its operating philosophy into each worker. Each team member is responsible for contributing to the success of the overall system. Being a part of the Toyota production system is a source of pride among the workers. All this indicates a holistic organization in which the whole is revealed by examining an individual part.

The following story illustrates Toyota's cooperative spirit at Georgetown. During a visit, we noted that one of the four stamping lines was having a quality problem. When the team leaders from the other two lines saw that the problem could not be remedied quickly, they left their lines and offered their assistance. The regularly assigned team leader examined the equipment while the other team leaders began inspecting the incoming blanks to the press line. As it turned out, the problem was due to excessive oil on the incoming blanks. With the additional help, the problem was resolved swiftly. This cooperative attitude among the team leaders is rarely found in traditional mass-producing plants with strong work rules. In these plants, many press operators (the working equivalent of a team leader) believe that helping other press operators is not part of their job. In addition, some press operators resist help from their coworkers because they consider it an indication that they are not capable of doing their job. However, in Toyota's case, the team leader freely accepted the help of the other team leaders, revealing a culture of true teamwork and shared responsibility.

Some experts believe that Georgetown has been able to create a productive culture because of a careful selection process in which prospective employees are evaluated regarding their potential to work as a team. Although this process has helped Georgetown, it is not essential to its success. Toyota appears to be adept at getting a "buy-in" from all employees, including managers and supervisors. This enables it to use its production system at all its plants, regardless of the background of the workforce. For instance, NUMMI, whose management hired up to 85 percent of the former GM workforce at the Fremont, California, plant (Adler, 1993), also was successful in creating a positive culture. The culture evident in the Toyota satellite plants thus is not necessarily attributable to worker selection but, rather, to a socialization process in which the workers are trained and, indeed, indoctrinated into the Toyota production system.

CONCLUSIONS

In this chapter, we presented many world-class practices and manufacturing methods. These practices can be transferred from the leading organizations to those companies trying to improve their competitiveness in many ways. We offer the following observations:

1. With the exception of the flexible assembly systems, the same body-in-white equipment (e.g., stamping presses) is being used by nearly all car manufacturers. Some companies, however, have not made the capital investments to modernize all of their equipment, even though the technology is available for them to use. There do not appear to be any limitations except the availability of capital regarding the transfer of body-in-white equipment.
2. The leading manufacturers have focused on minimizing dimensional variation. They have established problem-solving teams and gained a high level of understanding about minimizing variation in their stamping processes through continuous improvement. They have recognized that classic SPC methods do not function well in stamping operations. For instance, adjusting a process back in control is not simply a matter of turning a knob, as it is in most machining operations. The standardization of processes, die and press maintenance, die setup, and die design appear to be much more effective approaches to reduce stamping variation.
3. The best examples of U.S. manufacturers making significant gains in reducing variations on body components are those cases in which companies have judiciously used the real-time monitoring of stamping and body-assembly processes in conjunction with cross-functional teams. These teams usually include an engineer with excellent formal education in statistical methods and process-

control techniques. This practice enables them to improve substantially their design, die-tryout, and process-control activities. Ultimately, companies should try to eliminate (or at least reduce) measuring finished-part dimensions on stamped components. But until they have better control of their processes, modern data-collection methods can help companies obtain essential manufacturing knowledge more quickly.

4. The leading manufacturers have been very open in explaining their systems and philosophies. Still, many organizations have had difficulty implementing these systems. Successful implementation means changes in job classifications, a better understanding of the techniques, and a constancy of purpose over several years. Many companies are pursuing these efforts, but in many instances, management and labor have lacked commitment and a sufficient understanding of what is required to make real changes.

5. Although the leading companies currently have a competitive advantage, they are continuing to make improvements. In the future, the appropriate use of feed-forward information systems such as variation simulation will help companies predict the manufacturability of components before they are assembled. This type of system is different from the typical case in which a manufacturer builds a car body using parts known to be outside the specifications to determine whether they will form an acceptable assembly.

6. Japanese satellite plants in the United States provide excellent opportunities for other organizations to benchmark their best practices, but these opportunities require extensive commitment in order to be successful. A one- or two-day visit will not suffice to achieve the necessary level of understanding. Successful technology transfer requires a detailed understanding of the processes being examined.

Making improvements in car bodies is a competitive issue. The leading producers of car bodies currently have a significant advantage in development cost, quality, new-product lead time, customer acceptance, and productivity. Companies trying to improve their body-in-white operations through technology transfer need a better understanding of the management, engineering, and manufacturing practices being used by the leading producers. This understanding is critical to determining which practices should be adopted and how they should be implemented. In many cases, the successful transfer of technology will require companies to make a substantial cultural change, in which management, engineering, and labor are truly committed to a new and improved production system.

REFERENCES

Adler, P. S. (1993, January-February). Time-and-motion regained. *Harvard Business Review*, 71, 97–108.

Baron, J. S. (1992). *Dimensional analysis and process control of body-in-white processes.* Unpublished doctoral dissertation, University of Michigan.

Ceglarek, D., Shi, J., & Zhou, Z. (1993). *Variation reduction for body assembly: Methodologies and case study analysis.* Unpublished manuscript, Department of Mechanical Engineering, University of Michigan.

Clark, K. B., & Fujimoto, T. (1991). *Product development performance—Strategy, organization, and management in the world auto industry.* Boston: Harvard Business School Press.

Industrial Development Division, Institute of Science and Technology, University of Michigan. (1991). *Product development systems—A key to world-class manufacture of automotive bodies.* Unpublished manuscript prepared for the Auto/Steel Partnership Program.

Ingrassia, P., & Lavin, D. (1993, April 23). Neon may be a bright light for Chrysler. *Wall Street Journal,* pp. B1–B2.

Nissan's "smart" car assembly. (1991). *American Machinist, 135,* 50–52.

Shingo, S. (1985). *A revolution in manufacturing: The SMED system.* Trans. Andrew P. Dillon, Trans. Cambridge, MA: Productivity Press.

Smith, D. (1991). *Quick die change.* Dearborn, MI: Society of Manufacturing Engineers, Publications Development Department.

Takezawa, N. (1980). An improved method for establishing the process-wise quality standard. *Reports of Statistical Application Research, JUSE, 27,* 63–75.

Toyota's Caelum CAD/CAM system. (1992). *Interplay.* Tokyo: Toyota International Public Affairs Division.

Womack, J. P., Jones, D. T., & Roos, D. (1990). *The machine that changed the world.* New York: Macmillan.

11

Japan's Development of Scheduling Methods for Manufacturing Semiconductors

IZAK DUENYAS,
JOHN W. FOWLER,
AND LEE SCHRUBEN

In this chapter we describe the methods used by some Japanese semiconductor manufacturing companies for long-term planning, short-term scheduling, and shop-floor control. We begin with an overview of semiconductor manufacturing and the role of planning and scheduling functions. Next we describe our research methods. We then attempt to answer the following questions: (1) What tools and techniques do Japanese companies use to plan long-term capacity in the highly competitive and capital-intensive world of semiconductor manufacturing? (2) What tools and techniques do Japanese companies use to schedule issues in the highly uncertain and volatile environment of wafer fabrication? In addition to a general discussion of our findings, we examine the specific efforts of four companies that we studied in some detail.

SEMICONDUCTOR MANUFACTURING

Semiconductor manufacturing is among the most complicated and capital-intensive manufacturing processes in the world. In this section, we first give an overview of wafer fabrication, which is the most complicated portion of semiconductor manufacturing. We then describe the role of planning and scheduling in this environment.

Overview of Wafer Fabrication

The process for manufacturing integrated circuits consists of four phases: wafer fabrication, wafer probe, assembly (packaging), and final testing. Wafer fabrication is the phase in which hundreds of circuits are layered through successive operations onto a smooth, typically silicon, wafer. In wafer probe, the individual circuits are tested electrically using thin probes. The wafers are cut into individual circuits, and those circuits that fail to meet specifications are discarded. The next phase, assembly, consists of placing the circuits in packages designed to protect them from the environment. A final test is then conducted before the integrated circuits are shipped (For a detailed overview of semiconductor manufacturing, refer to Sze, 1988.)

Wafer fabrication is the most costly phase of semiconductor manufacturing. It is a complex sequence of processing steps, with the number of operations typically in the hundreds. These operations must be performed in a very clean environment (called a *clean room*), and the operators must wear special clothing to avoid introducing contaminants. Wafers move through the wafer-fabrication facility in lots (collections of wafers).

Some processing steps are performed on single wafers; some steps are performed on an entire lot; and some steps can process several lots at the same (i.e., they are batch processes). A wafer may go through each of several steps many times as the layers of circuitry are built up on the wafer. The sequence of steps may vary considerably for different products. Producing a particular type of circuit requires a specific sequence of processing steps (deterministic, with the exception of rework), with unique processing times at each step for that product type. Each processing step normally follows a very strict "recipe," so that processing times are essentially constant. However, wafer fabrication–processing equipment is highly unreliable (a machine availability of only 60 to 75 percent is common), and the yield losses are often very large, resulting in a highly stochastic production environment.

Planning and Scheduling in Wafer Fabrication

Semiconductor manufacturing is a highly competitive business. In the past, the competition has been primarily in the product design arena, but in the last several years the cost to manufacture integrated circuits has become an important competitive factor. As we indicated earlier, wafer fabrication is very capital intensive, with the cost of the next generation of wafer-fabrication facilities expected to reach nearly $1 billion. In addition to these costs, the increasing pace of product innovation places a premium on an organization's ability to plan for the long term (Shimoyashiro, 1992). The magnitude of the required investment makes it imperative to use the equipment effectively, and the time to manufacture a product is becoming more important. Short-term scheduling addresses these needs.

Long-term planning is concerned with a set of problems that will occur within the next few months to the next several years. Fordyce and his colleagues (1992) indicated that the following issues are addressed by long-term planning functions: (1) decisions about the impact of changes in the product line, (2) decisions about the types and numbers of equipment necessary to produce a given amount of product, (3) decisions about which manufacturing processes should be used to manufacture products, and (4) decisions about the manpower required. The fact that products' life cycles are relatively short and that they overlap with one another makes long-term planning a challenging endeavor. Long-term planning has traditionally been done using spreadsheets in both the United States and in Japan. In the last several years, robust performance-analysis techniques such as queuing-network theory and discrete-event simulation have become increasingly popular.

Short-term scheduling is concerned with the problems of the next hour to the next several months. The issues addressed by short-term scheduling include decisions about (1) when jobs should be released into the manufacturing line, (2) how much of each product should be produced on a given day, (3) how much overtime will be necessary on a given day or week, (4) what priorities should be assigned to the different jobs competing for the same resource and for late jobs, (5) when preventive maintenance should be performed, (6) how to reduce time lost to setups, (7) how to reroute product flows when machines are down, and (8) which machines to use for a given operation, given the yields for operations on different machines (Fordyce et al., 1992).

Most of the literature that addresses the long- or short-term planning and scheduling issues in wafer fabrication has appeared in the last five years, no doubt because of the greater industrial emphasis on manufacturing. Uzsoy, Lee, and Martin Vega (1992a, b) and Johri (1993) recently highlighted the difficulties in planning and scheduling wafer-fabrication facilities, and they also surveyed the literature on these topics. The main emphasis of much work on scheduling has been on static systems with deterministic processing times. In wafer fabrication, however, the system is dynamic and highly stochastic. A performance evaluation of wafer-fabrication facilities using queuing theory also is very difficult. The manufacturing flow in wafer fabrication is represented by a reentrant flow line (Graves, Meal, Stefek, & Zeghmi, 1983). Essentially, the same wafer visits a particular machine (or machine group) as many as 15 to 25 times, and the required processing of the wafer at that machine is different at each visit. Performance-evaluation methods using queuing theory have traditionally focused on lines without reentrant flows; very little work has been done on evaluating the performance of lines with reentrant flows.

Furthermore, the research on good sequencing policies in wafer fabrication is not extensive. At any one time, a typical machine in a wafer-fabrication facility has several different types of jobs waiting to be processed whose next operation is at a variety of different machines. Choosing an inappropriate job to process at a given machine could lead to the starvation of a bottleneck downstream. Similarly, it is important to control, when possible, the release of new jobs to the system, in order to avoid starving bottlenecks. Releasing jobs too late can lead to the starvation of bottlenecks, whereas releasing jobs too early can lead to high levels of work-in-process (WIP) inventory and noncompetitive cycle times.

A few significant papers have addressed this issue of release and sequencing control in wafer fabrication and have had some influence on the strategies used by U.S. semiconductor-fabrication firms (Hogg & Fowler, 1991). These strategies include the bottleneck starvation–avoidance technique (Glassey & Resende, 1988) and the workload-regulating release and sequencing policy (Wein, 1988). Lu and Kumar (1991), Perkins and Kumar (1989), and Kumar (1993) have drawn up effective dispatching rules. U.S. semiconductor-manufacturing companies have also been influenced by the *kanban*-release policy (an example is Fordyce et al., 1992, in which the implementation of a *kanban*-like policy at an IBM facility is described) and by closed-loop release policies, through which the WIP in the facility is kept constant by releasing a job only when one has been completed. (There is a case study describing the implementation of such a policy in Miller, 1990.) The purpose of our study was to identify the tools and techniques that Japanese companies use for long-term planning and short-term scheduling and to highlight the differences among the approaches taken by U.S. and Japanese companies.

OBJECTIVES OF OUR INTERVIEWS WITH THE COMPANIES WE VISITED

The Operational Modeling Department of SEMATECH (a research consortium composed of 11 semiconductor manufacturers) has been studying the challenges faced since 1988 by U.S. semiconductor companies in planning and scheduling wafer-fabrication facilities. These topics have been a major focus of seven SEMATECH modeling and simulation workshops during that time. In mid-1992, SEMATECH tried to determine what had been done in this area throughout the world. We first visited several semiconductor manufacturers in Europe. In early 1993, we conducted extensive interviews with a large number of employees either currently or previously responsible for planning and scheduling at six large Japanese semiconductor-manufacturing companies. We asked representatives from each company to describe the methods they use for planning and scheduling. When possible, we were given demonstrations of the actual software in use at the "fab."

We concentrated on the following issues during our interview: (1) What are the problems in planning and scheduling that the companies believe are important and for which they are developing models? (2) How are new projects on planning and scheduling initiated at the company (e.g., are they initiated by the demands of the fab manager or by the suggestions of the research staff), and how does the company decide to commit resources to develop a planning and scheduling model (e.g., do projects have to be justified on a return-on-investment [ROI] basis?)? (3) What tools do these companies use (e.g., simulation, queuing theory)? Why did they decide to use these tools? (4) How is a model for planning and scheduling evaluated at the company? Who does the evaluation? (e.g., upper management or the actual users of the model in the fab), and (5) What are the future objectives of the planning and scheduling departments?

PLANNING AND SCHEDULING MODEL DEVELOPMENT AND TOOLS

In this section, we report our findings on the questions posed in the previous section. We first describe those problems that the companies we visited felt were important and were trying to address through their planning and scheduling projects. We then focus on how planning and scheduling projects are initiated and evaluated at these companies. Finally, we look at the models and tools used by the companies we visited.

Objectives

All the companies we visited were developing models to address both long-term planning and short-term scheduling issues. Long-range production-planning objectives included product-mix planning, equipment-utilization planning, capital-investment planning, and personnel planning. An important consideration was developing models to identify the bottlenecks in the production process and the ways that capital should be invested to improve the bottleneck processes. An important consideration was the magnitude and variability of the production lead times. All companies cited the reduction of lead times as a significant objective.

The most common short-term scheduling consideration was the creation of a system that would tell operators what job to do next. Giving operators and supervisors correct and timely information was regarded as one of the most important objectives of any tool developed by the scheduling staff. One company told us that the problem with one of the earlier versions of their scheduling software was that it was so slow that by the time it told each operator what to do for the next several hours, the system status had changed, and the jobs that the operators were supposed to work on had moved elsewhere. Avoiding setups when possible and making good batching decisions are common objectives of the scheduling software.

Another objective was estimating whether lots would be completed on or before their delivery due date. We were told that managers were interested in knowing which lots might be late and that the development of models that could provide this information would be welcomed. Another objective was to decrease WIP inventory levels. We were told at every company that decreasing WIP inventory levels was a very high priority of upper management. In fact, we were told by one company representative that at one time, management measured WIP levels on certain days, and so the operators made sure that WIP levels were acceptable on these days.

Other objectives included understanding the impacts of hot lots on cycle-time variability. *Hot lots* are those jobs assigned high priority by upper management, and they tend to increase cycle times for other jobs as well as the variability of general cycle times. The final consideration was what actions to take after equipment failed.

Project Initiation, Development, and Evaluation

One issue that we explored during our interviews was how companies decide to undertake a certain planning or scheduling project and how its success or failure is determined. Although each company uses different procedures to evaluate the value and success of projects, we found some common characteristics as well.

Project Initiation

We found that the top-down initiation of projects is common, although companies also have mechanisms by which the planning or scheduling group can propose a certain project and upper management decides whether to undertake it. For example, at nearly all the companies we visited, upper management was concerned about lead times and WIP levels and thus started projects to reduce them. Other projects were undertaken because a member of the staff had proposed them. For example, at one company that we visited, a major annual event for the corporate research department is an exhibition for the operating divisions. At this R&D "open house," the researchers demonstrate and present their work and pitch their proposals. A project is then approved if the operating divisions think it will be beneficial.

Clear Definition of Customers and Objectives

We found that the members of the planning and scheduling groups in Japan always started a project with a clear definition of the objectives and the customers. At nearly all the companies that we visited, the R&D staff closely interacted with the plant managers and operators. The planning and scheduling R&D staff were aware that the ultimate users of the methods and software that they developed would be the operators at the semiconductor-fabrication facilities and so emphasized the importance of plant managers and workers "buying in" to the project.

There was a clear emphasis on making the planning and scheduling staff's projects easy to understand and user friendly. Furthermore, visualizations, charts, and statistics were used extensively in order to make the results easier to understand. All the Japanese companies we visited, however, avoided animation in their wafer-fabrication models. Animation was regarded as providing little information, compared with charts and statistics.

We found it very common for the tools devised by the planning and scheduling staff to be used at the R&D fabs first. If this implementation were successful, then the second stage of the implementation would be refining the tools for the production fabs. There was a significant effort to keep plant managers and operators involved in the development of scheduling tools from the early stages of the project. Although some U.S. companies emphasize close interaction between plant staff and R&D staff, some U.S. semiconductor manufacturers still have large R&D departments that appear to interact little with the actual production facilities.

Stable Teams

We observed that the planning and scheduling groups in Japanese semiconductor-manufacturing firms were very stable. In all but one of the companies that we visited, we were able to talk to the staff members who had been involved in the original scheduling tools developed over the last five to 10 years. The staff and the long-term outlook of the management were stable in all the companies we visited. The planning staff regarded their projects as part of a continuous, long-term improvement project. Each planning group was thus able to explain what they wanted to accomplish in the next three or four years and what milestone the current project represented. This is also in contrast with U.S. semiconductor-manufacturing firms at which assignments tend to be much more short term and planning and scheduling staffs tend to change more rapidly. In fact, in our conversations with the heads of planning and scheduling departments of U.S. semiconductor-manufacturing companies, they repeatedly cited the lack of stable teams as an important reason that they relied on vendors for most of their planning and scheduling software.

Reliance on "Locally Developed" Programs

We found that Japanese companies usually create their own tools and software, instead of using commercially available software. This is different from the situation in the United States, where most semiconductor-manufacturing companies use commercially available software. Although the staff at the Japanese companies that we interviewed were aware of the commercially available software specifically written for the semiconductor-manufacturing environment, all but one of them had decided against using it. The three reasons most commonly given for this choice were

1. *Dissatisfaction with the available software.* Nearly all the Japanese companies we visited had tried (or at least evaluated) some commercially available soft-

ware and found it unsatisfactory. A frequent complaint was that the commercially available software for keeping track of WIP on the shop floor was too slow. Interestingly, a major U.S. semiconductor-manufacturing company that we visited recently converted one of its fabs to what it called a "paperless" fab. In this fab, operators have to look at the computer to decide what to do next, and at the finish of each operation, the data must be entered into the computer. The WIP tracking program used at this fab is a commercially available package for tracking WIP. We were told by the plant manager that the bottleneck in the fab is the computer. In fact, for some processes, the time spent retrieving and entering data from the computer is greater than the processing time. The plant manager told us that the company is considering buying faster computers.

2. *Flexibility.* A big reason given by the companies for developing their own software was flexibility. Although the development of software in house required a larger investment of time and resources in the beginning, the companies felt that it was easier to improve software developed in house. By creating it in house, the companies also would be able to incorporate their own know-how and company procedures. Clearly, the long-term corporate commitment and stable team membership facilitated the in-house development and improvement of software.

3. *Engineering pride.* Interestingly, pride was also a reason for deciding to develop software in house. The planning and scheduling staffs emphasized the strong sense of pride in their work and stated that they much preferred using software they created themselves.

Project Evaluation

The planning and scheduling groups at all the companies we visited stressed that they did not have to justify a project by performing some sort of return-on-investment (ROI) computation. This is in contrast with the United States, where such calculations are rather important to deciding whether a project will be undertaken. In fact, the planning and scheduling groups in Japan also cited the difficulty of making such calculations. For example, the development of a shop-floor control mechanism can be useful because it leads to better WIP tracking and data collection, and it is very hard to quantify the benefits of better data collection. Also, the knowledge gained while working on one project can be useful on other projects. For all these reasons, the Japanese companies did not seem to rely on ROI computations when deciding whether to initiate a project.

Evaluation of a project's success also is not based on a simple numerical comparison of the money spent on the project versus the benefits accrued. Rather, at each of the companies, we were told that the success of a project was related to the company's long-term objectives and how the project fit with those objectives. Interestingly, we were told at several companies that their R&D staff were encouraged to publish their findings in practitioner publications and, in fact, that these publications and the interest they generated were often regarded as important to the success of a project. The planning and scheduling R&D staff at one company explained that their company believed that "potential" customers who saw these publications would be impressed, and hence these publications served as some sort of advertisement. A staff member of the planning and scheduling group at another company noted that corporate R&D staff are evaluated according to the 3–P system: patents, publications, and performance.

Models and Tools

In this section, we provide brief case histories for the planning and scheduling projects at four Japanese firms. Although we visited several other companies, we have not included them for reasons of confidentiality. The discussion of our work at NEC is based on a number of articles written by NEC personnel and associated university professors and not on our interviews.

Toshiba

Toshiba's current project to develop planning and scheduling tools for semiconductor manufacturing dates back to 1989. Initially, queuing networks were used to model fabs. The emphasis was on identifying bottlenecks and WIP inventories. After the project began, upper management became interested in lowering WIP levels in the fabs. Queuing-network models were used to show that fabs could achieve target throughput levels with much less WIP than they had at the time. These queuing-network models were based on approximate mean value analysis (Reiser & Lavenberg, 1980). Later, queuing-network analyzer (Whitt, 1983) and open queuing-network models were used to plan capacity, in which optimal-capacity parameters such as the number of machines were computed automatically by means of simulated annealing. One result of this phase of the project was a recommendation that the release policy practiced in the fabs (which was similar to the closed-loop release policy in which new work is introduced only when jobs have been completed) be more strictly applied. This recommendation was followed, and the amount of inventory in the fabs fell without a loss of throughput. Furthermore, the models were used to predict steady-state, long-term, aggregate performance measures, but they could not predict how individual lots would behave.

Management's interest in a tool to predict the behavior of individual lots (e.g., if a particular lot will be completed before its due date) led to the second phase of the project. A simulation program in C was developed and was designed to run everyday. The program downloads the current status of the fab from a database and then estimates when each order will be finished, given its current priority. If an important order is predicted to be late, then its priority can be changed, and the simulation is run again. Because each simulation run takes only about five minutes, this process can be repeated many times until a more satisfactory schedule (i.e., one in which important orders are not expected to be late) is obtained.

The simulation program has led to better data collection and tracking. Each time the program is run, the fab is simulated for one month. The system was first used for wafer fabs and was later extended to assembly and testing operations. Because the assembly lines are not necessarily at Toshiba, the scope of the model encompasses multiple companies. All variables in the model are deterministic. Machine failures are taken into account by inflating processing times. Yield is also taken into account by means of predetermined percentages. The developers of the model and the simulation program explain that random phenomena were avoided so that (1) results could be interpreted easily, (2) a single (and hence short) run would suffice, and (3) the task of data gathering would be facilitated.

The main drawback of the current deterministic simulation program is that it cannot be used to assign due dates to incoming orders at a desired confidence level. That is, the information on the current status of the shop floor cannot be used to predict customers' due dates that can be met a desired percentage of the time. We were told that management had recently become interested in a tool that would help predict customers' due dates, and there are plans to develop such a model.

The planning and scheduling staff at Toshiba have tried to provide models and software that are easy to understand and use by the production staff at the fabs. We were told, however, that the production staff and the operators at the fabs do have their local agendas and are sometimes more interested in "locally optimal" solutions. Accordingly, they accept new models, methods, or software only if they make noticeable improvements. In any case, simple, straightforward models are preferred at all levels of the organization, which is one reason that the models being used are deterministic. In fact, probably the most powerful aspect of the model and software in use at Toshiba is the simplicity and the speed with which it solves problems. (Further details on this project can be found in Fujihara and Yoneda, 1992.)

Mitsubishi

Mitsubishi's project leading to the development of a petri net–based simulator, View, started around 1988. Two objectives led to this fab simulator: (1) the workload prediction in the fab as a function of the release schedule, tools being down, and WIP; and (2) the design and capacity analysis of future factories in terms of the required number of tools and desired throughput levels. The project's customers were thus both fab operating personnel and fab designers.

View accepts inputs from the current factory configuration and input schedules and recipes (with setups). Input parameters that can be varied for analysis are (1) input quantity by product, (2) dispatching rules at each workstation (including due dates), (3) current WIP values, (4) maximum total WIP levels, and (5) a deterministic schedule of tool calibrations, failures, and repairs.

View offers output, presented numerically and with graphics, for (1) tool utilizations, (2) dynamic WIP charts for multiple work centers, (3) dynamic charts of throughput by work station, and (4) cycle times by product. This output is then used to control workload and process and to make major factory design changes.

The View system is centered on a computer-aided scheduling environment for a manufacturing system that uses both humans and computers to schedule operations. The scheduling editor consists of four components: modeling, simulation, evaluation, and editing. A novel approach is taken in the editing component, which incorporates an interactive system that allows an engineer to make and freely modify a desired schedule on a computer display while at the same time satisfying the constraints of the particular systems.

In View, a job-shop production system is modeled. The particular properties include the variety of machines, the variety of products produced, and complex process routings. The manufacturing system's performance can be evaluated in many ways, depending on the products or the manufacturing systems. The objectives include high utilization of machines and a smooth distribution of work over the entire system. In addition, strong constraints (which must not be violated) and weak constraints (desired but not necessary) are included in the scheduling process. The approach is not aimed at determining an optimal solution but it is focused on the cooperation between human and computer, in which the decision to accept the schedule is made by the human.

The scheduling task of manufacturing systems can be broken down into three subtasks: (1) monitoring the current status of facilities and jobs, (2) clarifying the requirements of the facilities and the jobs, and (3) deciding the processing order of jobs. Clearly, the last two are the most difficult. To avoid the combinatorial explosion associated with a mathematically optimal solution, Mitsubishi proposed this human–computer cooperative approach, using computer simulation and an interactive interface. The human's role is to evaluate and edit the schedule on a computer display. The computer's role is to handle the complex propagation of constraints arising from editing the schedule. The graphics interface was created on an engineering workstation, which executes the simulation and on which the user can modify the schedule as desired.

With regard to simulation modeling, a timed petri net is used to facilitate recognition and analysis of the behavior of complex manufacturing systems. Petri-net modeling is used because it allows the representation of a complex production line and the simulation of the behavior of system dynamics with very simple, but inflexible, components. This is the only use of petri-net factory modeling we found in this industry.

The decision to base the simulation on petri-nets was made many years ago after an international conference on petri nets held in Tokyo. The use of petri nets results in a system that allows fab models to be constructed very easily by choosing product and tool icons from a menu and dragging and linking them into a model. The interface does not use physical animation but, rather, relies on dynamic graphical representation of the relevant performance-evaluation information and statistics.

The View system has been used by Mitsubishi to design fabs, and it is currently in use in its fabs to predict production workloads. (Further details of View are available in Fukuda, Tsukiyama, and Mori, 1989.)

Nippon Telegraph and Telephone Corporation (NTT)

The Manufacturing Systems Technology Laboratory of NTT's LSI Laboratories has developed a Semiconductor Manufacturing Line Simulator (SEMALIS) for facility design and operational planning. SEMALIS is written in the general-purpose simulation language SLAM-II, with considerable use of FORTRAN subroutines. NTT has used SEMALIS to study (1) the influence (in terms of throughput and cycle time) of additional bottleneck equipment, (2) the effect of equipment failures and maintenance on line performance, (3) the influence of time-constrained processing between process steps (time-constrained processes are those that have to be repeated unless the next process is performed within a certain time limit; such processes are very important in wafer fabrication), and (4) the change in line performance when "hot" lots are introduced into steady-state manufacturing lines. This tool has been used for long-term planning, and NTT is devising separate tools for scheduling. A 220–day (one-year) run of SEMALIS on a Sun Sparc Station takes approximately one hour of CPU time; the fact that SEMALIS can provide answers relatively quickly makes it possible to evaluate many different alternatives. SEMALIS output provides data on turnaround time, throughput, equipment utilization, and lot queuing times at each workstation. We were told that fabs use some sort of closed-loop release policy in which a maximum WIP limit is set for the fab.

Two interesting facts differentiate NTT's project from the other companies' projects. First, SEMALIS was written in a general-purpose simulation language, although the software was developed in house. Second, the reliability of equipment in SEMALIS is simulated by randomly generating equipment downtime periods. As we have noted, all the other companies used deterministic models, for simplicity and speed. The current focus at NTT is on developing the capability to do on-line modeling. (A detailed description of SEMALIS and some of the results of using it can be found in Nakamura, Hashimoto, Mori, and Nose, 1992.)

NEC

Even though we did not interview NEC personnel, we include this section (based on articles in the literature) because of the obviously high quality of NEC's work.

The development of planning and scheduling tools at NEC dates back to the early 1980s. In this section we concentrate on the simulation-based PLAN-LSIP set of production-planning and evaluation tools. At first, the corporate research staff apparently evaluated some U.S. simulation languages, but they elected to develop their own tools. They followed the typical path from FORTRAN-based text systems to C-based graphics systems using X-Windows and UNIX. This project emphasized the graphical dynamic presentation of information to assist the production staff. Dynamic and colorful Gantt and WIP charts are widely used. NEC appears to focus on the end users of the system and the importance of the human–system interface.

PLAN-LSIP was developed to help decision makers plan and schedule production in the complex environment of semiconductor manufacturing. This decision-support system is intended to facilitate both long-term planning and short-term scheduling in wafer fabrication. Essentially, PLAN-LSIP is a deterministic simulation. The current status of the shop floor is downloaded (via Ethernet) from the shop-floor control system. PLAN-LSIP then simulates the system to predict the performance for the time period of interest. This information is displayed to the users via preprogrammed graphical presentation tools, or they can create their own graphs and tables. This information is used to help in planning and scheduling. For example, users can assess the effect of adding a machine for a certain operation by running two simulations and comparing the performance measures of interest with and without the additional machine. The simulation provides answers very rapidly (in part because of the use of deterministic models). Hence, many different alternatives can be evaluated in a relatively short time. Promising quantitative and qualitative results were achieved using the PLAN-LSIP system with a large-scale semiconductor-manufacturing plant: Turnaround time was reduced by 30 percent; long-range decision making was improved; and on-time delivery performance was enhanced. (Further details of the PLAN-LSIP system can be found in Homma et al., 1991.)

CONCLUSIONS

In this chapter, we described the methods used by some Japanese semiconductor-manufacturing companies for long-term planning and short-term scheduling. Some common characteristics of all the companies that we visited were

1. The importance given by all the companies to reducing lead time.
2. The view of technical projects as part of long-term continuous improvement rather than short-term fixes.
3. An emphasis on developing their own software and using simulation in planning and scheduling wafer-fabrication facilities.

4. A clear identification of each project's customers and an emphasis on having plant managers and operators participate in the development of scheduling tools from the early stages of the project.

All the companies that we visited had clearly defined long-term objectives for their projects and very stable teams who were aware of the history of the company's continuous efforts at improvement. Arguably, the main difference between Japanese modeling practice and many U.S. semiconductor-manufacturing companies is *not* that the Japanese choose to develop their own modeling software but the fact that they *can* develop their own tools. In all Japanese companies we visited, we observed a lack of management or professional interest in "quick" models and "dirty" analysis, an emphasis on stable team membership, strong connections with academic and professional communities, and very strong computing and analytical skills. All these factors enable these companies to develop software in house to meet specific needs of the project and thus improve their competitive position.

ACKNOWLEDGMENTS

We would like to thank Professors Susumu Morito of Waseda University and Robert Leachman of the University of California at Berkeley for their help in setting up our visits. This chapter is a revised version of a paper that appeared in the *Journal of Manufacturing Systems,* vol. 13, no. 5 (1994) (with permission of the Society of Manufacturing Engineers).

REFERENCES

Fordyce, K., Dunki-Jacobs, R., Gerard, B., Sell, B., & Sullivan, G. (1992). Logistics management system: An advanced decision support system for the fourth decision tier dispatch or short-interval scheduling. *Production and Operations Management, 1,* 70–86.

Fujihara, M., & Yoneda, K. (1992). Simulation through explicit state description and its application to semiconductor fab operation. (pp. 899–907). *Proceedings of the Winter Simulation Conference.* Phoenix.

Fukuda, T., Tsukiyama, M., & Mori, K. (1989). Scheduling editor for production management with human–computer cooperative systems. *Proceedings of the Sixth Symposium on Information Control Problems in Manufacturing Technology,* (pp. 179–83). Madrid: IFAC.

Glassey, C. R., & Resende, M. G. C. (1988). Closed-loop job release control for VLSI circuit manufacturing. *IEEE Transactions on Semiconductor Manufacturing, 1,* 36–46.

Graves, S., Meal, H., Stefek, D., & Zeghmi, A. (1983). Scheduling of re-entrant flow shops. *Journal of Operations Management, 3,* 197–203.

Hogg, G., & Fowler, J. (1991). Flow control in semiconductor manufacturing: A survey and projection of needs. *SEMATECH Non Classified Document No. 91110757A GEN.*

Homma, M., Miyatake, N., Miyajima, Y., Kikuchi, I., Tohnai, S., Ueno, J., Torii, T., Enomoto, M., Ninami, N., Fuyuki, M., & Inoue, I. (1991). Line productivity improvement using simulation system for VLSI manufacturing. *Proceedings of the Seventh International Symposium on Automated IC Manufacturing.* Phoenix: Electrochemical Society.

Johri, P. K. (1993). Practical issues in scheduling and dispatching in semiconductor wafer fabrication. *Journal of Manufacturing Systems, 12,* 474–85.

Kumar, P. R. (1993). Re-entrant lines. *Queueing Systems: Theory and Applications, 13,* 87–110.

Lu, S. H., & Kumar, P. R. (1991). Distributed scheduling based on due dates and buffer priorities. *IEEE Transactions on Automatic Control, AC-36,* 1406–16.

Miller, D. J. (1990). Simulation of a semiconductor manufacturing line. *Communications of the ACM, 38,* 98–108.

Nakamura, S., Hashimoto, C., Mori, O., & Nose, J. (1992). Discrete-event simulator for evaluation of line performance of semiconductor manufacturing lines. *Proceedings of the SEMI Technology Symposium,* (pp. 131–38). Chiba: Semiconductor Equipment and Materials International.

Perkins, J. R., & Kumar, P. R. (1989). Stable distributed real-time scheduling of flexible manufacturing/assembly/disassembly systems. *IEEE Transactions on Automatic Control, AC-34,* 139–48.

Reiser, M., & Lavenberg, S. (1980). Mean-value analysis of closed multichain queueing networks. *Journal of the ACM, 27,* 313–22.

Shimoyashiro, S. (1992). Manufacturing system for LSI wafer fabrication. *Proceedings of the SEMI Technology Symposium,* (pp. 147–54). Chiba: Semiconductor Equipment and Materials International.

Sze, S. (1988). *VLSI technology.* (2nd ed.). New York: McGraw-Hill.

Uzsoy, R., Lee, C. Y., & Martin Vega, L. A. (1992a). A review of production planning and scheduling in the semiconductor industry. Part I: System characteristics, performance evaluation, and production planning. *IIE Transactions, 24,* 47–61.

Uzsoy, R., Lee, C. Y., & Martin Vega, L. A. (1992b). A review of production planning and scheduling in the semiconductor industry. Part II: Shop floor control. Research Report, Purdue University.

Wein, L. M. (1988). Scheduling semiconductor wafer fabrication. *IEEE Transactions on Semiconductor Manufacturing, 1,* 115–30.

Whitt, W. (1983). The queueing network analyzer & performance of the queueing network analyzer. *Bell Systems Technical Journal, 62,* 2779–2843.

12

U.S.–Japanese Manufacturing Joint Ventures and Equity Relationships

JOHN E. ETTLIE
AND PETER SWAN

Recent headlines read "GM to Sell Its 50% Stake in GMF annual, a Robotics Firm, to Japanese Partner" (*Wall Street Journal*, June 4, 1992, Business Briefs section) and "IBM, Toshiba, Siemens to Team Up" (*Ann Arbor News*, July 13, 1992). The dissolution and formation of joint ventures (JVs) in manufacturing continue to be high drama in the world competitive scene, but the reasons for formation and dissolution of these ventures are still not well understood.

Interest in domestic manufacturing JVs was heightened during the last decade with the substantial increase of the Japanese presence in very visible industries like the automobiles, steel, and aircraft. Celebrated examples include the New United Motor Manufacturing, Inc. (NUMMI), which is a JV between General Motors Corporation and Toyota (Adler, 1992), and the Boeing Company's 20 percent nonequity partnership with three Japanese companies—Mitsubishi, Fuji, and Kawasaki-Heavy Industries—for the new 777 project (Stevenson, 1992). Japanese direct investment in the United States totaled $69.7 billion in 1989 (second only to Great Britain) in manufacturing (Japan Economic Institute, 1991). But beyond the celebrated cases of U.S.–Japanese manufacturing alliances, what do we really know about the broad range of Japanese equity investments in the United States? Although the number of new Japanese wholly owned subsidiaries in the United States peaked in 1988, the number of new Japanese JVs did not decline until 1990. In Figure 12.1, the number of start-ups and the type of ownership for Japanese direct investments are plotted by year. New, partially owned start-ups in the form of equity positions appear to have dropped even more dramatically in 1990. These Japan Economic Institute (JEI) data trends have been rationalized as caused by the political

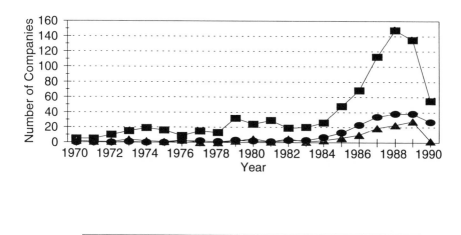

Figure 12.1. Japanese direct investment by year and type.

pressure that Japanese investors have encountered in recent years to share direct-venture enterprises and the generally decreasing availability of capital in Japan for investment. Although we did not investigate the political and global finance issues that appear to be at least partially responsible for the increased appearance of alliances and JVs, they constitute a significant context of this research. For example, figures compiled by the U.S. embassy in Tokyo (1993) show that whereas 85 percent of Japanese investments in the United States are wholly owned subsidiaries, only 67 percent of Fortune 500 firms are structured in this way in Japan. And whereas 31 percent of Fortune 500 firms in Japan are JVs, only 7 percent of the top 500 Japanese companies' investments in the United States are JVs (Japan Economic Institute, 1989).

In this chapter we propose and test a model that relates several factors to Japan's direct investment in manufacturing firms. Direct investment affects the choice of ownership structure and the capital position (if a position other than total ownership is selected). We conclude that although R&D intensity may not affect a Japanese firm's decision to use total ownership, it does affect the equity position and the type of structure (other than total ownership) used. Specifically, Japanese firms use partial stock purchases and lower equity positions for high-tech firms and JVs with higher equity positions for low-tech firms. The results suggest further avenues of research on the stability of JV governance structures as moderated by the size and history of the JV's partners, core technology characteristics, and political forces in play at the time of partnering.

THE JOINT-VENTURE LITERATURE

Although a great deal has been written about JVs, the literature appears in bursts of activity separated by long periods of neglect. After a great deal of activity in the late 1970s and early 1980s, the subject is just now enjoying a comeback in popularity. A selective review of the JV literature appears in Table 12.1. The literature also suffers from unevenness in its treatment of innovation issues. To overcome this limitation (cf. Berg, Duncan, & Friedman, 1982), we organized the literature into those contributions in the high-tech versus low-tech economic sectors and those that concentrate on resource issues versus other theories of joint activity. Contributions that compare high tech and low tech appear in the high-tech box (see Table 12.1).

Low-Tech, Resource Theories

Perhaps the best-known book that discusses JVs is that by Pfeffer and Salancik (1978), positioned in the low tech, resource theory box (Table 12.1). Their treatment concentrates on controlling resource dependency, and they outline three theories of why two or more firms form JVs. The first is an economic theory which states that JVs are established to share risk, to combine facilities to obtain economies of scale, or to generate capital. The second two theories are sociological or organizational. Professional or more complex organizations are more likely to establish JVs because they are better able to maintain autonomy in a partnership arrangement. The third theory is similar to the merger rationale, which suggests that JVs reduce uncertainty and promote stability in an organization's environment.

Pfeffer and Salancik (1978) reviewed empirical findings germane to these three theories of JV motivation and concluded that the sociological theory is supported by Aiken and Hage (1968). In addition, Pate (1969) found that most joint ventures are not undertaken to spread financial risk; rather, 80 percent of all JVs were between competitors or were buyer–seller relationships. Boyle (1968) found little evidence to support the notion that JVs are undertaken because of resource limitations.

Pfeffer and Salancik's (1978) own empirical test of the uncertainty-reduction hypothesis includes the idea that JVs are undertaken for reasons of interorganizational coordination. They found that this decision to coordinate depends on the industry's structure: Firms in industries with intermediate concentration are exposed to the greatest uncertainty and so have the greatest need for interfirm cooperation. They accounted for 60 percent of the variance in JVs with this model for FTC data (1966–69). Pfeffer and Nowak (1976) also found that firms form JVs with partners when there is industry interdependence and high technological intensity (sales and purchases). Sales interdependence predicts JVs best in intermediate-

Table 12.1. Summary of Joint-Venture Literature

	Resource Theories	Other Theories
High-tech	Kogut (1991): JVs respond to future. Koh & Venkatraman (1991): JVs stimulate market value.	Osborn and Baughn (1990): The form of governance varies with intensity of R&D. Daniels and Magill (1991): Only 12 percent of high-tech firms use global JVs. Abo (1992): Japan's first choice for governance is always direct ownership. Lynn (1991): Cognitive approach to managing JV varies by culture, especially the definition of efficiency.
Low-tech	Pfeffer and Salancik (1978): Firms in intermediate-concentration industries are most risky, and JVs vary. Christelow (1989): U.S.–Japanese JVs are mainly in Japanese industries in which Japan has advantage or equity. Tyebjee (1988): Offers typology of JVs based on need and markets. Egelhoff (1992): Small firms commit more to JV R&D. Hennart (1991): Discusses transaction costs. Blodgett (1991): Partner's contribution are linked to equity share.	Adler (1992): Population theory does not support NUMMI. Brannen (1992): Paper-mill that Japanese bought has hybrid structure. Auster (1990): The stage of industry and investment form is related, with JVs most common in growing industries. Weiss (1992a, b): Negotiation theory supports for auto JVs.

concentration industries and is used more often than mergers to coordinate competitive independence, allowing partners to exchange resources. This independence does not take into account the possibility that industries exert strong cultural influences on firms' behavior (Gordon, 1991).

Next, Christelow's (1989) study is summarized in Table 12.1. He suggests that most U.S.–Japanese JVs are established in industries in which Japan has a comparative advantage or at least parity in its economic position. Therefore, the U.S. partner has much to gain from this type of partnership. The cases used to support this view are drawn from JVs in the automotive (NUMMI) and television industries. One interpretation of this study is that U.S. partners would allow a greater equity position—say up to a 50–50 joint venture because they perceive more potential gain or have a greater need. The complement of this theory is discussed later.

Tyebjee (1988) studied many Japanese–U.S. JVs and developed a typology to explain the different types of relationships. He sees such JVs as falling into one of four categories: adoption, rebirth, procreation, and family ties. Adoption concerns a small U.S. firm in search of expansion capital.

Rebirth JVs are formed when a Japanese parent helps a large U.S. firm whose competitive position is deteriorating because of obsolete technology. Procreation describes a JV that is formed during the emergence of a new market for a product requiring several technologies. Family ties describes the restructuring of buyer–supplier relationships into a JV. Tyebjee believes that adoption and rebirth JVs are usually dominated by the Japanese partners, whereas procreation and family ties JVs may show more balanced control.

Egelhoff (1992) studied the technical alliances in the semiconductor industry and found, among other things, that the size of the firm is the strongest predictor of the percentage of R&D spent on the partnership. According to Egelhoff (1992, p. 16), "Firms with $100 million or less in semiconductor sales spent, on average, 41% of their R&D budget on technical alliances. Firms between $100 million and $1 billion spent on average 16%, and firms over $1 billion spent on average 9%." That is, firm size, rather than business strategy, was a better predictor of collaboration dependence for new technology development. Of course, if a minimum amount of funds is required for meaningful R&D, then small firms with lower absolute resources or less access to funds are likely to spend a greater proportion of their funds on R&D as well as a larger proportion of their R&D budgets on alliances to offset uncertainty, as Pfeffer and Salancik (1978) predicted.

Hennart (1991) examined the decision of Japanese companies to organize companies in structures other than wholly owned subsidiaries. He used transaction costs theory to explain the decision in terms of the comparative cost of sharing resources versus buying or creating needed resources or assets. Many variables were found to affect this decision. Companies that represented diversification for the Japanese parent decreased the probability that the parents would use total ownership, because JVs might provide access to technology new to the parent. Greater experience of the parents in the United States was found to increase the use of total ownership, because this is an asset that is costly or time-consuming to acquire. Required access to natural resources was found to decrease the propensity of creating wholly owned subsidiaries because of the cost of acquiring total ownership of resources. No relationship was detected between the parents' R&D expenditures as a ratio of domestic sales (R&D ratio) and the propensity to form wholly owned subsidiaries. Hennart suggests that parents with high R&D ratios should prefer wholly owned subsidiaries because they are willing to invest to create new technology. But he also points out that R&D-intensive parents might seek to acquire complementary technology from the United States via JVs.

Blodgett (1991) shows that equity positions in JVs are the result of the partners' differing contributions. She analyzed the investment decision using transaction cost theory and bargaining models. By assuming that equity ownership amounted to a proxy for management control, she found that both technology and government policies affected the equity positions of the dominant partners in foreign JVs.

Low-Tech, Other Theories

Adler's in-depth study of NUMMI appears in the low-tech category of other theories. Here the straw-person model is Hannan and Freeman's (1984) ecological theory of the substitution of new firms for failing older firms. Interestingly, like so many other recent articles on technological or regulatory change and industry structure (e.g., Ginsberg & Buchholtz, 1990; Osborn & Baughn, 1990), a hybrid theoretical explanation emerges after the data are examined. In Adler's (1992) study, the case study of the General Motors Corporation and Toyota JV resulted in the conclusion that although the NUMMI model is preferred to its predecessor, GM–Fremont, it also accommodates "greater worker and union power" (p. 85). This is what Adler calls a "more democratic form of Taylorism" (p. 86). Despite the lack of specificity of these terms, some conclusions can be drawn from this research: Hybrid forms do emerge from JVs, in this case a learning bureaucracy. Second, and perhaps in the broader perspective, many observers hypothesized that Toyota would eventually buy GM out of the NUMMI JV when it expired in 1996. Ironically, the two companies recently announced that they would build trucks at NUMMI after 1996. Third, Near (1989) studied nearly 7,000 U.S. and Japanese production workers and found Japanese workers to be *less* committed to their jobs. This finding implies that JV organization structures are not integrated and may have a strong influence on JVs' outcomes. Adler and Cole (1993) determined that NUMMI is a more effective model for learning than is the Uddevalla plant of Volvo. Earl (1992) found that JVs are more successful alliances than are project-by-project cooperative arrangements, using case data from GM, Nissan, Toyota, Honda, and Rover.

Brannen's (1992) dissertation presents an ethnography of a Japanese takeover of a Massachusetts paper mill. In this case, the merger of the two companies followed a unique pattern, as compared with the landed Japanese transplants in the automobile industry. Staffing patterns (line versus staff) were interspersed with Japanese and American professional and managerial personnel, whereas the typical Japanese transplant places its home-country personnel, with the exception of general managers, in staff positions only. Therefore, the hybrid, integrated structure leads to a unique, hybrid culture in this mature industry firm and, for example, avoids the "contradiction" of culture in statistical process control (SPC) quality programs.

The next entry in Table 12.1 is the study by Auster (1990) of 412 cases of U.S.–Japanese alliances from the Japanese External Trade Organization (JETRO) in nine industries in 1984/85. The author found support for the theory that the form of resource investment and the stage of the industry's evolution are related. Emerging industries use low-resource investment (i.e., technology exchange or joint R&D). JVs, which represent high-resource investments, are used in growing industries, whereas direct investment is used for some growing industries but mostly for mature industries. Weiss (1992a,b) studied international JVs using negotiation theory and found that the differences in the Toyota–GM–Ford negotiations were quite predictable.

High-Tech, Resource Theories

Kogut (1991) proposed that JVs are options for one or more partners to expand into new markets, therefore suggesting that JVs are unstable organizations. JVs are often used as a path to acquiring an existing company. In concentrated industries, a JV can also thwart competitors by tying up one of only a few potential acquisition targets. During the JV, the divesting party is contracted to pass on technology and information and, after a time, obtains full ownership.

Koh and Venkatraman (1991) found that announcements of JVs generally increased market value and were more successful than other types of governance for the information-technology sector from 1972 through 1986.

High-Tech, Other Theories

Osborn and Baughn (1990) studied 153 U.S.–Japanese technology alliances recorded in Japanese archives and found that the form of interorganizational governance varies according to the intent to conduct R&D and technology intensity as moderated by the size of the parent organizations. The intensity of the high technology leads to contracts that govern technology exchange, whereas intentions to conduct R&D lead to JVs.

Daniels and Magill (1991) observed that only 12.3 percent of high-tech industry firms use global JVs. All the JVs in their small sample ($n = 14$) had an indefinite life span but were in areas evaluated as low in strategic importance to the U.S. partner. One explanation of these results is that for high-tech firms, JVs are the worst of both the market and the hierarchy theories; that is, they have no market or organization advantage to reduce the JV's transaction costs.

In their case studies of nine high-tech firms in 14 international JVs (e.g., drugs and computers), Daniels and Magill (1991) found that seven were with Japanese firms. Ownership varied from 40 to 70 percent by the U.S. partner. They assumed that the locus of control usually went to the parent with the greatest interest, and this paralleled the use of other control mechanisms (staffing of expatriates is the exception). Little R&D takes place in these JVs. This research is consistent with Osborn and Baughn's (1990). The implication in this case is that the research and development stream has already been established for high-tech firms and that JVs would only erode the technical advantage. Trust usually springs from previous dealings based on similar values and the reputation of the partner. If foreign conditions are seen as very different from those in the home country, high-tech firms will take a partner to do business. For the same reasons, however, these ventures tend to be more stable and sustainable for the two partners, because there is little pressure, either technologically or financially, for one partner to take over the other.

Abo (1992) hypothesizes that "when Japanese firms apply their technological advantages to foreign countries" (firm-specific advantage in MNE theory), they will face problems in adapting to their local environment ("location-specific factor") (Abo, 1992, p. 304). In a study of 34 transplants, he found that most were a hybrid of U.S. and Japanese operational styles but that there were substantial differences across industries. Auto parts and auto assembly lean toward the "application side"; consumer electronics is shifted toward the adaptation method; and semiconductor plants are in the middle of the ratings between application and adaptation. For example, auto parts plants have "applied almost the identical practices as at their parent plants in Japan (although not so successfully as just-in-time in Japan)" (Abo, 1992, p. 305). One of the most important conclusions and interpretations of Abo's work is that Japanese, and perhaps all foreign investors in manufacturing, always prefer 100 percent ownership of plants and revert to JVs only when forced to do so because of political conditions (e.g., host-country rules or pressure for joint ownership), which supports the JEI data trends on JVs in the United States.

Interestingly, when size and age of firm are controlled, the Japanese firms in the Egelhoff sample spent among the lowest percentages (5 to 5.5%) of their R&D budget on technical alliances. Interviews revealed that larger firms did not want to depend on external sources for "crucial elements" of either their product or their process technology in semiconductors. Collaborative R&D was seen as "augmenting rather than substituting for strong internal R&D efforts" (Egelhoff, 1992, p. 16). Yet the cultural differences between Americans and Japanese create many problems when they actually implement their JVs (Lynn, 1991).

Success and Failure of JVs

Perhaps the most complex and controversial aspects of the JV research question is conceptualizing and measuring the success of this form of governance. Data are available on "changes" in governance from the JV form to other forms, including the "failure" of these investments. A sample of these statistics is presented in Table 12.2.

Domestic JVs (45.9% changed structure) and all international JVs (45 to 50% changed structure) appear to have the highest "failure rate." The latter statistics were based in part on U.S.–Indian JVs (Reynolds, 1984) and a sample of 66 firms of JVs in developing countries (Beamish, 1985), which are summarized in Datta (1988).

Table 12.2.   Survivability of JVs

Study	Time Elapsed	Firms	Structure Changed	Percentage Change
Domestic JV[a]	6 years	148	68	45.9%
Domestic JV with Japan[a]	6 years	23	8	34.8%
JVs of U.S. MNEs[b]	75 years	2378	728	30.6%
Owned subsidiaries of U.S. MNEs[b]	75 years	3555	558	15.7%
All international JVs[c]	—	—	—	45–50%

Sources:

[a] Kogut, 1988, pp. 39–52.

[b] Gomes-Casseres, 1987, pp. 97–102.

[c] Beamish, 1985, and Reynolds, 1984, reviewed in Datta, 1988.

Domestic JVs with Japan (34.8% changed) and all U.S. multinational enterprise JVs (30.6% changed) fare somewhat better if change is used as a negative indicator. Owned subsidiaries (like Japanese transplant direct investments) of U.S. multinational enterprises (MNEs) have the least amount of structural change, only 15.7 percent.

Yet these statistics do not take into account that in many countries JVs are forced on the investor by local laws or implied trade agreements. Furthermore, many companies like IBM and Ford have stated global strategies and policies that they will manufacture where they sell products; that is, their market-entry strategy forces foreign investment of some form in manufacturing facilities. These companies would likely alter their form of governance to fit local laws and custom as needed to implement their global strategies. What was a direct 100 percent investment today might easily be converted to a JV tomorrow. It is not clear how one should measure the success of a JV when one takes these trends into account. Measuring internal JVs' outcomes provides one multivariate alternative (Shortell & Zajac, 1988) which includes R&D investments.

Considerable case evidence on both sides (positive and negative) suggests that JVs are either a curse or a blessing for their parents. An outstanding early success in automotive supply is the TKS JV between TRW and Koyo (see Table 12.3). Established in Vonore, Tennessee, in April 1988 as a venture starting from scratch with 51 percent TRW ownership, the firm currently has 365 employees and six major customers and produces 1 million steering gears for these companies.

These performance numbers emphasize customer delivery (100%), quality improvement (line returns and scrap rates), and increasing speed of program launches, typical of a Japanese manufacturing firm.

Blodgett (1992) used event-history analysis to analyze 1,025 JVs formed by 69 companies from mergers and acquisitions from 1971 through 1981 and changes in ownership percentages from 10–K reports of the U.S. partners. She found that JVs are more stable when partners start out with

Table 12.3. Results to Date of the TRW–Koyo (TKS) Joint Ventures to Procedure—Power Rack and Pinion Gears and Other Steering Components

	1990	1991/92	1993
Customer delivery (%)	100	100	100
Line returns (PPM)	670	280	55
Machining scrap (%)	4.6	3.4	0.9
Program launches			
Installation (weeks)	4	1	0.3
Capability (months)	12	2	1
Production levels (months)	14	2	1

Source: Korde, 1993.

equal ownership (50–50) and when contracts have been renegotiated before. Contracts are more likely to be renegotiated, and therefore greater JV stability is promoted in open economies that impose few restrictions on direct investment.

Propositions

Many investigators have sought to explain investment as a choice between totally owned subsidiaries and JVs (e.g., Christelow, 1989; Gomes-Cassores, 1987; Hennart, 1991; Kogut, 1991). Although Osborn and Baughn (1990) looked at a wider range of arrangements for joint R&D, few writers have considered equity arrangements other than JVs and wholly owned subsidiaries. Although Tyebjee's (1988) typology of reasons for the formation of JVs provides a more detailed explanation of JV formation, he does not believe that the different reasons for formation might produce different equity arrangements. In particular, Tyebjee's adoption JVs do not seem to be JVs. These so-called JVs often do not share resources in the beginning but appear to be more an option to expand, as outlined by Kogut (1991), or attempts to access technology (Hennart 1991).

There are at least three different ownership structures, including the two used by other investigators (total ownership and JV) and a third that we call *partial ownership*. This third capital structure is characterized by two forms. In older firms, the Japanese partner may buy a substantial block of stock of the target (adopted) U.S. firm. This block may or may not represent de facto control of the target company in the beginning. In newly developed firms, partial ownership is represented by sharing equity in the new firm with individual investors, who usually are officers in the new company, rather than with officers in existing corporations.

This difference in structure may affect the Japanese parent's ability to influence the company and to acquire it at a later date. The relative bargaining power of the individual investors may be less than the bargaining power of the corporations that are partners in JVs. The determinants of these partial buyouts should be different from those for regular JVs with other corporations.

Taken together, these data and theories offer several propositions for testing. First, several contributions (especially Auster, 1990; Christelow, 1989; Daniels & Magill, 1991; Egelhoff, 1992; Osborn & Baughn, 1990) appear to converge on the theory that there is a salient relationship between type of industry—high tech versus low tech—and the proportion of Japanese investment in domestic manufacturing JVs, defined broadly. This convergence is expressed in the following propositions:

> Proposition 1: The more intense the R&D of the manufacturing industry is, the more limited will be the proportion of Japanese participation in firms that are not wholly owned subsidiaries. This should be reflected in the propensity to adopt (Tyebjee, 1988) high-tech firms. Such investments use a smaller "partial" equity position rather than JVs.

Because high-tech firms tend to be in less mature industries, it also follows that the organizational size will enter the predictive equation for JVs. That is, small firms initiate industries; they tend to stress product over process innovation (Utterback & Abernathy, 1975); and they are likely to be dependent on technical, human, and financial resources for survival and growth (Balkin & Gomez-Mejia, 1987).

JVs in concentrated (mature) industries would be preludes to acquisition; that is, larger firms should have a higher proportion of Japanese ownership (Kogut, 1991). Larger JVs usually acquire existing industries, following a "rebirth" JV in which the Japanese partner is dominant (Tyebjee, 1988).

> Proposition 2: Japanese equity investments structured as partial or JV equity positions are likely to be small in small firms and greater in larger firms for domestic manufacturing alliances.

Pfeffer and Salancik (1978) found that firms with suppliers in industries of medium concentration were more likely to form JVs, because of the increased uncertainty of companies in medium concentration industries. Tyebjee (1988) found that such JVs between supplier and customer were common and described them as "family ties" JVs.

> Proposition 3: Japanese investments in firms operating in industries with medium concentration take the form of JVs more often do than investments in industries with high or low concentration.

Christelow (1989) pointed out that high-visibility industries such as steel and auto favor ownership positions other than wholly owned, in order to fend off public criticism of foreign ownership.

> Proposition 4: Japanese investments in industries that have threatened or are threatened with import restrictions are more likely to be lower than are investments in firms in other industries.

Other performance outcomes are possible. Japanese processing technology might actually be superior in general, although U.S. product technology might dominate. One can only speculate on the implications of these strategic marriages. Exploration of cohort effects seems warranted as well (e.g., the recency of Japanese entry might reflect learning and prevailing economic conditions).

METHODOLOGY

As an alternative to cross-national comparisons (Lynn, 1991) and laboratory simulation (Adler & Graham, 1989), the data for this study were obtained from two sources: (1) for secondary analysis, from the Japan Economic Institute (1989) report on direct investment in U.S. manufacturing and (2) from case studies conducted using interviews on site with representatives of U.S.–Japanese JVs in manufacturing, as well as company records and published reports. These data were the most recent available at the time of this writing. According to the JEI report, Japanese direct investment in U.S. manufacturing peaked in 1988 and totaled $67.8 billion in 1989. This is second only to that of the United Kingdom, which totaled $119.1 billion in the same year. The majority of Japanese investment is in 100 percent ownership investments, whether in start-ups or acquisitions. Seventy-one percent (870 cases) of Japanese direct investments were total ownership.

The remaining 354 cases varied from 10 percent to 95 percent equity investment positions, with the majority being 50–50 partnerships (104, or 8.5%). Most of the 1,224 cases of direct Japanese investment were new-company starts (780, or 63.7%). The range between 100 and 95 percent was deleted because this range is usually considered complete ownership. All domestic cases were used regardless of whether the non-Japanese partner was a U.S. company or a foreign firm.

The major variables available from the JEI report include year formed, acquired versus new firm, employees, factories, location, product, SIC(4), parents, and percentage owned. From these variables, we created variables for a total percentage of Japanese ownership and a total percentage of U.S. ownership. Unfortunately, the data apply only to the start up (acquisition) of the JV. We do not have data on the stability of these firms. In fact, we know that some firms in the study now have significantly different ownership structures.

R&D intensity was determined by linking the SIC(4) code for each firm with a 1991 listing of R&D intensity. R&D intensity is defined as the R&D investment as a percentage of net sales. We used the figures published by Schonfeld & Associates, Inc. (1991), for this purpose, as they provided the best accuracy and were published for each four-digit SIC.

The natural log of the number of employees working at each firm is used to represent the variable of SIZE of each firm. Ettlie, Bridges, and O'Keefe (1984) found this to be a better representation of size than the number of employees in studies of product and process innovation. Two other variables were also tested as rival explanations of variance in Japanese ownership. These are Group Year formed (bought) and New (start-up versus acquisition).

Industry concentration was calculated by linking the SIC(4) code for each firm with a 1987 listing of industry concentration. The amount of sales attributed to the four largest firms was used as the industry concentration. We used the figures published by the U.S. Department of Commerce (1989) for this purpose, and we used three dummy variables to represent the lower, middle, and upper groups (LOWC, MIDC, and HIC).

The variable NEW indicates whether JVs were new companies or were acquired (0 = acquired and 1 = new). If new companies are riskier than existing companies, then new JVs should have lower Japanese ownership if they are being used to spread the risk. This would support the economic theory of JVs described by Pfeffer and Salancik. Year represents a control for changes in investment policy over time.

Dodwell Marketing Consultants (1990), JETRO (1992), and the Japan Chamber of Commerce and Industry (1991) were consulted to determine whether any Japanese parents manufactured a product in Japan that is similar to the venture's product(s) in the United States. This is reflected in the variable MAKE, a dummy variable with a value of 1 for Japanese parents with similar products.

The variable OYEAR represents the maximum number of years of experience in U.S. manufacturing for the Japanese parents at the time the investment is made.

Three variables were used to represent industry effects. Christelow (1989) stated that JVs are used in response to political pressure resulting from foreign inroads into important U.S. industries, such as autos and steel. Import restrictions have been threatened or used for both these industries. The variable POLIT represents ventures involved with auto or steel manufacturing (1 = involvement). The variable HITECH refers to firms in medical, biotech, airplane, telephone, and computer industries. These are high-tech industries in which U.S. companies hold some advantage over Japanese firms. Firms involved in publishing printed or recorded material are reflected in the dummy variable PUB. These resources should be difficult to appropriate by means other than purchasing companies in the short term.

The variable MRD represents the R&D intensity for firms having a medium concentration. Although we performed regression moderated by concentration group (LOWC, MIDC, and HIC), we present the significant result as an interaction term between medium concentration grouping and R&D to simplify Table 12.4. In Table 12.4, the results of two weighted least squares regressions compare the percentage of Japanese ownership in domestic ventures with various independent variables. The first model includes wholly owned subsidiaries, but the second one does not.

Although both models show significant relationships, the inclusion of wholly owned subsidiaries does provide some different results because of the size of the sample and the different strategies for direct investment represented by wholly owned subsidiaries.

In the first model, three factors are related to a lower percentage of total Japanese ownership. The variable POLIT representing firms in automotive and steel industries had a total Japanese investment that was 8.8 percent less than for ventures in other industries. The beta for this dummy variable was $-.132$ ($p < .001$). Firms with higher R&D intensity had a lower total Japanese ownership, but only for firms belonging to the middle-third concentration group (MRD beta $= -.205$ and $p < .001$). For firms in the lower- and higher-concentration groups, R&D intensity was not a significant factor.

Three factors were related to a higher percentage of total Japanese ownership. Firms that had a Japanese parent making a similar product had a total Japanese investment that was 11.5 percent more than that in other firms. The beta for MAKE was .146 ($p < .001$). Firms with newly developed sites had a total Japanese ownership that was 10.1 percent higher than that in existing firms that were invested in (beta $= .188$ and $p < .001$). Firms in publishing books and music also had a greater total Japanese ownership, which amounted to 11.2 percent (PUB beta $= .083$ and $p < .01$).

The overall explanatory power of the model was limited (Adj. $R^2 = .097$, $F = 12.74$, $p = .0001$). The low R^2 could be predicted, given the conflicting strategies represented by JVs, partially owned companies, and wholly owned companies.

The results for the second model had some differences and some similarities. Independent variables with similar values included MAKE and MRD, with betas of .243 ($p < .001$) and $-.327$ ($p < .01$), respectively. The betas for NEW and PUB were not significant. POLIT resulted in a higher percentage of Japanese ownership (beta $= .144$, $p < .05$), which is the opposite of the first model.

Two variables not significant in the first model were significant in the second. SIZE was negatively related to total Japanese ownership (beta $= -.230$, $p < .001$). HITECH firms had 12.0 percent (beta $= .285$, $p < .001$) more total Japanese ownership than other firms did. The overall explanatory power of the second model was better than the first (Adj. $R^2 = .227$, $F = 9.91$, $p = .0001$). Table 12.5 compares of the number of direct investments distributed by SIC(4) concentration and investment type (JV, partial ownership, and total ownership). The Cochran–Mantel–Haenszel statistics show a significant correlation between concentration level and investment type ($p < .01$), although the correlation is negative for medium concentration and JV formation. That is, the percentage of direct investment which takes the form of JVs is lowest (rather than highest, as expected) for companies manufacturing products with SIC(4s), which have mid-level concentration.

Table 12.4. Weighted Regression and Correlation Summaries

	Beta Entries for Models	
Independent Variable	All Firms (N = 1205)	Excluding (N = 334) Wholly Owned Firms
SIZE	.146***	−.230***
MAKE	.188***	.243***
NEW		
HITECH		.285***
PUB	.083**	
POLIT	−.132***	.144*
MRD	−.205***	−.327**
MIDC	.107*	
ADJUSTED R²	.097	.227***

Correlation Matrix: All Firms (sample size varies, pairwise deletion, max N = 1205)

	OJ	SIZE	RD	MAKE	NEW	OYEAR	HITECH	PUB	POLIT	LOWC	MIDC	HIC	MRD
OJ	1.00												
SIZE	−.018	1.00											
RD	−.050	.003	1.00										
MAKE	.190**	.032	−.164***	1.00									
NEW	.201***	−.238***	−.189***	.228***	1.00								
OYEAR	−.085**	.175***	.029	−.163***	−.120***	1.00							
HITECH	−.031	−.009	.385***	−.218***	−.161***	.016	1.00						
PUB	.094**	.025	−.090**	−.006	−.015	.021	−.120***	1.00					
POLIT	−.074*	.118***	−.331***	.121***	.235***	−.009	−.290***	−.101***	1.00				
LOWC	.035	−.164	−.066*	.030	.077**	−.033	−.242***	.010	.073*	1.00			
MIDC	−.044	−.060*	.043	−.028	−.083**	−.035	.215***	−.018	−.191***	−.469***	1.00		
HIC	.012	.213***	.019	0.00	.012	.066*	.101	.009	.124***	−.459***	−.569***	1.00	
MRD	−.112***	−.084**	.368***	−.121***	−.144***	−.014	.348***	−.042	−.238***	−.381***	.811***	−.462***	1.00

Correlation Matrix: Excluding Wholly Owned Firms (sample size varies, pairwise deletion, max N = 334)

	OJ	SIZE	RD	MAKE	NEW	OYEAR	HITECH	PUB	POLIT	LOWC	MIDC	HIC	MRD
OJ	1.00												
SIZE	-.192	1.00											
RD	-.213	-.050	1.00										
MAKE	.255***	-.025	-.285***	1.00									
NEW	.218***	-.228***	-.363***	.364***	1.00								
OYEAR	-.081	.098	.072	-.181***	-.217***	1.00							
HITECH	.008	-.101	.437***	-.404***	-.318***	.060	1.00						
PUB	.094	-.068	-.119*	.003	.074	-.020	-.066	1.00					
POLIT	.175**	.158**	-.464***	.248***	.344***	-.040	-.388***	-.065	1.00				
LOWC	.126*	-.156**	-.170**	.128*	.309***	-.065	-.369***	.156**	.132*	1.00			
MIDC	-.243***	-.120*	.195***	-.117*	-.218***	-.016	.265***	-.079	-.254***	-.455***	1.00		
HIC	.127*	.262***	-.038	0.00	-.066	.075	.075	-.065	.132*	-.463***	-.578***	1.00	
MRD	-.319***	-.119*	.485***	-.210***	-.295***	.025	.358***	-.066	-.330***	-.380***	.836***	.483***	1.00

* = p < .05
** = p < .01
*** = p < .001

Table 12.5. Investment Type

Concentration Group	Joint Venture	Partially Owned	Wholly Owned	Total
High (top third)				
Frequency	86	35	270	391
Percent	7.03	2.86	22.06	31.94
Row Percent	21.99	8.95	69.05	
Col Percent	39.27	25.93	31.03	
Medium (middle third)				
Frequency	55	59	302	416
Percent	4.49	4.82	24.67	33.99
Row Percent	13.22	14.18	72.6	
Col Percent	25.11	43.7	34.71	
Low (bottom third)				
Frequency	78	41	298	417
Percent	6.37	3.35	24.35	34.07
Row Percent	18.71	9.83	71.46	
Col Percent	35.62	30.37	34.25	
Total				
Frequency	219	135	870	1224
Percent	17.89	11.03	71.08	100.0

Cochran–Mantel–Haenszel Statistics

Statistic	Alternative Hypothesis	DF	Value	Prob
1	Nonzero correlation	1	5.044	0.025
2	Row mean scores differ	2	5.053	0.080
2	General association	4	15.085	0.005

DISCUSSION

The purpose of comparing the proportion of Japanese ownership in U.S. domestic manufacturing ventures and doing case research on JVs is two-fold. First, we would like to gain more insight into the reasons for forming JVs. Second, we would like to offer insight into the effects of forming JVs. Such knowledge would be useful in both academia and industry.

Motivation for Formation

According to our case studies, the JV is almost universally the governance mode of last choice for all participants. If this is true, then why has the formation of JVs increased so dramatically during the late 1980s? Our data offer a likely reason. The political pressure on the Japanese to use more U.S. content in automobiles sold in this country has led to many JVs in this industry. Similar pressure also has led to the same results in the steel industry.

Although we have shown a significant inverse relationship between R&D and the proportion of total Japanese investment in U.S. manufacturing ventures, this involvement does not seem to be related to JVs for high-tech industries (industries with an R&D ratio of more than 6%). Instead, ownership in high-tech companies that are not wholly owned seems to be more closely related to partial ownerships. For high-tech ventures that make products not manufactured by any of their Japanese parents, none of the firms in our sample was a JV. For all categories except low-tech ventures that make products manufactured by at least one Japanese parent, the partially owned firms outnumbered the JVs.

These results suggest that JVs traditionally have not been used by the Japanese to gain access to technology or new products; rather, total ownership and partial ownership appear more desirable under these conditions. Whether this trend persists is a matter of speculation.

This use of partial ownership is particularly interesting because it has not been given much attention in the literature. It is also interesting because the governance and control of partially owned firms are very different from those of JVs. In partially owned firms, Japanese parents may gain substantial control if the firm is new and the offspring has difficulty raising capital elsewhere.

A similar situation may exist with partially owned firms that are new start-ups. According to our case studies, these firms appear to attract private investors who also manage the venture while cooperating with Japanese parents who supply capital and often technology to the venture.

The issue of the relationship between control of a venture and ownership of it cannot be ignored. To date, the dominant mode of direct investment in manufacturing is through wholly owned subsidiaries (about 70% of firms fall into this category). Factors that negate this trend toward wholly owned subsidiaries appear to be based on resources. Such factors include access to markets, access to technology, access to new products, domestic content, and freedom from import restrictions. Our case studies show that JVs are not used unless there is some reason for coordinating and cooperation with another corporate entity.

Control appears to be very important, even when partial ownership and JVs are used. The results showing noticeably higher ownership for PUB or property rights companies, MAKE or ventures making products similar to Japanese parents, and HITECH or R&D-intensive industries in which the United States holds some advantage suggest that control is important. Even when a JV is formed, we observed that Japanese parents often retain substantial control over such enterprises by licensing their technology and controlling their markets. Thus the issue of control of JVs is more complex than just a percentage of ownership. Contradicting this trend of JVs' being used only as necessary to enter markets and gain access to technology is the literature that recommends interorganizational cooperation as a good and necessary process to maintain competitiveness. Pfeffer and Salancik (1978) assert that there are substantial benefits to such coordination. Osborn and Baughn (in Chapter 5 in this book) agree that although JVs and coordination agreements may have short life spans, the relationship between partner companies often continues after individual coordinations have been terminated. They also discovered that JVs are being used less to rob technology from other firms and more to keep abreast of current technology, to avoid being left behind. Koh and Venkatraman (1991) found that JVs are most profitable when they overlap existing products and markets to acquire complementary technologies and strengthen product–market scopes.

Finally, those of our results that seem to contradict those of Pfeffer and Salancik (1978) may not be as contradictory as they appear on the surface. First, for ventures that make products unlike any products made by their Japanese parents, the percentage of wholly owned subsidiaries is lowest for ventures in medium-concentration industries. Second, there may be a selection bias in our data in that they include only Japanese direct investments.

Third, Pfeffer and Salancik's data covered earlier JVs from U.S. Department of Commerce data. The factors concerning foreign JVs and more recent JVs could be very different. Also, the effect of industry concentration reported by Pfeffer and Salancik was insignificant. Finally, it is clear that ventures in medium concentration industries are different. The result showing that total investment is negatively related to R&D intensity in such ventures suggests that high-tech, medium-concentration industries may be unstable, as suggested by Pfeffer and Salancik.

Management Implications

Our case studies show that JVs have several implications for management. The operating results for our case studies were relatively good in most cases and outstanding in some. It appears to us that JVs offer an opportunity to use the best practices of Japanese and U.S. management to obtain excellent results and greater learning. This success is by no means guaranteed, however. A relatively successful JV is harder to obtain than a relatively successful subsidiary is, but the payoff for a successful JV can be substantially higher as well.

Our case studies highlight several areas of difficulty in running a JV. First, although JVs are usually negotiated over long periods of time and in great detail, their goals often change rapidly after they are formed. This rapid succession of goals often strains the relationships between the JV and its parents. Therefore, the motivation of the JV's parents is to choose partners that want a long-term relationship. Lane and Beamish (1990) found that this was the most important consideration when establishing a JV.

The structure of the JV often must be changed to reflect economic reality. Usually the U.S. parents force a downsizing, whereas the Japanese parents are often willing to support poorly performing JVs for relatively long periods of time. It is not clear, however, that this trend will continue with the changing economic environment in Japan.

The choice of people to run a JV and the structure of management also are important. Based on our case study and Brannen's (1992) ethnography, an interlocking structure in which Japanese and U.S. managers report to each other is recommended. To make this work, the managers must be chosen carefully. Although this recommendation may appear self-evident, it is not easy for a company to entice its best people to handle risky assignments at JVs.

Weick (1979) suggests that companies that tolerate differing opinions in their personnel can better learn from and react to changes in their environments. The ability of a parent company to provide good managers to run a JV may be related to its ability to tolerate heterogeneity in its personnel. In those companies that do not tolerate divergent opinions, people going to JVs are often seen as outsiders in the parent company, and consequently, the more qualified managers often reject such positions. This idea can be traced to the principle of requisite variety in general systems theory (Ashby, 1962), with the reminder that maintaining this divergence has a cost—variety is not free. Furthermore, managers at large parents may view a transfer to a JV as a risky career move. Therefore, it is not certain that the person best suited to running a JV will always agree to do so.

Related to the issue of heterogeneity is a company's ability to learn from JVs. According to Weick, the ability of a company to learn is also related to its ability to tolerate divergent opinions, which may be why most of the U.S. personnel in our case studies reported disappointing levels of indirect learning resulting from their experiences in JVs.

Although the pattern of governing JVs indicates that management control is important to the Japanese, operating JVs suggests something else. In almost all the JVs we studied, their management was left to the U.S. partners. This is especially interesting to us because the practices used appear more "Japanese" than American. Such practices include promotion from within, large investments in personal growth, and job rotation. It was not clear whether these practices resulted from suggestions by the Japanese parents or whether the JV gave the U.S. parents an opportunity to try new methods that they could not try in the parent company.

From what we have seen, the performance of JVs in terms of quality and efficiency is usually good, often better than that of U.S. competitors. We have heard many stories of how company performance was enhanced by using the best practices of both U.S. and Japanese management.

An example of this trend is that U.S. managers found that Japanese managers sometimes took forecasts or customers' requests too literally. Not only did the Japanese managers tend to build in too much capacity for predicted demand, but they also were reluctant to suggest design changes to U.S. customers that would result in a product of greater value.

Although the formation and management of a JV are formidable tasks, the rewards for success can be proportionally higher. Although we have not seen evidence that companies form JVs for the sake of interorganizational coordination alone, it is not clear that this is always the case.

Table 12.6. Summary of Joint-Venture Case Studies

	Company L	Company W	Company D	Company C
Industry	Telecommunications	Auto supply	Auto supply	TV tube glass
Technology	High-tech (4%)	Low-tech (2.4%)	Low-tech (0.5%)	High-tech (4%)
Ownership	51–49%	50–50%	60–40%	50–50%
Structure	Hybrid	Segregated	Segregated	Segregated
Management	U.S. partner	U.S. partner	U.S. partner	U.S. partner
Contributions	U.S. product	U.S. marketing	U.S. process	Shared technology
Motive	Market/patent	Market/alliance partnership	License	Market/technology
Technology performance	Best in class	Good	Good, but . . .	OK
Technology transfer	Excellent	Little	None	Good
Production performance	Good	Good (CpK > 1.5)	OK, downsized	OK, downsized
Culture	Port in a storm; accommodation	Japanese persistence	Japan versus U.S. customer: ex-pectation, trust	Rapid change
Lesson learned	Hybrid structure works	Technological specifications/ overdesign	U.S. negotiators weak	Technology not an end
Survival of JV	?	?	In jeopardy	OK

Industry R&D intensity (R&D expenses as a percentage of sales) and other factors.

CASE STUDIES

Using interviews (see the interview guide in the Appendix), company records, and published documents, we compiled four case histories of U.S.–
Japanese JVs in manufacturing, which are summarized in Table 12.6. First
we discuss each case separately, and then we present our general observations.

Company L

Company L was formed in 1988 as a 51–49 percent (U.S.–Japanese) JV
between two large parent companies. The Japanese partner had been manufacturing a high-tech telecommunications product in the United States
but lost a patent infringement suit in 1986 to the U.S. firm that originated
the technology in the industry. The Japanese company approached a U.S.
competitor with alternative technology and patents to form a partnership.
The two firms had prior relationships that facilitated the negotiation.

During the first four years of operation, the JV achieved the world-class
benchmark standard in three critical technical parameters for the product,
thereby equaling or surpassing the parents and the original U.S. firm in the
industry. Three of the first four years were profitable.

The JV's organization is an integrated structure with representatives
from the two parents alternating in the hierarchy. The president is Japanese, and the executive vice president and chief technical officer are American, and so on. Yet even with this very integrated structure, Company L
exercises considerable autonomy in decision making and planning.

This structure and culture sharply contrast with that described by Adler
(1993) for the JV between Toyota and General Motors: NUMMI in Fremont, California. Adler calls NUMMI a learning bureaucracy, but the
structure is hardly integrated in the way that Company L is. This and
other preliminary evidence suggest that high-tech and low-tech JVs present
quite different management challenges.

This current structure differs from the structure of the forerunner firm,
originally 100 percent owned and operated by the Japanese parent. In its
first incarnation, this firm had problems supplying its customers (even one
customer on site)—in a timely fashion, and there were complaints from
the U.S. employees that the firm had public and private agendas for decision making. The U.S. employees reported gathering information for a major equipment purchase decision, even though the decision had already
been made by the Japanese management of the predecessor firm.

Another remarkable accomplishment of this JV is that the firm's technology is already being transferred to a U.S. plant of the U.S. parent. These
rather rapid, second-order technology effects of the JV are extremely rare.
The president of the JV, an employee of the Japanese parent company,
told us that the motivations for venturing with this U.S. partner were that

the Japanese market would eventually have to open to the world, and to prepare for this gradual transition, his company needed to establish relationships with prestigious U.S. companies that were already well known and experienced in dealing with his firm.

The remaining challenge for this firm is that the world market in this product category is predicted to grow about fifteenfold during the next five to 10 years, and gearing up a relatively small JV firm and its production to meet this demand and still maintain this high level of quality and unique hybrid culture will be a formidable task. Just meeting short-term shipment targets seems to be a large order. The JV has already outgrown its main customer and now must come up with an expansion strategy that can be sustained.

Company W

Company W is a first-tier automotive supplier of engine components. The JV was initiated as a direct result of the oil crisis in the late 1970s. It was predicted that engines would have to be redesigned to be high performing, light, and more fuel efficient, and both parents' organizations were looking for ways to exploit this anticipated increase in the need for components that would foster this design trend. A distribution agreement was signed in 1978 between the two parents. The Japanese parent was looking for an entrée into the North American market, and the U.S. partner did not want to invest what was required in this high-tech product in order to enter the market. The distribution group was first located at the U.S. partner's headquarters.

The American partner assumed management of the firm from the beginning when it was formalized as a 50–50 JV in 1980, and in 1982 the plans for a "lights-out" factory were in place for the new plant. This plan was scaled back significantly, and a very "medium" technology plant was actually built when the market became soft. During this period, the U.S. partner acquired a leveraged-buyout status, and the JV was kept alive with export business and the continued financial support of the Japanese parent that had invested in the technology.

As it was in other automotive technology reports (e.g., Sestok, 1993), the Japanese partner was viewed as very conservative in its approach to design, often seen as "overdesigning" the product. Americans tend to regard the design process as obtaining a solution that is "good enough" to meet the specification. But as others, like Sestok from the Chrysler Corporation, have noted, this Japanese conservatism usually pays off in the product's increased durability and lower costs over the life cycle of the car, an approach that Chrysler adopted in its LH platform in late 1992 and subsequent product programs. This difference in the "culture" of design is often a sticking point in dealings between partners from the United States and Japan in the auto industry.

The organizational structure of this JV has changed several times during its history, but usually one Japanese engineer reporting to the JV manager or engineering was the only noteworthy feature. At one point during the firm's history (late 1980s), a Japanese joint general manager was appointed as part of the continuing support agreement with the Japanese parent. This Japanese manager assumed some of the firm's major marketing tasks while the U.S. manager continued to handle operations—sort of a role reversal but an opportunity for the Japanese parent to learn some of the business's market aspects.

An unanticipated side benefit of this structure, with a resident Japanese product engineer on staff, is that the JV has a built-in advantage in negotiating with Japanese transplant automobile companies and their Japanese suppliers. In the end, however, the management and implementation of the JV are essentially American, with no real integrated structure, as in the case of Company L.

In 1986, the products supplied for Ford engines were 80 percent Japanese and 20 percent American. For the current GM program, the mix is 25–30 percent Japanese content, and operating characteristics of the small plant (40 employees in a rural area) are quite good, with CpKs in the 1.33 to 2.0 range. The manager of the JV reported that the company should make a profit for the first time in its history by the end of 1992, and it is unlikely that the JV would still exist if the partner had not been this particular Japanese company.

Company D

This JV in the automotive-supply industry (rated first by its assembly-plant customer, the GM Saturn Corporation, for on-time delivery) was formed as the result of a license agreement that the two parents drew up in Japan in 1986. The U.S. partner licensed its technology to the Japanese partner and then was asked by this company to deliver products in the United States. Because the license applied only to the Japanese market, the production agreement had to be renegotiated for the U.S. market.

The JV was structured as a 60–40, U.S.-managed company, located near the assembly plant. The actual supply of the product was through original processing at the Japanese partner's plant in the Midwest, postprocessed at the JV, and then warehoused at the Japanese partner's facility, which was adjacent to the JV near the assembly plant.

Perhaps the most important point that emerged in this case was the differences between the two parents in their perception of what the assembly customer wanted and needed in order to be successful. The U.S. partner listened carefully to what the customer said it wanted and then compared its delivery needs with the production plan and noted the discrepancy. In addition, the U.S. partner's way of doing business was to act in the customer's best interest, even if it were at odds with the company's stated mission, but in consultation, of course. The Japanese partner took the customer's word as gospel.

This difference in dealing with customers led to significant problems in managing this JV. To show a profit in 1993, the temporary employees of this JV (about 30% of the workforce) had to be released. Not only did they interfere with regular production operations, but they also were not expected to be needed in the near future.

The U.S. partner admitted that a lesson learned in this experience was that it did not have the negotiation skills needed to manage this partnership. The Japanese operating group running the JV, which was a different group of people than those who negotiated the agreement, attempted to rewrite the JV partnership agreement for issues like the terms of payment.

Yet the actual operation of the JV has been quite successful recently because of a bonus system for productivity established by the U.S. partner and the addition of a new Japanese liaison manager to the JV (vice president for quality). In addition, Japanese engineers from the parent visited the operation "in waves" but could not suggest improvements that would substantially enhance operations not already simplified and modified by the three work-crew teams on the floor. Continuous improvement does cause stress in the operation, but with the new bonus system in place, based on reduction of scrap (which was 13%, reduced to 0.2%) and improvement in yield, it appears to be paying off. Inventory turns have been increased to 230 per year.

The JV team has made significant improvements in the U.S. equipment supplied to the production facility, many times over the recommended operating characteristics of the supplier's specified technical parameters. The unique design requirements of the assembly customer favored the Japanese company as a sole source, but to meet these world-class specifications, yields had to be low in the original production process that ships products to the JV. Therefore, the future of the JV is in doubt.

Company C

This JV was formed out of a necessity to participate in the global picture-tube market for color televisions. The Japanese partner wanted access to the U.S. partner's technology, and the U.S. partner wanted access to the Japanese partner's customers and technology, but the JV rapidly shifted to a market-driven partnership. The 50–50 JV started as a 66–33 JV in 1988 after a 30–year relationship between the two large parent companies. Significant process improvements (e.g., $200 million integrated factory facility) necessitated greater Japanese participation in the partnership. The Japanese parent is the same company as the parent in the previously cited case (Company D), and ultimately, this JV also had to be downsized in order to be profitable.

The JV enjoys very successful operating characteristics. Yields have improved from 8 to 26 percent, resulting from a typical Japanese strategy of a "war on waste." Both parents contributed significantly to the technology of the JV. Since the plant started up, there has been a 22 percent reduction in manufacturing costs. Product quality has improved 42 to 121 percent, depending on the component. Malcolm Baldrige Award criteria were used for quality improvement during 1992/93, even though the U.S. parent's total quality management (TQM) program was begun at this location in 1983. Inventory turns have tripled, and product-development time has been reduced by 50 percent.

The plant and the JV won a prestigious industry award for computer-integrated manufacturing but still had to downsize significantly during 1992 to meet the stringent goals of the U.S. parent (30% return on equity). Although these targets were achieved, they resulted in significant downsizing, as in the case of Company D.

The challenge the company faces now is the next generation of technology, high-definition television (HDTV). Can the JV compete? Will cost and quality continue to be issues? Will the potential conflict in U.S. and Japanese standards for HDTV pose problems? Stay tuned.

Summary of Cases

Although this is clearly a very limited set of JV case histories, some generalizations and common themes merit attention. First, the classic stereotype of the Japanese manufacturing partner bringing production know-how and the U.S. partner bringing product and marketing presence to a JV is generally supported by these cases. All four JVs had excellent operating characteristics, like cost of quality and delivery records. Making a profit was a different matter, however.

This profitability issue is the second point brought out by these cases. For example, the last two JVs had the same Japanese parent, and both had to be downsized by the U.S. (managing) partner in order to survive. If there is one notable Japanese cultural influence here, it is the tendency to overdesign technology that seems to lead to a tendency to overdesign the entire venture. By the same token, the Japanese partner stuck with the troubled JVs in this small sample long after most other partners would have bailed out. Striking a successful balance between these two views is a major challenge of managing this type of JV in the United States.

The third issue is an echo of the analysis of the JEI data: There seem to be noticeable differences between high-tech and low-tech JVs. Low-technology companies seem to be more difficult to manage. In either case, the motives for forming a JV often are quite different from the motives for sustaining the venture. Despite the problems of joining two company cultures and two national cultures, this strategy can be an effective "jump start" for cultural change in manufacturing operations.

Fourth and finally, an integrated organization structure appears to be preferred in these JV cases, holding the degree of R&D intensity constant. Company L is a prime example of how effective this structural approach can be, in both managing day-to-day operations and transferring technology to the parent operations. A global, long-term strategy appears to reinforce this hybrid structural approach.

We also raise several questions that could not be answered with secondary data. For example, how successful were these JVs? Second, what determines their success? Third, how should we interpret counterintuitive findings in the literature (e.g., Daniels & Magill, 1991) that suggest that high-technology JVs actually engage in less joint R&D, which calls into question the technology-sharing motivation for forming JVs in these R&D-intensive industries? Fourth, how stable are these JVs as organizations, and has the dominant partner changed over time? More research into the stability of the JV as a form of governance seems warranted.

A number of ancillary questions beg to be answered. For example, the results of this research, when compared with the findings of Osborn and Baughn (1990) (e.g., U.S.–Japanese technology alliances for the purpose of conducting joint R&D lead to JVs), call attention to the issue of whether U.S. and Japanese manufacturing firms do business differently depending on where the manufacturing facility is located. Most U.S.–Japanese JVs in the United States are single-plant investments. Do the landed transplant firms and 100 percent ownership ventures do business differently than JVs do?

Perhaps two of the most interesting questions raised by this study are (1) the nature of the challenge of the JV when there is parity (50–50) in the investment profile and (2) the success and failure of high-tech versus low-tech ventures. There often are reports of dissatisfaction on both sides of JVs—hidden and evolving agendas. The selection of key human resources and the strategies of parents (e.g., Intel) that limit long-term alliances because of the volatile nature of some industries' technologies are nearly always issues. This problem has obviously not stopped companies like Toshiba, IBM, and Siemens from forming partnerships, because the cost of developing the next generation of technology is so high. Is the JV a permanent, versus a transitory, form of governance forced by circumstances? Are the challenges so great to managing a JV for technology that only a few, very successful surviving companies will be able to master them and make them the key competitive weapon in the next decade? These questions need to be investigated.

ACKNOWLEDGMENTS

Work in this area was supported by the Japan Technology Management Program at the University of Michigan and the U.S. Air Force Office of Scientific Research. The opinions are those of the authors and do not necessarily reflect the official position of the funding agency. Comments on an earlier version of this chapter from Professors Brian Talbot and Tom Roehl are greatly appreciated.

REFERENCES

Abo, T. (1992, September 7–9). International application-adaptation of Japanese production system: Cases of Japanese automobile and electronics plants in the United States. *Proceedings* (pp. 304–7). Tokyo: IFSAM.

Adler, N. J., & Graham, J. L. (1989). Cross-cultural interaction: The international comparison fallacy. *Journal of International Business Studies, 20,* 515–37.

Adler, P. S. (1992). The "learning bureaucracy": New United Motor Manufacturing, Inc. In B. M. Staw & L. L. Cummings (Eds.), *Research in organizational behavior,* vol. 15, (pp. 111–194). Greenwich, CT: JAI Press.

Adler, P. S. (1993). Time-and-motion regained. *Harvard Business Review, 1,* 97–108.

Adler, P. S., & Cole, R. E. (1993). Designed for learning: A tale of two auto plants. *Sloan Management Review, 34,* 85–94.

Aiken, M., & Hage, J. (1968). Organizational interdependence and intraorganizational structure. *American Sociological Review, 33,* 912–30.

Ashby, W. R. (1962). Principles of the self-organizing system. In H. Von Foerster & G. W. Zopf (Eds.), *Principles of Self-organization,* (pp. 255–78). New York: Pergamon Press.

Auster, E. R. (1990). The relationship of industry evolution to patterns of technological linkages, JVs, and direct investment between U.S. and Japan. *Academy of Management Best Paper Proceedings,* August, 96–110.

Balkin, D. B., & Gomez-Mejia, L. R. (1987). Toward a contingency theory of compensation strategy. *Strategic Management Journal, 8,* 169–82.

Beamish, P. W. (1985, Fall). The characteristics of JVs in developed and developing countries. *Columbia Journal of World Business,* 13–19.

Berg, S., Duncan, J., & Freedman, P. (1982). *JV strategies and corporate innovation.* Cambridge, MA: Olegeschlager, Gunn & Hain.

Blodgett, L. L. (1991). Partner contribution as predictors of equity share in international JVs. *Journal of International Business Studies, 22,* 63–78.

Blodgett, L. L. (1992). Factors in the instability of international JVs: An event history analysis. *Strategic Management Journal, 13,* 475–81.

Boyle, S. E. (1968). An estimate of the number and size distribution of domestic joint subsidiaries. *Antitrust Law and Economics Review, 1,* 81–92.

Brannen, M. Y. (1992). *Culture, a critical factor in the successful implementation of statistical process control: A case study in intercultural change.* Working paper, University of Massachusetts.

Christelow, D. B. (1989). U.S.–Japan JVs: Who gains? *Challenge, 32,* 29–38.

Daniels, J. D., & Magill, S. L. (1991). The utilization of international joint ventures by United States firms in high technology industries. *Journal of High-Technology Management Research, 2,* 113–31.

Datta, D. K. (1988). International joint ventures: A framework for analysis. *Journal of General Management, 14,* 78–90.

Dodwell Marketing Consultants. (1990). *The structure of the Japanese auto parts industry.* Tokyo: Dodwell Marketing Consultants.

Dodwell Marketing Consultants. (1991). *Industrial groupings in Japan* (9th ed.). Tokyo: Dodwell Marketing Consultants.

Earl, P. E. (1992). The evolution of cooperative strategies: Three automotive industry case studies. *Human Systems Management, 11,* 89–100.

Egelhoff, W. G. (1992). *International technical alliances in the semiconductor industry: Some conceptualization and hypotheses.* Working paper, Fordham University.

Ettlie, J. E., Bridges, W., & O'Keefe, R. (1984). Organizational strategy and structural differences for radical versus incremental innovation. *Management Science, 30,* 632–95.

Ginsberg, A., & Buchholtz, A. (1990). Converting to for-profit status: Corporate responsiveness to radical change. *Academy of Management Journal, 33,* 445–77.

Gomes-Cassores, B. (1987, Summer). Joint venture instability: Is it a problem? *Columbia Journal of World Business,* 97–102.

Gordon, G. G. (1991). Industry determinants of organizational culture. *Academy of Management Review, 16,* 396–415.

Hannan, M. T., & Freeman, J. (1984). Structural inertia and organizational change. *American Sociological Review, 49,* 149–64.

Hennart, J.-F. (1991). The transaction costs theory of joint ventures and empirical study of Japanese subsidiaries in the United States. *Management Science, 37,* 483–97.

Japan Chamber of Commerce and Industry. (1991). *Standard trade index of Japan 1991–92.* Tokyo: Japan Chamber of Commerce and Industry.

Japan Economic Institute. (1989). *Japan's expanding U.S. manufacturing presence, 1989 Update.* Washington, DC: Japan Economic Institute.

Japan External Trade Organization (JETRO). (1992). *Japan trade directory 1992–93.* Tokyo: JETRO.

Kogut, B. (1988). A study of the life cycle of joint ventures. *Management International Review, 28,* 39–52.

Kogut, B. (1991). Joint ventures and the option to expand and acquire. *Management Science, 37,* 19–33.

Koh, J., & Venkatraman, N. (1991). Joint venture formations and stock market reactions: An assessment in the information technology sector. *Academy of Management Journal, 34,* 869–92.

Korde, A. M. (1993, August 2–3). *Quality journey: The TKS story.* Pages presented at the University of Michigan Quality Assurance Seminar, Traverse City, MI.

Lane, H. W., & Beamish, P. (1990). Cross-cultural cooperative behavior in joint ventures in LDCs. *Management International Review, 30,* 87–102.

Lynn, L. H. (1991, October 27–31). Cultural differences and the management of engineering in U.S.-Japanese joint ventures, (pp. 473–475). *Proceedings of the Portland International Conference on Management of Engineering and Technology.* Portland, Oregon.

Near, J. P. (1989). Organizational commitment among Japanese and U.S. workers. *Organization Studies, 10,* 281–300.

Osborn, R. N., & Baughn, C. C. (1990). Forms of interorganizational governance for multinational alliances. *Academy of Management Journal, 33,* 503–19.

Pate, J. L. (1969). Joint venture activity, 1960–1968. *Economic Review, Federal Reserve Bank of Cleveland, 54,* 16–23.

Pfeffer, J., & Nowak, P. (1976). Joint ventures and interorganizational interdependence. *Administrative Science Quarterly, 21,* 398–418.

Pfeffer, J., & Salancik, G. R. (1978). *The external control of organizations: A resource dependence perspective.* New York: Harper & Row.

Reynolds, J. J. (1984, Summer). The "pinched shoe" effect of international joint ventures. *Columbia Journal of World Business,* 23–29.

Schonfeld & Associates, Inc. (1991). *R&D ratios & budgets.* Lincolnshire, IL: Schonfeld & Associates, Inc.

Sestok, C. (1993, April 13). *Quality: A product durability perspective.* Paper presented at the Automotive Seminar Luncheon, Office for the Study of Automotive Transportation, University of Michigan, Ann Arbor.

Shortell, S. M., & Zajac, E. J. (1988). Internal corporate joint ventures: Development processes and performance outcomes, *Strategic Management Journal, 9,* 527–42.

Stevenson, R. W. (1992, March 15). Will aerospace be the next casualty? *New York Times,* (Business sec.), pp. 1, 6.

Tyebjee, T. T. (1988). A typology of joint ventures: Japanese strategies in the United States. *California Management Review, 31,* 75–86.

U.S. Department of Commerce (1989). *Concentration ratios in manufacturing industries.* Washington, D.C.: Government Printing office.

U.S. Embassy, Tokyo. (1993, April 7). *IMI–Japan Fortune 500 in Japan and Japan's top 500 companies in the United States* (telegraphic copy). Tokyo: U.S. Embassy.

Utterback, J. M., & Abernathy, W. J. (1975). A dynamic model of process and product innovation. *Omega, 3,* 639–56.

Weick, K. (1979). *The social psychology of organizing.* New York: Random House.

Weiss, S. E. (1992a). Analysis of complex negotiations in international business: The RBC perspective. *Organization Science, 3,* 1–32.

Weiss, S. E. (1992b). *Explaining outcomes of complex international negotiations: The Ford/*

Toyota and GM/Toyota cases. Paper presented at the International Business Research Seminar at the University of Michigan, Ann Arbor.

APPENDIX: INTERVIEW GUIDE

PROJECT DESCRIPTION

The purpose of this project is to contribute to the knowledge base on domestic Japanese–U.S. JVs in manufacturing. To do this, we would like you to tell a story about your company, to be used in a case study. Of particular interest are the effect of culture on domestic JVs and the use of technology in developing the venture.

CONFIDENTIALITY

All interviews on this project will be kept confidential. We will not associate any data or opinions with the names of people, plants, companies, or products. If you ever have a question about this research, please call, write, or fax John E. Ettlie.

FEEDBACK

The business case developed from this interview will be given to the participating company for comment and revision. No information from these interviews will be released without permission from the participating company. Please contact John E. Ettlie for any questions about this study.

HISTORY AND MOTIVATION OF THE JV

Why was the JV chosen over other possible relationships?

What did each parent contribute to the formation of the JV?

What did each parent hope to gain from forming the JV?

How was the percentage of ownership decided by the parents?

If you were going to advise two parents (U.S. and Japanese) considering a JV in domestic manufacturing, what would you tell them?

TECHNOLOGY RELATIONSHIP

Which parent(s) provided the technology needed to establish the JV?

What is the continuing technology relationship between the parties?

Does technology flow into and out of the JV, or is it primarily one way?

How has culture affected this technology relationship?

MANAGEMENT PRACTICES

Which parent is more responsible for managing the JV?

What techniques are used in managing the JV?

How have these techniques changed over the life of the JV?

To what extent does culture influence the way that the JV is managed?

MEASURES OF SUCCESS

What are the major barriers to and facilitators of the JV's success?

How well does the JV's performance measure up to the desires of its parents?

How well does the JV's performance compare with that of its major competitors?

What is the current challenge for the JV?

GENERAL INFORMATION

Do you have any published newspaper or magazine articles that you can share with us?

Do you have any annual reports that you can share with us?

Organizational chart? Parental origin of management and/or staff?

What is the total number of the JV's full-time, year-round employees?

What is the JV's R&D ratio (R&D expense/net sales)?

Can you share sales figures with us?

Can you share profit figures with us?

IV

TECHNOLOGY DEPLOYMENT AND ORGANIZATIONAL LEARNING

13

Culture, Innovative Borrowing, and Technology Management

JOHN CREIGHTON CAMPBELL

A recent page-one story in the *Wall Street Journal* was headed, "Shifting Gears: Some Manufacturers Drop Efforts to Adopt Japanese Techniques." American companies "realize that some of these systems, however useful in lifting productivity in Japan, haven't achieved much in their own plants," the article goes on to say. "The Americans were hampered by cultural differences, and, they acknowledge, by misapplication of what they saw in Japanese plants" (Naj, 1993, p. 1).

In fact, the misapplication of cultural lessons and the misperception of cultural differences have long been big problems when Americans seek to learn from Japan. Misled by journalists and business gurus—and often enough by Japanese businessmen and writers themselves—many American executives have come to believe in a benign, romanticized picture of how organizations really work in Japan.

The result is inevitable. American managers pick up on some Japanese marvel (e.g., QC circles, *kaizen, JIT*) and try it out in their plants, usually by bringing in a high-priced consultant with a briefcase full of secret techniques and jargon. Everyone is enthusiastic; it seems to work for a time; and then the complaining starts. Soon, the new program is seen as a failure.

What went wrong? The usual explanation is that the cultures in America and Japan are too different. It is said that Japanese trust one another; they naturally work hard; they are loyal to the group rather than being individualists; and they are harmonious and cooperative. With a workforce like that, no wonder all those Japanese techniques work so well. American workers are different, we think.

But is Japan's real advantage its trusting, loyal, and cooperative workforce? If so, how did these workers get that way? Are these attitudes somehow bred into them? Does being Japanese automatically make that person

311

group oriented, just as being born an American makes one an individualist?

The conventional wisdom, the way people usually think about U.S.–Japan differences and the impact of culture, answers yes to these questions. This outlook itself is a big part of the problem. In fact, first, the *attitudes* of Japanese and Americans are not different in the ways usually believed. Second, although their *behavior* may be different, this difference is due more to differences in structures (e.g., the way that companies are organized) than to differences in the way that the people in those organizations *think*. The next section illustrates these two points.

Does this difference mean that the concept of culture is useless or that cross-national differences in attitudes or ways of thinking are not important? Many social scientists either take such a view or argue that cultural factors are secondary in importance to structural explanations. My judgment is different: A more operational conception of culture and a more accurate picture of Japan can help the readers of this book understand why Japanese techniques work in Japan and then, perhaps, how these same techniques can work in the United States.

HOW DO THE JAPANESE REALLY THINK?

Americans and Japanese usually have rather similar perceptions about differences in attitudes (i.e., how people think) between the two countries, but these perceptions are often incorrect. Three examples illustrate this point.

Trust

The usual view is that Japanese can deal with one another easily because they trust one another, perhaps because they have such a homogeneous population. However, in 1980, the Japanese public television network asked large national samples in both countries a set of questions aimed at uncovering differences in ways of thinking (Richardson & Flanagan, 1984, p. 174). Two questions were relevant to trust:

	Japan	United States
Would you say that most of the time people are helpful or that they are mostly just looking out for themselves?		
Try to be helpful	25	59
Look out for themselves	75	41
Do you think that most people would try to take advantage of you if they got the chance, or would they try to be fair?		
Take advantage	71	33
Try to be fair	29	67

Compared with Americans, Japanese do not appear to have a very optimistic view of how they are likely to be treated by others; it would seem that there is not much basis for trust.

Loyalty

Perhaps Japanese have little regard for people as individuals (even other Japanese individuals), but surely they have a strong feeling of identification with the group. In particular, Japanese are thought to have deep emotional ties with their companies. How deep? A survey of manufacturing workers in Japan and the United States, carried out in 1981–83, included some relevant questions (Lincoln & Kalleberg, 1990, pp. 64–65). (An "Undecided" category, which in the original table also included weak responses on either side, is omitted here.)

	Japan	United States
I am willing to work harder than I have to in order to help this company succeed.		
Agree	54	74
Disagree	17	7
My values and the values of this company are quite similar.		
Agree	19	42
Disagree	41	27
I feel very little loyalty to this company.		
Agree	19	22
Disagree	50	58

The difference in the last question is in the expected direction, but the conventional wisdom would see Japanese workers as far more loyal than American workers, not the trivial gap shown here.

Work Ethic

If there is one thing Americans think they know about the Japanese it is that these people work hard and get more out of their jobs than Americans do. But look at some more data from the same survey:

	Japan	United States
I have other activities more important than my work.		
Agree	44	31
Disagree	30	44
All in all, how satisfied would you say you are with your job?		
Satisfied	18	34
Dissatisfied	16	5

	Japan	United States
Knowing what you know now, if you had to decide all over again to take the job you now have, what would you decide?		
Take it again	23	59
Not take it again	40	8

It appears that Japanese workers do not seem quite so happy in their work as Americans imagine.

Measuring attitudes is tricky. One never quite knows how a question will be interpreted by the respondent, especially when trying to ask the same question in different countries and languages. The findings of lower job satisfaction in Japan than in the United States have been confirmed in other studies (cf. Cole, 1979), however. At a minimum, the superior performance of Japanese companies is not adequately explained by more positive attitudes among Japanese workers. So what is the secret?

WHY SO HARDWORKING AND LOYAL?

Take hard work, for example. Visitors to Japanese *factories* are invariably impressed by the sustained energy levels of blue-collar workers. Visitors to Japanese *offices* are sometimes impressed by the long work hours of white-collar workers but are less impressed with the ratio of actual work to tea drinking and other time-wasting activities. Visitors to Japanese *universities* are never impressed by any sign of hard work by college students—often they seem to idling around the campus (if they show up at all).

That is, hard work is situational in Japan: Rather than being innate to the Japanese personality, this behavior depends on how the individual person perceives his or her environment. For that matter, the tendency to work hard is also situational in the United States. Perhaps there is some difference in the average inclination to work hard between Americans and Japanese, but even if there is, the size of this gap is dwarfed by the great differences *among* Japanese, or *among* Americans, in different situations. This point indicates that we need to look more at environments, or structures, than at attitudes.

Loyalty is another example. There is ample evidence that more Japanese workers will behave as if they are more loyal to their companies than American workers will. The data cited earlier indicate that loyalty is not a natural trait among Japanese any more than it is among Americans. Therefore, there must be a different explanation for the difference in behavior.

Consider the Japanese firm (in Japan and to some extent even the "transplant" organizations in the United States)—what are its operating principles (e.g., Clark, 1979)?

1. Highly selective recruitment, with examinations and interviews to pick the right people even for blue-collar as well as managerial jobs.
2. A lengthy apprentice period both to teach skills and to indoctrinate members

into the ways of the firm, with slogans like "for harmony and strength" (cf. Rohlen, 1974).

3. "Permanent employment" for core workers, with regular promotions, though always the possibility of being left behind (Pucik, 1984)

4. The expectation that members of a work group, even bosses and subordinates, will socialize together after hours.

These characteristics of Japanese companies are quite distinctive, at least when compared with those of American organizations. For example, Japanese workers report socializing with their coworkers more than twice as often as do American workers; they also socialize with their superiors *six times* more often (Lincoln & Kalleberg, 1990, p. 88).

All these operational principles appear designed to foster loyal behavior. In fact, the attention and resources devoted to these practices, compared with those at the typical American company, indicate clearly that Japanese managers themselves do not believe in any innate Japanese propensity to loyalty. If workers were going to be loyal anyway, management would not be so careful about picking, indoctrinating, and controlling them.

Perhaps such techniques can work only in Japan: "American workers don't stand up and salute," the *Wall Street Journal* quotes a GE executive who tried and failed to implement quality-control circles (Naj, 1993, p. 1). But do Americans never salute?

The most American of Americans are marines, and they salute all day. Compare the operational principles of Japanese companies just noted with those of the U.S. Marine Corps: "We're looking for a few good men," intense socialization in boot camp and beyond, slogans like *"semper fi"* and "one for all and all for one," highly regularized promotion combined with intense competition, and a strong expectation that units will stick together even when—maybe especially when—out on the town.

The result should be, for the marines or any well-functioning military unit, a cohesive group whose members behave loyally and effectively when times get tough, even if cut off behind enemy lines, say, when top-down supervision is lacking. Again, that is how members of Japanese companies like to see themselves. If creating such tight organizational bonds is seen as important, similar techniques should work in the United States as well as in Japan.

In fact, many Japanese manufacturing companies have achieved the same levels of quality and productivity in their American transplant factories as they have back in Japan. In these cases, personnel practices vary, but for the most part some Japanese-style principles have been introduced and have been effective. Clearly these results do not depend on some unique personality of native Japanese workers.

TOWARD A USEFUL CONCEPTION OF JAPANESE CULTURE

It seems that the values and attitudes of Japanese and American workers are not so different. Japanese *organizations* are different, but it is possible to create Japanese-style organizations with American personnel if management uses Japanese-style techniques. It would seem to follow that Japanese companies choose to use these Japanese-style techniques much more often than do American firms. Why?

In my view, the answer has to do with culture, but culture in a sense different from such superficial notions as "Japanese are loyal" or "they work hard." This more basic sense of culture can be explained through another cliché about Japan: the notions of "harmony" and "consensus."

It is clear that in Japan, harmony is an important value and that consensus is seen as the best way to operate. Both concepts are evoked all the time. One might therefore jump to the conclusion that harmony is seen as natural by Japanese and that Japanese think they naturally do better at reaching a consensus than Americans do.

Quite the opposite is the case. In my experience, the reason that Japanese talk about harmony all the time is that they see it as desirable, perhaps vital, but as quite *un*natural. If Japanese workers naturally got along with one another, managers would not talk about harmony all the time. If consensus came easily, the Japanese would not have to work so hard at it.

Fundamentally, it seems to me that most Japanese understand how the world works somewhat differently than most Americans do, in two ways.

First, Japanese tend to be pessimistic about human nature; they see people as egotistical and prone to fighting all the time unless they are constrained by self-discipline or social controls. Many Americans are more optimistic about human nature and assume that people can get along naturally.

Second, Japanese see situations essentially as matters of concrete human relationships, in cases in which Americans often think in terms of material things, individual motivations, or abstract principles (Lebra, 1976).

A good illustration of the second point is the way that the American automotive industry (particularly General Motors) reacted to the threat from Japan in the early 1980s. The solutions the Americans thought they should learn from Japan about how to manufacture cars included

1. Buying more robots (material things).
2. Getting the workers excited about quality (individual motivations).
3. Reorganizing the company (abstract principle).

Reorganizing a company into new divisions might seem to be a concrete, pragmatic action, but in the case of GM it made sense only when gazing at organization charts and thinking schematically. There was little consideration of the human relationships within and across those parts of the organization that actually made the company work. These relationships were badly disrupted, leading to intense, debilitating conflict just when the company's real problems needed everyone's attention (Keller, 1989). A Japanese executive, bent on improving performance, would have first thought carefully about those human relationships.

WHAT IS JAPANESE-STYLE TECHNOLOGY MANAGEMENT?

To Americans steeped in the classical literature of business management, this Japanese tendency to look at relationships first may sound like what used to be called the *human-relations school,* as opposed to the *scientific-management school.* An oversimplified characterization of the human-relations school is that good performance depends on keeping workers satisfied. Certainly, many slogans associated with Japanese-style management (putting people first, concern for workers' careers, permanent employment) sound like ideas from the human-relations school.

This impression is misleading. As noted previously, Japanese workers are not especially satisfied, and the techniques that Japanese managers typically use are not mainly aimed at workers' attitudes. Rather, they are aimed at behavior. In fact, Japanese workers use scientific management often, including breaking a task into its components through time-motion studies and devising the most efficient routines.

The key is that although Japanese techniques are conceived in terms of human relationships, the objective is not to make workers comfortable. Quite the opposite, it is to keep them pressured. High-pressure techniques pervade Japanese approaches to management, even in areas that in this country would be seen as matters of technology.

A good example of the manipulation of human relationships to apply pressure directly to workers' behavior is the just-in-time or *kanban* approach to inventory. As a United Technologies executive told the *Wall Street Journal's* reporter Naj, "The primary motive in just-in-time isn't reducing inventory"; it is "to expose the weak points on the manufacturing line" (Naj, 1993, p. 1). With no extra parts as a buffer, the assembly-line worker is directly dependent on the supplier to make the part perfectly and on the trucker to deliver it on time. The relationships among these workers have been changed in a way that *forces* the desired behavior, regardless of whether their attitudes are happy and cooperative or quite surly. The same techniques can work with relationships among companies (cf. Dore, 1988).

Quality circles are similar in that they mobilize peer pressure to make workers identify and solve problems. Circles often have failed in the United States, partly because of executives' failure to think through the political problems caused by their introduction, in particular, the circles' threat to the power and role of the first-line supervisors. Japanese executives, with their tendency to see human relationships as the key factor, are more likely to recognize such problems and deal with them directly rather than hoping optimistically that people can simply work them out on the shop floor (Cole, 1989).

Concurrent engineering provides another good example (cf. Chapter 8 by Ward and his colleagues in this volume). Imposing a tight deadline for product design forces engineers from various departments to communicate intensively. An American cross-functional team might be formed on the assumption that all these participants should be able to cooperate if they are properly motivated to believe in collective rather than departmental goals. A Japanese manager is more likely to realize from the start that participants from different departments are bound to get into conflicts, whatever their motivations, and so he will pay more attention to figuring out where disputes will arise.

Not all disputes are worth worrying about. Japanese organizations are notorious for trying to suppress or paper over arguments if they are not crucial. But when a working agreement between, say, marketing and manufacturing engineering is needed to develop a product quickly, much effort will be devoted to building a framework for resolving differences of opinion. Off-the-job social relationships like drinking together after work are one element of this process. When such techniques are carried out skillfully, the sort of intense communication and trust required for "set-based" design techniques in concurrent engineering become possible.

A final example appears at first glance to be entirely technological, but it is actually based on similar principles of organizational pressure. Japanese manufacturing firms in such areas as automotive-body engineering are noted for their careful attention to tolerancing. The benefits in terms of ease of assembly, rapid die changes, and so forth have been amply documented (cf. Chapter 10 by Hammett and his colleagues). Beyond that, stressing proper tolerances throughout the design, engineering, and actual manufacturing processes imposes strict discipline on the participants. Sloppy work shows up immediately and causes trouble for others. Workers are forced to work hard and carefully without direct supervision, which is the essence of effective high-pressure management.

Many of these Japanese-style techniques include a higher level of involvement by blue-collar workers, engineers, and middle managers than Americans are used to. The common error in trying to learn from these techniques is to imagine that involvement is effective because it makes people happier or more satisfied. Again, it often does not; it makes people feel more pressured. In the end, these workers see no alternative to behaving in the way that management wants. Although working in this way is likely to be more interesting for workers and engineers, and thus perhaps more fulfilling in a deep sense, it is also more frustrating and stressful. *Kaizen*, permanent improvement, does not make for a very comfortable life.

CROSS-CULTURAL LEARNING

A Cadillac engineer, quoted in the *Wall Street Journal* article mentioned previously, observed that "the Japanese were very creative in the application of the things they learned here. . . . We brought back what we saw in Japan and tried to execute them mechanically" (Naj, 1993, p. 1). In fact, the Japanese wrote the book on how to borrow management ideas, and Americans could learn something about how to learn by looking at their historical experiences (cf. Chapter 14 by Brannen; Westney, 1989).

In the mid-nineteenth century, Japan was desperate to catch up with the West. Conservatives called for "Western technology and Eastern ethics," that is, the superficial adoption of modern techniques without changing fundamental cultural patterns. This viewpoint is analogous to that of American executives who think that some technique like *kaizen*, JIT, quality function deployment, concurrent engineering, or quality circles can just be plopped into an existing organization to get quick results.

Liberal Japanese intellectuals thought the opposite. They believed that Western techniques were embedded in Western culture, and so Japan would have to become Westernized in order to modernize. They relied on education and propaganda to try to change basic Japanese ways of thinking. The analogous belief in American companies holds that a new "corporate culture" is vital and that the way to get there is through intense campaigns urging workers to devote themselves to quality or to put customers first. The assumption is that cultural change at the level of individual attitudes will lead to changes in individual behavior and that eventually the entire organizational structure will be transformed.

In Japan, in many cases, neither school of thought turned out to be correct. The key sequence for many important aspects of modernization was that new organizational structures (e.g., the army or the post office) were imported from abroad and implemented without much preparation. Over time, the behavior of managers and workers adapted to the structure, and eventually a new set of understandings about how the world works was created. In short, structural change led to behavioral change, which led to cultural or attitudinal change.

This historical experience in Japan implies three lessons for today's American firms.

First, techniques can be imported. Cultural change may be required in the long run, but the new ways of acting called forth by the imported techniques themselves are far better mechanisms for changing attitudes than is any amount of exhortation from the top. Again, the rigorous application of such innovations as JIT or close tolerancing over a period of time will, inevitably, change the culture of the company.

Second, in contrast, these techniques simply cannot be seen as tools. They are best seen as new organizational routines or operating procedures that crucially change the ways that people and groups relate to one another. These changes can be considered *organizational learning*, which is a very different matter from individual learning (cf. Cole, Chapter 16 in this volume).

Third, the new techniques are bound to be difficult to implement, and they will require adaptations as people get used to how they operate. This is precisely what the Cadillac engineer meant by "the Japanese were very creative in the application of the things they learned here." Americans should think more about concrete problems of adaptation rather than simply following formulas in textbooks.

In my view, as I noted earlier, Japanese do have a cultural advantage over Americans in this area. They tend to see human relationships rather than material things or abstract principles as the most fundamental level of reality. In particular, despite the usual interpretations of Japanese management techniques heard in the United States, they do not share Americans' faith in the magical efficacy of changing individual attitudes. Changing the structure will change behavior, and attitudes will follow—that is the Japanese assumption. There is no reason that this lesson cannot be effectively employed by American managers.

REFERENCES

Adler, P., & Cole, R. E. (1993). Design for learning: A tale of two auto plants. *Sloan Management Review, 34:* 85–94.

Clark, R. (1979). *The Japanese company.* New Haven, CT: Yale University Press.

Cole, R. E. (1979). *Work, mobility, and participation.* Berkeley and Los Angeles: University of California Press.

Cole, R. E. (1989). *Strategies for learning: Small-group activity in American, Japanese, and Swedish industry.* Berkeley and Los Angeles: University of California Press.

Dore, R. P. (1988). *Flexible rigidities: Industrial policy and structural adjustment in the Japanese economy, 1970–1980.* Stanford, CA: Stanford University Press.

Keller, M. (1989). *Rude awakening: The rise, fall, and struggle for recovery of General Motors.* New York: Morrow.

Lebra, T. S. (1976). *Japanese patterns of behavior.* Honolulu: University of Hawaii Press.

Lincoln, J. R., & Kalleberg, A. L. (1990). *Culture, control, and commitment.* Cambridge: Cambridge University Press.

Naj, A. K. (1993, May 7). Shifting gears: Some American manufacturers drop ill-starred efforts to adopt Japanese techniques. *Wall Street Journal,* p. 1.

Pucik, V. (1984). White-collar human resource management: A comparison of the U.S. and Japanese automobile industries. *Columbia Journal of World Business, 19:* 87–94.

Richardson, B., & Flanagan, S. C. (1984). *Politics in Japan.* New York: HarperCollins.

Rohlen, T. P. (1974). *For harmony and strength: Japanese white-collar organization in anthropological perspective.* Berkeley and Los Angeles: University of California Press.

Westney, E. D. (1989). *Imitation and innovation: The transfer of Western organizational patterns to Meiji Japan.* Cambridge, MA: Harvard University Press.

14

Does Culture Matter? Negotiating a Complementary Culture to Support Technological Innovation

MARY YOKO BRANNEN

On October 7, 1989, a group of American and Japanese managers joined by members of the union committee performed a modified ritual of the traditional Japanese ground-breaking ceremony to celebrate the completion of the 40 million dollar expansion of the plant. Traditionally, a Shinto (the aboriginal religion of Japan) priest would have blessed the new machinery by performing a formal "baptismal" in the context of a Shinto ritual to ensure prosperity for the plant. Mindful of the strong Catholic composition of the work force, TSP's Japanese president decided upon a middle-of-the road approach which blended Western and Japanese ground-breaking rituals. The Western portion of the ritual was comprised of a traditional ribbon-cutting and white-gloved starting up of the machinery by the Japanese chairman of the board. The Japanese portion of the ritual was the "sake" (Japanese traditional rice wine) cask-breaking ceremony where Japanese managers were joined by their American counterparts and union officials in donning "happi"—coats—and performing a song and hand-clapping ceremony to celebrate the success of the expansion. (Brannen, 1993, p. 107)

In December 1989 the Dexter Paper Company, located in a small town in western Massachusetts, was acquired by the Tomioka Paper Company of Japan. Japanese management rehired most of the former American workforce and renamed the plant the Tomioka Specialty Papers Company (TSP). The primary goal of TSP's management during the first two and a half years after the acquisition was to transform the plant into a state-of-the-art specialty paper–production facility concentrating on capturing a lion's share of the facsimile paper market in North American as well as the newly developing market for thermal and pressure-sensitive label technology.

The groundbreaking ceremony for the completion of the $43 million expansion marked the success of the management team in realizing this goal. The successful operations of the newly transformed plant rested not only on the transfer of technology from Japan, which was housed in the expansion in the form of leading-edge mixing and coating machinery, but also, and most important, on the successful transfer of the organizational processes necessary to support the technology. The cross-cultural transfer of technology and organizational processes cannot be made unilaterally but requires an adjustment of the original forms in order to fit into the new organizational context. The anecdote at the opening of this chapter is but one example of the ongoing cultural negotiation that took place at the plant to facilitate operations in a bicultural context.

In this example, the issue around which the cultural negotiation revolved was how to celebrate the successful conclusion of the expansion. Neither the traditional Japanese religious ritual nor the traditional Western groundbreaking ritual seemed to fit. Aspects of the parent company's cultural ritual did not make sense in the new cultural context and even threatened to offend constituents of the U.S. subsidiary's home culture (as in the case of the religious element of the Japanese ceremony). Yet certain aspects of the Japanese cultural ritual needed to be retained in order for Japanese employees (both at TSP and from the parent company) and extraorganizational Japanese contributors to the expansion (contractors, bankers, and suppliers) to feel that the accomplishments of their joint efforts were properly acknowledged. The negotiated result was therefore a hybrid ritual blending important elements of both traditions.

The issue of the transferability of Japanese organizational processes and the accompanying "Japanese management techniques" [1] (as they are commonly referred to in the popular business press) emerged as a core theme from the inception of the ethnography. Once Japanese decision makers from the home office ascertained that the U.S. plant had the capacity in terms of space requirements for expansion, capable existing technology to meet product-line requirements, and a solid raw material–sourcing base, their attention turned to the social-technical issues in implementing the technology. Of primary concern to both Japanese and American members of the new management team was whether there existed an organizational culture (or a *culture of work,* as Tak Wagatsuma, the newly appointed Japanese president of the plant, called it) that would support the successful implementation of statistical process control (SPC), the key technological innovation that was to be introduced at TSP.

The success of TPC Japan's strategic plan for TSP U.S.A. to capture the lion's share of the facsimile paper market in North America well within three years of the acquisition rested on the successful implementation of a total quality-control program that was centered on SPC technology. The SPC technology was vital to the successful running of the no. 20 coater, a state-of-the-art thermal coating machine, and the new "color kitchen," a state-of-the-art mixing facility; both innovations would be housed in a $43 million expansion at the plant. The issue of quality control has general and specific implications for this study. Generally, quality is seen as the source of competitive advantage to U.S. businesses that have been losing market share and presence in industries to Japanese competition. Specifically, quality-control issues were the most pressing concerns of the new management team at TSP in the transitional phase directly following the acquisition. Early on, the management team identified what they saw as cultural barriers to the successful implementation of the technological innovations at the plant. This chapter describes the cultural negotiation that took place in the immediate wake of the acquisition to foster a "culture of work" complementing the new management's agenda of total quality control. I also discuss the cultural barriers to change and the steps that the management team used to break down these barriers.

THE CROSS-CULTURAL TRANSFER OF TECHNOLOGY

> In the transfer of organizational patterns across societies, both conscious innovations and unconscious innovations produce departures from the original model. No matter how much a new organization's founders may want to build an exact copy of a model drawn from another society, they can never replicate it completely in the new setting. This is hardly an astonishing assertion. We would expect that changes would be necessary when social structures are transferred across cultures. But ascribing any and all departures from a model to the influence of culture does little to advance our understanding. By identifying more precisely the range of factors behind these departures, we can grasp more quickly how culture and new organizational patterns interact and how the processes of cross-societal emulation shape the development of organizations. (Westney, 1987, p. 25)

In the international management literature, the word *culture* often refers to national culture. In this article, however, I will draw on current anthropological theory (Geertz, 1973; Ong, 1987) to define culture in a different sense. By the words *culture* and *cultural,* I mean a historically situated and an emergent system of negotiated meanings and practices common to the people in an organization. *Culture* in this sense is endogenous, not given to a particular firm but developed and shaped by the ongoing interactions of the people in the firm as well as by the strategic choices that these people make.

Cultural barriers to change have become an increasingly relevant research topic as U.S. industries have begun to lose their competitive advantage in the global marketplace. The loss of market share to international competitors in traditional, mature industries such as automobiles, clothing, and, more recently, shoes provoked a catalytic reaction among American decision makers considering radical changes in management techniques.

The preoccupation of both management scholars and practitioners with Japanese management styles is a case in point. William Ouchi's *Theory Z,*

Ezra Vogel's *Japan as Number One,* and Pascale and Athos's *The Art of Japanese Management* are just three examples of best-sellers in the management literature. Spurred by Japanese competition, American managers have begun to look more seriously at the human side of technology for answers to the problems of sluggish productivity growth, poor quality, and fading competitive capability. Quality circles and suggestion boxes were introduced to include the worker as a valued team member in the decision-making process. But when such attempts to use Japanese management techniques do not immediately meet with favorable results, decision makers and researchers alike generally conclude that there are Japan-specific, nontransferable, cultural, and historical reasons that the techniques fail in the United States. Such a conclusion only perpetuates the mystique surrounding the Japanese culture, emphasizing its difference and blinding us to what we might otherwise learn from the Japanese. In this view, *culture* is narrowly defined in nationally specific terms, as the very phrase *Japanese culture* implies. This underlying sentiment is echoed in the common refrain "We are not Japanese, so their techniques simply cannot be transferred to our workforce."

If we are to conclude from this statement that nothing can be transferred from the Japanese experience to an American setting, how are we to understand the many cases in which Japanese expatriate managers have been successful in using some form of "their" managerial techniques with American workers in Japanese-owned businesses in the United States? Cases such as the Kyocera company in San Diego, in which Japanese management techniques were implemented with a largely Asian workforce, are rare. In most successful cases of Japanese-owned companies in America (e.g.., the YKK Zipper plant in Macon, Georgia, the Kawasaki Motorcycle factory in Lincoln, Nebraska, and the Honda of America plant in Marysville, Ohio), management has favored a middle route in applying Japanese management techniques.

Nevertheless, these techniques obviously would not work in the United States if there were something essentially "Japanese" about them. Indeed, with the advent of Japanese takeovers of American companies and with more instances of Japanese management techniques being successfully implemented by American workforces, we are seeing the successful turnaround of factories that were previously struggling to stay alive.

The TSP plant located in the northeastern United States is an example of this phenomenon. Before the Japanese management acquired the plant, it had been operating three days a week, and hourly workers were regularly laid off an average of 12 weeks per year. In the final five years of U.S. management, 30 of the 116 office workers were given termination-of-employment notices, and the relationship between management and the union was strained and characterized by a reported average of three grievances a month. Just two and a half years after the takeover, the plant was operating seven days a week; there had been no layoffs or terminations of employment since the change in management; and grievances were down to two in the last year. In addition, the plant underwent a $43 million expansion of its facilities to house state-of-the-art equipment that would increase total plant capacity by more than 100 percent and provide approximately 60 new jobs for the community.

The bottom-line measure of the plant's success under the new management was the marked improvement of the product's quality. Three and a half years after the change in management, the percentage of sales reimbursed to clients for poor-quality merchandise had fallen from 3 percent to 0.9 percent, which translates into $1.3 million in annual savings for the company. Internal deviations in product quality had dropped from 30 to 40 to five to 15 per month, resulting in a 5 percent reduction in waste.

FACTORS AFFECTING THE SUCCESSFUL IMPLEMENTATION OF NEW TECHNIQUES

Cases such as these, in which Japanese managers have successfully managed *American* workforces toward increased productivity, make it clear that the lack of success in implementing newer operation-management techniques cannot simply be explained by the workers' national cultural differences. Management scholars have thus sought alternative ways of explaining the success of Japanese management with American workers. For example, in an article on Japanese manufacturing techniques, Andrew Weiss stated, "The superior productivity of Japanese workers compared with their U.S. counterparts is commonly attributed to cultural reasons. This is not true. . . . [T]he reality is that some straightforward management decisions explain the high productivity of Japanese workers" (1984, p. 120).

Weiss asserted that manifestations of behavior attributed to the inherent cultural proclivities of the Japanese worker such as lower absenteeism, greater corporate loyalty, and harder working employees are myths. His suggested alternative "realities" of Japanese productivity are more engineers per worker, selective hiring, benefits from steep wage profiles, substantial pay differences, and a unique capital structure. He indicated that there were simple management techniques that could be learned from the Japanese that can increase productivity. This point of view is not new. Ebrahimpour (1985) examined quality management in Japan and the United States and offered nonculturally specific recommendations for improving quality in American firms. Moreover, in a literature review of practitioner-oriented journals and business magazines in the last five years, 65 out of 78 articles focusing on quality-control management in Japanese-owned manufacturing settings (in the United States and Japan) shared Weiss's and Ebrahimpour's views.

Another popular explanation for the success of Japanese takeovers in the United States is that the Japanese have large amounts of money to make the technological changes necessary for a positive turnaround. This suggests that if enough money is pumped into a system, success is ensured.

Although these culturally nonspecific views of Japanese management techniques help demystify the Japanese success story, they fail to consider important differences between U.S. and Japanese attitudes toward work that are key to the successful implementation of innovations.

CULTURE AND TECHNOLOGICAL CHANGE

The theme of culture and its effect on change is not new. The earliest attempts to join the two themes in the field of organizational studies are available in the socio–technical systems literature (Emery & Trist, 1965; Katz & Kahn, 1966; Trist & Bamforth, 1951). More immediate anteced-ents to this theme come from the organizational culture literature, which describes a way of seeing and consequently understanding organizations in which language, symbols, images, rituals, and anecdotes become the data used in uncovering the underlying shared beliefs and assumptions that guide behavior (Frost et al., 1985; Schein, 1985; Smircich, 1983). Much of the research in the organizational culture literature also deals specifi-cally with cultural change in work environments (Allen, 1985; Barney, 1986; Gagliardi, 1986; Kilmann, 1985; Lorsch, 1985; Martin & Meyer-son, 1988; Pettigrew, 1985; Wilkins & Dyer, 1987). The authors of the cultural change literature generally focus on the relationship between a firm's culture and its strategy. They examine the efficiency of a firm's cul-ture in helping the organization realize its strategic goals. These writers therefore tend to concentrate on looking for gaps between a firm's existing culture and its needed culture and identifying plans of action for cultural change programs.

Although the cultural change literature could contribute greatly to our understanding of how culture might help in the successful implementation of technological innovations, none of the researchers has directly investi-gated this issue. Moreover, the organizational change literature that deals specifically with the introduction of innovations has focused on the struc-tural effects of such innovations rather than the human resource side of the issue (Damanpour & Evan, 1984; Terreberry, 1986; Woodward, 1965). In addition, most of the scholarly research on innovation in organizations is multivariate analyses of survey data that assess the relationships between a number of organizational variables and the decision to adopt an innova-tion. A study of publications in academic journals on organizational stud-ies over the past five years shows no reported collaborative work between production-operation scholars and organizational management scholars. An examination of 19 current textbooks covering the field of production and operations management found, in most cases, no mention of the sociotechnical approach to operations. Only six texts mention the topic briefly (Buffa & Sarin, 1987; Chase & Aquilano, 1989; Meridith, 1987; Schroeder, 1989; Vonderembse & White, 1988).

In a review of operations strategy, Anderson, Cleveland, and Schroeder (1989) indicated that workforce and organization problems require imaginative solutions by managers in the fields of operations management and organizational behavior. In the absence of such interdisciplinary studies that might serve as a basis for understanding culture as a key variable in the successful implementation of technological innovation, I decided to explore this issue by conducting on-site research at a production facility undergoing such a change.

THE TRANSFER OF TECHNOLOGY TO JAPAN FROM THE WEST: A HISTORICAL PERSPECTIVE

Japanese history from 1868 to 1871, a period commonly referred to as the Meiji Restoration—which was a series of events that included the opening of Japan's doors to foreign trade, the reestablishment of imperial power, and the consequent formation of a unified nation-state—led to basic reforms fashioned to expedite Japan's rapid ascension to modernization. During the era that followed (1868–1911), Western organizational models played an important role in ensuring Japan's successful modernization. In her book *Imitation and Innovation,* Eleanor Westney traces the crosssocietal organizational transfer of three Western technologies that were critical to the rebuilding of modern Japan: the postal system, the newspapers, and the police system. Other organizational forms successfully adapted from the West were the banking, educational, and transportation systems. Westney argues that the transfer of these organizational forms from the West was successful not because of a keen sense of organizational planning by Japanese decision makers at the time or because of a natural fit between the transferred forms and the new social environment. Rather, it was the "capacity of the new institutions for transforming the environment" (Westney, 1987, p. 24).

The postwar era (1945–55), or Japan's "American Year," marked the second wave of foreign impetus for change and modernization in Japan. Japan continued to successfully transfer foreign technology during this period until its recovery was complete by 1955, when Japan had the seventh-largest GNP in the world economy. American influence on business included the breakup of the great *zaibatsu* (large organizational conglomerates) to decentralize the economy, foster antimonopoly regulation, and encourage the formation of labor unions to counterbalance the power of management, as well as complex land and educational reforms. Again, during this wave of technology influx from abroad, Japan successfully adapted the new organizational forms. Of particular note is Japan's nationwide adaptation of the quality-control philosophy and techniques introduced by W. Edwards Deming in the 1950s, which launched a national campaign to improve quality and productivity in Japan. Whether Japanese managers could indeed implement foreign technologies in Japanese work organizations with Japanese workers or whether there was simply a good fit between the new organizational forms and the Japanese culture never seems to have been a cause for debate.

TRANSFERRING TECHNOLOGY FROM JAPAN TO THE UNITED STATES

In the late 1970s, however, with the emergence of Japan as an economic world power and with the success of Japanese manufacturers in turning around the negative image of poor quality associated with Japanese products by winning global recognition for their high-quality standards, scholars and practitioners of management began to question whether Japanese management techniques could be transferred. The debate over whether Japanese quality consciousness and production techniques can be transferred has continued to the present time and can be said to be the principal source of interest in Japanese management in the business community. Now, when the United States is the recipient rather than the transmitter of technology, issues of fit between the transferred technology and work culture have become hot topics in the debate. It is interesting that it is only now when the United States has become the target of technology transfer that the issue of imitability has become salient when (as discussed earlier) the Japanese have for centuries successfully adopted Western technology into a cultural and an industrial context quite distinct from the transmitting cultures of the West. Indeed, the differences between Japanese and Western industrial cultures have never been less distinct than now, when Japan has become a peer among the worldwide industrialized community. One might argue, therefore, that it should be easier now than ever before to make cross-cultural transfers of technology between Japan and the West.

FIELD-SITE RESEARCH: THE CASE OF TSP

The TSP plant is an ideal research site for investigating this sociotechnical issue, because the decision makers are Japanese and the workforce is American. The successful implementation of technological innovation therefore cannot be attributed to national culture factors alone. If Japanese managers can work successfully with an American workforce to turn around a factory, it seems likely that the management techniques could be applied in other circumstances. The argument that there is something about an American workforce that impedes the implementation of Japanese management techniques would be disproved.

This study began as a series of on-site visits by an interdisciplinary research team in which I (then a doctoral student of organizational behavior and human-resource management), accompanied by a professor of operations management, met with the vice president of operations to discuss production issues related to changes in management. These visits triggered a five-year qualitative research project to document the cross-cultural dynamics of the venture. The methodology we used is *ethnography* (see Van Maanen, 1988, for a detailed description of this method), an anthropological term describing a qualitative process of inquiry using on-site participant observation, unstructured and semistructured interviews, and informal conversations to uncover and trace emergent themes. We chose this methodology because of the exploratory nature of our study, with its aim of uncovering cultural assumptions that act as barriers to change.

We found that questions about the transferability of Japanese management techniques occupied, from the inception of the takeover, a central concern in the minds of both Japanese management as well as the American workforce. The former group (with the marked exception of the president) were primarily concerned about the attitude (*kangaekata*, literally, "way of thinking") of the American workers—whether they would be as loyal, reliable, and hardworking as their Japanese counterparts. The latter group had mixed feelings of fear that the plant would be run in the "Japanese hell camp model" (explained later in the section "Cultural Barriers to Change") as well as exhilaration that the new owners had the resources to put new life into the plant.

In the interviews we conducted with those persons responsible for making technological changes at the plant, it became clear that both "culture-bound" and "culture-free" ideas about the transferability of Japanese management techniques were circulating at the plant. The American vice president of operations, Jim LaForet (the former plant manager), after having come back from a tour of the Japanese production facilities, explained his view:

> The first order of importance is to reach a reasonably even level of production with a challenge of zero defects. Only then can we launch a larger-scale effort of total quality management to a working relationship with suppliers. . . . But we have a long way to go in establishing work norms that can bring about this change. . . . The Japanese have an entirely different attitude toward work.

He then picked up a round red Japanese doll with skinny arms and legs adorned with a headband with the inscription *katsu zo*, the Japanese phrase for "we shall win!" that was given to him as a gift from the chairman of the Japanese parent company, the Tomioka Paper Company (TPC). He patted the doll on the head, which caused it to jump up and down and yell in either English or Japanese one of many phrases to encourage victory, such as *gambatte* (let's try harder), *yoisho* (let's go; yo, heave ho!), or even its namesake *katsu zo* (we shall win). The doll was a kind of *daruma,* an embodiment of Bodhi Dharma, the founder of Zen Buddhism, who is said to have meditated for so many years to reach a transcendental state that his arms and legs atrophied. As a cultural icon, the *daruma* (as it is known in Japan) has come to represent perseverance and earnest work efforts and is therefore the spiritual embodiment of the Japanese idealized work ethic. At the U.S. plant, it could be seen as a bicultural ideal in which the vocalized work ethic is translated smoothly from Japanese into English. Jim LaForet's view was, however, that "it won't be easy to find an American hourly worker jumping up and down saying that!"

Indeed, Jim's skepticism was echoed by many of the Japanese management team. The refrain heard in a two-and-a-half-hour focus-group interview one year after the takeover was that the American workers had work orientations very different from those of the Japanese. By far the most common phrase echoed in describing the American hourly worker was *ugokanai* (literally, "they don't move"; that is, they appeared to be unmotivated, as if they had no drive). Other phrases used were *musakurushii* (shabby or tacky, referring to their sloppy dress habits), "me"—*wabakari* or *jibun no koto shika kangaenai* (both meaning that they were prone to think of "me" [themselves] only), *kane de ugoku hito* (motivated principally by money), and *jiritsu-shin no tsuyoi hito* (people with a strong spirit of independence).

On the other hand, the Japanese president of TSP, Tak, had different ideas. He felt that the workforce held strong work values, were diligent, and cared about the product but that they had worked under such difficult conditions under the previous management that it would take time to rebuild the trust necessary to create a culture of work congruent with the goals of the new venture. His faith in the workforce came from both a generalized respect for production-line workers and a contextually based knowledge of this particular workforce. The quality-control manager at TSP agreed: "The Japanese are real believers in people, and really go out of their way to get them on their side. . . . They have the highest respect for operators—and listen to them." The workforce at the plant was composed predominantly of western Massachusetts natives who were of either Polish or French-Canadian descent, whose families had been working at the plant for generations, and who therefore could be characterized as having a historically based commitment to the plant. In addition, the plant had been the number one employer in the small town, and lateral transfers to competing firms had not been a viable alternative for the employees, thereby resulting in a structural impetus for organizational commitment.

What was implicit in the Japanese president's strategy for the management of technology was an understanding that there would have to be a "culture of work" congruent with the successful implementation of the technology. He was able to prioritize which organizational cultural attributes were crucial to the successful implementation of the new technology and which were tangential.

The success of the Japanese management team in turning around the plant within the first two and a half years after the takeover can be attributed mainly to the successful management of the human side of the technology transfer.

The rest of this chapter is devoted to identifying the cultural barriers to change that were considered to be hindering the successful implementation of technology. These factors represent the items on what might be called the *docket for negotiation* in negotiating a work culture that complements technological innovation. They are what Westney called "the range of factors behind [the] departures [from the original, Japanese (in this case) model]." By identifying and tracing the way in which the new management strove to break down these barriers and implement new cultural patterns, I show in this instance of technology transfer "how culture and new organizational patterns interact and how the processes of cross-societal emulation shape the development of organizations" (Westney, 1987, p. 24).

THE HISTORY OF THE U.S. PLANT

The original U.S. plant was founded in 1916. The plant was run like a family business: The founders were "good with people" and ran an organization characterized by benevolent yet authoritative leaders. Under this management, employees enjoyed company parties three times a year—at Christmas, in the spring, and at a summer barbecue. In 1954, the company was merged with another company, and in 1957 it became a wholly owned subsidiary of a manufacturing and sales company. As a result of the consolidation, the new corporation became an organization with a total of six manufacturing plants. Between 1954 and the mid-1970s the plant experienced much growth before its productivity declined. It was the city's second-largest employer, grossing $20 million in sales in 1979.

The corporate headquarters operated the facility on an extremely tight budget, "only spending money on equipment if it were broken." From 1981, there were no social gatherings; hourly workers were regularly laid off; and many office staff members were fired. Management was characterized by a hierarchical structure, with the senior and middle managers supervising a unionized workforce made up of 120 second- and third-generation workers of mostly Polish or French-Canadian ancestry. The most common metaphor used by the hourly workers to describe the American management style was "hammer and sickle." The relationship between management and the unions had deteriorated to an all-time low by 1981: Grievances were up to an average of 12 per month, and a strike closed the plant for six weeks. In 1983, the plant was sold to a holding company. From 1983 until the takeover by the TSP Company in 1986, the predominant concern of the employees was job security.

THE HISTORY OF THE JAPANESE COMPANY

TPC was founded in 1948 and has grown to become the eighth-largest company in its field in Japan. The company's home office is located in Tokyo. Its operations include a central warehouse that distributes finished goods throughout Japan, a primary manufacturing and converting plant, and international distribution centers.

TPC's entire operation uses the *kanban* system of inventory control, which is based on a customer-order "pull" system. At each plant, fully automated warehouses store no more than 72 hours' worth of finished goods, which are then distributed by truck and rail to customers in the nearby areas or are shipped to a separate warehousing facility for distribution throughout the world. All machines in the plant are equipped with SPC monitors that ensure that outputs conform to specifications and inform quality-control specialists of the nature or source of any problems arising in the production process.

Eighty percent of TPC's workers are high school recruits. Most were trained in *kogyo koko* (factory-oriented technical high schools). The mills are based on the "factory town" model, with a TPC community including a day-care center and kindergarten, an infirmary, single men's dormitories and cafeteria, married employees' apartments, children's playgrounds, club houses, guest quarters, parking lots, and leisure facilities such as a small golf course, a baseball diamond, and a company beach. This community surrounds the actual factory.

TPC employees up through the rank of *kacho* (section head) are members of the company union, an enterprise union. All employees wear company-provided uniforms that do not distinguish among ranks. All employees are paid a salary. At the midmorning and midafternoon work breaks, TPC employees typically do Japanese radio exercises.

THE TAKEOVER

When the sale was final, the new Japanese management replaced top management and promoted the previous plant manager and marketing manager to senior positions while retaining the American middle management and hourly workers. The new management rehired approximately 170 of the 206 blue- and white-collar workers from the previous company (the remaining 36 employees were transferred as an entire division to another plant of the former owner). There are currently 206 employees at the plant: 91 office workers and 115 hourly workers. Of the nine Japanese employees, three are in top-management positions.

According to the new management, the determining factor in deciding to buy the U.S. plant was the equipment and the already trained workforce. In addition, a venture started from scratch would have cost much more than the acquisition price, and it would have taken up to two years longer to get a new plant operating smoothly.

After the acquisition, the company was renamed Tomioka Specialty Papers. TSP took special care to gain the goodwill and support of both the community (a large part of whom are World War II veterans) and the U.S. employees during this changeover. During the summer before the takeover, TSP hosted for the community a "get acquainted" picnic in the parking lot of the factory. The new president introduced himself to each person with a handshake and a word of goodwill. The only setback to the goodwill during the takeover was the collective-bargaining agreement with the union. Hourly workers were angry that each lost an average of two weeks of paid vacation leave as well as the portability of their pension plan.

THE TECHNOLOGY: STATISTICAL PROCESS CONTROL

Statistical process control (SPC is also known as statistical quality control) was developed in the United States in the 1940s as a means of quantitatively controlling manufacturing processes so that outputs would conform to specifications. The introduction of SPC to postwar Japan by W. Edwards Deming in 1950 was the catalyst for a national campaign to improve the quality and productivity of Japanese manufacturing (Ishikawa, 1985). The implementation of SPC at a national level was carried out in various forms, including public and company-specific educational programs and a national awards program. The latter included the still much coveted Deming Award for Quality Excellence (which exists in Japan but, ironically, not in the United States) and the now well-known quality-control circles which were established in Japan to institutionalize at the factory level the use of SPC in conjunction with total quality–improvement programs (Gibson, 1982). Whereas quality-control circles continue to be used for their original purpose in Japan, attempts to implement them in U.S. factories in the 1970s uncovered underlying workforce hostility and feelings of alienation toward management on the shop floor, which led to a refocusing of the quality circle away from statistical training and output quality-control discussions to a discussion forum for improving working relationships, group problem solving, and participative decision making (Bushe, Danko, & Long, 1984). U.S. companies have continued to try to implement SPC systems, but they have generally done so independently of quality-control circles (Bushe, 1988).

SPC is a method that provides quantitative data to help managers and on-line workers understand the critical variables and their intercorrelations in each sequence of the manufacturing process. The process uses basic statistical tools, such as graphing means and range charts and simple correlational statistics. TSP's two paper-manufacturing facilities in Japan use a sampling inspection plan for continuous production. SPC is used not only for outgoing quality control but also for process-maintenance control, by bringing attention to defect-producing conditions as they occur. SPC equipment is a standard feature on all paper coaters at TPC Japan and is also used in the mixing departments to control the quality of coating material and color. At TSP, SPC was implemented solely on the new thermal-coating machine (no. 20 coater) and the "color kitchen," the mixing area, which was refurbished at the time of the $43 billion expansion. This approach is to use a control chart in order to find the causes of substandard material and improving the production processes. Control charts for TSP include information about the following variables: coating weight, coated-surface moisture content, curl of coated paper (too much curl indicates not enough moisture), and the pressure, thickness, and smoothness of the application of coating. A final qualitative inspection is made after finishing and converting, when the product might be embossed, cut to appropriate size, and packaged. This inspection checks the curl and the existence of wrinkles in the product and assesses the general appearance of the product. At TSP's factories in Japan, each person in the work crew (one team per paper coater) is trained to read computer-generated SPC charts to ensure that any deviations from specifications are quickly readjusted. This process virtually guarantees that all finished products will meet specifications. In addition, it tells workers where major deviations may occur so that they can make improvements in the tolerances and capabilities of processes, thereby continually improving product quality and productivity (Ishikawa, 1985).

To some scholars of technological change in production operations, SPC is not regarded as a genuine technological innovation because it primarily affects aspects of the management function involving process rather than the physical input of the production function itself. But when SPC is used as an ongoing procedure to maintain and monitor product quality (as is the case at TSP), it directly affects the product inputs as well as the outputs, as the statistics on quality improvement suggest. Even though managers and engineers consider SPC to be a rather simple technological innovation, which is taught to undergraduates in third-year college industrial engineering courses, large-scale attempts at implementing SPC have not been successful in the United States (Bushe, 1988).

A recent study in which researchers investigated the use of SPC systems in the United States demonstrates this point. Bushe (1988) examined Honeywell, Boeing, Xerox, General Motors, and Ford—all large enterprises that had pumped money into the latest technology of quality control. Despite this effort, Bushe found no case in which SPC had become an accepted way of doing business. Conversations with manufacturing personnel in various locations over two years revealed that very few operations managers appreciated the social systems aspects of this technology and that none had considered it in the planning and implementation stages of the process. Having found that capital to invest in sophisticated SPC equipment was not the remedy for U.S. manufacturers' quality problems, Bushe conducted a qualitative field study to examine the barrier to the introduction of SPC in U.S. manufacturing. The study showed that the failure to implement SPC could be blamed at least partially on cultural barriers to change. The case study of introducing SPC at the TSP plant provides a natural arena to examine further this issue of culture and the strategy of innovations. We discuss next the cultural barriers to change at TSP and the steps that were taken to break them down.

CULTURAL BARRIERS TO CHANGE

The cultural barriers to change at TSP that directly related to the successful implementation of new quality-control techniques can be broken down into four categories: (1) negative images of the Japanese, (2) residual assumptions of the previous management regarding work, (3) differences in Japanese and U.S. unionized labor structures, and (4) different interpretations by Japanese and U.S. employees of quality control. All four cultural barriers are described in Table 14.1.

Table 14.1. Cultural Barriers to Change at TSP

1. Negative Images of the Japanese
   a. Media "hell camp" images.
   b. Residual negative stereotypes and attitudes from World War II.
   c. Other local loss of work to "oriental" competition.

2. Residual Assumptions of Previous Management Regarding Work
   a. Individualism fostered by history of labor antagonism.
   b. Performance versus learning culture: maximize output, minimize change, adaptation, and learning.
   c. Segmentalism of job categories, responsibilities, issues, and problems.

3. Differences in Unionized Labor Structure
   a. Implications of enterprise versus industry unions.
   b. Percentage wage increases versus wage parity.
   c. Flexible job transfer versus job categorization.
   d. Supervisors as union members versus nonmembers.
   e. Similar dress versus dress differences.
   f. Union leader to manager progression versus union leader hierarchy.

4. Different Interpretations of Quality Control
   a. Quality control by line (including lowest levels) versus quality control by staff or not at all.
   b. Zero defect challenge versus periodic quality check.
   c. Quality control at the source (established with a working relationship with suppliers) versus finished product–quality checks by quality-control function.

NEGATIVE IMAGES OF THE JAPANESE

To pave the way toward successful implementation of changes at the plant, the TSP management had the immediate task of breaking down barriers and resistance to Japanese management, fostered by "horror stories" in the media likening Japanese-owned factories to "hell camps" where employees were forced to conform to Japanese practices such as uniforms, exercises, workaholism, and putting the company first, above family. The year before the takeover was one in which the media were flooded with programs on Japan focusing on issues of Japanese–U.S. trade relations. Some coverage of Japan was flattering, some neutral, and some quite unfavorable. A movie hit at the box office during the year before the takeover, *Gung-ho,* was a rather humorous yet poignant depiction of what one might expect life to be like as an American employee of a Japanese corporation.

To make matters worse, some hourly workers had relatives employed at the local athletic-shoe factory who were experiencing layoffs and salary cuts because the company was losing market share to factories in other "oriental" countries employing laborers who would work at cut-rate prices. For example, one worker voiced this concern in a preliminary focus-group interview: "Yeah, I don't especially like the fact that I'll be working for 'The Enemy.' But you know, I don't have much choice if I want to make money for my family."

The issue of family-versus-company loyalty was especially important in this locale because it was a small-town community made up of predominantly Catholic residents who valued strong family ties and lived within an extended family. Many employees lived with three generations of their family, and the majority of others who did not nonetheless got together regularly with nearby relatives. The image of the Japanese worker who puts in a 12-hour day and staggers home after late-night drinking sessions with the team was, therefore, not particularly enticing to most of the employees at the plant.

RESIDUAL ASSUMPTIONS OF PREVIOUS MANAGEMENT REGARDING WORK

The "manufacturing culture" of the previous owners encouraged three barriers to change: individualism, performance norms, and segmentalism of job categories.

An individualism-versus-group orientation is an often-quoted significant difference between American and Japanese cultural orientations. Interestingly, the historical accounts of the U.S. company under its founding owners characterize the original "manufacturing culture" of the plant as group centered and familylike. But this original cultural norm was shattered by the lengthy history of animosity and lack of trust between management and the workers in the second phase of the U.S.-owned company's history. What resulted from the prolonged adversarial relationship between management and union workers was that the employees exhibited an extreme version of the individualistic response to a conflict-plagued work environment. They felt that all they owed the old management was their time (because "management gives us nothing extra; why should we give them more?"). The result of the individualistic work orientation was that there were no group-centered programs such as quality-of-work-life projects practiced at the factory. Safety programs, suggestion boxes, and problem-solving groups, which are a way of life for TPC workers in Japan, were foreign to the American factory workers before the takeover.

A related issue stemming from individualistic cultural values is that the American workers were operating from what might be called output-oriented norms of work behavior. The factory was previously organized in such a way as to maximize output at the expense of change, adaptation, and learning. The resultant standard operating procedure for the workers under the former management was to produce as much as possible with the least amount of downtime. This attitude led to a manufacturing culture that encouraged the worker to spend little to no time solving problems. In addition, maintenance was seen as a post-hoc operation in which machinery was attended to only when a problem emerged. As one of the maintenance crew put it, "Our motto might as well have been, 'we don't fix it if it's not broke.' "Consequently, the existing coating machines were in considerable misalignment, and the plant's physical condition was below safety standards in regard to lighting as well as general clutter and upkeep.

In contrast, the Japanese factory workers, trained in SPC processes, expected a public display of on-line problems (one function of the SPC monitor) and a worker-based problem-solving approach. In addition, maintenance worked together with production and quality control to establish a preventative-maintenance operating norm.

A final issue related to cultural norms is that the American workers were steeped in the tradition of segmented job categories. This work orientation led to the tendency to compartmentalize information and problems and thereby to let each department or workstation deal with its own problems in isolation from other departments. In contrast, SPC takes a comprehensive approach that requires cross-functional thinking and problem-solving procedures.

DIFFERENCES IN MANAGEMENT–LABOR STRUCTURES IN THE UNITED STATES AND JAPAN

The basic difference between the Japanese and U.S. labor-relations systems is that Japan has enterprise (or company) unions, as opposed to industry unions in the United States. All other disparate traits between the two systems can be traced to this basic conceptual difference. The manifestations at TSP of the differences because of the enterprise/industry union split between U.S. and Japan labor structures are as follows: First, American trade unions demand wage parity, whereas their Japanese counterparts are concerned with "base-up" or percentage wage increases. Second, American unions are generally organized on an industrial or occupational basis and emphasize the systematic categorization of jobs, whereas Japanese company unions reject this type of categorical rigidity and favor a flexible job-transfer system within the company. Third, Japanese management and labor are distinguished differently from U.S. management and labor. There is an overlap or slight blurring of the hierarchy and of the line between blue- and white-collar workers. Japanese workers are union members up through the rank of chief supervisor. This rank includes the positions of foreperson and superintendent, which are nonunion in the United States. This point is further emphasized in the differences between management and labor dress habits in American and Japanese companies. In the U.S. factory the norm was that as soon as one became "management," one donned a dress shirt and tie, whereas at TPC Japan there is no distinction in dress between management and labor. This distinction also leads to a pattern of mobility between labor and management at TPC Japan, at which a large number of managerial personnel have held positions of leadership in the company union.

DIFFERENT INTERPRETATIONS OF QUALITY CONTROL

The basic difference in quality-control processes in U.S. and Japanese companies is that whereas in most American factories it is regarded as a staff function, in Japan it is carried out by line personnel who have the necessary training to engage in such functions (Bushe, 1988; Juran, 1978, 1981a,b). Originally, when the U.S. company was operating profitably, it had a quality-control department staffed with three quality-control technicians who worked closely with maintenance and R&D staff persons. But in 1981, when the company's profitability began its severe downward turn, the U.S. company did away with the quality-control department entirely.

Quality control at TSP is designed to promote the principle that every product sold should be perfect—100 percent defect free. TSP workers follow the philosophy that they will do everything possible during their entire eight-hour shift to produce a perfect product. This is the challenge. The key to implementing this philosophy is that each worker has a standard manual for his or her job: The worker makes sure that the process and products for which he or she is responsible falls within the specifications, by means of an ongoing, careful examination of the product itself and by reading and interpreting the display on the SPC monitors. The worker passes a detailed log of events to his or her supervisor after the shift is completed and stays an extra 15 minutes to discuss with the following shift members how the operation is running. The following shift members also come to work 15 minutes early for the overlap discussion. If there is a problem, the worker writes down when he or she saw the problem, to whom it was reported, and the action taken to correct the problem. A problem report is issued in addition to the daily log sheets, on which the worker states the nature of the problem and his or her thoughts about its cause. At TPC Japan, work manuals include quality definitions in addition to the standard operating and maintenance instructions. At the time of the takeover, the U.S. company addressed the issue of quality solely by using specification charts distributed to each line supervisor.

STEPS TAKEN TO BREAK DOWN THE BARRIERS

As Eleanor Westney observed, the success of Japanese managers in transferring Western organizational forms into a Japanese cultural context is mainly due to the "capacity of the new institutions for transforming the environment." These steps that the Japanese management took toward transforming the microenvironment of the plant to overcome the barriers to change are discussed next and in Table 14.2.

OVERCOMING BARRIERS CAUSED BY NEGATIVE IMAGES OF THE JAPANESE

The first step taken by the Japanese management to overcome prejudices against and misperceptions about the Japanese was to make it clear that TSP would be run as an "American" factory. There were to be no company exercise rituals and no mandatory company uniforms (although they were provided to those employees who wished to wear them). The primary language used at the plant was English, and the Japanese president encouraged the Japanese management team to speak in English as much as possible, even among themselves while at the plant. However, this edict was frequently violated at company meetings when Japanese managers would often begin speaking in their native language to clarify or to expedite the discussion. To encourage the Japanese management team to "Americanize," the president situated each manager and his family in different towns, located, as a rule, no closer than 20 miles to one another so that they would be forced to interact daily on their own with Americans. Another significant act on the part of the president in regard to the "Americanization" was his decision on how to conduct the groundbreaking ceremony for the $43 million expansion as cited at the beginning of this chapter.

The second step was to educate the employees about Japan. To do this within the first year, the TSP management sent all the top American executives at the plant to Japan for a three-week acculturation program that

Table 14.2.   Cross-Cultural Change at TSP: Overcoming Barriers

1. Overcoming Negative Images of Japanese
    a. Active community outreach agenda.
    b. TSP run as an "American" factory.
    c. In-depth cross-cultural training for executives, including trips to Japan and language training.
    d. Cross-cultural workshops for all interested employees.
    e. Product and Japanese client training for sales personnel.

2. Overcoming Residual Assumptions
    a. Reinstated company parties (Christmas, New Year's Day, summer celebration).
    b. Safety programs, suggestion boxes, quality-control groups, preventive maintenance.
    c. Cross-functional job assignments (engineers in sales and maintenance departments).

3. Resolving Labor Relations Issues
    a. Monetary issues
       Increased earnings because of full operations, seven-day-per week continuous operations.
       Optional 12-hour shifts plus weekend overtime.
       Renovations and expansions interpreted as indication of job security.
    b. Trust issues
       Grievances down.
       A perception of more open communication.
       Management's encouragement of participation.
       Union-approved "working foreperson" and "flexibility language."
       No layoffs or terminations of employment during first four years.

4. Resolving Quality-Control Issues
    a. Hired culturally congruent quality-control manager.
    b. Interdepartmental (R&D, quality control, maintenance) production of quality-control manual.
    c. Quality-control trainers brought from Japan.
    d. Teams of workers and working forepersons sent to Japan for training.

was meant to teach them not only about Japanese culture but also about TSP's manufacturing culture. In addition, I conducted workshops entitled "Working with the Japanese" for all employees on a per-interest basis. In-depth, ongoing cross-cultural training was given to the American executives and administrative assistants who would have the most contact with Japanese staff persons and clients. TSP sales personnel attended separate training workshops to inform them of the new product lines and to help them deal more effectively with their new Japanese clients.

OVERCOMING RESIDUAL ASSUMPTIONS OF PREVIOUS MANAGEMENT REGARDING WORK

To instill a group-versus-individualistic orientation toward work, the new management reinstated the tradition of company parties (Christmas, New Year's Day, and a summer picnic outing). In addition, a safety program (which included safety shoes for all and hard hats when needed) was installed; suggestion boxes were put in place; and quality-control groups were introduced. The cultural barriers to change resulting from an output orientation and segmentation of job categories were treated as a management–labor structure issue.

OVERCOMING BARRIERS CAUSED BY DIFFERENT INTERPRETATIONS OF MANAGEMENT–LABOR STRUCTURE

TSP's management concentrated on two issues to overcome the labor structure barrier, monetary stability and trust.

Monetary Issues

Because of the seven-day-a-week, continuous-operation schedule for the first three and a half years after the change in management, the workforce was making more money than ever. Instead of having to scrimp and save for the 12 weeks a year that they would typically be laid off under the old management, the hourly workers had been able to spend more freely without the worry of leaner times to come. The management allowed the workforce to continue working a 12-hour shift schedule, whereas a typical worker worked three days in a row and then was off for four days. This 12-hour system meant time and a half for many employees who work weekends regularly; therefore, they had even more opportunities to make money.

In addition, the new management renovated all machinery and made major capital expenditures to expand the plant. In one staggering case, the new management spent $70,000 over four months to realign a thermal-coating machine. In this case, money did "talk," and to these workers, it said "job stability." There is also an issue of pride in one's job, which plays a part in the workers' favorable attitude toward management as a result of the renovations and expansion. All the workers were very proud to have well-maintained and even cutting-edge machinery to work on.

Trust Issues

Grievances were down, to an unprecedented two in 1989. The hourly workers attribute this to more open communication between management and workers. If there is a problem, the workers felt that they could talk to their supervisors about it and that something would be done to correct the problem. Since the change in management, the workers had many instances of proof in the new management's sincerity. All the workers that I interviewed said that they felt that their complaints and suggestions were heard and acted upon by the new management. Steps taken by the management to ensure the workers' participation in making decisions included a suggestion box system and management's regular appearance at the union committee meetings.

Overcoming this rather formidable barrier led to a successful outcome of the collective bargaining in December 1988 and again in December 1991, in which two new "Japanese" concepts were incrementally accepted by a majority vote of the union membership at TSP. These two concepts were that of the working foreperson and flexibility language. The working foreperson was an on-line attempt by the Japanese management to blur the distinction between administrative and production jobs. The working foreperson was a nonunion position that allowed him or her to do hands-on work along with the operators on his or her team. Flexibility language was introduced into the new contract so that management could reserve the power to choose the crew (versus job bidding) on the new machines. In the future, it is expected that flexible work assignments and job rotation will be the rule for all the work teams at the plant. Both concepts help break down the individualism and segmentation barrier and to make quality control an on-line, team effort at TSP. These concepts were first introduced in a trial area of production (the newly expanded portion of the plant) in 1988 and then fully implemented at the plant in 1991.

RESOLVING DIFFERENT INTERPRETATIONS OF QUALITY CONTROL

The first step was to hire a quality-control manager and send him to Japan for a three-week training program. Next, an interdepartmental team of Japanese and American employees from research and development, quality control, and maintenance was asked to write a quality-control manual that would be distributed to all hourly workers. Weekly production meetings to address issues of quality control were introduced.

Quality-control trainers were brought from Japan to instruct the on-line workers and their managers in new issues in quality control. In addition, teams of hourly workers were sent to Japan for a three-week to one-month hands-on training program on coating machines equipped with SPC monitors. Finally, after the quality function at the plant itself was operating smoothly, management extended its quality-training program to its main raw materials supplier, by funding an all-expenses-paid trip for a five-member team of quality and production managers to undergo specialized supplier quality training at TPC's factories in Japan. The TSP management also paid for predeparture training in Japanese survival language and business culture for the team.

CONCLUSION

The case of the technology transfer at TSP is an example of how cultural issues may be considered in a change process such as the implementation of quality-control techniques. TSP used a holistic approach to change that gave equal attention to both the technological and the human issues affecting the successful implementation of an innovation. The Japanese management's tacit assumptions about culture that I have conceptualized as their culture of work enabled them to succeed in implementing a technological innovation. The concept of a culture of work allowed the Japanese management to identify those barriers that otherwise would have prevented their success, either by reducing the potential gains from their innovations or by making the entire innovation a failure.

This research has three implications for the further study of international takeovers and intranational takeovers. First, although I believe that the Japanese have what might be called a specifically "Japanese" culture of work, their concept of culture can be applied to non-Japanese organizational contexts. The fact that the Japanese management team at TSP has been successful in dissolving the cultural barriers to change and in implementing a technological innovation suggests that these techniques can be initiated by other management teams, regardless of nationality. Second, this concept of culture also can be applied on international contexts, in which there already is an internally heterogeneous culture in a single nation-state like the United States, mainland China, and India.

Finally, this concept of culture is not a panacea. Some Japanese companies, of course, fail, and some companies that succeed sometimes falter in other areas, just as TSP has struggled in the area of middle management. The takeover can generate problems that the new management does not know how to resolve. These problems will arise because a given definition of culture always is bound to its context. Even now, while I am making the Japanese concept of work culture explicit in giving it a name, I too am creating the concept from a particular perspective and context. Were this concept that I have called a *culture of work* to be transferred to a different organizational situation, there would no doubt be a new set of frictions for which it could not account. What makes this context-bound notion of culture a useful one is finally that it both enables one to see potential problems that one would otherwise not see and also to anticipate that there will be certain areas of blindness that one can only begin to identify in the context of the specific organizational interaction. The dual nature of this concept makes it valuable to both researchers and practitioners.

NOTE

1. The phrase "Japanese management techniques" is in quotation marks because it is not clear whether an objectively quantifiable set of techniques exists or, for that matter, whether it can be attributed to a Japanese national work culture. I use the phrase throughout this chapter because my informants regularly used it.

REFERENCES

Allen, R. F. (1985). Four phases for bringing about cultural change. In R. H. Kilmann et al. (Eds.), *Gaining control of the corporate culture* (pp. 332–50). San Francisco: Jossey-Bass.

Anderson, J. C., Cleveland, G., & Schroeder, R. G. (1989). Operations strategy: A literature review. *Journal of Operations Management, 8,* 133–58.

Barney, J. B. (1986). Organizational culture: Can it be a source of sustained competitive advantage?" *Academy of Management Review, 11,* 656–65.

Brannen, M. Y. (1993). *Your next boss is Japanese: Negotiating cultural change at a western Massachusetts paper plant.* Unpublished doctoral dissertation, University of Massachusetts at Amherst.

Buffa, E. S., & Sarin, R. K. (1987). *Modern production/operations management.* New York: Wiley.

Bushe, G. R. (1988). Cultural contradictions of statistical process control in American manufacturing organizations. *Journal of Management, 14,* 19–31.

Bushe, G., Danko, D., & Long, K. (1984). A structure for successful worker problem-solving groups. In D. Cleland (Ed.), *Matrix management systems handbook* (pp. 714–31). New York: Van Nostrand Reinhold.

Chase, R. B., & Aquilano, N. J. (1989). *Production and operations management.* Homewood, IL: Irwin.

Damanpour, F., & Evan, W. M. (1984). Organizational innovation and performance: The problem of organizational lag. *Administrative Science Quarterly, 29,* 392–409.

Ebrahimpour, M. (1985). An examination of quality management in Japan: Implications for management in the United States. *Journal of Operations Management, 5,* 419–31.

Emery, F. E., & Trist, E. L. (1965). Causal texture of organizational environment. *Human Relations, 19,* 21–32.

Frost, P. J., Moore, L., Louis, M. R., Lundberg, G., & Martin, J. (Eds.) (1985). *Organizational culture.* Beverly Hills, CA: Sage.

Gagliardi, P. (1986). The creation and change of organizational cultures: A conceptual framework. *Organization Studies, 7,* 17–134.

Geertz, C. (1973). *Interpretation of cultures: Selected essays.* New York: Basic Books.

Gibson, P. (1982). *Quality circles: An approach to productivity improvement.* New York: Pergamon Press.

Ishikawa, K. (1985). *What is total quality control? The Japanese way.* Trans. D. J. Lu. Englewood Cliffs, NJ: Prentice Hall.

Juran, J. M. (1978, November). Japanese and Western quality: A contrast in methods and results. *Management Review,* 27–45.

Juran, J. M. (1981a, June). Product quality—A prescription for the West. Part I: Training and improvement programs. *Management Review,* 9–14.

Juran, J. M. (1981b, July). Product quality—A prescription for the West. Part II: Upper-management leadership and employee relations. *Management Review,* 57–61.

Katz, D., & Kahn, R. L. (1966).*The social psychology of organizations.* New York: Wiley.

Kilmann, R. H. (1985). Five steps for closing culture-gaps. In R. H. Kilmann et al. (Eds.), *Gaining control of corporate culture* (pp. 351–69). San Francisco: Jossey-Bass.

Lorsch, J. W. (1985). Strategic myopia: Culture as an invisible barrier to change. In R. H. Kilmann et al. (Eds.), *Gaining control of corporate culture* (pp. 84–102). San Francisco: Jossey-Bass.

Martin, J., & Meyerson, D. (1988). Organizational culture and denial, channeling, and acknowledgment of ambiguity. In L. R. Pondy, R. J. Boland, Jr., & H. Thomas (Eds.), *Managing ambiguity and change* (pp. 93–125). New York: Wiley.

Meridith, J. R. (1987). *Management of operations. 3rd* edition. New York: McGraw-Hill.

Ouchi, W. A. (1981). *Theory Z: How American business can meet the Japanese challenge.* Reading, MA: Addison-Wesley.

Ong, A. (1987). *Spirits of resistance and capitalist discipline: Factory women in Malaysia.* Albany, NY: SUNY Press.

Pascale, R. T., & Athos, A. G. (1981). *The art of Japanese management.* New York: Simon & Schuster.

Pettigrew, A. M. (1985). Examining change in the long-term context of culture and politics. In J. M. Pennings et al. (Eds.), *Organizational strategy and change* (pp. 269–318). San Francisco: Jossey-Bass.

Schein, E. H. (1985). *Organizational culture and leadership: A dynamic view.* San Francisco: Jossey-Bass.

Schroeder, R. G. (1989). *Operations management.* 3rd edition. New York: McGraw-Hill.

Smircich, L. (1983). Concepts of culture and organizational analysis. *Administrative Science Quarterly, 28,* 339–58.

Terreberry, S. (1986). The evolution of organizational environments. *Administrative Science Quarterly, 12,* 590–613.

Trist, E. L., & Bamforth, K. W. (1951). Some social and psychological consequences of the Longwall method of coal-getting. *Human Relations, 4,* 3–38.

Van Maanen, J. (1988). *Tales of the field.* Chicago: University of Chicago Press.

Vogel, E. (1979). *Japan as number one: Lessons for America.* Cambridge, MA: Harvard University Press.

Vonderembse, M. A., & White, G. P. (1988). *Operations management.* St. Paul: West.

Weiss, A. (1984, July–August). Simple truths of Japanese manufacturing. *Harvard Business Review,* 119–25.

Westney, D. E. (1987). *Imitation and innovation.* Cambridge, MA: Harvard University Press.

Wilkins, A. L., & Dyer, W. G. (1987). *Toward a theory of cultural change: A dialectic and synthesis.* Paper presented at Third International Conference of Organizational Symbolism and Corporate Culture, Milan.

Woodward, J. (1965). *Industrial organization: Theory and practice.* Oxford: Oxford University Press.

15

Institutional Pressures and Organizational Learning: The Case of American-Owned Automotive-Parts Suppliers and Japanese Shop-Floor Production Methods

THOMAS Y. CHOI
AND S. NAZLI WASTI

This chapter focuses from an institutional perspective on the dynamics of U.S. automotive suppliers learning Japanese shop-floor production methods (see Suzaki, 1993). We first take the broad perspective that the pressure to adopt these methods was "institutional" for U.S. manufacturing companies (see Zucker, 1987, for a review). Proponents of institutional theory argue that the impetus for organizational changes comes from external institutions rather than the technical reasoning of internal actors. According to this perspective, an organization makes changes when they are sanctioned by other, more powerful institutions in the same industry.

The data collected from our research support this perspective. All companies have sole U.S. ownership, and they were selected to represent three key areas of the automotive-supplier business: powertrain, body parts, and interior parts. Two companies were chosen from each of the three areas. It was interesting to discover that almost all the Japanese shop-floor production methods in these companies were implemented in the late 1980s, and that only after the Japanese gained a reputation in the U.S. auto market during the 1980s as world-class manufacturers and their production methods were thus legitimized did U.S. companies begin to adopt their methods.

Although the traditional institutional thinking (Meyer & Rowan, 1977; Zucker, 1987) suggests that there is no learning at the organization's tech-

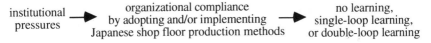

Figure 15.1. An institutional model of organizational learning.

nical core because of an institutional process, the more recent literature (e.g., Choi & Liker, 1992) posits that true learning can take place even when changes are institutionally motivated. Our goal was to discover the organizational elements that assist in the learning process in an environment with institutional pressure, using the case of Japanese shop-floor production methods. We identified the various types of production methods adopted and examined the levels of learning that took place. We did this by first interviewing managers to find out the Japanese shop-floor production methods they had adopted. (The methods are adopted when management consciously decides to learn them, and they are implemented when the adopted method is actually used on the shop floor.) Then we asked workers and line leaders about how often they actually used the methods on the shop floor. We limited our study to such shop-floor methods as housekeeping, quality-control (QC) circles, preventive maintenance (PM), and statistical process control (SPC) that have direct implications for the shop-floor operations. We excluded such methods as quality-function deployment (QFD) or failure modes and effects analysis (FMEA) from our consideration because these methods are related more to engineering than to shop-floor applications.

In the first section, we focus on the first and last stages of the model, as depicted in Figure 15.1: institutional pressures and three levels of learning for the case of Japanese shop-floor methods. Next we look at what happened in the intermediary stage of the model: the organizational compliance with the institutional pressures that led to the actual learning. We describe six U.S. auto suppliers' reactions to institutional pressures and how different reactions led to different levels of learning. Finally, we discuss the lessons we learned from the research.

INSTITUTIONAL PRESSURES AND ORGANIZATIONAL LEARNING

Proponents of institutional theory argue that organizations make changes when faced with external pressures. Such organizational changes are, however, viewed as dissociated from shop-floor activities (Meyer & Rowan, 1977). On the other hand, Choi and Liker (1992) contend that institutional compliance with the adoption of technology can, in fact, be closely associated with shop-floor activities, meaning that organizational learning can be substantive even under institutional pressures. This instance of learning is viewed as occurring at two levels, single-loop and double-loop learning, based on Argyris's (1976, 1984) terminology. (These terms are defined later in this section.)

Institutional Pressures

Two observations justify our claim that the adoption of Japanese shop-floor production methods was an institutional process for U.S. manufacturers. First, according to our data, U.S. companies did not adopt Japanese shop-floor production methods until they became "legitimated elements" (Meyer & Rowan, 1977). Then, as predicted by institutional theorists (DiMaggio & Powell, 1983), the institutional process led U.S. companies to exhibit similar characteristics in their shop-floor practices.

Legitimization of Japanese Shop-Floor Production Methods

The use of shop-floor production methods by the Japanese was largely the result of technical reasoning. These methods were developed mainly in the United States (Schroeder & Robinson, 1991) by Deming (1952) and Feigenbaum (1961) and were further refined in Japan by practitioners such as Ohno (Womack, Jones, & Roos, 1990) and academicians such as Ishikawa (1985). The rationale for these methods was convincing to the Japanese manufacturing companies that implemented the ideas of farsighted U.S. thinkers and, hence, succeeded in increasing their core competencies. Legitimization differs from technical reasoning in that it stems from people's perceptions. These methods were not legitimized in the United States until the 1980s, when the Japanese captured a large share of the U.S. auto market, overcame their image as inexpensive auto manufacturers, and later challenged the luxury lines. Deming (as discussed in Gabor, 1990) had tried to convince the American companies in a technically rational way to use statistical QC mechanisms. But only after the Japanese legitimized this approach did the managers of U.S. companies begin to consider it.

This phenomenon is much like what happened to the safety programs in the United States in the mid-1970s. After the Occupational Safety and Health Administration (OSHA) was formed, many corporations began to establish "safety programs." The technical reasoning cited for the safety programs was to reduce injuries and lost workdays, but if this were correct, the corporations would have introduced the programs long before the emergence of OSHA. In fact, it was only after the federal government legitimized safety programs through the establishment of OSHA did corporations scurry to install them. The adoption of safety programs in the 1970s, therefore, could be accurately construed as an institutional rather than a technical process. Japanese shop-floor production methods have undergone much the same process. Had the implementation of these methods been a technical process, U.S. manufacturers would have introduced them before the emergence of Japan's manufacturing prowess.

Our data support this observation. There are all together 62 cases of adoption of Japanese shop-floor production methods among the six companies. Of the 62, only five were implemented before 1985. Considering the inherent benefits of these methods, we found a strong institutional pressure to motivate the companies to start adopting them. Moreover, four of the five cases adopted SPC-related methods, and all four cases came after American original-equipment manufacturers (OEMs) legitimized them by touting their usefulness and by urging their suppliers to adopt them.

Isomorphism in U.S. Manufacturing Companies

Isomorphism is one of the key dependent variables in institutional processes (Zucker, 1987). It describes a way in which organizations become increasingly similar as they are affected by institutional pressures (DiMaggio & Powell, 1983). That is, the legitimizing pressures are applied to all companies in an industry, and as the companies comply, albeit at varying rates, they begin to resemble one another regarding the effects of these pressures.

The six companies that we included in our research resembled one another in their adoption of Japanese shop-floor production methods. The companies had no business ties among them and were not aware of one another's shop-floor practices, although they introduced similar Japanese shop-floor methods, albeit at different times. The companies began to resemble one another in that they all formed housekeeping, statistical process control, and some kind of group-based problem-solving teams. Because the walls of most of the companies, which only a few years ago stood bare (i.e., the companies began to implement visual management about five years ago), are now covered with information, one can hardly miss this apparent sign of isomorphism.

Organizational Compliance: Three Levels of Learning

We have argued that the adoption of Japanese shop-floor production methods in the United States has been an institutional process. According to this perspective, the boundaries of organizations in the same industry or field are thought to be uniformly exposed to institutional pressure. Having said this, we now look inside the organizational boundaries and examine the learning that is manifested. Although organizations may be exposed to the same type of broad, industry-level environmental pressures, the intraorganizational pressures to learn will surely vary, depending on the particular organizational context. For example, the books published on Japanese shop-floor production methods have been available to all organizations, but the internal pressure to use this knowledge source has varied from organization to organization.

The learning that takes place within organizations is thought to occur at three levels. At the lowest level, no learning occurs. This view is largely supported by institutional theorists such as Meyer and Rowan (1977), who argue that compliance comes at the administrative level and is "decoupled" from the organization's technical core. In other words, the organization's goal is to maintain its reputation and comply only on the surface, in which case no real learning can take place on the shop floor. One example of this is SPC. American OEMs demanded that their suppliers begin using SPC in the early 1980s. The suppliers complied by sending their workers to SPC training sessions and, in some cases, even installing specialized computer systems. Consequently, many of these companies won the OEMs' quality awards, but our data indicate that in many cases, these companies still do not practice SPC on the shop floor, except to collect data to send to their customers.

The flip side of this scenario is that true learning takes place within organizations, which, in turn, results in technical benefits. Argyris's concept of learning (1976, 1984) can be applied to the ways in which company members can learn Japanese shop-floor production methods. Argyris distinguished between "single-loop" and "double-loop" learning. In single-loop learning, the focus is on learning one thing at a time, to keep the organization on track and to correct deviations from this goal as learning takes place (Morgan, 1986). This type of learning tends not to lead to additional learning. Accordingly, single-loop learning takes place when a company adopts a new production method but does so rather mechanically. For example, company management can use QC circles to solve problems without understanding the additional "governing variables" (Argyris, 1984) (e.g., production pressure or individual persons' hidden agendas) that affect the success of this new program. The extent of learning in this case is merely the use of QC circles to solve problems. Double-loop learning, on the other hand, takes place when the organization begins to learn about the governing variables that affect its performance. The organization is able to question other factors that affect learning (Morgan, 1986). Given the observation that all Japanese production methods (e.g., QC circles, TPM, *kanban*) are interrelated and hence can work as governing variables for one another, evidence of holistic thinking (or what Senge, 1990, called *the fifth discipline*) is viewed as a key indicator of double-loop learning.

THE PROCESS OF LEARNING

Methodological Approach

We spent two days interviewing at each of the six companies. The number of people we interviewed in each company was typically about 15, including both managers and workers. We interviewed the managers on the first day, spending at least one hour per person, and we interviewed the workers on the second day, spending up to one hour with each person. We asked the managers to identify (1) the Japanese shop-floor production methods that the company had adopted and (2) the sequence in which they adopted these methods. We asked the workers and line leaders (1) to review the level of implementation of each shop-floor production method identified by the managers as having been adopted by the company and (2) to confirm the sequence of its implementation as it was introduced on the shop floor. At the end of each interview, we asked the workers and line leaders to rate the level of effectiveness for each shop-floor production method on a five-point scale, with five designating high effectiveness. After we compiled the preliminary reports for all six companies, we mailed them to the companies for a review and the correction of any factual errors. All six companies subsequently returned the reports.

In addition to the interviews we took two steps to determine the level of learning during the two-day interviews. First, we investigated any evidence of learning. "No learning" meant a minimal implementation of Japanese shop-floor production methods and a discrepancy between the managers' and the workers' accounts of what had been implemented. Our aim was to see what was taking place on the shop floor (i.e., implementation) and not what the managers claimed they had done (i.e., adoption). Second, once we had identified a company as having "learned a production method," we noted any evidence of single-loop learning or double-loop learning from the interviewees. For single-loop learning, we looked at whether the interviewee showed evidence of a rather myopic perspective of learning. For instance, if an interviewee discussed learning one production method with no reference to how it related to other methods or to the overall production process, we regarded this response as an indication of single-loop learning. Some examples of what respondents said were, "We made it work, but nothing really came out of it"; "Yes, we do keep a clean ship [referring to their housekeeping program], but a lot of cleaning is done by the full-time janitor"; "We do collect SPC data, but the only people who look at it are the quality people." We also noted whether the interviewee provided evidence of double-loop learning, for example, if an interviewee discussed how one Japanese shop-floor production method (e.g., quick die change) depended on the success of another shop-floor production method (e.g., standardization). Some of the examples used as evidence for systems thinking were, "We knew that without making this one work first, we could never get [the other method] to work"; "It is incredible how these things all are interrelated"; "I work with [another person] closely because what I do [implementing a new shop-floor production method] depends so much on what [the other person] does."

Among the six companies, one company seemed to exhibit overall double-loop learning; another company, partial double-loop learning; three other companies, single-loop learning; and one, no learning. The key dependent variable is the extent to which the companies actually learned Japanese shop-floor production methods. In other words, the dependent variable is not overall organizational performance. When we use words like *success,* we only are implying the success of implementating the Japanese shop-floor production methods. Next we describe each company in descending order of their extent of learning.

Six Cases of Learning

We assigned pseudonyms to the six automotive-supply companies in order to maintain confidentiality. Lerntech is the only company displaying overall double-loop learning; hence, we gave it that label to represent its employees' learning of production methods. Leanshow indicates partial double-loop learning, with the managers displaying double-loop learning and other employees showing elements of single-loop learning. Leanshow is short for "lean showcase" because of its status as a showcase plant with its successful implementations of lean Toyota production-system (TPS) practices. Target, Honpress, and Tridrive are the companies showing evidence of single-loop learning. Target was given this pseudonym because its efforts to introduce Japanese shop- floor production methods were driven primarily by the tight target pricing imposed on it by Honda. The next company is called Honpress because the pressure on it to implement various activities was brought by Honda either directly (through target prices and recommendations) or indirectly (through Honda's training programs). The implementation of Japanese shop-floor production methods in Tridrive was driven by three different sources (engineering, union, and corporate management), which resulted in our selection of this pseudonym. Forge-M exhibited very limited organizational learning according to our institutional model. This company has traditionally been a GM supplier; hence, we named this company Forge-M, which stands for "For GM."

To ensure further anonymity of the participating companies, we offer only general descriptions of their products. Moreover, the names of the Japanese automotive-parts supplier companies for whom they work are not disclosed (e.g., Nippondenso, Tokai Rika). However, all six companies agreed to reveal the names of all OEM customers, whether American or Japanese, for whom they work.

Lerntech

Lerntech is an indirect supplier with 100 employees and annual sales of $11 million in 1992, of which 65 percent was from first-tier automotive suppliers. Its principal products are stampings and springs. Since 1985, Lerntech has acquired accounts from eight Japanese transplants, currently constituting 10 percent of its sales.

The company has shown particular success in implementing of Japanese shop-floor production methods. A few learning approaches separate this company from the others. First, despite its status as an indirect supplier that mainly supplies to the domestic market, the vision of its management always has been the global market. According to one manager, "We knew we had to compete against the best, so we always tried to learn the world-class manufacturing." According to another manager, "We have always had our sight on the global market." It appears that this world-level perspective greatly motivated the company to strive to learn what the Japanese had to offer. The management also has focused on "cultural issues over cost-related issues." According to the CEO, "We believe people cause everything. We invest in our people. . . [even] during bad times." As evidence of this, the company continued to expand its training program in the late 1980s even when one of its main products was being phased out and the company's survival was being threatened. This adherence to training brings out another aspect of this company's learning approach: Its training program is characterized by repeated training on the same topics and emphasis of their utilization on the shop floor. Because the main obstacle to achieving "world-class manufacturing" was determined early as a lack of training, the company began offering extensive training, which ranged from SPC and problem-solving techniques to quality-related seminars and visits to successful plants. To use the methods, the employees (workers and managers alike) were subjected to repeated training sessions on various topics of Japanese shop-floor production methods and were given ample opportunities to practice what they had learned.

As a consequence, the interviewees exhibited a good understanding of various Japanese shop-floor production methods and their usage. Moreover, they displayed a keen comprehension of how the production methods worked as governing variables for one another, thus showing evidence of systems thinking, or double-loop learning. Referring to Japanese shop-floor production methods, one typical comment of the interviewees was, "The things we do are all interrelated. We cannot overlook one area and think we will be successful in another area." As evidence of this statement, Lerntech is the only company among the six companies that has a working PM program. The importance of PM can be understood only through a systems perspective indicating how closely PM is tied to other methods (such as housekeeping, just-in-time delivery, standardization, and even problem solving). Without understanding this, maintenance will be viewed as nothing more than maintenance that has no bearing on delivery.

It is also interesting that all the learning approaches that helped Lerntech achieve double-loop learning are characterized by an internal locus of motivation, as opposed to an external one. Lerntech's global perspective, cultural focus, and commitment to training all were generated internally and driven by the company's management. In the other four cases of single-loop learning, as we will show, the learning of Japanese shop-floor production methods was largely driven by Japanese customers.

In addition, Lerntech is the only company among the six that uses many alternative sources of learning. Lerntech's concentration on training resulted from a rather academic exercise of the theory of constraints (Goldratt & Cox, 1986) provided by a local college professor. In addition, the company invited many guest speakers through a local consortium of manufacturers. It also has been working with a world-renowned manufacturing consultant who recently began to help introduce a "minicompany" concept on the shop floor. Although the other five companies also have used sources other than their customers, the importance of these alternative sources was explicitly discounted, whereas the importance of learning from the Japanese customers was emphasized.

Leanshow

From being simply a "metal" plant bending, molding, and soldering metals to build metal frames, in eight years Leanshow has expanded into assembly and has developed a production line controlled by the state-of-the-art, computerized *kanban* method. Leanshow employs 550 people, and its main products are seat frames and complete seat assemblies. At the present time, virtually all of its products are supplied to Japanese customers.

Leanshow first experimented with visual management, inventory reduction techniques, and work cells in the mid-1980s. Nonetheless, its "partnership" with Toyota, which officially began in 1988, and the emphasis on Toyota production systems (TPS) have been major driving forces behind the new methods at Leanshow. Many of the interviewees told us, "They [Toyota] have really worked with us and we have learned a lot from them" and "We are all dedicated to do[ing] what Toyota wants us to do. We are completely customer focused." A *kanban* system was implemented at the outset in the assembly area used for the preparation and quick shipment of orders broadcast electronically to the plant by Toyota. *Kaizen* also was stressed on the shop floor, for which management set aside a separate budget for all continuous improvement–related activities. Changes such as andon lights and cross-training followed. Technical-service managers from Toyota maintained contact with Leanshow, advancing training in areas such as *jidoka* (stopping work if any abnormality), *pokayoke* (devices to aid worker in doing task right), work standardization, quick die change, pareto charts, fishbone diagrams, and other aspects of TPS.

As one interviewee put it, the company currently gets "a lot of publicity for being a showcase plant." The shop-floor production methods have no doubt been well taught through honest and deliberate leadership, and management seems to have shown good systems learning. Their undertaking and financial support of a complete implementation scheme (i.e., TPS) reflects their holistic perspective.

But the workers in general do not seem to reflect the holistic perspective that the managers exhibit. Rather, they are preoccupied with using various shop-floor production methods in a rather disjointed way (i.e., on an individual basis). Although the workers showed pride in the company's *kanban* system by talking about how well it works, they made no reference to how it was related to other aspects of TPS. According to the workers, "[SPC] has been around but doesn't get used much"; "We are not using it [andon lights] to the full potential. It gets ignored sometimes"; and "[The cross-training board] is not kept up-to-date." Statements like these reveal a more fragmented, technique-oriented learning at the worker level than the integrated learning necessitated by the double-loop learning approach.

Target

Target entered the stamping business in the 1960s, and currently 90 percent of its sales come from the automotive market. The company manufactures various types of metal stampings and stamped assemblies. The company employs 160 full-time and 40 temporary employees. Since starting work for Japanese transplants in 1988, it has acquired 15 transplant accounts, and its annual sales reached $23 million in 1992. Currently, 80 percent of Target's jobs come from Japanese transplants, with 40 percent of its total sales going to Honda and its Japanese suppliers.

Target is one of the first U.S. stampers to carve out a niche in supplying Japanese transplants, and the learning-curve effects have been substantial. One person observed, "Working for the Japanese has prompted us to look deeper into the meaning of quality." Working with different Japanese customers, in particular with Honda, seems to be a key factor in the company's attempts to learn Japanese shop-floor techniques. Honda's target price allowed only a "very tight" profit margin and thus pressured the company into devising internal ways of lowering costs and widening the profit margin. For example, raw materials inventory was reduced by negotiating with suppliers; the use of temporary workers was expanded; a companywide freeze was placed on hiring workers for non-value-added work; and the amount of overtime was reduced significantly. The company emphasizes good housekeeping and obtained training on problem-solving techniques from a local college professor. It also worked closely with a representative from Honda, who introduced "the ideology of continuous improvement, performance quality, elimination of waste, and associate involvement."

On the other hand, the impact of Japanese customers such as Honda is less evident on the shop floor than at the management level. Despite the previously mentioned activities, a number of Target employees who work on the shop floor commented that the continuous-improvement (CI) attitude was not as widespread among workers as it was among engineers and that the problem-solving techniques were not well understood by anyone. Other statements indicated that some employees did not use visual management and that the use of SPC was limited to the quality department. The adoption of certain production methods (e.g., *jidoka*) has been supported by a particular department but was not tied to other core processes, with shop-floor workers learning the least about their interrelations. These findings indicate, in regard to shop-floor production methods, disjointed considerations that lead to a lack of systems thinking and a neglect of the interrelationships across functional and departmental boundaries.

Honpress

Honpress entered the automotive sector by selling parts to Honda and a major Japanese supplier in 1985. Now more than 90 percent of its sales come from this market. Its sales in 1992 were $25 million, and it currently has 300 employees. Honpress produces a wide array of plastic molded parts for interior and exterior automotive use. Forty percent of its sales are to Honda and another 40 percent to two major Japanese transplants. In 1988, the company was bought out by a larger automotive supplier that wanted to "get into the transplant business." Since the change in owner-ship, the emphasis seems to be on retaining the Japanese accounts that were obtained earlier.

The real impact on the company's shop-floor operations came when the company began supplying the automotive market. The company discov-ered that the automotive market in general "required more stringent qual-ity requirements," noting, in particular, the quality requirements of Honda and other Japanese suppliers. The new parent company spent additional capital to upgrade the machinery, in order to be able to respond to the customers' insistence on quality. The company has also stressed housekeeping activities and problem-solving teams.

Honpress subsequently received BP (better productivity, better partner, etc.) training from Honda in 1990 and on Honda's recommendation, in-troduced visual management to enhance "communication with associ-ates." Judging by comments made in the interviews (e.g., "People are not afraid to talk to each other, and management has an open door policy"; "We are constantly brought up to date on what is going on"; "Managers are easy to talk to."), this implementation has been particularly successful. Other changes include problem-solving techniques, QC circles, work cells, and an employee-involvement program.

Honpress employees, on the other hand, noted some barriers to success in the implementation of such changes. First, they indicated some lack of "prethought" and "up-front strategy," suggesting a lack of overall guid-ance and purpose. Another problem they mentioned was the speed of growth, which left most people with no sense of direction and no time to figure it out. Some techniques were neglected, as indicated in the following statements: "No one on the floor really knows how to do problem-solving techniques" and "Everybody got trained [in SPC], but we never got to use what we learned." These symptoms imply that an integrated systems perspective was not included in the implementation of the changes. Fur-thermore, without actual use of the shop-floor production methods, it is safe to assume that such a perspective will not be fully understood, and thus its links to production methods in other areas will not become appar-ent. This situation constitutes a serious barrier to double-loop learning.

Tridrive

Tridrive is a subsidiary of a multibillion-dollar corporation. Its key prod-ucts are powertrain parts, most of which are sold in the auto aftermarket, with the rest being sold to OEMs. Tridrive employs 1,050 people. The company's Japanese customer base to date is fairly limited, with Nissan and a major Japanese supplier making up less than 1 percent of its total sales.

Japanese shop-floor production methods have been implemented through three major programs: various projects for Japanese customers, an employee-involvement (EI) program, and a total quality leadership (TQL) program. These programs were rather disjointed, with no real connection to one another. The three programs had different origins, and the impacts they have had on the shop floor are not interrelated. Changes made because of the Japanese customers, the EI program, and the TQL program came from engineering, the union, and corporate management, respectively, and the implementation of each program took place without clear reference to the implementations of the other programs. This finding suggests a mechanistic approach to change rather than a holistic one.

Tridrive had to concentrate on developing its engineering capability to manufacture parts with a special metal alloy for its Japanese customers, because they required "perfect parts, [that are] functionally flawless and aesthetically pleasing." Such technical requirements from Nissan led Tridrive to purchase dedicated machinery, tooling, and measuring equipment and even to deploy dedicated input materials. These changes were made as isolated events only for Nissan, although the company is "planning" eventually to apply them to all areas. The impact to date of these purchases on the shop floor has been only in the use of dedicated machines and materials for Nissan.

In 1988, the company designed an EI program. In this union-driven program, EI teams began to stress housekeeping and the CI attitude, and the number of suggestions submitted rose sharply. The interviewees told us that "the managers now allow the teams to make their own decisions"; "The workers are eager to get involved in teamwork"; and "The EI program has brought the workers together and started a good working culture." The EI program, however, focused mostly on quality-of-work-life (QWL) issues and "has lacked analytical training" that is more directly applicable to shop-floor operations.

The company also recently initiated a TQL training program in which several shop-floor problem-solving techniques were introduced and more analytical training was provided. It is still too new to have had any substantial impact on the shop floor, according to such statements as "We learned some [problem-solving techniques] at the TQL training, but we have not made a regular practice of using them yet" and "The line supervisors are being asked to change their roles from supervising to coaching and cheerleading, but they need more training."

Forge-M

Forge-M has traditionally been a GM supplier; in fact, its sales for GM reached 75 percent of its total business. However, because of the recent decline in orders from GM, the company wanted to broaden its customer base. Accordingly, its nonautomotive sales increased from 3 percent in 1991 to 11 percent in 1992. The company's sales to the Japanese are currently at 1 percent, but they are expected to increase sharply in the next few years. Forge-M is a custom-contract machining-services company, operating in job-shop fashion with 160 employees. The company produces high precision–machined components.

The company's effort to implement Japanese shop-floor production methods came largely from its once-premier customer, GM. The company conducted training on SPC, preventive maintenance, and problem-solving techniques and more recently established an EI program called *synchronous organization*. Nonetheless, Forge-M had the fewest Japanese shop-floor production methods of the six companies (about five identifiable Japanese shop-floor production methods, whereas the others showed an average of about 10). Moreover, with the exception of housekeeping, which Forge-M has emphasized internally for well over 10 years, all other Japanese shop-floor production methods implemented because of GM's pressure are used at a rather low level.

The company's recent encounter with a major Japanese supplier also seems to have had minimal impact on its shop-floor operations. Noting that this particular Japanese supplier "does not give explicit mandates for [production-method] implementation," Forge-M has been reluctant to introduce Japanese shop-floor production methods, which can be partly explained by its rather fragmented organizational context. Although the five other companies encountered some resistance from workers, this has been most prevalent at Forge-M. Many interviewees indicated that many workers still have a biased view of the Japanese. A few commented that the company has a "closed community" atmosphere, quite "inflexible" toward change. A few noted that there is a discernible communication gap between upper management and workers on the manufacturing floor and that all key decisions are made by upper management. A certain amount of "fear" of certain members of top management also was expressed.

These observations suggest that workers resist production methods when they are associated with Japan, that the techniques are imposed on the workers in a top–down fashion, and that the workers do not fully understand the new production methods they are supposed to use. Their fear of the Japanese ("Some say the Japanese are going to come in and take things from us and then drop us") and management ("Workers fear saying certain things to the management") may make them even more reluctant to recognize the necessity and role of the Japanese shop-floor production methods. This attitude, in turn, will lead to less learning, less comprehension, and hence more reluctance to change.

DISCUSSION

This chapter has provided a model of organizational learning based on institutional theory. To explain the factors contributing to the extent of learning, we used the model to examine modes of implementation observed under similar institutional pressures. Through observations and interviews, we highlighted some of the organizational elements (e.g., training, selection of techniques, sources of learning) that contribute to learning Japanese shop floor production methods.

The study's qualitative data support the institutional model of organizational learning in six automotive-supplier companies. The industrywide institutional pressure to implement Japanese shop-floor methods, though leading to isomorphism across the companies we observed, resulted in varying degrees of organizational learning. Whereas one company showed almost no learning, other companies showed evidence of single-loop learning by implementing certain tools and techniques, albeit mechanically, and yet another was able to achieve double-loop learning. The company that achieved double-loop learning demonstrated an understanding of the interrelation of the techniques with one another and it maintained a holistic perspective of the implementation of production methods.

From this study, we arrived at two conclusions: First, in agreement with Choi and Liker (1992), our study shows that substantive learning can take place in an institutional environment, allowing the organization to reap the benefits brought by the shop-floor production methods. Second, although single-loop learning is common and can lead to increased efficiency, double-loop learning is the more desirable form. Because Japanese shop-floor production methods are inherently interrelated and work as governing variables for one another, these interrelations can be fully understood only by a holistic perspective that paves the way for double-loop learning.

The necessity of double-loop learning also has been voiced by other experts in the field. Garvin (1988) noted that although programs, tools, and techniques have proliferated in U.S. companies, a lack of understanding has impeded their progress. The principal factor he identified in the progress of the Japanese firms is an overriding philosophy that encourages "a holistic approach rather than a focus on technique." Suzaki (1987), in his discussion of Japanese shop-floor production methods, emphasized the need for all production methods to "fit together." Instead of simply regarding the implementation of each method as a separate project, he proposed that all methods be effectively integrated and directed under the overarching goals of the whole organization as a system.

Mechanical compliance with the institutional pressures to implement certain Japanese shop-floor production methods may lead to some increased efficiency but not a company's use of its full potential. Rather, a company must understand and use the entire system of applications, plus the interrelations of implementations, to gain optimal implementation of these changes. Unfortunately, there seem to be many who still confuse the difference between these two levels of learning. A recent *Wall Street Journal* article (Naj, 1993) is a case in point. The author portrayed Japanese shop-floor production methods as "fad idea(s)" and characterized U.S. companies as being "disenchanted" with them. What is correct about this portrayal is that institutional adoptions of these methods can appear faddish and lead to inefficiency, as many institutional theorists (e.g., Zucker, 1987) have pointed out. What Naj neglected to say was that the varying levels of learning may result from such an institutional process. If a company introduces one or two Japanese shop-floor production methods as isolated projects, it will most likely lead to single-loop learning or even to no learning. The following quotation from this article provides evidence of this problem: A director of one company remarks, "We brought back what we saw in Japan and tried to execute [these processes] mechanistically" (Naj, 1993, p. A12). In such a situation, it is likely that the companies will not gain all the benefits they anticipated from implementing these methods.

The Pressure to Learn and Its Effects on Learning

So what really affects learning? The case studies in this chapter help identify some patterns in organizational learning under the pressures to which an organization is exposed. In the Lerntech example, there was internal pressure to learn, as opposed to external pressure, which is associated with double-loop learning. This internal pressure was nurtured by the company's incorporation of a global perspective. Proponents of this perspective seek world-class manufacturing capability and emphasize a people-oriented "cultural" focus to cultivate in their employees. Lerntech subsequently offered extensive and repeated training and used several channels of learning. As a result, Lerntech is the only company in our sample that manifested overall double-loop learning; that is, all the employees demonstrated a good understanding of how each method tied in with the others and how the success of one method depended on the others.

The data also provide evidence that external pressure from Japanese customers leads to single-loop learning. In the cases of Honpress, Tridrive, and Target, the implementation of new production methods was primarily the result of external pressure from their Japanese customers. The recommendations and training regarding the use of production methods came mainly from these customers. In these companies, an internally motivated use of alternative sources of learning was limited. Instead, the main motivations for the learning were cost reduction and overhead reduction for Target, the retentiion of existing Japanese accounts for Honpress, and the acquisition of such accounts for Tridrive. These companies displayed single-loop learning: Their production methods and their interrelationships were not fully understood by everyone, and some methods were not used regularly or to their greatest potential.

Forge-M showed very limited learning (categorized here as "no learning") and the fewest Japanese shop-floor production methods. What differentiates this company from the others is the source of the pressure to learn, which was mainly generated by a U.S. customer. The desire to win the quality awards of this OEM played an important role in the adoption of its production methods. A possible reason for the low level of learning is the differing approach of U.S. OEMs from Japanese OEMs: U.S. OEMs traditionally use an arm's-length approach toward their suppliers. This approach can easily induce decoupled institutional compliance, in which no substantive learning takes place in the technical core.

The institutional model of learning introduced in Figure 15.1 can now

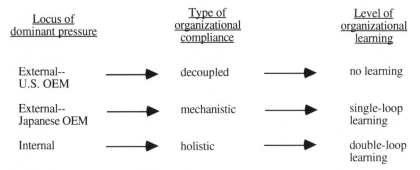

Locus of dominant pressure	Type of organizational compliance	Level of organizational learning
External--U.S. OEM	decoupled	no learning
External--Japanese OEM	mechanistic	single-loop learning
Internal	holistic	double-loop learning

Figure 15.2. An organizational model of response to pressure to change.

be revised to reflect the dynamics at the organizational level. Rather than starting with the institutional pressures at the industry level, as in Figure 15.1, this modified model starts with the immediate pressures on organizations. Subsequent types of compliance and levels of organizational learning are more explicitly categorized in Figure 15.2.

General Observations of Learning

Housekeeping activities and the adoption of visual management were typically at the top of the list of production methods implemented across our sample. One possible explanation for the proliferation of housekeeping is that having a clean, orderly workplace is in harmony with traditional thinking about quality of work life and is also associated with workplace safety, thus making it appealing to both unions and management. In regard to visual management, employees at all levels desire easy access to information, and displaying information on the walls is a simple way of providing immediate results.

These also are highly cost-effective applications (i.e., their impact per dollar spent is relatively high, mostly because of the relatively low investment required for their installation). This low cost most likely makes it easier to convince management to adopt them. It seems that for companies contemplating the adoption of Japanese shop-floor production methods, focusing on these methods at the outset would be helpful in overcoming the initial resistance typically present in organizations to adopting new methods. Of course, the interrelation of these methods with the production process must be emphasized in order to lay the groundwork for double-loop learning. For example, housekeeping is closely tied to machine maintenance and the reduction of work-in-process inventory. What typically happens is that as the shop floor is cleaned and organized, the oil leaks on the floor are more readily noticed, and the inventories between workstations become more prominent, thus forcing management and workers to deal with these problems.

Although SPC is one of the oldest production methods (generally several years old in our sample), it has turned out to be one of the least used. The effective utilization of SPC requires a full grasp of how it relates to overall production, not just to so-called quality control, and without this understanding, few companies are willing to practice it when they are under pressure to manufacture products. One commonality among the companies is the source of pressure to implement SPC. All companies were prompted by their American customers, through either a direct request or more subtle pressure. In our cases, SPC is used mostly for documentation. The reports are sent to customers who require them, but their internal use is minimal. When used, the data are put to reactive rather than proactive purposes. Instead of looking for trends and patterns of defects, workers mechanically look for points out of bounds, and when a problem does occur, quality personnel are called in. Even then, workers complained that they "do not get the quality people right away."

Another interesting observation is the conspicuous absence of preventive maintenance on the shop floor in the five companies that did not achieve double-loop learning. The successful implementation of preventive maintenance requires knowing how it is tied to other production methods, such as SPC, housekeeping, reduction of setup time, and problem solving. It is, therefore, our opinion that the true value of methods such as preventive maintenance is not immediately apparent without the holistic outlook that is present in double-loop learning.

Recommendations

We observed that in an institutional environment, companies tend to comply superficially just to satisfy requirements. This compliance leads to no substantive learning, because the main motivation for change is to maintain reputation and gain legitimacy. Although there are benefits associated with a good reputation and legitimacy, institutional decoupling in an organization represents non-value-added activity from an operational perspective. In other words, it is wasteful to do something for show and then to do something else at the technical core. We recommend, therefore, that when companies adopt new Japanese shop-floor production methods, their managers carefully review their motivations. If the interest is merely institutional, the firm should be aware that the implementation can easily become superficial and turn wasteful.

When companies react to institutional pressures, the effect is at two different levels of learning: single-loop and double-loop. As shown in Figure 15.2, single-loop learning is achieved when the change is externally motivated, and double-loop learning takes place when the change is mainly internally motivated. In the single-loop learning environment, the organization seems to focus more on reacting to environmental pressures. For example, Target cut its overhead in order to widen its profit margin under pressure from Honda's target-pricing practice. On the other hand, Lerntech (the only case of overall double-loop learning) had internal organizational pressure to learn. This association makes intuitive sense in that an internal pressure to learn would help the workers understand the links among the production methods. Even as companies try to react to external pressures as best they can, they must develop programs from *within*. In order to succeed in making changes not only to satisfy customers on the outside but also to capitalize on their own learning, they must ensure that workers and management participate together to build up this internal pressure.

It also appears that management's vision needs to extend beyond satisfying its immediate customers. When companies concentrate on merely complying with a customer's specific demands, this compliance leads to a mechanistic approach to learning. Companies may succeed in satisfying the customer, but this focus may, in fact, hurt their abilities to achieve double-loop learning. Their perspective may remain overly focused, which does not allow them to gain a holistic perspective. Rather, management's vision should be at the global level; these executives should consider not only present customers but also potential customers. This sort of far-reaching vision enables companies to consider more than mechanistic compliance, which leads to single-loop learning, and comply more holistically, which leads to double-loop learning.

Another element that leads to double-loop learning is training, but not the training that is given once on a single topic. Rather, the key is repeated exposure to the same topics through the use of multiple training sources (e.g., lectures, workshops, plant tours, publications). If employees observe the same shop-floor method in different contexts or from different perspectives, this will give them a better understanding of how to use the technique and how it fits together with other applications.

The observations in this study, although limited to the implementation of shop-floor production methods in automotive suppliers, provide an interesting starting point for researchers and practitioners to understand ways to achieve better learning as a result of institutionally driven changes. These observations also offer evidence that institutional pressures can result in both single-loop and double-loop learning. Although short-term organizational efficiency and current customer satisfaction can take place through single-loop learning, long-term organization efficiency and potential customer satisfaction can take place only through double-loop learning.

ACKNOWLEDGMENTS

Our research was funded by the Japan Technology Management Program at the University of Michigan and the U.S. Air Force Office of Scientific Research.

REFERENCES

Argyris, C. (1976). Single- and double-loop models in research in decision making. *Administrative Science Quarterly, 21,* 363–75.

Argyris, C. (1984). How learning and reasoning processes affect organizational change. In P. S. Goodman (Ed.), *Change in organizations* (p. 446). San Francisco: Jossey-Bass.

Choi, T. Y., & Liker, J. K. (1992). Institutional conformity and technology implementation: A process model of ergonomics dissemination. *Journal of Engineering and Technology Management, 9,* 155–95.

Deming, W. E. (1952). *Elementary principles of the statistical control of quality: A series of lectures.* Tokyo: Nippon kagaku gijutsu remme.

DiMaggio, P. J., & Powell, W. W. (1983). The iron cage revisited: Institutional isomorphism and collective rationality in organizational fields. *American Sociological Review, 48,* 147–60.

Feigenbaum, A. V. (1961).*Total quality control: Engineering and management.* New York: Free Press.

Gabor, A. (1990). *The man who discovered quality.* New York: Times Books.

Garvin, D. A. (1988). *Managing quality: The strategic and competitive edge.* New York: Free Press.

Goldratt, E. M., & Cox, J. (1986). *The goal: A process of on-going improvement.* Croton-on-Hudson, NY: North River Press.

Ishikawa, K.(1985). *What is total quality control? The Japanese way.* Englewood Cliffs, NJ: Prentice Hall.

Meyer, J. W., & Rowan, B. (1977). Institutionalized organizations: Formal structure as myth and ceremony. *American Journal of Sociology, 83,* 340–63.

Morgan, G. (1986). *Images of organization.* Newbury Park, CA: Sage.

Naj, A. K. (1993, May 7). Shifting gears: Some American manufacturers drop ill-starred efforts to adopt Japanese techniques. *Wall Street Journal,* p. A12.

Schroeder, D. M., & Robinson, A. G. (1991). America's most successful export to Japan: Continuous improvement programs. *Sloan Management Review, 32,* 67–81.

Senge, P. M. (1990). *The fifth discipline: The art and practice of the learning organization.* Garden City, NY: Doubleday.

Suzaki, K. (1987). *The new manufacturing challenge: Techniques for continuous improvement.* New York: Free Press.

Suzaki, K. (1993). *New shop floor management: Empowering people for continuous improvement.* New York: Free Press.

Womack, J. P., Jones, D. T., & Roos, D. (1990). *The machine that changed the world.* New York: Macmillan.

Zucker, L. G. (1987). Institutional theories of organization. *Annual Review of Sociology, 13,* 443–64.

16

Reflections on Organizational Learning in U.S. and Japanese Industry

ROBERT E. COLE

Organizational learning is a concept that has become extraordinarily fashionable in the last few years (Senge, 1990). The purpose of this chapter is to examine the nature of organizational learning in Japanese and American manufacturing firms. I identify broad differences in their characteristic approaches and propose some approaches to maximizing corporate performance in this area.

Unfortunately, the popularity of the organizational learning concept is not matched by any great intellectual rigor in its application. The distinction between individual and organizational learning is often not clearly made. Interestingly, it is a concept that captivates scholars as well as managers and thus has the potential for serving as a bridge between the two communities. The interest in organizational learning stems from the premise that flexibility and speedy response are characteristic of learning organizations, and these are seen as critical to organizational survival and success in the new world of global competition. Learning organizations are adaptive organizations, and under the best circumstances they develop organizational practices that help them learn how to learn (cf. Argyris, 1992). We can call the latter *generative learning* (McGill, Slocum, & Lei, 1992).

Perhaps the most obvious example of the critical significance of organizational learning is the organization's ability to learn from past product design generations. After all, new products are the lifeblood of a business organization. Consider the American auto industry from about 1960 to 1980: After a new car was designed, it often had the same irritating defect as the previous model did, because there was not much organizational learning. By contrast, the Japanese entered the American auto market in part through a successful strategy of rapidly introducing new models, each one incrementally better than the previous one (e.g., Stalk & Hout, 1990). Nor is this issue of organizational learning limited to traditional mass production industries. If anything, it is more critical to rapidly evolving industries. In the computer and semiconductor industries, success over the last few decades has involved successfully "scaling down" from one product generation to the next. Those firms that could apply their experiences from one generation to the next (i.e., those firms capable of the greatest organizational learning) were among the most successful. This result suggests that organizational learning, even at the simple level of adaptive learning, is a critical issue with strong consequences for productivity and competitiveness.

To discuss organizational learning, it is first necessary to distinguish it from individual learning. Many researchers and managers confuse individual learning with organizational learning or use the terms interchangeably. This is a big mistake.

We tend to assume that individual learning is the basis of organizational learning, but consider the following case of programmers in the software industry: U.S. programmers have traditionally seen programming as an art, with a company's success limited only by their ability and creativity. In short, individual learning is seen as the key to success. These people often resist the idea of standardization. But what has been happening over the last decade is a gradual transformation of the industry. Standardization of design, tools, and products is increasing (Cusmano, 1991). These developments, however, reduce individual skill levels and learning opportunities for many programmers. In short, organizational learning sometimes takes place at the expense of individual learning. We are reminded again that there is a big difference between individual and organizational learning. Contrary to the conventional wisdom, one does not presume the other. Until this difference between individual and organizational learning is well understood, the concept of organizational learning will have little value.

A simple analytic framework distinguishes between individual learning and organizational learning. Figure 16.1 shows four logical possibilities in the relation between individual and organizational learning. At the lower right are organizations in which there is minimal individual learning and minimal organizational learning. The upper right shows organizations high on individual learning but low on organizational learning. The lower left shows organizations in which there is a fair amount of organizational learning but in which individual learning is low. Finally, the top left shows organizations in which there is a lot of both individual and organizational learning. This simple categorization can serve as a guide for subsequent discussion, but first we need to clarify what is meant by the term *organizational learning*.

To grasp the concept of organizational learning, we start from the assumption that organizational learning is based on routine. Work routines (what people actually do in the organization) are the basis for organiza-

Organizational Learning

	High	Low
High		
Low		

Individual
Learning

Figure 16.1. Framework for relationship between individual and organizational learning.

tional memory (Nelson & Winter, 1982). These routines make up organizational networks and processes. The routines are independent of the individual actors who enact them, although individual persons do contribute to their formation and sustenance (see Levitt & March, 1988).

This process by which we transmit and evolve organizational routines is organizational learning. We, of course, can learn good and bad things. We want, however, to define organizational learning in terms of identifying and creating best-practice work routines, standardizing these practices, diffusing them (i.e., actualizing them) throughout the organization, and then renewing the process. These routines include best-practice routines for coordinating the activities of the organization's various functional units.

Organizational learning also means developing improvement routines, specific routines for bringing about change. Of particular interest are those improvement routines that lead organizational personnel to reflect on the appropriateness of past assumptions and activities and to reflect on what they might learn from failure. The emphasis is also on which improvement routines work and why they work. We are interested in the mechanisms and processes by which all of this can occur: Professionalization, socialization, peer shoptalk, training, feedback, imitation, problem-solving routines and information-sharing routines, and personnel movement are some mechanisms that come to mind. Whatever the mechanism, how well an organization carries out this process is one of the central issues determining the quality of an organization's products and services and has a profound impact on organizational productivity as well. How well an organization learns has a great impact on competitiveness.

A word about the term *individual learning* is necessary. Individual learning means the continuous development of the skills necessary to perform changing job demands. More generally, it is about employees at all levels demonstrating behaviors of openness to change, flexibility, systems thinking, creativity, self-efficacy, empathy, cooperative behavior, and problem-solving skills. There are three conditions for converting individual learning to organizational learning: motivation, capability, and opportunity. All three are critical ingredients, and any one or two are necessary but not sufficient. Too often, managers settle on one or two and wonder why individual learning has not occurred. Thus, in the early 1980s, many U.S. firms invested millions of dollars in quality-training programs for all their employees over a short period of time without giving serious attention to providing immediate opportunities for applying the training. As a result, the training was quickly forgotten, and so this large investment had no lasting value. Similarly, many manufacturing firms decided to implement top–down corporatewide total quality-management programs, setting up quality councils, training each layer of company employees, collecting data from external customers, doing a Baldrige diagnostic, and so forth, without any attention to whether these activities were meeting the needs of employees at the different levels of the organizations. By ignoring the motivational element, they contributed greatly to the employees' labeling such efforts as superficial and "flavor of the month."

Keeping in mind that there are many internal national differences as well as industry differences, let us turn now to an overview of learning emphases in modal-performing large American and Japanese manufacturing firms. Figure 16.2 reports my evaluation based on the literature as well as my own research activities. As the figure shows, the modal-performing manufacturing firms in the U.S. tend to fall into the top right category—high on individual learning for selected employees but low on organizational learning. The modal-performing manufacturing organizations in Japan fall in the top left category—high on both individual learning and organizational learning. This statement is subject to qualification because these modal-Japanese firms often limit and channel (critics would say distort) individual learning in order to achieve better organizational learning.

Organizational Learning

		High	Low
Individual Learning	High	Modal large Japanese manufacturing firms*	Modal large U.S. manufacturing firms
	Low	Tayloristic organizations in stable environments	Ideal organization for monopolistic labor and product markets

*With the qualification that individual learning is often limited so as to better serve organizational learning.

Figure 16.2. Hypothesized relationship between individual and organizational learning.

That is one reason that we do not see the kind of individual creativity that is often manifested in U.S. firms.

It is a reasonable hypothesis that in the future, the most dynamic markets, turbulent environments, and successful organizations in both countries will be those organizations that fall into the top left—high individual learning and high organizational learning. Although this is not the modal-American behavior, many of the best U.S. firms, like Motorola, can already be characterized as manifesting a strong focus on both individual and organizational learning. However, generally speaking, the Japanese appear to have a head start.

In the lower right box of Figure 16.2, we can imagine monopolistic or oligopolistic situations in which the value of a learning organization is quite low and the costs of creating such an organization exceed the benefits. In the lower left box, we see the traditional Tayloristic organization with its stress on limiting individual learning and deskilling employees while standardizing work. This bureaucratic form works best in relatively stable, routinized environments.

How does organizational learning occur from a structural perspective? Organizational learning occurs along two dimensions: (1) bringing information into the organization and (2) identifying and diffusing best practices within the organization.

Let us start with bringing information into the organization. This is a critical element of the learning process. The outside environment of the firm, both inside and outside the nation, is composed of competitors, customers, government, and external developers of new technology. This environment contains a variety of signals to the organization that will confer competitive advantage on the firm if it can pick up the right messages, decode them, and act on them in a timely and effective fashion.

Table 16.1 reports the differences between the approaches of U.S. and Japanese manufacturing firms in bringing information into the organiza-

Table 16.1.   Bringing Information into the Organization

Characteristic U.S. Approaches	Characteristic Japanese Approaches
Personnel movement across firms	Learning from customers, competitors, *keiretsu* members, and long-term employees
Specialized personnel assigned to task	Mobilizing largest possible number of employees to meet outside challenge
Heavy use of consultants	Cooperative corporate activities
Strong role for professional associations	Push from government
Merger and acquisitions	Hiving off (spinning off) from established companies, licensing technology

tion. These categories describe central tendencies, and there is a lot of variation around the means.

The U.S. firms rely heavily on moving people as bearers of information. It is expected that the rapid movement of personnel across firms will lead to the successful fertilization of each company's efforts to develop new technology and rapidly incorporate it into new organizational routines. Perhaps the quintessential example of such benefits lies in the success of the Silicon Valley in building and evolving the computer industry away from its mainframe origins. The job hopping not only of successful entrepreneurs but also of legions of middle-level technical personnel has been well documented and clearly has been a major factor in the dynamism of the industry.

A second characteristic of the U.S. approach is to assign specialized personnel to the task of monitoring the environment and collecting the needed information. The tradition of specialization is strong in U.S. industry, and it applies no less in this area. In many organizations, the marketing department, for example, has a monopoly on collecting information from the customer. We assume that specialized personnel can do this job better and then simply transfer that information to those who will use it.

Another typical U.S. mode of collecting information from outside the organization and trying to build it into best-practice routines requires relying on outside consultants. No matter what the organizational issue—from accounting practices to downsizing to quality improvement—in the United States there are legions of outside consultants ready to help. Indeed, as we see in the current reengineering movement, they are ready to create the demand. It is presumed that consultants are the most rapid diffusers of best practices. They are marketers par excellence. The analogy is to bees going from flower to flower (firm to firm), fertilizing each one with the latest best practice.

Another characteristic of U.S. economic life that has an impact on organizational learning is the role of professional associations and a sense of professionalism. These associations, whether they be of lawyers, engineers, or chemists, tend to be oriented toward the professional advancement of their members. People join these organizations to stay on the cutting edge of their professions. The education of young professionals is similarly oriented. What do we value most in a Michigan or Berkeley engineering Ph.D.? The answer is individual creativity. Later, at the workplace, there is a great stress on achieving individual success by learning professional expertise. In short, professional organizations in the United States are particularly important to fostering individual learning.

Finally, a tried and true method over the last three decades in particular lies in merger and acquisition as a strategy for bringing information into the organization. Instead of building a competence, a company buys it.

A newcomer to the approaches adopted by U.S. firms, and a very promising one, is the rapidly increasing use of benchmarking. When well done, it is a focused approach to collecting and acting on information about world-class competitive products, especially business processes. Much benchmarking, however, is done badly, with those assigned to the task running around looking for numbers without understanding the process that generates those numbers. Because of its relative newness, I did not include benchmarking in Table 16.1.

Although there are benefits to each of the traditional U.S. emphases, there also are problems. Lots of personnel movement across firms means that when one firm is acquiring new valuable personnel, another firm is losing them, and that often means a loss of organizational memory. Loss of organizational memory, in turn, negatively affects cooperative activities and thereby quality and productivity. On a different level, because the overwhelming bulk of the personnel of U.S. firms are U.S. nationals, those firms hiring experienced personnel tend to learn only those best practices associated with other U.S. firms. With U.S. firms increasingly facing global competition, this approach is becoming more vulnerable because it lacks the variety present in the broader competitive environment.

Specialized personnel may be good at acquiring information from the outside environment, but they often have great trouble getting key people in the firm outside their specialty to listen to them. Communicating and cooperating with colleagues in different functional departments are critical to using the information intelligently and effectively. Design engineers, for example, often react negatively to recommendations from marketing personnel. In contrast, consultants often have their own interests at heart. When consultants leave, knowledge and learning often leave with them.

Emphasis on professionalism can lead to a greater focus on individual rather than organizational learning. A classic case is U.S. engineering, in which prestige among fellow engineers is awarded to those on the cutting edge of technology. Those on the cutting edge are those doing "real engineering work," as opposed to solving mundane, everyday problems and then incorporating their solutions into organizational practice and seeing that their solutions are institutionalized (Thomas, 1994).

The problem with relying on merger and acquisition to acquire knowledge and capability from the external environment is that the knowledge and capability of the new firm are hard to absorb. Key people from the acquired company often leave. The company doing the acquiring often behaves in a way that kills the capability of the newly acquired company. Replication is difficult (Nelson & Winter, 1982). As a result of these varied considerations, the new knowledge and capability have a tendency to evaporate.

Let us turn now to the Japanese case and consider the approach of the many large export-oriented manufacturing firms shown in Table 16.1. These firms stress learning from long-term employees, customers, competitors (especially foreign competitors), and *keiretsu* members (employees borrowed from suppliers, a Japanese version of using personnel movement). There is a strong emphasis on using long-term employees to collect information about the external environment through a variety of methods.

As a late industrializer, Japan was behind the West and has been playing catch up for more than 100 years. Thus there was a strong emphasis on learning from abroad, and many mechanisms evolved for doing that (e.g., the role of trading companies)

The Japanese firm's approach to absorbing information from the outside especially stresses learning from customers. In a recent cross-national study, researchers asked representatives of responding firms (including automotive, computer, banking, and health care organizations) how often their department translated their customers' expectations into the design of new products and services. Fifty-eight percent of the Japanese managers responded *always* or *almost always,* compared with 22 percent of the U.S. managers (Ernst & Young, 1991). The greater focus on customers on the part of responding Japanese managers for just the computer and automotive industry also was apparent (Ernst & Young, 1992a, b). The Japanese stress what they call the *market-in strategy,* which requires a firm to internalize the market into as many areas of the firm as possible. It means building some degree of uncertainty into the firm rather than trying to insulate it from uncertainty (cf. Cole, Bacdayan, & White, 1993). As practiced in the best Japanese firms, employees try to diffuse information about the outside environment as broadly as possible within the firm in order to mobilize as many employees and cooperating suppliers as possible to focus on satisfying current and potential customers. When a company is faced with an external problem or challenge, the Japanese approach is to magnify it and to mobilize as many employees as possible to deal with it.

The Japanese strategy is not to leave information acquisition from the outside to a specialized group. It is common, for example, to arrange for design engineers, not just marketing staff, to get into the field to collect data on customers. That more than one group collects data from the outside or has had that experience gives the firm different perspectives and makes it easier to sell the final evaluation inside the corporation to the various critical constituencies. The customer, in short, becomes the common language of the different functional groups.

The Japanese, not burdened by laissez-faire ideology, emphasize cooperative corporate activities to speed up the organizational learning process. A good example is the Japanese Union of Scientists and Engineers (JUSE). This organization, based on corporate membership, was formed in the late 1940s to promote quality improvement in its member companies. That is, JUSE is oriented toward quality improvement in firms, not individual advancement or professionalism of quality specialists per se. That is JUSE is interested in individual learning only to the extent that it contributes to organizational learning. Even when the Japanese participate in international professional associations, they tend to treat them differently than do their U.S. counterparts. Consider how the Americans and Japanese use participation in the International Solid State Circuits Conference (ISSCC) and the International Electron Devices Meeting (IEDM) (Nishi, 1993). Although they both use the meetings to share technical information, the

Americans use the meetings as an important opportunity for researchers and/or engineers to demonstrate their technical achievement and capabilities and for technical professionals to fulfill their personal career-development steps. Participation is primarily at the initiative of the individual researcher. For the Japanese, however, participation in the meetings is strongly encouraged and supported by top management, and presentation is used as one measure of an R&D manager's capability and as a cheap way to maximize engineers' morale and growth. Japanese semiconductor firms pin their key milestone for R&D activities by committing to paper the submission deadlines. They use the meetings to calibrate technology choice and progress vis-à-vis others. At the same time they see the meetings as a cheap signaling device, making known their intentions and capabilities to potential customers and suppliers. In short, these meetings for the Japanese are much more a part of the organizational learning process than they are for the Americans.

Many examples have been reported of the Japanese government's role in the learning process, and therefore we have no need to repeat that account (Johnson, 1982). Although the role of the Japanese government may well have been exaggerated in some accounts, it clearly has been an important support (e.g., Okimoto, 1984). It was a role that was especially strong earlier in the century and in the early post–World War II period (e.g., Lynn, 1982).

In sum, we have seen a lot more cooperation among Japanese firms, sometimes as a result of a government push to bring about a kind of collective organizational learning. Such examples are in far fewer supply among U.S. firms.

As one might expect from companies that concentrate on building core competencies rather than on buying expertise, Japanese firms display a tradition of hiving off (spinning off) newly established business areas that are not seen as central to the mission of the parent firm (Gerlach, in press). This process is not a matter of individual entrepreneurs quitting to start their own company à la Silicon Valley but, rather, corporate-managed spin-offs with continuing relationships. The Japanese also have been very effective at strategically using licensing to build competitive advantage (Lynn, 1982).

Although there are advantages to the Japanese approach, there also are downsides: Cooperative corporate activity sometimes leads to collusion at the expense of the public. The government can sometimes guess wrong in its efforts to force cooperation in certain areas, an area that the *Wall Street Journal*'s editorial writers seem to delight in pointing out in as exaggerated a fashion as possible. Even the customer's focus, if carried to an extreme, can create problems. As apparent in the auto industry, excessive emphasis on the customer led to excesses in model and features variation in the late 1980s. Moreover, it is increasingly recognized in Japan that a customer's focus can lead to unreasonable demands and sacrifice on the part of employees in the name of satisfying the customer.

In closing this section, it is important to note that it is not a matter of one response's being right and one's being wrong. Both the U.S. and Japanese responses were quite rational in light of the environments they faced and their respective institutional histories. It just turned out that the Japanese response was better in responding to the environment of the 1970s and 1980s.

Now we turn to the second arena for organizational learning. Bringing relevant information from the environment to the organization is the first task of a learning organization. The second task is applying that information and developing internal ideas to create best practices and then diffuse those best practices to all potential work sites to which they can be applied. Diffusion of best practices in turn requires standardization. It is hard to diffuse and improve what you have not standardized.

Viewed from this perspective, what can we say about the performance of progressive U.S. and Japanese companies? Here is a place where the Japanese have clearly outperformed the Americans. Table 16.2 shows the respective approaches to diffusing information within the organization. What is apparent in the best U.S. firms is a great emphasis on individual learning, particularly for management employees. This is reflected in the large expenditures for individual management training. Individual employees also take relatively large responsibility for their career learning plans (Lynn, Piehler, & Zahray, 1989). There is much less attention paid to thinking about how this individual training and learning will be translated into organizational learning.

The very concept of standards and standardization is something to which Western managers and engineers tend to react negatively, as it conjures up images of dusty, unused manuals and stifling bureaucracy. On the Japanese side, however, we see impressive attention paid to organizational learning. Standardization is understood to be an important objective and one that, if handled properly, can be compatible with innovative behavior because it is seen as a key element in the cycle of process improvement. One has to standardize a process as part of the method of improving it. The Japanese firms that I have studied tend to think of standardization as spreading best practice—standardization is about spreading best practice—not how we usually think of the concept of standardization! And the Japanese have developed some innovative approaches to doing that. For exam-

Table 16.2. Diffusing Best Practices Within the Organization

Characteristic U.S. Approaches	Characteristic Japanese Approaches
Focus on individual learning for selected employees; assume it is translated into organizational learning	Focus on organizational learning through standardization and improvement routines
Reliance on formal training	Reliance on on-the-job training
Reliance on hierarchical structure to identify and diffuse best practice	Reliance on peer-to-peer learning

ple, the use of cross-functional team organization brings about a broad information sharing, ensuring that the same information is available to all in the group. Quality-function deployment makes a similar contribution.

Consider the question of how an organization persuades technical personnel throughout an organization to recognize and adopt best practices. It is a tough problem. Some common obstacles include people saying, "It's different in my department, and therefore it doesn't apply," or "we need to invent our own solutions." To the extent that U.S. firms explicitly attack this issue, they opt often to carry out training activities through traditional hierarchical authority structures. They typically use a hierarchical structure to enforce practices that those up the chain decide are best practice.

Many of the 20 Japanese manufacturing firms that I studied in 1989, however, were organized through more horizontal peer-to-peer learning activities. Consider the following observations that grew out of two contrasting ways of organizing research laboratory employee interactions: Figure 16.3 describes the organizational interactions in R&D observed by Makoto Kikuchi, formerly of MITI's Electrotechnical Laboratory (ETL) and later head of R&D at Sony. He spent considerable time at MIT and Bell Laboratories. One sees in Figure 16.3 an emphasis on peer learning in the Japanese system, as opposed to relying on the hierarchical structure for information flows, as in the U.S. system (Kikuchi, 1983).

For an example from a different part of the organization, consider the following: In large, export-oriented manufacturing firms, it is common practice that once a month in the workplace, engineers present to their peers their problem-solving activities relating to some specific project (Cole, 1992). This is a major form of training for engineers. By proceeding in this fashion, the firms diffuse not only best-practice solutions but also

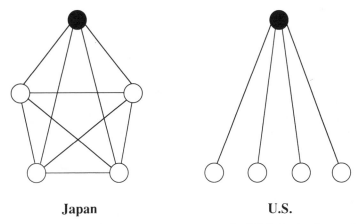

Japan   **U.S.**

Figure 16.3. Comparative management patterns for R&D in the electronic industry in the United States and Japan.

problem-solving methods and failure modes. This approach is a low-cost and highly effective mode of transfer that sidesteps the hierarchical structure.

What about the downsides of the Japanese approach to organizational learning? First, although standardization is important, it can and often does lead to bureaucratic behavior and a rigidity that does not add value to the firm. Excessive rules and regulations slow response time and inhibit innovative behavior. The Japanese are not immune to these problems. I recall a young employee of a company that had just won the Deming Prize telling me how he watched in shock when his fellow employees built a bonfire the day after the prize was announced and burned a lot of the documentation associated with winning the prize. He was totally disillusioned. Much of the data and documentation were only for show!

At the same time, one of my observations from recent interviews in the U.S. and Japanese semiconductor equipment industry is that employee ownership of the process is a critical variable. If the employees operating the process own the process of standardization, it is a much better recipe for avoiding the bureaucratic downside of standardization. The Japanese, on average, seem to do a better job—not a perfect job—of organizing in that fashion.

In one of the American semiconductor equipment companies where I conducted interviews, top management decided that its product-development costs were out of control and that they needed to gain control over those costs. To that end, they appointed a staff person to create their first formal product-development process, with appropriate sign-offs at each stage. They saw this as a way to give them the chance to kill poor projects earlier, thus reducing costs. The staff person was given by a vice president a one-page blueprint of the desired process and then told to interview all the involved engineers in various departments to come up with a proposed design for product development. He described the interview process to me as one of both listening to the engineers and selling them the new approach that had been suggested. The final approach he arrived at looked very much like that originally suggested by the vice president. Top management chose not to approve the plan formally but, rather, de facto to begin implementation. Thus began the real process of trying to gain the employees' buy-in. It went very slowly for the next year. In other words, we see here a pseudoparticipation, and predictably, the working engineers were very suspicious of the outcome because they had had little to do with the design of the new system. The kind of change process described here would be less likely to occur in a Japanese counterpart firm because it would have more seriously involved the working engineers in the redesign process. Over the last decade, many U.S. manufacturing firms have learned that it pays to involve production workers in the redesign of their work; it seems odd that we have not always applied that understanding to high paid, highly skilled engineers.

This brings us to the second problem—and in the end perhaps the most fundamental problem—associated with the Japanese approach to organizational learning, that individual learning and creativity are often sacrificed on the altar of what is best for the organization. In the days of abundant labor, in which employees were grateful just to be employed in a large, stable organization and when the primary task of many business organizations was simply to catch up with Western practices, the almost complete control of individual learning by the firm could be accepted by employees. Increasingly, however, employees have better ideas about what they expect from the organization, and they are less content to leave their career-training plans in the hands of management. There are also fewer and fewer easy foreign models to adopt, and ever more creative solutions to organizational problems are required. In this environment, the continued sacrificing of individual needs and objectives to meet organizational objectives will be counterproductive. More and more companies are starting to respond to this changing environment. Fujitsu, for example, announced in 1994 a new management-training program, along with a new merit-reward salary system. The old program required middle managers to take a six-week training course in specified subjects. But under the new program, these middle managers will be allowed to select the courses' content at their discretion. It is hard to imagine another industrial nation in which increases in an individual employee's ability to choose training directions would be subject of national media attention (*Nihon keizai shinbun*, 1994).

The challenge for the Japanese in the future is tapping individual creativity and individual potential for growth and learning, without losing the teamwork that has proved so effective for Japanese companies. The challenge for the U.S. firms is just as clear. They need to concentrate on getting a higher conversion rate from individual learning assets to organizational learning assets.

Given our focus on organizational learning, it is appropriate in closing to identify the organizational strategies that are most effective in turning organizational learning into corporate core competence. The following are strong candidates:

1. Identify organizational learning as problematic, and show strategic corporate intent to pursue.
2. Actively manage job rotation and career-development policy to maximize organizational learning—especially across functional specialties.
3. Maximize individual learning opportunities that contribute to organizational learning.
4. Work to create a common language of problem-identification and problem-solving methods, using customers as the focus of the efforts.
5. Take "snapshots" of important things that the organization has recently learned and publicly show them to a broad cross-section of employees (use visible management tactics). Use information technology to share information in many places at the same time.

6. Instead of sharing information and decisions on a need-to-know basis, share information as widely and deeply as possible within the organization to educate and involve employees. Emphasize both formal and informal communication.
7. Select employees for employment and promotion according to criteria emphasizing team participation and leadership.
8. Stress entrepreneurship and empowerment with accountability and structured processes.
9. Create reward systems that promote organizational objectives and process performance. Work to eliminate reward systems that optimize individual or small-unit performance at the expense of the larger organization.
10. Celebrate successes in organizational learning.
11. Use structured peer-based learning to identify and diffuse the best practice.
12. Eliminate organizational complexity, especially unneeded layers that distort, retard, and destroy organizational learning.
13. Aim for cross-functional management of major business processes to ensure learning across departmental boundaries.
14. Create closed feedback loops to ensure that the organization learns from customers and important performance outcomes.
15. Design work facilities to maximize opportunities for organizational learning.

When we examine the approach to bringing information into the organization, as well as how the organization uses information to devise and spread best practices, we see two distinct models. The Western model is one in which there is a great emphasis on individual learning for selected employees but not much focus on how to translate that individual learning into organizational learning. The Japanese approach is one in which there is a great emphasis on organizational learning, but individual learning and creativity are often either sacrificed or channeled solely toward corporate ends. In the future, more turbulent environments will ensure that corporate success goes increasingly to those organizations that develop their potential to maximize both individual learning and organizational learning.

REFERENCES

Argyris, C. (1992). *On organizational learning.* Oxford: Basil Blackwell.
Cole, R. E. (1992). Issues in skill formation in Japanese approaches to automation. In P. Adler (Ed.), *Technology and the future of work* (pp.187–209). New York: Oxford University Press.
Cole, R. E., Bacdayan, P., & White, J. (1993). Quality, participation, and competitiveness. *California Management Review, 35,* 68–81.
Cusmano, M. (1991). *Japan's software factories.* New York: Oxford University Press.
Ernst & Young (1991). *International quality study: Top-line findings.* Cleveland: Ernst & Young.
Ernst & Young (1992a). *International quality study: Automotive industry report.* Cleveland: Ernst & Young.
Ernst & Young (1992b). *International quality study: Computer industry report.* Cleveland: Ernst & Young.

Gerlach, M. (in press). Economic organization and innovation in Japan. *Journal of Economic Behavior and Organization*.

Johnson, C. (1982). *MITI and the Japanese miracle: The growth of industrial policy*. Stanford, CA: Stanford University Press.

Kikuchi, M. (1983). *Japanese electronics*. Tokyo: Simul International.

Levitt, B., & March, J. (1988). Organizational learning. In R. Scott (Ed.), *Annual Review of Sociology*. (vol. 14, pp. 319–40). Palo Alto, CA: Annual Reviews.

Lynn, L. (1982). *How Japan innovates: A comparison with the U.S. in the case of oxygen steelmaking*. Boulder, CO: Westview Press.

Lynn, L., Piehler, H., & Zahray, W. (1989). *Engineering graduates in the United States and Japan: A comparison of their numbers, and an empirical study of their careers and methods of information transfer*. Final Report of the Project American and Japanese Engineers: A Comparative Study of Indicators of Their Number, Quality and Utilization, National Science Foundation Grant No. SRS-845099836.

McGill, M., Slocum, J., Jr., & Lei, D. (1992). Management practices in learning organizations. *Organizational Dynamics, 21*, 5–17.

Nelson, R., & Winter, S. (1982). *An evolutionary theory of economic change*. Cambridge, MA: Belknap Press.

Nihon keizai shinbun. (1994, April 18). Fujitsu says: Bosses, be ambitious. *Nikkei Weekly*, p. 9.

Nishi, Y. (1993). A comparison between Japanese and American technology management practices. In R. Cutler (Ed.), *Technology management in Japan* (pp. 31–48). Boston: American Association for the Advancement of Science.

Okimoto, D. (1984). The political context. In D. Okimoto, T. Sugano, & F. Weinstein (Eds.), *Competitive edge: The semiconductor industry in the U.S. and Japan* (pp. 78–133). Stanford, CA: Stanford University Press.

Senge, P. (1990). *The fifth discipline: The art and practice of the learning organization*, Garden City, NY: Doubleday.

Stalk, G., Jr., & Hout, T. (1990). *Competing against time*. New York: Free Press.

Thomas, R. (1994). *What machines can't do*. Berkeley and Los Angeles: University of California Press.

17

Managing Technology Systemically: Common Themes

JEFFREY K. LIKER,
JOHN E. ETTLIE,
AND ALLEN C. WARD

Our original intent for this book was to compile the work of a diverse collection of researchers studying technology management in Japan—a very general topic indeed. This group of professionals comes from different disciplinary backgrounds (engineering, operations management, organizational theory, business strategy, business history, sociology, anthropology, and political science), has different research interests, and has varying levels of exposure to Japan. In some cases, their studies are aimed at confirming or disconfirming conventional wisdom about Japan, but each is a highly focused effort, rigorous in the framework of the parent discipline. In assembling the book, we based some natural groupings of chapters on the stage of the technology life cycle of the phenomenon studied. However, we expected to struggle with the problem of identifying cross-cutting themes in these disparate chapters.

Nevertheless, to our surprise, we found a number of novel and coherent themes or lessons emerging from the discussion among the members of this group. All these themes can be viewed as an outgrowth of a more basic observation, that Japanese managers tend to think in terms of *systems*. That is, whereas U.S. managers usually focus on individual skills, techniques, departments, disciplines, and organizational structures, Japanese professionals and managers tend to concentrate on the connections among these elements. When tasks cannot be managed in their entirety by particular people or groups, the problems can always be broken down into smaller units, but the connections among these units still are not lost in this dissaggregation.

This observation is enunciated in this book in different ways by different writers, partly depending on their disciplinary background. For example, the social scientists emphasize the importance that Japanese managers place on social relationships and interorganizational linkages, whereas the engineers are struck by the Japanese engineers' skill in systems design. However, none of our authors was previously in a position to recognize the breadth of the systems thinking indicated by their independent observations. In this final chapter, we describe the common themes, with examples from several chapters of this book. But first, we briefly review some of the basic concepts in systems theory that form the foundation for the observations that follow.

THE FOUNDATION UNDERLYING SYSTEMS THINKING

Our convergence on systems thinking as the paramount difference that we observed between U.S. and Japanese technology-management approaches needs to be put into the perspective of the rich tradition of writing and thinking on general systems theory (GST). GST is considered by many to be the unifying discipline of science, and its application to systems engineering and to problem solving in this arena should be examined.

Von Bertalanffy (a biologist by training) first introduced the idea of GST in 1937 at the University of Chicago, in Charles Morris's philosophy seminar (Von Bertalanffy, 1968). But his seminar notes were not published until after World War II, when model building and abstract generalizations became more fashionable in science. Von Bertalanffy (1968, p. 91) stated that GST tries to derive "concepts characteristic of organized wholes such as interaction, sum, mechanization, centralization, competition, finality, etc., and to apply them to concrete phenomena."

The basic contribution of systems thinking is an emphasis on the fit between pieces of the system rather than a focus on the pieces themselves. Systems thinking is often contrasted with Frederick Taylor's *The Principles of Scientific Management* (1911), which focuses on optimizing the pieces. For example, work is fragmented into highly specialized jobs, each performed by a separate specialist; the management function of thinking is segmented from the worker function of executing; research is separated from development, which is separated from manufacturing; and so on. Some specialists deal with customers; others design products; and still others manufacture those products.

What we see in the Japanese system is a relatively integrated web of relationships within and between firms and with the marketplace. Campbell observes in Chapter 13 that perhaps the central feature of Japanese culture is the attention paid to *social relationships*. Whereas the Western tradition is to concentrate on the tasks and the technical capabilites of individual people to perform those tasks, Japanese companies stress the relationships *across* people, as well as relationships *across* tasks. This may be why Japanese managers seem to go to extraordinary efforts to cultivate long-term relationships and why they screen new persons or companies before allowing them to join their carefully cultivated network of relationships.

Japanese managers do not see technology as an issue separate from their business plans or their people. The best Japanese managers look first at the core work processes needed to make products that satisfy customers and then identify the technology needed to support the people who do this work. Support systems are just that—support systems for the core work processes—not little empires to serve their own agendas. In these ways, the Japanese management system fits well with the tenets of sociotechnical systems theory, which tries to find a balance between the core technical and social processes needed to achieve the organization's purpose (Taylor & Felten, 1993). Like Japanese total quality-management methods, STS analysis begins with the environment and then identifies the organization's mission, generally defined as satisfying the customers' needs. The focus is then on describing the core task and social processes needed to carry out the mission (Pasmore,1988).

STS is based on open-systems concepts, which means that organizations are influenced by and influence the environment, but this is not to say that there are no boundaries. In fact, defining the boundary between the inside and the outside of the organization and within the organization is central to STS analysis and design. STS theorists realize the importance of boundaries to keep organizations manageable, but they also realize that there is a cost in lost efficiency and information whenever a boundary must be crossed. Thus, they stress that boundaries be designed to include all processes needed to accomplish autonomous tasks (Davis, Canter, & Hoffman, 1955). The self-managing work group is the basic building block in STS and should be designed to include all the core skills needed to perform routine tasks and make routine decisions in the course of the workday. Scientific management divides tasks functionally and places boundaries between different thinkers and doers working on interrelated tasks. Japanese management practices place more of the responsibilities for day-to-day problem solving on the shop floor. Japanese managers seem to realize that trying to integrate people across departments and companies is difficult, and so they create segmented organizations around self-contained tasks. This was described by Liker and his colleagues (Chapter 7) in the case of assigning self-contained bundles of tasks to outside suppliers. The important thing is that the segmentation be in terms of relatively discrete stages in the design and production process rather than across different functional groups needed to perform a set of interrelated tasks.

The best Japanese firms are "learning systems" characterized by continuous improvement or *kaizen* (Imai, 1986; Senge, 1990). Many little improvements to the system add up to major system gains in the long term. But as Cole noted in Chapter 16, in order for these improvements to be codified and broadly applied, they must become part of organizational learning. It is not enough for individual persons to improve their work processes independently. There must be communication among them, agreement about the new work methods, and some degree of conformance to standardized systems in order for improvements to last and have a systemic impact.

We believe that many of the attributes commonly associated with Japanese management can be explained as examples of systems thinking, including a focus on the customer, the Toyota Production System, long-term employment, *keiretsu,* the integration of suppliers into product development, the development of broad, internal competencies, the wide distribution of quality responsibility, the development of global alliances, and the recent trends toward environmentally safe manufacturing. Certainly, systems thinking is central to the quality philosophies of the late Edwards Deming.

This is not to say that Japanese managers have studied systems thinking or would talk about what they do in these terms. But some combination of culture, the influence of U.S. "gurus," and historical circumstance seems to have led Japanese companies in this direction. The five themes that cut across the chapters in this book each elaborate on some aspect of systems thinking evident in Japanese companies.

COMMON THEMES

In looking across chapters, we found five themes related to systems thinking. The following subsections synthesize observations throughout the book as they relate to the five themes. These are not the only common themes in the book, and they are not mutually exclusive; rather, they are interrelated. But for purposes of exposition we feel that they bring out many of the interesting points made by the chapters' authors.

1. Developing Broad Internal Competencies

Japanese business organizations seem to stress developing core internal strategic capabilities as a means of integrating the parts of their companies. Technical skill becomes a central organizing agent rather than a specialist commodity. Thus, breadth is encouraged in addition to depth.

Broad internal competency is manifested in a number of ways. Cross-training is one of the more common and obvious (Lynn, Piehler, & Kieler, 1993). For example, Japanese engineers starting work at Toyota might find that their first assignment is to sell cars at a dealership or to work on a production line. Also at Toyota, by interviewing stamping-production personnel and body engineers (for Chapter 8, on set-based design), we discovered that all the body engineers had experience in stamping. Fruin (Chapter 9) makes similar observations about the importance of cross-training in Toshiba's multifunction, multiproduct factories. In all these cases, the important competencies that seem to be developed intentionally are a range of technical knowledge that is highly product focused, rather than in-depth specialist knowledge that is then applied to a variety of different products. Fruin also notes that in this context, knowledge and practice are inseparable: "Their connection and fusion may be reworked, even strengthened, through annealing processes of repeated knowledge acquisition and application."

Another manifestation of the development of internal competence is the tendency of Japanese firms to create or customize technology for in-house needs rather than to buy it "off the shelf" from outside. Whitney (1992) observed this trend across a number of Japanese companies in the development of in-house computer-aided design (CAD) systems. Despite the broad availability of commercial CAD systems, he found that large Japanese companies like Sony, Toyota, and Nissan developed their own CAD systems and allied engineering-analysis and data-management programs, often based on a modification of a commercially available software package (e.g., IBM CADAM). Sometimes the software is commercialized and other times simply used in house. Duenyas, Fowler, and Schruben (Chapter 11) discovered a similar trend in the use of production-scheduling software in Japanese electronics industries: Simulation software is used to customize applications in house.

This practice also extends to production technology, according to Whitney (Chapter 6). Nippondenso, like Honda and Matsushita, has production-technology development departments that create new capabilities. For example, Nippondenso has customized robots just for internal use. Whitney attributes this practice to the priority that Japanese companies place on integrating the technology with their unique product and process capabilities. For example, he argues that the design process is "usually carefully cultivated and idiosyncratic to each company, and it is tightly linked to, and drives, the capabilities of the supporting software." Another explanation is a more political view, that by developing technology in house, the Japanese companies avoid the trouble that can come with being dependent on an outside group, an explanation more consistent with the views expressed by Campbell in Chapter 13.

Developing internal competencies that are focused on products becomes necessary, according to Fruin (Chapter 9), if time to market is a significant competitive factor. He argues that in this context, localizing and integrating knowledge resources are critical to success. Toshiba does this through its knowledge works. All the core functions needed to design and build a wide range of products are confined to a single location centered in a factory. This centralization is especially important when engineering and technical progress is intimately tied to manufacturing practice. This is certainly the case for the "subsystems suppliers" to the Japanese auto industry, described in Chapter 7 by Liker, Kamath, Wasti, and Nagamachi. They note that in order for the suppliers to react quickly to the strong customer pressure to rapidly develop and test customized prototypes, these suppliers have created "full service technical capabilities," the ability to perform all key product-development tasks in house.

In a different vein, Methé, in a study of the electronics industry, and Roehl, Mitchell, and Slattery, in their study of the pharmaceutical industry, independently contend that Japanese companies are working quickly to develop new competencies needed to cope with a changing environment. Japanese companies in these rapidly changing, technology-dependent industries are concerned about their *lack* of internal competence in basic research. They have done and will continue to do a good job of developing finely honed systems for using technologies developed externally and of rapidly deploying their products based on these technologies. But more and more they are finding a need to create internal innovative capabilities, whether because the rate of technological change is outpacing their ability to borrow from others or because conventional sources have become more guarded in offering access to their new technology. Thus, Japanese companies need to construct a pipeline of fundamental technology and are finding innovative ways to evolve routines for basic research. Methé's and Roehl and his colleagues' studies make clear that pharmaceutical technology managers regard knowledge of the connections between the basic and development R&D units as important. Even when technological specialization was needed, they consciously attempted to provide variety in the experience, often by also requiring basic researchers to spend some time working on drug-development projects.

Two systems principles are illustrated by these cases. First, the principle of requisite variety (Ashby, 1962) states that the complexity of internal competencies in an organization must match the complexity of its environment. Japanese companies have built a complex internal web of technical skills to deal with an external environment that demands high-quality products, at a reasonable cost, that can be delivered on schedule. We saw evidence that they are attacking with equal vigor the problem of more fundamental technological innovation.

Second, many Japanese companies seem to have found a balance between differentiation and integration (Lawrence & Lorsch, 1967). In all these cases, the force driving the development of competence seems to be the drive to integrate the expertise into the entire system of the company. For example, Toyota might attract better programmers by buying commercial CAD packages. But those programmers could not possibly understand and support the Toyota system as well as Toyota's own programmers can. They have gained considerable specialized, in-house expertise in these programs, which is well integrated into the rest of the organization and clearly targeted to explicit company goals. Again, Campbell's political explanation suggests that Japanese organizations generally fear developing a dependence on outside "experts" who might build up a power base or hold an ideology that might diverge from the organization's goals.

2. Being Flexible Within Clear Boundaries

Japanese companies combine organizational innovation and creativity with highly disciplined processes. They establish plans and boundaries at high levels of abstraction, allowing for variation within the boundaries at lower levels of abstraction. The closer one gets to routine processes on the shop floor, the more tightly constrained the boundaries are, yet there is still room for innovation, even within these tight boundaries.

Ward, Sobek, Cristiano, and Liker (Chapter 8) make this phenomenon explicit in their theory of set-based design. They found that Toyota, internally and with its suppliers, begins with sets of possibilities that fall within certain boundaries and then innovates within those boundaries. For example, an approved clay model of the car body does not represent the final, detailed design but, rather, a range of variation is understood to be acceptable. Body designers and die makers communicate with one another about constraints (i.e., boundaries) and eventually decide on a specific design. Similarly, Toyota listens to its suppliers to understand their constraints and trade-offs in setting components' specifications. These specifications then become targets, which are often modified as the supplier explores the design space. Over time, the boundaries become increasingly tight until they converge toward a single design.

The Japanese approach to black-box sourcing, as described by Liker, Kamath, Wasti, and Nagamachi (Chapter 7), facilitates this process. Suppliers receive clear and steady signals from their customers about critical performance specifications, as well as hard dates for delivering prototypes. They then have the autonomy and obligation to design subsystems that satisfy the specifications within their customers' tight time schedule—flexibility within tight constraints. Toyota's constraints are more flexible in that they communicate to the suppliers the reason for the constraints, for example, by showing the suppliers the spatial layout of adjoining parts, and the suppliers are welcome to suggest changes in the layout that will make their part cheaper and better. But even Toyota's suppliers know that Toyota takes these constraints very seriously and that they must have a very good justification for their suggested changes.

Functional build, as practiced by the leading Japanese auto makers (see Hammett, Hancock, and Baron in Chapter 10) also indicates recognition that the initial body design is not engraved in stone—that there is still a need for some degree of flexibility. Parts are stamped in the die tryout and assembled as a screw body, and as long as the body looks good and satisfies the designer's intent, it is acceptable. No attempt is made to grind the dies so they exactly match the original nominal dimensions. In the past, U.S. automakers spent a great deal of effort (one could argue, wasted effort) grinding the dies so the stamped parts would be at the nominal dimensions. This practice seems to be a misplaced emphasis on accuracy rather than on satisfying the intent of the design. Accuracy becomes paramount in stamping in the dimensional control of body stampings, when instead, painstaking attention to detail is needed to ensure that the process can be repeated. For example, when changing a die to run a new batch of a previously run part, the exact conditions of the former die set must be reproduced to minimize the lot-to-lot variation. Thus, Japanese automakers have established detailed, standardized procedures for changing dies, with input from the workers.

Whitney (Chapter 6) describes Nippondenso's (ND's) approach as standardized flexibility. ND's business was originally dominated by Toyota, and Toyota demanded an enormous variety of different parts, in some cases with only hours of advance notice. ND's first attempt was to invest in technology and procedures to enable rapid production changeover, but this had reached its limit. The solution was to identify the boundaries of the customer's needs, for example, the minimum and maximum likely sizes and the heat-reducing capability of radiator cores. Given this understanding of the limits of required variation, ND engineers innovate furiously, investigating many possible design approaches. Their goal is a set of standardized components that can be combined to meet any customer's need within the understood limits and that can be produced and assembled on the same equipment. Customers can order any of those standardized combinations at a lower price, compared with the alternative of a completely customized design. Thus, standardization provides boundaries within which options are available.

In the case of basic research in Japanese companies, perhaps the boundaries have been overly tight. Methé (Chapter 2) notes that research in Japanese companies is predominately "pulled" by market demand rather than "pushing" new products onto theoretically possible markets, what Methe calls *pulling on a string*. In fact, an important characteristic of systems thinking is keeping the organization focused on a common purpose (Ackoff, 1957/58; Taylor & Felten, 1993). Thus, Japanese companies have been very good at persuading even scientists in R&D to attend to the firm's main business. Ironically, this apparent strength in systems thinking is also a weakness, because as a result, most R&D is closer to the development side of the R&D continuum. Japanese R&D is normally very time and target oriented, with a particular target date and known targets for innovation characteristics at the start of a project. Although this approach has led to an enviable number of products brought to market from research, it has also heavily restricted creativity and innovation. Methé points out that Hitachi has intentionally built a new laboratory, separated from the rest of the company physically and organizationally, to reduce the "lure of pulling on the string."

An example not from this book is the case of job design in Toyota factories. Adler and Cole (1993) compared the Toyota production system as it is practiced at the Toyota–GM joint venture (NUMMI) in California with the team approach at a Volvo plant in Uddevalla, Sweden. They observed at Toyota a far more standardized system: Toyota wrote highly detailed, step-by-step instructions for performing each job in automotive assembly, whereas the Volvo plant had far longer cycle times, with teams of workers building an entire subsystem and workers being encouraged to do the job as they chose. In fact, Toyota considers the standardization of jobs as part of the foundation of the Toyota Production System. Nonetheless, these detailed job designs are not created solely by industrial engineers, as Frederick Taylor would have advocated, but with input from workers. Moreover, workers are continuously encouraged to improve their jobs. Thousands of workers' suggestions are routinely used to modify formal procedures.

Adler and Cole argue that standardization and flexibility are in fact not mutually exclusive but can go hand in hand. Standardized procedures enable the workers at NUMMI to find opportunities for improvement and incorporate those improvements into the standard operating procedures. It seems that there was more organizational learning in this plant than in the more laissez-faire environment of the Volvo plant. Without the standard operating procedures, any innovation by one worker would not be passed on to other workers. Thus there would be no organizational learning, only individual learning. By all available measures of productivity, quality, and even employee satisfaction, NUMMI outscored Volvo.

In Chapter 16, Cole states that the very concept of standards and standardization has a negative connotation in contemporary U.S. management culture. There is much attention in Japan to developing standardized approaches, and if properly handled, standardization can be compatible with innovative behavior. Imai (1986) contends that standardizing the process is essential to continuous improvement. In the learning organization that Cole describes, standards are not viewed as fixed procedures but, rather, are subject to change, and improvements by those people expected to follow these standards.

"Systems thinkers" have long emphasized the idea of focusing on boundaries between "black boxes" in the system to treat the system at a high level of abstraction. There is then room for variation within the black boxes: The boundaries make clear what kinds of innovation are acceptable and what kinds of behavior are not. Each phenomenon observed here can be viewed as an instance of just such behavior.

3. Carefully Constructing Social Boundaries

Van de Ven (1986) called the management of part–whole relations the most significant problem in managing innovation in complex organizations. Japanese companies somehow seem to be good at it, if nothing else, judging by the quality of fit and finish of the final product. The U.S. interpretation of this skill is often that Japanese are more "teamy" and naturally cooperate toward a common goal, even with "partners" in other firms, government, and education. But Campbell believes that this is far from the truth. If anything, cooperation across boundaries happens more "naturally" in the United States. Because the Japanese believe that people and organizations are naturally self-serving, they pay much attention to carefully constructing boundaries and creating strong relationships across boundaries only when they are essential to success. Thus, the boundaries are "permeable" in an open-systems sense but are carefully guarded and not open to any stranger who happens to be passing by.

Fruin (Chapter 9) notes this point. Drawing on an earlier paper (Fruin, 1994), he argues that strong boundaries can in fact be useful and necessary but that they must be selectively erected and selectively permeable. Without any boundaries, there would be no opportunity for different parts of the system to develop distinctive competencies and make strong contributions to the whole. Not everyone can be an expert on everything. For example, outside suppliers that are part of the customer's *keiretsu* are encouraged to be independent and to supply other customers in order to get new ideas and maintain an incentive to be innovative. However, as Liker and his colleagues assert (Chapter 7), there is an intentional effort to develop mutual interdependence between customers and their *keiretsu* partners. Suppliers are carefully monitored for their reliability and trustworthiness. There is a great deal of interpenetration across the boundaries that separate customers and key suppliers. In some cases, customers own a share of the supplier, not enough to dictate the supplier's policies but enough to have some control over a supplier's directions that may be unfavorable to the customer.

There are many examples in this book of the close connections across departments in a firm. Fruin writes about the close connection between product development and manufacturing in the "knowledge works." Whitney (Chapter 6) also notices this close connection at Nippondenso, where engineers view manufacturing as a strategic capability that is exploited through appropriate product design. Hammett, Hancock, and Baron (Chapter 10) see the close connections among body designers, die designers, and stampers that integrate design and manufacturing in world-class body-in-white engineering. Once again, these relationships do not necessarily happen naturally in Japanese firms. But job-rotation policies, lifetime employment that locks employees into the firm as well as commits the firm to its employees, strong hierarchical relations, and slow promotion and monitoring by the hierarchy link the goals of the employees to the goals of the firm as a whole.

Years ago, Galbraith (1974) observed that one way to deal with integration across boundaries is to reduce the need for information processing, by dividing big tasks into relatively self-contained smaller tasks. Von Hippel (1990) calls this *task partitioning*. This process is precisely what Liker and his colleagues (Chapter 7) found Japanese auto customers doing when dealing with parts suppliers. "Sourcing in chunks" is a way of reducing the interdependence of different parts suppliers on one another and on the customer. Specifications are communicated in a highly structured, formalized way, and suppliers are sent to develop their chunk and bring it back at a preset time and place for prototype testing. This procedure is far from the image of a cooperative brainstorming session in which everyone kicks around free-flowing ideas in hopes of reaching a consensus. Liker and his colleagues found that the interdependence of customers and suppliers does not always lead to more communication but can be selective enough to actually decrease the need for communication. As Firdman (1991, p. 203) explains,

> As paradoxical as it may seem, good coordination means giving people less information less frequently in a shorter time rather than more information more frequently in a longer time. In other words, coordination should provide opportunities and means for communication and information exchange; but the information infrastructure must determine how much information is exchanged, how frequently, and for how long.

Highly permeable boundaries and integration are not always an advantage. In Chapter 2, Methé discusses the dynamic tension between connecting the basic-research group to the organization and insulating it from the pressures that such connections will bring. If there are no fences between the basic-research group and the rest of the company, even scientists supposedly in basic-research groups may become highly focused on short-term product-development projects with definite time lines and targets. On the other hand, if the fences around basic research are too high and impenetrable, then it may be irrelevant to the company's business goals.

Roehl, Mitchell, and Slattery (Chapter 3) believe that the resource constraints of relatively small Japanese pharmaceutical companies have led them to develop cohesive research organizations to compete with larger, more bureaucratic rivals. These firms need to be innovative, yet they cannot afford research for its own sake. Consequently, they make great efforts to allow researchers a degree of freedom while creating mechanisms for communication between the labs and other parts of the organization. In addition, senior managers pay close attention to the development process and, when necessary, steer development efforts toward corporate goals.

Aldrich and Sasaki's (Chapter 4) discussion of collaboration of competitors through consortia also indicates that the "fences" separating competitors in Japan remain high and strong, though selectively permeable. Concentrated research efforts aimed at pushing technological frontiers in ways needed for particular streams of product development are jointly undertaken, and they are approved by the federal government. Then the competitors take that knowledge back to their sides of the fences and begin competing to manufacture specific products.

Chapter 5, by Osborn and Baughn, presents a rather complex picture of the various ways that Japanese companies both protect and allow penetration of their boundaries across firms in high-technology alliances. The three types of boundary-spanning relationships they describe—dominance, turbulence, and international hybridization—vary in rigidity and the degree of penetration across the "fences." These alliances use different governance forms, have different forms of knowledge flows, vary in their degree of stability, and are used to different degrees in different technological areas. The extent and nature of boundaries differ with the firm's strategic intent. In all these cases, although the boundaries are real, they can be penetrated in certain ways. Points of penetration are strategically selected to establish the most important connections.

4. Regarding "Japanese Methods" as Consequences of Attention to Designing Systems for Local Conditions, Not as Stand-Alone Tools

"Japanese techniques" are not universally practiced in Japan, nor are they essential in and of themselves. In fact, Japanese managers and engineers are often surprised to find that the world is so interested in "Japanese" methods. They are likely to say that rather than a Japanese approach there *is* a "Toyota way" or a "Sony way." In fact, Campbell (1988) interprets this belief as an effort to distinguish between inside and outside: Organizational slogans and mission statements are often seen by insiders as unique even when they sound strikingly similar to those of other companies. Whether real or perceived, the importance of creating an internal culture and adapting tools and methods to local circumstances cannot be overemphasized. U.S. managers often borrow the techniques and miss the structural and cultural conditions that make the techniques effective.

This point is made best in Chapter 15, by Choi and Wasti. All the U.S. companies they identified as receiving little or no lasting benefit from Japanese quality methods view these methods as individual tools. The adoption of Japanese practices in the United States has largely been an "institutional process." Companies have mimicked faddish methods to impress their customers that they are "progressive." But the mimicked methods often turned out to have little substance. Only one company in Choi and Wasti's study benefited significantly because it saw, and adopted, the pieces as part of a whole. In fact, not only the managers but also the workers saw the connection between individual pieces and the broader systems approach. For example, they could articulate how suggestion systems can improve job design and make Just-in-Time systems work effectively.

Liker and his colleagues (Chapter 7) also found that firms can imitate individual structural features of Japanese manufacturer–supplier relationships without gaining many benefits. For example, reducing numbers of suppliers, sole sourcing, and bringing suppliers into the design process at an early stage are not likely by themselves to lead to noticeable benefits. Strong system-engineering capabilities and conditions of mutual dependence are the underlying systems allowing effective black-box sourcing. U.S. companies, however, often copy practices like early sourcing and sole sourcing without also including the underlying systems competencies or mutual dependence.

In Chapter 8, Ward and his colleagues write that Toyota does not apply the set-based approach in a single way across all suppliers. Only those suppliers that have the maturity and technical capability to deal with the flexibility are given specifications as ranges. Other suppliers are given more rigid targets.

Cole (Chapter 16) discusses this issue from a somewhat different perspective. He points out that individual learning in U.S. companies is strong and that individual people may learn specific tools, methods, or routines, but the problem is weak organizational learning. The practices are not disseminated widely across the firm and adopted at an organizational level. Thus their implementation is spotty, and an integrated approach is lacking.

These examples illustrate the danger of pulling any individual tool or management method out of its company and national context and assuming that it will work in the same way in a foreign context. Although Japanese companies have a reputation for borrowing technologies and management concepts from other countries, they seem to be able to adapt them to local circumstances—"local" at the national level, the company level, and even the plant level. And they have institutionalized these approaches at an organizational level, rather than depending on individual learning by "experts" or specialist departments.

This is not to say that the entire Japanese system must be implemented to achieve any benefits. Rather, individual tools or management methods must be seen in the wider context of the company's system, and managers must understand how this fits into their system. Systems thinking emphasizes fit and adaptation rather than a static view of plugging a tool into a fixed organizational structure.

5. Increasing Global Connectivity

Japan has historically been a very insulated, homogeneous society; that was the case by design before the Meiji era. Yet we find evidence in many chapters of this book that Japanese companies are becoming increasingly connected globally and have become a formidable global competitor.

Osborn and Baughn (Chapter 5) write about various forms of global alliances. Japanese companies seem to be unmatched at choosing the form of the alliance and its accompanying changes that fit with their business strategy. For example, what often started in the 1980s as "international hybridization," a relatively equal partnership between firms, often became a dominant–subordinate relationship as Japanese companies bought out their partners when they acquired enough knowledge and resources to run the operation alone. We expect this practice is less prevalent with the tight cash of the 1990s.

Ettlie and Swan (Chapter 12) analyze joint ventures in the United States, documenting the well-known increases in Japan's direct investment in the United States in the late 1980s, which then subsided in the 1990s. They found that the type of investment varied according to the characteristics of the partner firm. Japanese firms were using partial stock purchases and low-equity positions to acquire know-how from high-tech firms and joint ventures with high-equity positions to acquire the production capabilities of the low-tech firms. Whether or not that high level of investment will continue in the United States, Japanese firms have acquired a foothold in selected industries and important competencies. At the time of this writing, Japanese companies are aggressively pursuing various kinds of alliances with firms throughout Asia.

Brannen (Chapter 14) describes the cultural adjustments needed by Japanese firms that acquire U.S. operations. Clearly, the Japanese expatriate managers do not typify the culture of their home country. That is, they speak English well and were undoubtedly selected to be sent to the United States because they are relatively cosmopolitan. They also are struggling to adapt to the U.S. culture of work. Yet what is most striking in Brannen's story of the evolution of management practices in the paper-products firm is the willingness and ability of the Japanese managers to adapt their management style to local circumstances. Although they did not do everything right from the start, they seemed to find ways to make core Japanese management practices palatable to U.S. employees.

These chapters on global alliances explain the learning process that takes place between parties. Japanese managers did not start out in global alliances as experts on working across cultures. In fact, in many ways they were quite naive. But in their struggle to be successful in the relatively alien U.S. culture, there is evidence of learning and adaptation. Knowledge of our language is obviously one advantage that Japanese expatriates have over most U.S. expatriates. The observations in Chapter 16, by Cole, suggest that as expatriates learn from their experiences in the United States, this learning is probably transferred back to the home organization at a higher level than at typical U.S. firms. That is, although U.S. expatriates may learn at an individual level, Japanese expatriates may be better at fostering organizational learning. The Japanese practice of intentionally transferring personnel to the United States for fixed terms (e.g., three to five years) and then rotating new people into these positions seems to encourage organizational learning.

MANAGEMENT IMPLICATIONS

Each chapter in this book contains many implications, but we will not review them here. Rather, we will look at five implications that follow directly from the five cross-cutting themes that we listed earlier in this chapter. The most general implication is that managers must be able to think in terms of systems and concentrate on designing and managing the systems for which they are responsible, paying attention to connections with other interrelated systems. In fact, we believe managers should be selected in part based on their capacity for systems thinking, a much broader criterion than specific technical or human relations expertise. More specifically, we offer the following five observations:

1. Develop Social and Technical Competencies That Tie the System Together

Islands of expertise should be avoided. Isolated departments with a particular functional focus are not likely to contribute to broader organizational goals. Even cross-functional teams that are responsible for only a particular piece of the product (e.g., a component assembly) must understand the relationship between their component and the entire product, as well as what the customer wants. Many recent efforts in the United States attempt to create broader *integrative competencies* through such programs as total quality management and concurrent engineering. At the same time, there is a need for specialized knowledge, and finding the right balance between specialist and generalist knowledge is difficult.

One of the most ambitious examples of organizational restructuring in the automobile industry was Chrysler's move in the early 1990s to platform teams for its new vehicle programs (*Ward's Auto World,* 1992). Chrysler eliminated most of its functional departments in product development, instead dividing them among four teams—large car, small car, minivan, and jeep/truck. Within these teams, subgroups focus on subsystems of the vehicle, for example, electrical/electronic systems or suspension systems. All these teams, including manufacturing representatives, are located in one building. Great pains have been taken to ensure regular communication within and across groups in a platform team as the product and manufacturing process is being developed. Accordingly, engineers have a wider view of their place in the total vehicle program and have learned from the other disciplines needed to design and build a car. There is some concern, however, that knowledge gained by a subsystem group in one platform may not be shared with subsystem specialists working on other platforms. For example, are electrical engineers sharing their knowledge of new technologies for electrical components with the other teams? Are they staying abreast of the latest technologies, or are they preoccupied with their current program? Chrysler has had limited success experimenting with approaches like technology clubs to bring together specialists across teams. But balancing specialist and generalist knowledge is a delicate task. (Incidentally, Toyota, often viewed as the model for organizing new-product development in a team approach, would not do anything nearly so radical as Chrysler because its functional departments are too important and powerful.)

2. Use Abstraction Boundaries to Combine Initiative with Discipline

The relatively organic, integrated systems observed in Japan are certainly not free-for-alls. Rather, they have definite boundaries and often conform strictly to them. This is true for many kinds of boundaries—target specifications for products, boundaries between levels of the hierarchy, boundaries between departments or sections, standardized ways to perform jobs, target goals and dates for R&D projects, and boundaries on appropriate social behavior. Some boundaries are not written down but seem to be understood and followed. Liker and his colleagues (Chapter 7) describe the role of windows for innovation in the automotive supplier case: Suppliers know that there are relatively brief windows of time in the concept stage during which they can influence innovative product designs for their components. Formal presentations are scheduled far in advance and are often the one shot at influencing the customer's decisions. After that, key technology decisions are made and are very difficult to alter.

The balancing act in defining boundaries is to keep them tight in areas that will directly affect the achievement of goals while loose enough to allow some degree of creativity and initiative. This balance is managed in the factory by devising strict standardized procedures to avoid lot-to-lot variation and allow for a high degree of predictability, as described by Hammett and his colleagues in Chapter 10, while creating an environment that permits employees to contribute to the development and improvement of the procedures through *kaizen* activities. As noted by Methé (Chapter 2), Japanese companies have had a harder time finding the right balance in basic and fundamental research. There, it seems that targets and deadlines have been overly constraining, particularly as the pace of technological change has increased in high-tech industries like electronics.

3. Establish Appropriate Connections Inside and Outside the Company

Two faces of Japanese companies appear contradictory on the surface. On the one hand, observers see networks of companies connected by "trust," for example, in the way that manufacturers and suppliers are bound together (Smitka, 1991). On the other hand, Japanese companies are often viewed as closed, almost impenetrable to outsiders, and other observers argue that the cutthroat world of manufacturer dominance of suppliers is anything but trusting (Sakai, 1990).

These views, in fact, are not inconsistent. The *keiretsu* is indeed a broader collection of closely linked businesses than we are used to seeing in the United States, and the relationships across companies and between government and industry are close in ways that are different from those in the West. On the other hand, Japanese companies carefully choose their partners in joint ventures and carefully consider the nature and scope of relationships they establish. As Campbell observes, largely because Japanese managers do not have faith in human nature and the cooperative spirit, they deliberately manipulate their relationships. For example, relationships with suppliers are carefully cultivated over many years, and the process that Liker and his colleagues describe for new suppliers to enter the business is torturous and slow. This is true for Japanese suppliers trying to break into business with new customers as well as for foreign suppliers. But Japanese companies are not willing to depend on blind faith in suppliers' intentions. Using controlled competition between two or three suppliers for each part and establishing small but significant equity relationships are ways to keep suppliers in line and motivated to accept demanding targets for improvement.

In Chapter 4 by Aldrich and Sasaki, we learn that Japanese R&D consortia are focused on specific technical goals and based on lower levels of investment than U.S. consortia are. As in the case of supplier management, relationships across boundaries in Japan are selective and strategic. The lesson from this is that although there is a need to develop strong linkages both inside and outside the firm, companies must determine what they need from those connections and to be economical in establishing them. In other words, the connections should be established selectively, but if they are important, they may merit large up-front investments of time and resources.

4. Do Not Blindly Copy, but Design the System

All the authors of this book believe that there is much that U.S. companies can learn from the Japanese. And all of them also believe there is little to gain from cookie-cutter copying. An important principle of systems thinking is that each system is unique. Combined with the principle that the fit between parts of the system is critical, it makes sense that what works well in one system will not work in the same way in another (Pasmore, 1988). It also means that even companies in the United States cannot blindly copy "best practices" from one another.

The importance of tailoring the methods to the system is underscored in Chapter 15 by Choi and Wasti. In those companies that adopted a practice because of external pressures, learning was superficial. Learning cannot be effective unless it is double-loop learning (Argyris, 1976), with an understanding of the underlying systemic relationships among the parts. In the case of shop-floor practices, this systemic understanding must be pushed all the way down to the shop floor.

Another implication is that it is more productive to model the underlying processes than to display those processes superficially. For example, set-based design, described in Chapter 8 by Ward and his colleagues, is a way of thinking about design. That is worth learning. To the extent that Japanese companies are using a set-based approach, they provide a concrete example. In general, companies are more apt to learn from concrete examples than from abstractions. But when they try to apply what they have learned, they need to apply the principle, not copy the example. It would be a mistake to learn from Toyota's approach to body engineering only that one should increase the number of clay models and prototypes.

That is likely to be inefficient and not improve the design. But the principles of exploring the design space, identifying constraints, and communicating boundaries and ranges are worth learning, with Toyota as one example of a company that has put these abstract concepts into operation.

Campbell, in Chapter 13, makes an important observation about the so-called Japanese work ethic. We frequently hear that Japanese managers have it easy because the workers are naturally motivated and feel obligated to contribute to the company. The company comes even before family. But Campbell shows through comparative survey data in the United States and Japan that Japanese workers are less likely to be strongly committed to their company, are less likely to say that the company comes before family, express lower levels of job satisfaction, and so on. Surveys over time show a steady decrease during the 1980s and early 1990s in workers' commitment to work relative to family and leisure. But according to Campbell, what appears to be a result of a natural work ethic is really the result of the structure of human-resource practices—structures such as lifetime employment, careful selection, intense socialization, semiannual bonuses, and slow promotion that bind the worker to the firm. Americans can and have applied these principles, and Campbell uses the U.S. Marines as an example. A compelling argument is also made by Haley (1989), that the U.S. Forest Service, a famous U.S. bureaucracy, contains all these characteristics.

5. Respond to the Whole, Global Environment

It has become a cliché to say that companies are operating in a global environment. It is no longer enough to become comfortable designing products for home markets and operating within the narrow confines of the home culture. But recognizing the importance of becoming a global player and thinking and acting strategically based on a global outlook do not always go hand in hand.

Nippondenso uses ingenious combinations of design and manufacturing capabilities as its primary strategic weapon (see Whitney, Chapter 6). When it sets out to develop a new version of its technology, it starts by identifying targets that will make it the global leader for the next 10 years. This change is made by benchmarking competitive products in the United States, Japan, and Europe. It then defines its combined customers' needs across the globe. In accordance with this definition, it selects targets for such characteristics as weight, performance, and cost. The key to standardized variety is to have sufficient variety to meet the needs of all customers globally, yet sufficient standardization to underprice all competitors globally.

We are not arguing that Japanese companies have cornered the market on knowing how to interact with the global environment. But as a late-stage industrialized country and one dependent on the import–export market, Japan has had to learn how to borrow ideas and technology from wherever it could and to try to understand the tastes of the consumers in its overseas markets. Perhaps what is most important to learn from the Japanese globalization experience is not their specific methods but their experimenting and their successes, and the obstacles to their success, with globalization.

CONCLUSIONS

This book should not be viewed as a description of the typical Japanese practices of typical Japanese companies. We fully intended to document technology-management practices of particularly successful firms. Companies like Toyota, Nippondenso, Hitachi, and Toshiba all are top corporate players in the world, including Japan. When we look at them, we see various manifestations of systems thinking. In this chapter, we have incorporated these manifestations into five themes.

The best Japanese firms develop social and technical competencies that tie the system together, use abstraction boundaries (e.g., standardized procedures) to combine initiative with discipline, establish appropriate connections inside and outside the company, do not blindly copy, design their own systems, and respond to the whole, global environment. In fact, the same can also be said about the best U.S. companies. Some excellent U.S. companies, for example, the Malcolm Baldrige Award winners, have adopted these methods in part by benchmarking the best Japanese companies which learned many of their quality-management approaches from the United States. So it is not surprising that to a degree we see a convergence of the best practices.

In the 1990s, the Japanese challenge seems far less daunting and overwhelming than it did just 10 years ago. The strong yen, the reduction in easily available and cheap capital, the recession in Japan, the Kobe earthquake, and the great strides made by U.S. companies in responding to Japan's competitive challenge all have contributed to a feeling that U.S. companies are resuming their leadership role. But there is a danger of complacency. Although U.S. firms have gotten better, Japanese firms are continuing to improve. In fact, economic hardship gives the Japanese further motivation to drive down costs and make their operations more efficient. There is some indication that the Ministry of Education is working to improve the university research infrastructure. Dollars spent on R&D have been holding their own. And so, it is dangerous to count out some of our most formidable competitors in Japan.

We believe that the United States also must continue to study and learn about its overseas markets, competitors, and partners. Even if we no longer view Japanese companies as the conquering giants that they appeared to be in the 1980s, we still ought to be watching them as they experiment and learn from both their successes and mistakes. It seems clear that the management of technology will be critical to the global economic battlefield. We hope that this book provides one useful window on some important aspects of technology-management practices in both Japan and the United States.

REFERENCES

Ackoff, R. L. (1957/58). Towards a behavioral theory of communication. *Management Science, 4,* 218–34.

Adler, P. S., & Cole, R. E. (1993, Spring). Designed for learning: A tale of two auto plants. *Sloan Management Review,* 85–94.

Argyris, C. (1976). Single- and double-loop learning models in research in decision making. *Administrative Science Quarterly, 21,* 363–75.

Ashby, W. R. (1962). Principles of the self-organizing system. In H.Von Foerster & G. W. Zopf (Eds.), *Principles of self-organization* (pp. 255–78). New York: Pergamon Press.

Campbell, J. C. (1988). *Politics and culture in Japan.* Ann Arbor: Center for Political Studies, Institute for Social Research, University of Michigan.

Davis, L., Canter, R., & Hoffman, J. (1955). Current job design criteria. *Journal of Industrial Engineering, 6,* 5–11.

Firdman, H. E. (1991). *Strategic information systems: Forging the business and technology alliance.* New York: McGraw-Hill.

Fruin, W. M. (1994). Good fences make good neighbors—Organizational property rights and permeability in product development strategies in Japan. In Y. Doz (Ed.), *Managing technology and innovation for corporate renewal.* New York: Oxford University Press.

Galbraith, J. R. (1974). Organization design: An information processing view. *Interfaces, 4,* 28–36.

Haley, J. O. (1989). Mission to manage: The U.S. forest service as a "Japanese" bureaucracy. In K. Hayashi (Ed.), *The U.S.–Japanese economic relationship: Can it be improved?* (pp. 196–225). New York: New York University Press.

Imai, M. (1986). *Kaizen.* New York: McGraw-Hill.

Lawrence, P. R., & Lorsch, J. W. (1967). *Organizations and environment.* Cambridge, MA: Harvard University Press.

Lynn, L. H., Piehler, H.R., & Kieler, M. (1993). Engineering careers, job rotation, and gate-keepers in Japan and the United States. *Journal of Engineering and Technology Management, 10,* 53–72.

Pasmore, W. A. (1988). *Designing effective organizations: The sociotechnical systems perspective.* New York: Wiley.

Sakai, K. (1990). The feudal world of Japanese manufacturing. *Harvard Business Review, 6,* 257–64.

Senge, P. M. (1990). *The fifth discipline: The art and practice of the learning organization.* Garden City, NY: Doubleday.

Smitka, M. (1991). *Competitive ties: Subcontracting in the Japanese automotive industry.* New York: Columbia University Press.

Taylor, F. W. (1911). *The principles of scientific management.* New York: Harper.

Taylor, J. C., & Felten, D. F. (1993). *Performance by design: Sociotechnical systems in North America.* Englewood, NJ: Prentice-Hall.

Van de Ven, A. H. (1986). Central problems in the management of innovation. *Management Science, 32,* 590–607.

Von Bertalanffy, L. (1968). *General systems theory.* New York: Braziller.

von Hippel, E. (1990). Task partitioning: An innovation process variable. *Research Policy, 19,* 407–18.

Ward's Auto World. (1992, March). Chrysler's LH team struts its stuff, pp. 37–60.

Whitney, D. E. (1992). State of the art in Japanese CAD methodologies for mechanical products—Industrial practice and university research. *Office of Naval Research Asia Scientific Information Bulletin, 17,* 83–171.

Index